D0801819

WHAT YOU DIDN'T KNOW
ABOUT THE BIBLE

Questions and Answers

WHAT YOU DIDN'T KNOW
ABOUT THE BIBLE
Questions and Answers

J. Carter Swaim, Ph.D., D.D.

Bell Publishing Company
New York

Copyright © MCMLXV by Edward Ernest, Inc.
All rights reserved.

This 1984 edition is published by Bell Publishing Company,
distributed by Crown Publishers, Inc., by arrangement with
The Vanguard Press.

Quotations from the Revised Standard Version of The Holy Bible
Copyright, 1952-1957
Used by permission of The Division of Christian Education of
The National Council of Churches of Christ in the U.S.A.

Manufactured in the United States of America
This book was originally published as
Answers to Your Questions About the Bible.

Library of Congress Cataloging in Publication Data
Swaim, J. Carter (Joseph Carter), 1904-
    What you didn't know about the Bible.
    Reprint of: Answers to your questions about the
Bible. 1965.
    Includes index.
    1. Bible—Examinations, questions, etc.   I. Swaim, J.
Carter (Joseph Carter), 1904-   Answers to your
questions about the Bible.   II. Title.
BS612.S753   1983   220.6'1   83-15659

ISBN: 0-517-428016

h g f e d c

TO
GERRIT AND GEORGEANNA
HEEMSTRA

*"A faithful friend is a sturdy shelter:
he that has found one has found a treasure."*

Acknowledgments

Our sincere thanks to all who participated in the preparation and production of this book, with special recognition to Mildred R. Vergara for preliminary editing and checking of scriptural references, to Bernice S. Woll for final editing and comparison of proofs, and to Dee Atkinson for compiling the index. Theirs has been a difficult and painstaking task performed with diligence and devotion. I would also like to thank Alfred G. Wilson, from whose idea the book stemmed.

We also gratefully acknowledge the courtesy of the Division of Christian Education of the National Council of Churches of Christ in the U. S. A. for permission to use the text of the Revised Standard Version in quotations.

J. Carter Swaim

Contents

THE APOCRYPHA

THE NEW TESTAMENT

WHAT YOU DIDN'T KNOW
ABOUT THE BIBLE
Questions and Answers

Introduction

Q. What is the origin of the word *Bible*?

A. *Biblion,* derived from the ancient city of Byblos, is a Greek word meaning papyrus roll. The plural *ta biblia* has given us the English word *Bible:* the Scriptures were originally written on papyrus rolls.

Q. What is the Bible?

A. The collection of sacred writings belonging to the Hebrew-Christian tradition; among the Jewish people, the Bible is sometimes used in the limited sense of the Hebrew Scriptures alone.

Q. What is the canon of Scripture?

A. Derived from the Greek word for measuring rod, the word *canon* describes the list of Scriptures that are considered authoritative.

Q. Who made the decision regarding the books to be considered authoritative?

A. Ecclesiastical dignitaries simply ratified the convictions arising out of the experience of believers. Regarding the Old Testament, three stages can be noted: the Law was canonized about 400 B.C., the Prophets about 200 B.C., the Writings about 90 A.D. Regarding the New Testament, a Festal Letter of Athanasius in 367 A.D. listed the twenty-seven books now found in our Bibles; this was formally ratified by the Council of Hippo, 393 A.D., and the Third Council of Carthage, 397 A.D.

Q. What books were included in the Law?

A. The five "books of Moses": Genesis, Exodus, Leviticus, Numbers, Deuteronomy.

Q. What books were included in the Prophets?

A. The "former prophets" (i.e., the historical books): Joshua, Judges, I and II Samuel, I and II Kings; and the "latter prophets": Isaiah, Jeremiah, Ezekiel, and the book of the Twelve.

Q. Why are works of history included among the Prophets?

A. Because of the basic nature of prophecy: it was not primarily an unrolling of the future but a forthright declaration of the mind and purpose of God. Prophecy is not so much foretelling as forthtelling.

Q. What works are included among the Twelve?

A. Hosea, Joel, Amos, Obadiah, Jonah, Micah, Nahum, Habakkuk, Zephaniah, Haggai, Zechariah, and Malachi.

Q. Why were the Twelve grouped together?

A. Because of their brevity they could all fit upon a single papyrus roll.

Q. What is meant by "major" and "minor" prophets?

A. These terms refer strictly to size and not to significance; the words *major* and *minor,* used in their original Latin sense, simply mean that some books (Isaiah, Jeremiah, and Ezekiel) are larger in size, some (the Twelve) are shorter.

Q. What books make up the Writings?

A. Books of poetry: Psalms, Song of Songs, Lamentations. Books of history: I and II Chronicles, Ezra, and Nehemiah. Stories of Hebrew heroes (Daniel) and heroines (Ruth and Esther). Wisdom literature: Job, Proverbs, Ecclesiastes.

Q. In what languages was the Bible originally written?

A. Except for portions of Daniel and Ezra, the Old Testament was written in Hebrew; the exceptions are in Aramaic, another Hamito-Semitic language deriving its name from Aram (Gen. 10:22). The New Testament was written in Greek.

Q. Why was the New Testament not written in Hebrew?

A. Alexander the Great had made the language of the Greek people the lingua franca, or common speech, of the Mediterranean world. Though most New Testament writers had a Hebrew background, they wrote in the tongue most widely used and understood.

Q. Where are the original manuscripts of the Bible?

A. None of them is known to exist; persecutors made a point of destroying sacred books, others perished through the processes of deterioration that beset all literary works.

Q. From what, then, do translators work?

A. From handmade copies of copies of copies (etc.) of the originals; these are available in photostat, and have been collated for use in printed Hebrew and Greek texts.

Q. Are private persons entitled to translate the Bible?

A. Certainly; anyone with the necessary linguistic skills is at liberty to make his own version; ministers would, in fact, be delighted if each member of the congregation made his own translation from the original languages.

Q. Where are the oldest copies?

A. The Isaiah Scroll discovered in the Dead Sea Cave and now located in the Hebrew University of Jerusalem, oldest text of the Old Testament, is a thousand years older than any previously known; it may date from the first century B.C. The oldest Greek Bibles are Codex Vaticanus, a fourth-century manuscript in the Vatican Library, and Codex Sinaiticus, fourth century, in the British Museum. Other ancient texts of the New Testament are Codex Alexandrinus, fifth century, British Museum; Codex Ephraemi Rescriptus, fifth century, Bibliothèque Nationale; Codex Bezae, fifth century, Cambridge University; Codex Washingtonienses, sixth century, Smithsonian Institution, Washington, D.C.

Q. In what ways can the historicity of the Scriptures be checked?

A. Monuments left by the Assyrians, the Egyptians, the Babylonians, and the Greeks sometimes serve to confirm Biblical reports of encounters that the Hebrews had with these peoples. Archaeological discoveries sometimes confirm the Biblical descriptions of encounters with the Canaanites. The Jewish historian Josephus provides a survey of Hebrew history often paralleling Biblical narratives. Tacitus, Suetonius, and Pliny are Roman writers who make incidental reference to Jesus.

Q. Do these outside sources confirm the truth of the Bible?

A. Historical details can often be verified. It is a mistake, however, to suppose that the essential truths of the Scriptures are to be determined by outside sources. The essential truths of Scripture have to do with reproducible human experiences that are ratified only through lives of faith and hope and love.

Q. What is the earliest translation of the Hebrew Bible?

A. The Septuagint, a Greek version made in Egypt in the third century B.C., arising out of the need for a Scripture that could be understood by Greek-speaking Jews far from home and no longer familiar with Hebrew.

Q. Why is it called the Septuagint?

A. This translation of the Hebrew Old Testament into the Greek language was said to have been done by seventy scholars. From this circumstance it derives its name, *Septuaginta* being the Latin word for seventy.

Q. What Greek translations of the Old Testament were made by Christians in the second century A.D.?

A. Those of Aquila, a Jewish proselyte of Pontus; of Symmachus, member of the Ebionite sect that repudiated Paul and used a Hebrew Gospel of Matthew; and of Theodotion.

Q. How were these early Greek translations brought together in the early church?

A. Origen, who was born about 185 A.D. and succeeded Clement as head of the catechetical school in Alexandria, conceived the idea of collecting all existing Greek versions, with a view to recovering the original text of the Septuagint. He assembled in six parallel columns the Hebrew text, the Hebrew transliterated into Greek letters, and the versions of Aquila, Symmachus, the LXX, and Theodotion.

Q. What name did Origen give to this work?

A. Hexapla (or sixfold); this term is echoed in Bagster's Hexapla, of the nineteenth century, which assembled in parallel columns six English versions: Tyndale, the Great Bible, the Geneva Bible, the Rheims New Testament, the Bishops' Bible, the King James Version; and in the twentieth-century Octapla (or eightfold work) in which eight English versions of the New Testament appear in parallel columns and on facing pages.

Q. What is the Samaritan Pentateuch?

A. That version of the Books of Moses that has been preserved by the Samaritan community since its break with the Jews, perhaps from the time of Nehemiah.

Q. What is the value of the Samaritan Pentateuch?

A. It is the only Scripture recognized by the Samaritans (cf. John 4:1-20). For non-Samaritans, it is important as being the earliest external witness to the Hebrew text that is in substantial agreement with that which has been handed down in the Jewish-Christian community.

Q. How does the Samaritan Pentateuch differ from the texts familiar to us?

A. There are some six thousand variations, many of which are simply scribal errors. Others arose from the desire of the copyists to avoid anthropomorphisms, to make corrections, and to harmonize related passages. Sometimes the text is amended to support distinctly Samaritan views, as when, in Deuteronomy 27:4, the word *Gerizim* is substituted for *Ebal*.

Q. What was the earliest Latin translation?

A. The Old Latin produced either at Carthage or at Antioch and now known largely through quotation by the Fathers.

Q. What is the most influential Latin version?

A. That of Jerome, made in the fourth century A.D.—the work of an irascible monk who reputedly is the only man ever canonized for his learning in spite of his character.

Q. Why is Jerome's version called the Vulgate?

A. From the Latin word *vulgas,* meaning "crowd": Jerome's work, intended for use by the common people, was put into the vulgar tongue.

Q. What is the special significance of the Vulgate?

A. For many centuries it was the only Bible authorized by the Western Church. Until the twentieth century, all Roman Catholic translations had to be made not from the Hebrew and Greek originals but from Jerome's Vulgate.

Q. What early translations were made into Syriac?

A. The Peshita or "simple" revision appears to have been made in the second century A.D.; the Harclean, in the seventh century, by Thomas of Harkel (or Heraclea).

Q. What was the earliest Egyptian translation?

A. There are two Egyptian, or Coptic versions: the Sahidic (current in es-Said, or Upper Egypt), from the third century; and the Bohairic (current in the Behera, northeast of Alexandria), from the seventh century.

Q. What was the earliest Ethiopic translation?

A. Ethiopic is the term applied to Geez, the classical language of the Abyssinians; the Ethiopic version appears to date from the fourth century, at which time Ethiopia became a "Christian" nation. Amharic is now the common language of Ethiopia. The first Amharic Bible was published in 1840 and revised in 1952.

Q. When was the earliest Armenian translation?

A. About the year 300, at which time King Tiridates III and the Armenian nation embraced Christianity.

Q. What was the earliest Gothic translation?

A. That made by Ulfilas, or Little Wolf, in the fourth century. Since the Goths had had no literature before this, Ulfilas had to invent an alphabet.

Q. What portions of the Bible did Ulfilas feel compelled to omit?

A. I and II Samuel, I and II Kings, since his own people were so warlike. In this matter, he argued, the Goths "needed the bit rather than the bridle."

Q. What of German translations?

A. The mystics made the earliest translations of the Bible into German. One of these was published at Strasbourg in 1466. Luther's translation (1522-34) became an important factor in fixing the language and unifying the culture of Germany. By 1546, the year of his death, the number of editions had risen to three hundred and seventy-seven.

Q. Who made the sixteenth-century Danish translation?

A. Christiern Pedersen, said to have been the first writer of importance to use Danish, and who wished his people to combine Christian faith, popular education, and acquaintance with Danish history.

Q. When was the first translation made into Icelandic?

A. By the middle of the sixteenth century the New Testament had been translated into Icelandic by German missionaries. Gudbrand Thorlaksson, bishop from 1570 to 1627, published a hymnal and an Icelandic translation of the Bible.

Q. When was the first translation made into Swedish?

A. In the sixteenth century a Swedish translation was made by a group of men, one of whom was Olavus Petri. The New Testament, in 1526, was the first book of importance to be printed in Sweden.

Q. When was the first Finnish translation made?

A. Isaac Rothovius, Bishop of Abo from 1627 to 1652, founded a university, advanced the idea of popular education, and caused a Finnish translation of the Bible to be made.

Q. By whom was the first Hungarian translation made?

A. In the sixteenth century, under the influence of John Huss, two priests made a Hungarian translation.

Q. What is the Dutch authorized version?

A. The Staten Bijbel, authorized by the States General in 1625, was completed in 1637. Franklin D. Roosevelt took the oath of office as President of the United States on the Roosevelt family Bible, an edition of this version published in 1686.

Q. What French translations of the Bible have there been?

A. John Calvin and others were interested in the French Geneva version, of which today's Lausanne version is a lineal descendant. A revision of J. F. Ostervald's La Sainte Bible was published in 1900. Another version of La Sainte Bible, translated under the direction of L'Ecole Biblique de Jerusalem and published in 1955, is often referred to as the Jerusalem Bible. The translation of Louis Segond is widely used.

Q. When was the Bible first translated into Welsh?

A. In 1588 the complete Bible was published in Welsh, the work of William Morgan.

Q. When was the Bible translated into the Turkish language?

A. Albertus Bobowsky, a Pole who had been kidnaped from his native land by Tartar raiders and sold as a slave in Turkey, renounced the Christian faith and embraced Islam, and eventually became the Sulton's dragoman. While at the court, he was persuaded by the Dutch ambassador to put the Scriptures into the Turkish tongue. The manuscript was sent to Leyden in 1660, where, for one hundred and fifty years, it lay unnoticed. Then the Russian ambassador, who had learned Turkish while serving in Constantinople, discovered it and began to update its vocabulary. After his death, Jean Daniel Kieffer completed the revision, which was first published in 1827. A version in modern Turkish was published in 1941.

Q. Who translated the Bible into modern Greek?

A. N. Bambas and others in 1844.

Q. When was the Bible first translated for use in Hawaii?

A. In 1840; under the influence of missionaries, Hawaii had the first schools, the first printing press, the first newspaper west of the Mississippi. Its first printing press was later sent to the Marcus Whitman mission in the Oregon territory.

Q. What of Rumanian translations?

A. From 1550 onward, sections of the Scripture were translated into Rumanian from the Slavonic; the first complete Rumanian New Testament was published in Transylvania in 1648.

Q. What Chinese translations have been made?

A. Karl Friedrich August Gützlaff, a German missionary from Pomerania, who lived from 1803 to 1851, translated the Bible into Chinese. This was later revised by a committee of five, including Edwin Edgerton Aiken, a Congregational missionary, and Andrew Sydenstricker, a Presbyterian. Sydenstricker, father of Pearl Buck, realized that revision of the Chinese Scriptures was imperative when he saw that his predecessors had not fully understood Chinese idioms. Elijah's chariot, for example, was translated "fire wagon." Since this term was later used for "railway train," Chinese readers were bewildered.

Q. Who first translated the Bible into the languages of India?

A. In 1793 William Carey translated the Bible into Bengali, the first of thirty-five Scripture versions made by him.

Q. What is the Gutenberg Bible?

A. The first large work produced from movable type in the Western world.

Q. What is the date of the Gutenberg Bible?

A. It came from the printing press of Johann Gutenberg in the German city of Mainz about 1452.

Q. In what language is the Gutenberg Bible?

A. Representing the translation made by Jerome toward the end of the fourth century A.D., it is in the Latin language.

Q. Is the Gutenberg Bible actually the oldest printed book?

A. It is believed that the much smaller Constance Missal, issued by the same printer, was a kind of preparatory work for the much larger one. Movable type appears to have been invented in China in the eleventh century. Earlier, done by the process of wood-block printing, Chinkang Ching, or the Diamond Scripture, of Buddhism was produced in China in the year 868. Between 175 and 183 A.D., some of the Confucian classics were engraved on a series of stone slabs; the ink rubbings made from them were an anticipation of the art of printing.

Q. By what other names is the Gutenberg Bible known?

A. It is sometimes called the Mazarin Bible because the first copy to gain the attention of the modern world was found in the library of Cardinal Mazarin, in Paris. From the circumstance that the folio pages have two columns, each usually with forty-two lines, the Gutenberg work is also referred to as the forty-two-line Bible.

Q. What are some distinctive features of the Gutenberg Bible?

A. Because verse divisions had not yet been devised, the work is divided only into chapters. Because all books known up to that time had been handwritten, the type face was made to resemble the writing of a scribe.

Q. How many copies of the Gutenberg Bible have survived into the twentieth century?

A. Of the approximately two hundred copies originally printed, forty-six are known to be still in existence. Of these, however, only twenty-two are complete.

Q. Where in the United States can Gutenberg Bibles be seen?

A. Complete copies are in the Library of Congress, the Widener Library of Harvard University, the Yale University Library, the Pierpont Morgan Library, the Library of the General Theological Seminary. Incomplete copies are in the New York Public Library and the Henry E. Huntington Library.

Q. What position is accorded the Gutenberg Bible in the Library of Congress?

A. It is exhibited in close proximity to the Great Bible of Mainz, a hand-lettered product done in the same city and at approximately the same time as the Gutenberg text. The Great Bible of Mainz was given to the Library of Congress in 1952 by Lessing J. Rosenwald, of Jenkintown, Pennsylvania. These volumes are said to form the most sought-after exhibit in the Library of Congress.

Q. What is the value of a Gutenberg Bible?

A. Although no copies are for sale, it is estimated that one would bring something like half a million dollars.

Q. What philatelic recognition has the United States Government made of the Gutenberg Bible?

A. In 1952 it issued a three-cent postage stamp (then the usual letter rate) showing the Mainz printing press and bearing the words, "500th Anniversary of the printing of the first book, The Holy Bible, from movable type, by Johann Gutenberg."

Q. At the inauguration of what American president was a facsimile of the Gutenberg Bible used?

A. On a copy now in Independence, Missouri, President Truman placed his hand as he took the oath of office January 20, 1949.

Q. When were the first efforts made to translate the Bible in England?

A. Caedmon, an Anglo-Saxon cowherd, was a poet remembered for his seventh-century paraphrases of Bible stories.

Q. What efforts were made in the eighth century to translate the Bible into Anglo-Saxon?

A. Eadhelm, bishop of Sherborne, translated the Psalms; Egbert, bishop of Holy Island, translated the Gospels; the Venerable Bede, the father of English history, died while translating the Gospel according to John. "I don't want my boys to read a lie," he said.

Q. What efforts were made in the ninth century?

A. Alfred, the only king to whom the British people have given the epithet "Great," had a section of the Hebrew law translated, and made it a part of his own legal code. He translated also a part of the Acts, and wished that all the freeborn youth of his kingdom "should employ themselves on nothing till they could first read well the English Scripture."

Q. Where in America is the work of King Alfred commemorated?

A. At Alfred University, in New York State, a region named by English travelers for its resemblance to Alfred's country in England. Alfred University's centennial pageant, in 1936, emphasized how the Anglo-Saxon king's love of learning and deeply religious spirit had "found an echo in the Alfred of today."

Q. What tenth-century efforts were there at Bible translation?

A. Archbishop Aelfric inserted English translations of some Scripture passages between the lines of the Latin Bible, to assist the clergy, who seemed to have little skill in interpreting the Vulgate. The Gospels, too, were translated for popular use.

Q. What put an end to this chapter in Bible translation?

A. The invasion of William the Conqueror, after which the Saxon clergy were replaced by priests of Normandy, who regarded the language of the defeated race as barbaric.

Q. What was the first complete English translation of the Bible?

A. That associated with the name of John Wyclif, a version which appeared about 1382; a revision by John Purvey and others was carried out between 1388 and 1395.

Q. Was Wyclif's translation made from the Hebrew and Greek originals?

A. No. These had been largely forgotten during the Middle Ages. Wyclif worked from the Bible generally used in Europe at that time, Jerome's Vulgate. Wyclif's version was thus a translation of a translation.

Q. What are some points at which Wyclif anticipated twentieth-century versions?

A. Words rendered in the King James Version as "verily, verily," Wyclif translated by "truly, truly," the phrase used in the Revised Standard Version, 1952. Wyclif's version of Luke 2:14: "Glori be to God in highest hevenes, and pees be to men in erthe which be of good wille" is much nearer to the Revised Standard Version than to the King James.

Q. What reception was accorded Wyclif's translation?

A. Archbishop Arundel in 1412 wrote to the pope concerning "that wretched and pestilent fellow John Wyclif, of damnable memory, that son of the old serpent, the very herald and child of anti-Christ" that "to fill up the measure of his malice, he devised the expedient of a new translation of the scriptures into the mother tongue." Another described Wyclif as "The devil's instrument, Church's enemy, people's confusion, heretics' idol, hypocrites' mirror, schism's broacher, hatred's sower, lies' forger, flatteries' sink."

Q. How did the established order further show its contempt for Wyclif?

A. His bones were dug up and burned and thrown into the little river Swift, on whose banks was the parish served by Wyclif at Lutter-worth. Of this desecration, an old historian says: "as the Swift bore

them into the Severn, and the Severn into the narrow seas, and they
again into the ocean, thus the ashes of Wyclif is an emblem of his teaching, which is dispersed over all the world."

Q. By what prayer is Wyclif remembered?

A. To his translation he affixed these words: "God grant us to ken
and to kepe Holi Writ and to suffer joiefulli some pain for it at the
last."

Q. Who was the first to translate the Greek New Testament into
English?

A. William Tyndale, whose New Testament was completed in
1525.

Q. How did the Greek New Testament become available?

A. Discovery of old manuscripts was a feature of the Renaissance.
Erasmus, the Dutch scholar and humanist, working from half a dozen
medieval manuscripts, edited the first Greek Testament ever published;
it appeared in 1516.

Q. What was the chief significance of Erasmus' work?

A. It made vernacular versions inevitable. "I totally dissent," he
wrote in his preface, "from those who are unwilling that the sacred
Scriptures, translated in the vulgar tongue, should be read by private
individuals. I would wish even all women to read the Gospel and the
Epistles of Paul. I wish they were translated into all languages of the
people. I wish that the husbandman might sing parts of them at his
plough, and the weaver at his shuttle, and that the traveler might beguile
with their narration the weariness of his way."

Q. Did the church authorities in England welcome the translation
made by Tyndale from the Greek Testament of Erasmus?

A. On the contrary, they refused to allow him to work ·in England,
banned the books when effort was made to import them from the Con-
tinent, and described Tyndale's translation as a "damnable and heretical
book."

Q. How were copies of Tyndale's work made available to the
people of England?

A. They were smuggled into the country in imports from the Con-
tinent.

Q. What famous utterance of Tyndale describes his spirit?

A. When he heard a learned man say it would be better to be without God's laws than the pope's, Tyndale replied: "If God spare my life, ere many years I will cause a boy that driveth the plough shall know more of the Scripture than thou doest."

Q. What price did Tyndale pay for his determination in carrying out this proposition?

A. He was burned at the stake on October 6, 1536.

Q. What was Sir Thomas More's opinion of Tyndale?

A. This supposedly liberal humanist described the Bible translator as "a beast discharging a filthy foam of blasphemies out of his brutish beastly mouth," one who learned his heresies "from his own father the devil," and insisted that he was one of the "hellhounds that the devil hath in his kennel."

Q. What ecclesiastical judgment was pronounced upon the work of Tyndale?

A. Johann Dobneck, who revealed to the English bishops the fact that Tyndale's New Testament was being secretly printed at Cologne, said: "The New Testament translated into the vulgar tongue is in truth the food of death, the fuel of sin, the vail of malice, the pretext of false liberty, the protection of disobedience, the corruption of discipline, the depravity of morals, the termination of concord, the death of honesty, the well-spring of vices, the disease of virtues, the instigation of rebellion, the milk of pride, the nourishment of contempt, the death of peace, the destruction of charity, the enemy of unity, the murderer of truth."

Q. What was the lasting effect of Tyndale's work?

A. He did more than any other to fashion the religious vocabulary of English-speaking people. It has been estimated that ninety percent of the King James Version was taken over from Tyndale.

Q. What were the martyred Tyndale's dying words?

A. "O Lord, open the King of England's eyes."

Q. How long before this prayer was answered?

A. In 1537, one year after Tyndale's burning, the second edition of Coverdale's Bible (the first appeared in 1535) was "set forth by the kynge's most gracious license." Coverdale was friend and colleague of Tyndale, and his Bible was largely Tyndale's.

Q. What was Matthew's Bible?

A. A version published in 1537 by John Rogers, this was a combination of Tyndale and Coverdale. The reason Rogers wrote under the name of Thomas Matthew is suggested when we remember that in 1555 he was burned alive at Smithfield, "the first martyr," says Foxe, "of all the blessed company that suffered in Queen Mary's time." Archbishop Cranmer prevailed upon the king to sanction the circulation of this version.

Q. What was distinctive about Matthew's Bible?

A. It was the first to introduce chapter summaries.

Q. Who revised Matthew's Bible?

A. A London lawyer, Richard Tavener, in 1539.

Q. What is an authorized version of the Bible?

A. A translation issued with the approval of a recognized ecclesiastical body.

Q. How many authorized Bibles have there been?

A. Five: The Great Bible, 1539; the Bishops' Bible, 1568; the King James Bible, 1611; the Revised Version, 1881-85; the Revised Standard Version, 1946-1952.

Q. What recognized ecclesiastical bodies have given their approval to Bible translations?

A. The hierarchy of the Roman Church, operating through the Papal Biblical Commission; the Church of England; Councils of Churches.

Q. What English Bible translations have been approved by the Roman hierarchy?

A. The Rheims-Douai, 1582-1609, revised by Bishop Challoner in 1749; the New Testament translation of Francis Aloysius Spencer (the first Roman Catholic translation made in America); the translation of Ronald A. Knox; the New Testament of our Lord and Saviour Jesus Christ, translated under the patronage of the Confraternity of Christian Doctrine; the Westminster Version of the Sacred Scriptures, edited by Cuthbert J. Lattey.

Q. How has the Church of England given its approval to Bible translations?

A. Under the ecclesiastical structure of the Church of England, the reigning monarch is its nominal head. It was the custom in the past for the monarch, acting in this capacity, to authorize Bible translations. More recently, the Convocation of Canterbury acts on its own initiative.

Q. What English Bibles were authorized by English kings?

A. The first authorized version was the Great Bible issued in 1539 with the approval of Henry VIII. The second authorized version, the Bishops' Bible, 1568, appeared in the reign of Queen Elizabeth I. The third authorized version, 1611, was sanctioned by James I of England, who was James VI of Scotland.

Q. What was the significance of the Bishops' Bible?

A. Matthew Parker, archbishop of Canterbury, was the prime mover in the work; many of those who assisted him were bishops. Never a popular translation, its importance arises from the acceptance by ecclesiastical authorities of the necessity for Bible translation. At a number of places where Tyndale had used the word "love," the Bishops' substituted "charity."

Q. What is the Saint James Version of the Bible?

A. Although one sees references to it in the writing of people who should know better, there is no such thing. King James was far from being a saint. One reason he initiated a Bible revision project was to divert his people from the addled policies of his reign. A Puritan preacher pointedly announced that he was preaching from James the First and Sixth—that is, James 1:6, which describes one who is "like a wave of the sea that is driven and tossed by the wind."

Q. What reception did the King James Version receive when it appeared in 1611?

A. The translators wrote in their preface: "Zeal to promote the common good, whether it be by devising anything ourselves, or revising that which hath been laboured by others, deserveth certainly much respect and esteem, but yet findeth but cold entertainment in the world. It is welcomed with suspicion instead of love." These words were prophetic of the objections that were to be raised. For seventy years after its publication, the volume was denounced as theologically unsound and ecclesiastically biased. The integrity of its translators was called into question. They were accused of "blasphemy," "most damnable corruptions," "intolerable deceit," "vile imposture."

Q. What Bible translations have been initiated by the Convocation of Canterbury?

A. In 1856 and again in 1870 the Convocation received motions looking toward what was to become known as the Revised Version. The New Testament appeared in 1881, the entire Bible in 1885. Representatives of the Church of England also served in planning The Bible: A New English Translation (New Testament, 1961). This project was launched in 1946 by the General Assembly of the Church of Scotland, which adopted overtures recommending that a translation of the Bible be made in the language of the present day.

Q. What were some features of the Revised Version of 1881-85?

A. The attempt was made to follow the order of the words in the original languages, a factor that deprived the work of readability; insofar as possible, all changed expressions were couched in the vocabulary of earlier versions.

Q. What reception did the Revised Version receive in America?

A. The long-awaited revision of the New Testament, brought to New York by ship, was sent by telegraph to Chicago, where the entire work was published two days later by two Chicago newspapers. Some two million copies of the New Testament were sold within a short time, and three million by 1887.

Q. What is the relationship of the American Standard Version, sometimes referred to as the American Revised Version, to the Revised Version?

A. The British revisers were in correspondence with an American Committee that felt that its choices of text and interpretation warranted a separate version in the United States. Out of deference to the British Committee, the Americans waited until 1901 to publish their work.

Q. What were some features of the American Standard Version?

A. More forward-looking than their British counterparts, the American revisers rejected "uncouth, unidiomatic, or obscure phraseology," even where it was thought to have "rhetorical force" and "antique flavor."

Q. What part have Councils of Churches played in initiating Bible translations?

A. In 1937 the International Council of Religious Education took steps looking toward a fresh revision of the Scriptures in English. By the time the work of its Standard Bible Committee was completed, in 1952, the originating organization had become the Division of Christian Education of the National Council of the Churches of Christ in the U.S.A. The Revised Standard Version was commended by the General Assembly of that body to its constituent communions. Two organizations sponsored the New English Bible: The Council of Churches for Wales, the United Council of Christian Churches and Religious Communions in Ireland.

Q. In addition to the Church of England, the Church of Scotland, and the Church Councils just named, what ecclesiastical bodies joined in authorizing the New English Bible?

A. The Baptist Union of Great Britain and Ireland, the Congregational Union of England and Wales, the London Yearly Meeting of the Society of Friends, the Methodist Church of Great Britain, the Presbyterian Church of England.

Q. What right have Councils of Churches to initiate Bible revision?

A. Church Councils are co-operative agencies of the constituent communions and have only such authority as comes from their ability to draw together scholars representative of Christendom's best learning.

Q. What men associated with the founding of denominations have made their own Bible translations?

A. John Wesley, whose movement within the Church of England led ultimately to the Methodist Church, published, in 1755, his own revision of the New Testament, with explanatory notes. Alexander Campbell, whose protest against some Presbyterian doctrines led to the founding of the Disciples of Christ, published, in 1826, a translation of the New Testament bearing his name. This rested largely upon the work of three British divines: George Campbell (the Gospels), James Macknight (the Epistles), and Philip Doddridge (Acts and Revelation).

Q. What members of the Standard Bible Committee issued their own translations?

A. James Moffatt, whose New Testament appeared in 1913 and Old Testament in 1926, is one of the few men who have undertaken singlehandedly to put into English both the Hebrew Old Testament and the Greek New Testament. Edgar J. Goodspeed published in 1923 The New Testament: An American Translation. In 1931 this was bound up with the Old Testament of Alexander J. Gordon, Theophile J. Meek, J. M. Powis Smith, and Leroy Waterman to form The Bible: An American Translation. In 1938 Dr. Goodspeed published The Apocrypha: An American Translation.

Q. Who are some of the men who made individual translations in the eighteenth century?

A. William Mace, William Whiston, Edward Harwood, Gilbert Wakefield.

Q. Who are some of the men who made individual translations in the nineteenth century?

A. Robert Young, H. T. Anderson, Farrar Fenton, Granville Penn, Joseph Bryant Rotherham, Samuel Bagster, Rodolphus Dickinson, Herman Keinfetter (pen name of F. Parker).

Q. Who are some of the persons who made individual translations in the twentieth century?

A. Richard Francis Weymouth, W. G. Ballantine, Mrs. H. B. Montgomery, J. B. Phillips, W. B. Godbey, Charles Williams, Charles Kingsley Williams.

Q. What was the first English Bible brought to America?

A. The Geneva Version, published in 1560. Made by English and Scottish exiles who worked in the Swiss city, the translation never had any formal authorization, yet was one of the most popular of all English versions. It was the Bible of John Knox, John Bunyan, John Milton, Oliver Cromwell, William Shakespeare, and the Pilgrim Fathers. Nearly two hundred editions were issued in England, where it continued to be printed until 1616. After that, some one hundred and fifty thousand copies were imported from Holland, where the last edition appeared in 1644.

Q. What were distinctive features of the Geneva Bible?

A. Seeking to be as far as possible its own commentary, it introduced such aids to study as maps, woodcuts, tables of weights, measurement, distance, etc., and an appendix of metrical psalms. It was also the first English Bible to have verse divisions.

Q. What is the Breeches Bible?

A. This name is given to the Geneva Bible, from its rendering of Genesis 3:7, which relates that Adam and Eve "made themselves breeches." Wyclif's version had used the same expression.

Q. What is the Treacle Bible?

A. This name is given to the Coverdale Bible, from its rendering of Jeremiah 8:22: "Is there no treacle in Gilead?"

Q. What is the Bug Bible?

A. A 1549 edition of Matthew's Bible, where Psalm 91:5 uses the work "bugges" in the sense of ghosts or evil spirits.

Q. What is the Wicked Bible?

A. A 1631 edition of the King James Version, in which the word "not" was omitted from the Seventh Commandment; for this error the printer was fined three hundred pounds.

Q. What are the Great He Bible and the Great She Bible?

A. Editions of the King James Version in which the sentence in Ruth 3:15 varies between "he went into the citie" and "she went into the citie."

Q. What is the Vinegar Bible?

A. An edition of the King James Version in which a column heading at Luke 20 inadvertently substituted "vinegar" for "vineyard."

Q. What was the first book printed in the New World?

A. The Bay Psalm book, a metrical version of the Psalter made by Richard Mather, John Eliot, and Thomas Weld. It was published at Cambridge in 1640 under the title *The Whole Book of Psalms Faithfully Translated into English Metre.*

Q. What was the first Bible translation made in the New World?

A. John Eliot's translation into the language of the Algonquian Indians. The New Testament appeared in 1661, the whole Bible in 1663.

Q. What word did this translation contribute to the vocabulary of American politics?

A. The word *mugwump,* an Indian term used by Eliot to translate the Old Testament word familiar to us as "judge." Among the judges of Israel were Deborah, Gideon, Sampson. Each of these was described in Eliot's version as "mugwump."

Q. What was the second complete Bible published in the New World?

A. A German Bible, issued in 1743 from the press established by Christopher Sauer at Germantown, Pennsylvania.

Q. What was the first English Bible printed in America?

A. The Aitken Bible, which appeared in 1782, in which year Congress passed a resolution calling for its use. This was not so much authorization of a Bible as determination to keep out editions published elsewhere.

Q. What early American patriot made his own translation of the Bible?

A. Charles Thomson, secretary of the Continental Congress, made his own translation from the Greek New Testament and the Greek Old Testament or Septuagint. Thomson's version was published in 1808.

Q. What is the Jefferson Bible?

A. In 1803, Thomas Jefferson purchased copies of the New Testament in English, Greek, Latin, and French, and constructed for himself a harmony of the Gospels from which he was accustomed to read each night before retiring.

Q. What American lexicographer wished to be remembered for his version of the Bible?

A. Asserting that "Whenever words are understood in a sense different from that of the original languages, they do not present to the reader the Word of God," Noah Webster made a revision of the English Bible consisting "of words expressing the sense which is most common in popular usage." The volume, issued in 1833, with revisions in 1839, 1840, and 1841, was entitled *Holy Bible with Amendments*. Webster regarded this as the "utmost undertaking" of his life, and wished to be remembered by it rather than by his dictionary or blue-back speller.

Q. What is the Twentieth Century New Testament?

A. Following a "Tentative Edition" issued in three parts between 1898 and 1901, the Twentieth Century New Testament appeared in 1904. Abandoning the traditional order of the books, it sought to present them in a more nearly chronological order.

Q. What is the Berkeley Version of the Bible?

A. A work combining the New Testament translation of Gerrit Verkuyl with an Old Testament translation done by a score of individuals. The footnotes contain "moralistic conclusions, quotations from modern poets and philosophers, parallels in modern history, and suggestions about memorization."

Q. What is the Bible in Basic English?

A. A translation of Old and New Testaments using a vocabulary limited to one thousand words, the eight hundred and fifty words of Basic English plus one hundred and fifty distinctively Biblical words.

Q. What is the Bible Designed to be Read as Living Literature?

A. A publication, primarily for college students, in which genealogies and duplicate narratives are omitted and each book is prefaced by an introduction. The basic text is that of the King James Version, though the Revised Version is used for Proverbs, Job, Ecclesiastes, and the Song of Songs.

Q. What is the New World Translation of the Hebrew-Christian Scriptures?

A. A version, made by anonymous translators, for the Watch Tower Bible and Tract Society, popularly known as Jehovah's Witnesses.

Q. What is the Authentic New Testament?

A. A translation by Hugh J. Schonfield, a Jewish scholar who felt that his knowledge of the Hebrew background gave him facility in re-creating the authentic atmosphere of the Christian faith.

Q. What factors make continuing Bible translation inevitable?

A. The discovery of older manuscripts, new knowledge about the Biblical languages, the changing nature of English speech.

Q. What older manuscripts are now available to scholars?

A. Twentieth-century translators have access to half a dozen rather complete manuscripts far older than any known to the King James translators.

Q. What are these more ancient Biblical texts, and where are they now located?

A. Codex Vaticanus, in the Vatican Library; Codex Sinaiticus, in the British Museum; Codex Alexandrinus, in the British Museum; Codex Ephraemi, in the Bibliothèque Nationale; Codex Bezae, at Cambridge; and Codex Washingtoniensis, in the Freer Gallery of the Smithsonian Institution, Washington, D.C.

Q. What is a codex?

A. A handwritten book with pages (in contrast to the earlier roll or scroll).

Q. Besides codices, what other ancient sources are available?

A. Portions of Old and New Testaments preserved on papyrus.

Q. What are some of the most important papyri?

A. The Chester Beatty Papyri; the John Rylands collection; the John H. Scheide Papyri; and those collected by Grenfell and Hunt.

Q. How has new light been shed on Biblical languages?

A. The discovery of non-Biblical documents dating from New Testament times has shown that the early Christian documents were written not in classical Greek but in the language of the common people.

Q. What are some illustrations of this?

A. The prodigal son did not simply "gather all together," but turned it into cash—so he could take it with him. Judas did not hold the bag, but carried a money box. Paul wrote to the Philippians not simply, "I have all, and abound," but "I have received full payment, and more."

Q. What are some illustrations of the changing nature of the English language?

A. Such words out of the King James Bible as *ouches* (Exodus 28:11), *pannag* (Ezekiel 27:17), *besom* (Isaiah 14:23), and *brigandine* (Jeremiah 46:4) are no longer intelligible to most people. Others are misleading: *ear* in the King James Version is a verb meaning "plow" (I Samuel 8:12); *angle* is a noun meaning "fishhook" (Isaiah 19:8); *bravery* refers not to courage but to feminine finery (Isaiah 3:18-23). Still other words convey now a meaning opposite to that they once had. *Prevent,* now meaning "preclude," once meant "anticipate" (as in the King James Version of Psalm 119:147: "I prevented the dawning of the morning"). *Let,* now meaning "permit," once meant "hinder" (as in the King James Version of Romans 1:13: "I purposed to come unto you, but was let").

Q. What is a Bible concordance?

A. An alphabetical index showing the places in the Scripture where each principal word occurs, including in each case the immediate context. Although such verbal indices are now available for many authors, the first concordances were for Bible study.

Q. Who made the first concordance?

A. The first alphabetical verbal index appears to have been devised by Cardinal Hugo, a thirteenth-century dignitary interested in helping people to use the Vulgate. He is said to have had the assistance of some five hundred monks.

Q. Who made the first concordance for the English Bible?

A. In the sixteenth century, John Marbeck published what the title page described as "A Concordance, that is to Saie, a Worke Wherein by the Order of the Letters of the A.B.C. Ye Maie Redely Find Any Words Conteined in the Whole Bible, so often as it is There Expressed or Mentioned." This was designed to aid in the study of the only English version authorized up to that time, the Great Bible of 1539.

Q. What eighteenth-century eccentric made a concordance to the King James Version?

A. Alexander Cruden, whose biography, written by Edith Olivier, is entitled *Alexander the Corrector*. Dissatisfied with the existing concordances, Cruden set himself to construct one that would be perfect and "complete."

Q. What later concordance claimed to include 118,000 references not found in Cruden?

A. Young's Analytical Concordance, listing not only English words but also Hebrew and Greek words.

Q. What concordance, originally designed for the King James Version, later took account of other versions?

A. Strong's Exhaustive Concordance, first published in 1894, later introduced comparative features taking into account renderings in the Revised Version and the American Standard Version.

Q. What electronic device has been used to construct a concordance in the twentieth century?

A. At the suggestion of the Reverend John W. Ellison, a Univac computer was set to work constructing a concordance for the Revised Standard Version.

Q. How does the time spent by a computer compare with that spent by a man in constructing a concordance?

A. James Strong is said to have spent thirty years making his Exhaustive Concordance. Univac's Complete Concordance to the Revised Standard Version required one hundred and twenty hours.

Q. How does a machine-made concordance compare with a man-made one?

A. Univac does not appear to be very well instructed in the Kingdom of God. It cannot distinguish between common nouns and proper nouns, and in early editions the name of Mark was listed indiscriminately with other kinds of marks. Univac, unable to tell the difference between nouns and verbs, cannot distinguish "might" as a word for power from "might" as a helping verb. Where Univac lumps all Biblical Josephs together, Cruden distinguishes Joseph the son of Jacob, Joseph the name of a tribe, Joseph the husband of Mary, and Joseph as "the name of divers men."

Q. What is a harmony of the Gospels?

A. An arrangement by which similar incidents from the several narratives are placed in parallel columns, to facilitate comparative study.

Q. Who made the first harmony of the Gospels?

A. Tatian, a second-century apologist who lived in Mesopotamia and was a pupil of Justin Martyr. Between 153 and 170 A.D., Tatian issued what he called *Diatesseron,* from the Greek words meaning "by means of the four."

Q. What Reformer prepared a harmony of the Gospels?

A. John Calvin; in 1584 there was published in London his *A Harmonie upon the Three Evangelists, Matthew, Mark, and Luke with Commentarie Faithfullie Translated out of Latine into English by E. P. Whereunto is also included a Commentarie upon the Evangelist S. John by the Same Author.*

Q. What are some harmonies using the King James Version?

A. One of the earliest was that of Samuel Craddock, who published, about 1668, *The Harmony of the Four Evangelists and Their Text Methodized.* About 1889, A. T. Pierson published what he called *The one gospel; or, the combination of the four evangelists, in one complete record.*

Q. What are some harmonies using the Revised Version of 1881?

A. Those by E. A. Abbott and W. G. Rushbrooke (1884); J. A. Broadus (1893); J. M. Thompson (1910).

Q. What are some harmonies using the American Standard Version of 1901?

A. Stevens and Burton published in 1904 *A Harmony of the Gospels for Historical Study—An Analytical Synopsis of the Four Gospels.* Walter E. Bundy's *A Syllabus and Synopsis of the First Three Gospels,* first published in 1932, was reissued in an anniversary edition in 1952.

Q. What are some harmonies using the Revised Standard Version?

A. Ralph D. Heim's *A Harmony of the Gospels,* 1946; Albert Cassel Wieand's *Gospel Records of the Message and Mission of Jesus Christ; Gospel Parallels, A Synopsis of the First Three Gospels,* based on Albert Huck's *Synopse der Drei Ersten Evangelien.*

Q. What are some Gospel harmonies using Roman Catholic translations?

A. In 1942, S. J. Hardegen issued *A Chronological Harmony of the Gospels, using the revised text of the Challoner-Rheims Versions.*

About the same year, J. E. Steinmueller published *A Gospel Harmony,* using the Confraternity edition of the New Testament.

Q. Why do some Gospel harmonies work with all four evangelists, some with only three?

A. The difficulty of harmonizing John with the other writers leads most contemporary students to treat it separately, as John Calvin did, seeking to harmonize only Matthew, Mark, and Luke.

THE OLD TESTAMENT

The Pentateuch

Q. What is the meaning of the word *Pentateuch*?

A. Derived from the Greek for "Five Rolls," this is the term applied collectively to the first five books of the Old Testament: Genesis, Exodus, Leviticus, Numbers, and Deuteronomy.

Q. What is the Hebrew name for these books?

A. The five of them together are known as Torah, which means "Law" or "Teaching," in the sense of Divine Instruction.

Q. Why are they called the Five Books of Moses?

A. Because they deal with the events culminating in the birth, education, public career, teaching, and abiding influence of Moses, of whom it is said in Deuteronomy 34:10: "there has not arisen a prophet since in Israel like Moses, whom the Lord knew face to face."

Q. Who is the author of the Pentateuch?

A. The title indicates that the fivefold work is about Moses, rather than by Moses; since Deuteronomy 34:5-7 contains an account of the death and burial of Moses ("Moses . . . died there in the land of Moab . . . but no man knows the place of his burial"), the entire contents could hardly have come from him. Although the work was probably put into its present form in the sixth century B.C., when the nation, deprived of its homeland, assembled the accounts that had come down through generations of the unique way in which God had dealt with His people, Israel, it enshrines the thoughts of many men and is not to be attributed to a single individual.

Q. What sources were used by the compilers of the Pentateuch?

A. Ancient stories of human origins, handed down through long ages; traditions of the patriarchs, Abraham, Isaac, and Jacob, and all whose lives were bound up with theirs; accounts of how the Hebrew people came to be in Egypt and of the miraculous deliverance from the land of bondage; narratives of the wilderness wanderings and the bestowal of laws to meet situations as they arose; the conquest of Canaan; the settlement in the Land of Promise and the division of the land among the tribes. Embedded in this material are songs celebrating great national events (such as the Song of Moses, Exodus 15:1-18, and the Song of Miriam, Exodus 15:21); songs associated with community occasions (such as the opening of a new water supply, Numbers 21:17f); songs commemorating the exploits of individuals (such as the Song of Lamech, Genesis 4:23f); collections of laws, such as the Ten Commandments (Exodus 20:1-17; Deuteronomy 5:6-21) and the Holiness Code (Leviticus 17-26); dramatic monologues, such as the Blessing of Jacob (Genesis 49:1-27) and the Blessing of Moses (Deuteronomy 33:1-29).

Q. What different strands or intertwined threads constitute the Pentateuch?

A. One strand called J (from the initial letter of Jahveh, its distinctive name for God) embodies traditions cherished in the southern kingdom of Judah; another strand, called E (from the initial letter of Elohim, its distinctive name for God), embodies traditions cherished in the northern kingdom of Israel. The ministry of Israel's prophets infused the law with a new breadth of compassion and inclusiveness, and reformers produced a strand, called D, which is spoken of as the Deuteronomic Code. Deprived of a national homeland and the privilege of worship at the temple in Jerusalem, the priests sought to strengthen Sabbath observance, the keeping of dietary laws, celebration of festival days, and produced a Priestly Code, referred to as P. Although the existence of these strands is generally recognized, there is no agreement regarding the precise limits of any one of them, and there are some who discern still other strands, as L (for Lay source) and S (for South).

Q. What are characteristics of the J document?

A. In addition to the name Jahveh, it employs such terms as Sinai, Israel, Canaanites, and such phrases as "find favor in the sight of," "call on the name of," "bring *out*" (from the land of Egypt); coming perhaps from the religious leaders associated with Solomon's temple, it does not require the miraculous in order to discern Jahveh's guiding hand in Israel's history; with subtle touches it portrays shades of character in men, and the infinite mercy of God.

Q. What are characteristics of the E document?

A. In addition to the name Elohim, it employs such terms as Horeb, Jacob, Amorites, the man Moses, and the phrase "bring *up*" (from the land of Egypt); coming from Ephraimite circles, it has a strong interest in the righteousness that God requires of his people: when the people sin, they must be called to repentance; there is an interest in outstanding personalities, with Moses as the chief; miraculous aspects of the nation's history are emphasized.

Q. What are characteristics of the D material?

A. D is fond of such phrases as "that your days may be long," "a mighty hand and a stretched-out arm," "the sojourner, the fatherless, and the widow," "with all your heart and with all your soul"; reflecting the reform under Josiah, in 621 B.C., it does not add to our knowledge of the character and work of Moses, but rephrases older regulations in the light of prophetic teaching.

Q. What are characteristics of P?

A. P uses such phrases as "to be gathered to" (one's ancestors), "be fruitful and multiply," "by their families," "their generations." Not concerned with the rigors of the wilderness wanderings, it is sure that the forms of worship envisioned for the second temple are so perfect and appropriate that they must have had their origins in more primitive times.

Q. What is the Hexateuch?

A. Because the strands of J, E, D, and P can be traced through the book of Joshua, some prefer to link this work with the five books of Moses and have a sixfold arrangement. The speech attributed to Joshua at Shechem (Joshua 24:2-13), as summing up the whole six books, has been described as a kind of Hexateuch in miniature: "I gave you a land on which you had not labored, and cities which you had not built, and you dwell therein; you eat the fruit of vineyards and oliveyards which you did not plant" (Joshua 24:13).

THE FIRST BOOK OF MOSES COMMONLY CALLED
GENESIS

Q. What two accounts of the creation are found in Genesis?

A. Genesis 1:1-2:3 gives a summary statement of the different orders of created beings; this account emphasizes the sovereign and originating power of God who eternally is, and who has appointed man and woman, made in his image, as trustees of nature's bounty. The second account (2:4-25), beginning "These are the generations of the heaven and the earth when they were created" (2:4), deals more specifically with man: the garden given to him "to till it and to keep it" (2:15); the lordship of man over other living things ("The man gave names to all"—2:20); the indissoluble companionship of husband and wife ("they become one flesh"—2:24); the conditional nature of all happiness (there is one tree of which "you shall not eat"—2:17).

Q. What words from the latter story are quoted in the New Testament?

A. "Therefore a man leaves his father and mother and cleaves to his wife and they become one flesh" (2:24) are made the basis for the teaching of Jesus (Matthew 19:5) and Paul (I Corinthians 6:16; Ephesians 5:31) on the nature of true marriage.

Q. How does the new translation of the Jewish Publication Society differ from many English versions in its rendering of 1:2?

A. In Hebrew, as also in Greek and other languages, one word serves for the two English terms, wind and spirit (John 3:8 contains a play on words based on the Greek). Contending that "the Spirit of God was moving over the face of the waters" reflects belief in the later doctrine of the Trinity, the 1962 translation of the Jewish Publication Society here reads: "a wind from God sweeping over the water."

Q. What are the main divisions of the book of Genesis?

A. Chapters 1-11 deal with the origins of life, arts, speech, civilization, all of which man has somehow managed to mar; chapters 12-36 deal with the origins of the Hebrew community in the lives and deeds of Abraham, Isaac, and Jacob; chapters 37-50 show how, through

Joseph's triumph over adversity ("you meant evil against me; but God meant it for good"—50:20), God was preparing for his people a distinctive period of training and discipline in Egypt.

Q. How does Genesis account for the origin of sin?

A. Man and woman in the garden overreach themselves in their attempt to "be like God" (3:5) and attain a quality of knowledge that rightly belongs to God alone. The subtlety of the temptation is symbolized by its embodiment in a serpent, a creature man now instinctively regards as his enemy, and by the appeal the serpent makes to the man's native endowments of taste ("good for food"—3:6), sight ("a delight to the eyes"—3:6), ambition ("to be desired to make one wise"—3:6), and desire to please ("she also gave some to her husband"—3:6).

Q. What other aspects of man's relationship to God are suggested by the story of the Fall?

A. The impossibility of running away from God ("the man and his wife hid themselves"—3:8; but "God called to the man"—3:9); man's reluctance to accept responsibility for his actions ("The man said, 'The woman . . . gave me fruit . . . and I ate' . . . The woman said, 'The serpent beguiled me' "—3:12f); the belief that "pain in child-bearing" (3:16), the difficulties of tilling the soil ("thorns and thistles it shall bring forth"—3:18), and frail mortality ("you are dust and to dust you shall return"—3:19) are the price man pays for his disobedience.

Q. What contrast does Paul draw between man's conduct in the garden and the life opened to him in Christ?

A. "For as by one man's disobedience many were made sinners, so by one man's obedience many will be made righteous" (Romans 5:19; cf. I Corinthians 15:45-49).

Q. In Genesis what follows man's revolt against God?

A. Man's strife against man, typified by the conflict between Cain and Abel (4:1-16).

Q. What word of Jesus covers both these situations?

A. "You shall love the Lord your God with all your heart, and with all your soul, and with all your mind . . . You shall love your neighbor as yourself" (Matthew 22:37,39).

Q. What elements in the Cain and Abel story indicate its representative and symbolic character?

A. Though one strand of Genesis suggests that the only inhabitants of the earth were these two and their parents, another presupposes the existence of other people: God must put a mark upon Cain, "lest any who come upon him should kill him" (4:15); going eastward, too, Cain finds a tribe to give him refuge and a wife (4:16). Cain, "a tiller of the ground" (4:2), typifies the agricultural mode of society; Abel, "a keeper of the sheep" (4:2), the pastoral. Abel's sacrifice is represented as more pleasing to God (4:4), apparently because the Hebrews, by this time a pastoral people, were sure that God was more pleased with "the firstlings of the flock" (4:4) than with products that were simply "the fruit of the ground" (4:3). Symbolically, the slaying of Cain takes place in the field (4:8).

Q. Cain is reported to have "dwelt in the land of Nod" (4:16); where was that?

A. It is pictured as "east of Eden" (4:16), but cannot be further identified.

Q. How is the song of Lamech (4:23f) echoed in the New Testament?

A. To his two wives, Adah and Zillah, Lamech, the swashbuckling son of Methushael (4:18) or Methuselah (5:25), boasted (4:24):

"If Cain is avenged sevenfold,
truly Lamech seventy-sevenfold."

Jesus bids Peter forgive not seven times, but seventy-seven times (the meaning of the Greek in Matthew 18:22).

Q. What distinctive character is introduced in Genesis 5?

A. Set amid the genealogical records indicating who begat whom and how long each lived is the brief and provocative biography of Enoch: "Enoch walked with God after the birth of Methuselah . . . Enoch walked with God; and he was not, for God took him" (5:24); and "By faith Enoch was taken up so that he should not see death; and he was not found, because God had taken him." (Hebrews 11:5).

Q. Who are the Nephilim (6:4)?

A. Many peoples have had stories of a race of giants who once dwelled upon earth. To this type of being the Hebrews gave the name of Nephilim. In Numbers 13:33 the returning spies report having seen the Nephilim in Canaan: "we seemed to ourselves like grasshoppers, and so we seemed to them"; Ezekiel 32:27 refers to "the fallen mighty men of old."

Q. What item among the Dead Sea Scrolls deals with the birth of Noah?

A. One of the documents tells how Noah at birth "rose up in the hands of the midwife and conversed with the Lord of righteousness," and when he opened his eyes they lighted the house "like the sun." Fearing that Noah might be the son of one of the Nephilim, Lamech inquired of his wife about it, but she reassured him.

Q. What were the dimensions of the ark Noah was commissioned to build?

A. "This is how you are to make it: the length of the ark three hundred cubits, its breadth fifty cubits, and its height thirty cubits" (6:15).

Q. What symbols of universal peace appear in connection with the story of the Flood?

A. The dove and the olive leaf (8:10f).

Q. What significance is attached to the rainbow?

A. A symbol of God's covenant never again to wipe out the life of mankind ("While the earth remains, seedtime and harvest, cold and heat, summer and winter, day and night, shall not cease" (8:22), it is to serve as a reminder to God as well as to man: "When the bow is in the clouds, I will look upon it and remember" (9:16).

Q. What uses does the New Testament make of the story of the Flood?

A. Jesus says (Matthew 24:37): "As were the days of Noah, so will be the coming of the Son of man"; he does not picture Noah's contemporaries as engaged in great evil: "they were eating and drinking, marrying and giving in marriage"—acting, in short, as if life held nothing more for anyone than food and drink and romance. Hebrews 11:7 tells how Noah "became an heir of the righteousness which comes by faith"; I Peter 3:20f represents the deliverance in Noah's ark, when eight persons "were saved by water," as the prototype of baptism.

Q. What is the meaning of the fact that, after the Flood, Noah "planted a vineyard; and he drank of the wine, and became drunk, and lay uncovered in his tent" (9:20)?

A. In these few words the author powerfully portrays two facts of human nature: (1) God's gifts are often turned to evil uses; and (2) liquor and sexual abuse often go together.

Q. What is the purpose of the genealogical tables in Genesis 10?

A. Grouping the peoples of the known world largely according to geographical location, the compiler traces the entire human family to a common origin in Noah and his sons.

Q. What archaeological finds are brought to mind by the Genesis story of "a tower with its top in the heavens" (11:4)?

A. Ziggurats found on the plains of Shinar indicate that this type of structure was common among the Babylonians.

Q. What is the purpose of the Tower of Babel story?

A. To explain why, since there is but one human family, there should be such diversity of speech.

Q. What allusions are there in the New Testament to the Tower of Babel?

A. Although it is not explicitly mentioned, the events of the day of Pentecost ("each one heard them speaking in his own language"—Acts 2:6) and the Seer's vision of "a great multitude" out of many nations, all joining in the same hymn of praise ("Salvation belongs to our God"—Revelation 7:10) are no doubt intended to indicate how the Spirit of God has enabled man to triumph over the curse of a divided speech.

Q. What is the most marked characteristic of Abraham?

A. His confident obedience in responding to the call of God ("he went out not knowing where he was to go"—Hebrews 11:8).

Q. What place does the New Testament assign to Abraham?

A. He is often referred to as the true father of all whose lives are lived by faith (cf. Romans 4:1-25; Galatians 3:6-9; James 2:20-23).

Q. What significance does the New Testament see in Abraham's having children by both Sarah and Hagar?

A. Sarah's offspring was progenitor in the true line of promise; Hagar's son turned out to be the father of the despised Ishmaelites, symbol of those who live in slavery to sin (Galatians 4:21-31). "Now this is an allegory: these women are two covenants . . . Hagar . . . corresponds to the present Jerusalem, for she is in slavery with her children. But the Jerusalem above is free, and she is our mother" (Galatians 4:24-26).

Q. What is the purpose of Abraham's being bidden to take his "only son Isaac . . . and offer him . . . as a burnt offering" (22:2)?

A. That the Hebrews should learn at the outset of their history that there are better ways of pleasing God than by human sacrifice.

Q. What do the Dead Sea Scrolls tell about Sarah?

A. They speak of her great beauty as manifest in her feet, her legs, her face, her hair: "And above all women she is lovely . . . and with all her beauty there is much wisdom in her."

Q. Who was Melchizedek?

A. A mysterious figure in 14:18f, he was "priest of God" and "king of Salem" who blessed Abraham after his victory over neighboring marauders. Described in Hebrews 7:3 as "without father or mother or genealogy," he suggests to the author of that Letter that there is a genuine priesthood other than the traditional one reserved for Aaron's descendants. So Christ is (Hebrews 7:17)

> " a priest for ever,
> after the order of Melchizedek."

Q. What is the significance of Sodom and Gomorrah?

A. Lot, given his choice of land, chooses the glamorous "cities of the valley" (13:12). These prove a poor place, however, in which to bring up children (19:1-13). When the cities are destroyed by volcanic action ("brimstone and fire from the Lord"—19:24), Lot's wife, looking back wistfully over the life that might have been, "became a pillar of salt" (19:26); the sorry sequel is that Lot lives incestuously with his daughters in a cave (19:30-38).

Q. What reference is made in the New Testament to the destruction of Sodom?

A. Warning the people of his own day that they were more scornful, insolent, and hardhearted even than the inhabitants of that city whose name has become synonymous with sexual perversion, Jesus says: ". . . it shall be more tolerable on the day of judgment for the land of Sodom than for you" (Matthew 11:24).

Q. What is the meaning of the name "Isaac"?

A. The Genesis narrative derives it from the Hebrew word for laughter, in remembrance of his parents' reaction at hearing that a child would be born to them in their old age (17:17,19; 21:1-7).

Q. What part does Isaac play in the patriarchal stories?

A. Less of a personality than the others, since he was overshadowed by a distinguished father, his principal function is to provide a link between the generation of his father Abraham and Abraham's famous grandson, Jacob.

Q. What was the outward sign of the covenant between God and Abraham?

A. Circumcision (17:11).

Q. What is the first piece of property acquired by Abraham?

A. A burial place for his wife, the Cave of Machpelah (23:1-20).

Q. Where did Abraham's servant find a wife for Isaac?

A. In the ancestral land of Mesopotamia (24:3f,10), he found Rebekah, a maiden "very fair to look upon" (24:16).

Q. Who were the twin sons born to Isaac and Rebekah?

A. Esau and Jacob (25:24-26).

Q. How did they differ?

A. "Esau was a skillful hunter, a man of the field, while Jacob was a quiet man, dwelling in tents" (25:27). From Esau the Edomites were descended; from Jacob, the Israelites.

Q. What incident between the brothers reveals their character?

A. Esau, the first-born, coming in hungry from the fields, forfeited his primogeniture when Jacob offered him in exchange "bread and pottage of lentils" (25:34).

Q. In what other way did Jacob get ahead of his brother?

A. With the connivance of his mother, he deceived his blind and dying father, and obtained the blessing that rightly belonged to the older (27:1-40).

Q. What happened to Jacob, the cheater?

A. He is cheated by his father-in-law, Laban, who foists upon him Leah, the older sister of Rachel, whom Jacob wanted to marry (29:9-30); Laban also managed by trickery to make off with the animals Jacob claimed as his wages (30:32-36).

Q. What experience of Jacob is enshrined in Christian hymnody?

A. Jacob's vision of the night (28:11-22), with angels "ascending and descending" (28:12) is the basis of the spiritual, "We are climbing Jacob's Ladder," as well as Sarah Flower Adams' hymn, with its lines:

> *"There let the way appear*
> *Steps unto heaven:*
> *All that Thou sendest me*
> *In mercy given:*

Angels to beckon me
　Nearer, my God, to Thee."

Q. What did Rachel steal (31:19)?

A. The "household gods." The term "household gods," in the Revised Standard Version, is a translation of the Hebrew term *teraphim*.

Q. What is the origin of the word *Mizpah*?

A. Genesis 31:48-50 identifies it as "Watchpost," the name given to the place where Jacob and Laban settled their differences.

Q. How is Jacob's name changed?

A. A vision of the night, in which Jacob "wrestled" with a mysterious figure beside the Jabbok, leads to his being called Israel, interpreted as "He who strives with God" or "God strives" (32:22-32).

Q. Why did Jacob favor Joseph over his other children?

A. Because he was "the son of his old age" (37:3).

Q. What mark of favoritism did Jacob bestow?

A. "He made him a long robe with sleeves," such as would be used on ceremonial occasions by one who might be expected to inherit his father's position.

Q. What effect did this favoritism have in the family?

A. Joseph's brothers "hated him, and could not speak peaceably to him" (37:4).

Q. How did Joseph intensify the hatred of his brothers?

A. By reporting to them a dream in which his sheaf "arose and stood upright" in the field, while the sheaves of his brothers did obeisance to it (37:5-8).

Q. How did the brothers take vengeance?

A. By selling Joseph to a caravan bound for Egypt (37:28,36).

Q. What happened to Joseph in Egypt?

A. He was sold to Potiphar, an officer at the Pharaoh's court, and "became a successful man" (39:2) whom Potiphar appointed "overseer of his house" (39:5).

Q. What perils beset Joseph in this position?

A. Potiphar's wife, rebuffed in her attempts to seduce him, lied about him and obtained his imprisonment (39:6-20).

Q. What happened in prison?

A. Joseph won the Pharaoh's attention and favor by his skill at interpreting dreams (41:39-44).

Q. What government post does Joseph obtain?

A. Second only in authority to the Pharaoh, he becomes food administrator in a time of famine (41:46-57).

Q. What effect does this have upon the Hebrews?

A. Joseph's aging father, learning that there is food in Egypt, sends his other sons there to ask for some (42:1-5). Thus Joseph is reunited with his brothers and through them with his father (42:6-46:7), and the Hebrews are established in Egypt.

Q. What happens at the end of Jacob's life?

A. He pronounces a blessing upon his sons and grandsons, summing up the character of each and assigning to each a portion of the Land of Promise (48:1-49:33).

Q. What happens after Jacob's death?

A. The body, embalmed after the ancient manner of the Egyptians (50:2f), was taken by Joseph to the Cave of Machpelah, the burial site acquired by Abraham (50:4-14). Joseph "reassured" his brothers "and comforted them" (50:21); when Joseph died "they embalmed him, and put him in a coffin in Egypt" (50:26).

Q. What English classic derives its theme from the Genesis story of the Fall?

A. Milton's "Paradise Lost."

Q. What are some twentieth-century literary works that have derived their titles from Genesis?

A. *Giants in the Earth,* by Rolvaag; *The Ark and the Dove,* by J. Moss Ives; *He Sent Forth a Raven,* by Elizabeth Madox Roberts; *Hagar's Child,* by Grace Naismith; *Call Me Ishmael,* by Lloyd Collins; *East of Eden,* by John Steinbeck; *Joseph and his Brethren,* by Thomas Mann.

Q. In what way does the book of Genesis set the pattern for the first six books of the Old Testament?

A. The books from Genesis through Joshua are designed to show how God fulfilled the promise made to the patriarchs in Genesis 12:7 and 13:15: "To you and your descendants I will give this land."

Q. What patriarchal altars are described?

A. That of Abraham at Bethel (12:8), Hebron (13:18), and Mt. Moriah (22:9); that of Isaac at Beersheba (26:25); that of Jacob at Shechem (33:20) and Bethel (35:7).

Q. What sacred spots are mentioned?

A. "Abraham planted a tamarisk tree in Beersheba" (21:33) and built an altar "by the oaks of Mamre" (13:18); Jacob erected a sacred pillar at Bethel (28:18) and at the place where he made a covenant with Laban (31:45); a well between Kadesh and Bered was called Beer-la-hairoi (16:14), meaning "the well of one who sees and lives."

Q. How does the creation story emphasize the littleness and the frailty of man?

A. By describing him (2:7) as formed of "dust from the ground."

Q. Dante recalls how Genesis pictures Art and Nature as the two sources of man's wealth; what is the basis for this?

A. "The Lord God took the man and put him in the garden [natural resources] to till it and keep it [art—that is, the labor of man]" (2:15).

Q. What is the Bible's earliest love song?

A. Adam's exclamation upon recognizing the woman as "counterpart and complement" of him:

"This at last is bone of my bones
    and flesh of my flesh;
she shall be called Woman
    because she was taken out of man" (Genesis 2:23).

Q. What is the meaning of the fall?

A. That man, having overreached himself, is up against evil that is too much for him.

Q. What is the meaning of the "flaming sword which turned every way, to guard the way to the tree of life" (3:24)?

A. That man cannot return to a state of innocence.

Q. What is the significance of the genealogies found in Genesis 5 and thereafter often in Scripture?

A. They emphasize the importance the Hebrews attached to family solidarity.

Q. What is the significance in Genesis 6:2,5 of the fact that when "the sons of God saw that the daughters of men were fair; and they took to wife such of them as they chose," the wickedness of man soon "was great in the earth"?

A. It suggests that evil is not simply a local and temporary thing but is cosmic in its extent and significance.

Q. How does the length of the ark, given in 6:15, compare with that of a ship like the *Queen Mary*?

A. The ark was about half as long.

Q. What two accounts of the Flood are given?

A. One narrative says, regarding the animals, "two of every sort" (6:20) went into the ark; the other says "seven pairs of all clean animals . . . and a pair of the animals that are not clean" (7:2).

Q. What words sum up the story of Abraham?

A. "And he believed the Lord; and he reckoned it to him as righteousness" (15:6).

Q. What New Testament passages allude to this?

A. Romans 4:3,9,22; Galatians 3:6.

Q. What passages in the Hexateuch suggest that Genesis 17:10 is a reading back into an earlier time of a practice that originated later?

A. Exodus 4:24ff says that circumcision began with Moses; Joshua 5:7, that it began with Joshua.

Q. What passage in the Apocrypha refers to the events described in Genesis 19?

A. Wisdom 10:7 says of Sodom and Gomorrah:
"Evidence of their wickedness still remains:
a continually smoking wasteland,
plants bearing fruit that does not ripen,
and a pillar of salt standing as a monument to an
    unbelieving soul."

Q. What popular belief lay back of the story in 30:14ff?

A. That the eating of mandrakes was an aid to conception.

Q. What was so serious about Rachel's stealing "her father's household gods" (31:19)?

A. The possession of these carried with it the right to his property.

Q. What is the universal significance of Jacob's wrestling with the unknown adversary (32:24f)?

A. The loneliness of the human spirit at grips with the unseen powers of the Universe.

Q. How does Joseph acknowledge an obligation to a morality greater than that of the community?

A. He is sure that to "do this great wickedness" would be to "sin against God" (39:9).

THE SECOND BOOK OF MOSES COMMONLY CALLED
EXODUS

Q. What is the meaning of the word *Exodus*?

A. It is a Greek term for "going out" or "departure"; the Hebrew title of the book, *we-eleh shemoth,* derived from the opening phrase, means "These are the names."

Q. What does the title refer to?

A. It refers to the deliverance God wrought for his ancient people, providing them a "way out" of Egypt; in original Greek, Luke 9:31, Jesus uses the same word in speaking of his own impending crucifixion, rather than a word meaning death.

Q. What is the date of the Exodus?

A. The events here recorded probably took place in the latter half of the thirteenth century B.C.

Q. What are the principal divisions of the book of Exodus?

A. 1:1 to 12:36 deals with the plight of the Hebrews, slaves in Egypt, with Moses' call, and with the wonders God wrought as evidence that he was with Moses; 12:37 to 18:27 deals with the actual escape from Egypt, and with subsequent wanderings in the wilderness; 19:1 to 40:38 deals with the covenant God made with Israel at Sinai, and the subsequent construction and equipping of the tabernacle.

Q. Genesis concludes with the story of Joseph, who had risen to great power in Egypt. What brought about the change in attitude on the part of the Egyptians toward Hebrews?

A. "Now there arose a new king over Egypt, who did not know Joseph" (1:8); he set taskmasters over them "and made their lives bitter with hard service" (1:14).

Q. What is the meaning of the word *Pharaoh*?

A. Egypt, governed by regions, had a central authority called "the great house," or *per-o;* the term came to be applied to the king himself, and the title passed into the vocabulary of the English Bible as Pharaoh.

Q. What population control device did the Pharaoh adopt in order to keep the Hebrew people in subjection?

A. He ordered the midwives to kill all Hebrew males at birth. "But the midwives feared God, and did not do as the king of Egypt commanded them" (1:17).

Q. How did a Hebrew boy get to the Pharaoh's court?

A. To protect her newborn son, a Hebrew mother set her child adrift in "a basket made of bulrushes" (2:3), with his older sister nearby to watch. "Now the daughter of Pharaoh came down to bathe at the river" (2:5), found the floating crib, took the child to her apartment, and employed the child's mother as nurse. Pharaoh's daughter "named him Moses . . . 'Because I drew him out of the water' " (2:10).

Q. What was Moses' first impulsive action toward freeing his people?

A. He killed an Egyptian whom he found oppressing his people, "and hid him in the sand" (2:12); for this "Moses fled from Pharaoh, and stayed in the land of Midian" (2:15), where he met and married Zipporah, (2:16-22), daughter of Reuel, the priest of Midian. Tending the flock of his father-in-law, Moses saw a bush "that was burning, yet it was not consumed" (3:2); there God commanded him to "bring forth my people, the sons of Israel, out of Egypt" (3:10).

Q. Under what name did God reveal himself to Moses?

A. "I am who I am" (3:14; cf. 6:3); Jesus later used the formula, "I am . . ." (cf. John 8:12,24,58; 10:7,11; 11:25).

Q. What was Moses' first response to God's call?

A. That he was not the man to lead the people from Egypt: "I am slow of speech" (4:10); God thereupon appointed Aaron, Moses' brother, to be spokesman for them both (4:11-16).

Q. What groups today perpetuate the custom begun by Moses when, realizing that in God's presence he was "on holy ground," he took off his shoes?

A. The Samaritans on Mt. Gerizim, and the Moslems upon entering a mosque.

Q. What family term, so important for Biblical religion, makes its first appearance in connection with the call of Moses?

A. Moses is instructed to say to Pharaoh, "Israel is my first-born son" (4:22).

Q. What is the Pharaoh's reaction to Moses' "Let my people go" (5:1)?

A. He laid yet heavier tasks upon the Hebrews, requiring them to produce as many bricks as before, but without providing them with straw (5:4-21).

Q. What theological concept having to do with deliverance first makes its appearance in this book?

A. Salvation is often spoken of in terms of redemption—which means literally "buying back." Through Moses, God here says to the people, "I will redeem you with an outstretched arm" (6:6). The song of Moses (15:13) contains the line: "Thou hast led in thy steadfast love the people whom thou hast redeemed."

Q. What assistance did God promise Moses?

A. "Great acts of judgment" (7:4), manifesting themselves in disasters that decimated the life of Egypt: the waters of "the Nile turned to blood" (7:20), and the fish died; frogs thereupon "came up and covered the land of Egypt" (8:6); then "there came gnats on man and beast; all the dust of the earth became gnats" (8:17); then "there came a great swarm of flies" and "the land was ruined by reason of the flies" (8:24); then "all the cattle of the Egyptians died" (9:6); next, there were "boils breaking out in sores on man and beast throughout all the land of Egypt" (9:9); then "there was hail, and fire flashing continually in the midst of the hail, very heavy hail, such as had never been in all the land of Egypt since it became a nation" (9:24); then "the Lord brought an east wind upon the land. . . . And the locusts came up over all the land of Egypt, and settled on the whole country of Egypt, such a dense swarm of locusts as had never been before, nor ever shall be again . . . not a green thing remained" 10:13-15); then "there was thick darkness in all the land of Egypt three days" (10:22), "a darkness to be felt" (10:21).

Q. What effect did these plagues have upon Pharaoh?

A. Sometimes it is said that "Pharaoh hardened his heart" (8:32); sometimes that "the Lord hardened Pharaoh's heart" (10:20); sometimes simply that "the heart of Pharaoh was hardened" (9:7).

Q. How was deliverance finally wrought?

A. When "At midnight the Lord smote all the first-born in the land of Egypt" (12:29), "the Egyptians were urgent with the people, to send them out of the land in haste" (12:33).

Q. How had the Hebrews prepared for this?

A. The blood of slain lambs was used to mark the lintels and door-posts of Hebrew homes, so that "the destroyer" did not enter (12:21-27). From their neighbors, the common people of Egypt, the Hebrews had "asked for" jewelry and clothing ("Thus they despoiled the Egyptians"— 12:36); the Hebrews hastily baked for themselves "unleavened cakes of the dough" that they had placed in "kneading bowls" fastened to their shoulders (12:34).

Q. How are these events remembered?

A. The departure from Egypt is annually recalled and relived in the Passover rite, in which a lamb is slain, unleavened bread is eaten, and the children are told: "It is the sacrifice of the Lord's passover, for he passed over the houses of the people of Israel in Egypt, when he slew the Egyptians but spared our houses" (12:27). The New Testament interprets Christ's death in similar terms: "Christ, our paschal lamb, has been sacrificed. Let us, therefore, celebrate the festival . . . with the unleavened bread of sincerity and truth" (I Corinthians 5:7f).

Q. How did the Hebrews escape from Egypt?

A. When the fleeing Hebrews came to a body of water, a part of the Red Sea, "the Lord drove the sea back by a strong east wind . . . and the people of Israel went into the midst of the sea on dry ground" (14:21f); the waters closed over the pursuing Egyptians, and "not so much as one of them remained" (14:28).

Q. How is this commemorated in Hebrew literature?

A. By the Song of Moses (15:1-18), beginning:

"I will sing to the Lord, for he has triumphed gloriously;
the horse and his rider he has thrown into the sea."

Q. Did the Hebrews take the shortest route to the Promised Land?

A. No. "God did not lead them by way of the land of the Philistines, although that was near. . . . But God led the people round by way of the wilderness" (13:17f).

Q. What hardships characterize the wilderness wanderings and how were they overcome?

A. Remembering that in Egypt they "sat by the fleshpots and ate bread to the full" (16:3), the hungry horde "murmured against Moses and Aaron" (16:2). Then migrating quails "came up and covered the camp" (16:13f), and there was daily gathering of "a fine, flake-like thing, fine as hoar-frost on the ground" (16:14); the latter was called *manna,* from the Hebrew phrase, "what is it?" Just when people were thirstiest, too, Moses struck a rock and water gushed out (17:1-7); Amalek and his people, coming out to fight, were repulsed, with Joshua making his debut as military leader (17:8-16); upon the advice of his father-in-law, Moses chose assistants who "judged the people at all times; hard cases they brought to Moses, but any small matter they decided themselves" (18:24-27).

Q. What code of laws was given for the ordering of the common life?

A. The Ten Commandments (20:1-17), bestowed at Mt. Sinai; these were elaborated into specific regulations concerning the treatment of slaves (21:11); punishment for acts of violence (21:12-27): "life for life, eye for eye, tooth for tooth, hand for hand, foot for foot, burn for burn, wound for wound, stripe for stripe" (21:23-25); injury to animals (21:28-22:1); the administration of justice (22:16-23:12); observance of the annual feasts (23:14-17; purity of worship (23:18-33).

Q. Why is the mountain of revelation sometimes called Sinai (19:20; 34:29) and sometimes, Horeb (3:1; 17:6)?

A. One may have been the name of the range, the other of the peak; or one may have been a Midianite name, the other a Canaanite.

Q. What response did the people make to the giving of the Law?

A. They pledged themselves: "All that the Lord has spoken, we will do, and we will be obedient" (24:7).

Q. What arrangements were made for keeping the Law continually before the people?

A. Its tablets were encased in "an ark of acacia wood" (25:10), kept inside a portable tabernacle appropriately designed, decorated, and furnished (26:1-27:21); over it the priests, clad in garments "for glory and for beauty" (28:2), presided (28:1-31:11).

Q. Did the people remain faithful to their pledge of pure worship?

A. No. They turned aside in the absence of Moses. Aaron took their gold earrings and fashioned a visible object, a molten calf, similar to the animals worshiped in Egypt (32:1-35). When Moses returned, he was infuriated that they had made for themselves "gods of gold" (32:31). "And the Lord sent a plague upon the people" (32:35). The enraged Moses smashed the tables of the Law "at the foot of the mountain" (32:19).

Q. How were the people governed after that?

A. A gracious God provided Moses once more with tablets of the Law, and renewed his covenant with the people (34:1-35). There followed additional regulations concerning appropriate offerings to the Lord (35:1-29), the fashioning of the tabernacle (36:2-37), the making of an altar (38:1-7), the furnishings of the place of worship (38:8-31), and the attire of the priests (39:1-31).

Q. The tabernacle, constructed "after the pattern . . . shown . . . on the mountain" (25:40; cf. Hebrews 8:5) was in "sight of all" and covered by a cloud. How did this serve them?

A. "Then the cloud covered the tent of meeting, and the glory of the Lord filled the tabernacle (40:34). Through all their journeys, whenever the cloud was taken up from over the tabernacle, the people of Israel would go onward" (40:36).

Q. What was the "tent of meeting" (33:7)?

A. A tent pitched outside the camp where people could come and receive from Moses answers to their solemn inquiries; the tent may have contained the ark mentioned in Deuteronomy 10:1-5 as enshrining the two tablets of the Law.

Q. What annual seasonal festivals are described?

A. The "feast of unleavened bread" (23:15), a reminder of the hasty exit from Egypt; the "feast of harvest" (23:16), at which the year's first fruits were offered to the Giver of all; the "feast of ingathering" (23:16), at the end of the year.

Q. How does the account in Acts differ from that in Exodus regarding the size of Joseph's family?

A. Exodus 1:5 says: "All the offspring of Jacob were seventy persons"; Acts 7:14 refers to "all his kindred, seventy-five souls."

Q. What use does the New Testament make of the magicians' explanation to Pharaoh of why they could not duplicate all the feats of Moses and Aaron?

A. Their explanation was, "This is the finger of God" (8:19). Jesus says in Luke 11:20: "If it is by the finger of God that I cast out demons, then the kingdom of God has come upon you."

Q. What promise in Exodus is basic to the book of Tobit?

A. "I send an angel before you, to guard you on the way and to bring you to the place which I have prepared" (23:20).

Q. What is the reason for the strict provision, "You shall not boil a kid in its mother's milk" (34:26)?

A. This was a practice associated with Canaanite religion, from which the Hebrews were to keep themselves aloof.

Q. What references does the New Testament make to the veil that "shall separate for you the holy place from the most holy" (26:33)?

A. At Jesus' death, according to Matthew 27:51, "the curtain of the temple was torn in two, from top to bottom." The author of Hebrews 9:11f sees symbolic significance in this: "Christ . . . entered once for all into the Holy Place."

Q. Why was the altar to have "horns . . . on its four corners" (27:2)?

A. To give a sense of security to those who sought sanctuary there.

Q. What element in the blending of incense does Paul apply to the believer's daily life?

A. The incense was to be "seasoned with salt" (30:35); so Paul says: "Let your speech . . . be . . . seasoned with salt" (Colossians 4:6).

THE THIRD BOOK OF MOSES COMMONLY CALLED

LEVITICUS

Q. What is the significance of the title *Leviticus*?

A. The sons of the tribe of Levi were priests in Israel (cf. I Kings 12:31); this book describes the position and duties of the levitical priests. The Hebrew title, derived from the first word, is "And he called," which is the word God first spoke "from the tent of meeting" (1:1).

Q. What matters are dealt with in the first five chapters of Leviticus?

A. The proper procedures for various forms of sacrifice: burnt offerings (in which the victim is entirely consumed, "a pleasing odor to the Lord"—1:3-17); cereal offerings, in which the products of the field are presented to the Lord (2:1-16); peace offerings, through which reconciliation is effected (3:1-17); sin offerings, to expiate wrongs unwittingly done (4:1-35); sacrifices to remove the stain of ritual defilement (5:1-19).

Q. What is the subject matter of Chapter 6?

A. The function of the priest in assisting the worshiper who presents a guilt offering (6:1-7); a burnt offering (6:8-13). a cereal offering (6:14-18); a sin offering (6:24-30); as well as the priest's own cereal offering (6:19-23).

Q. What is the subject matter of Chapter 7?

A. The philosophy and effects of the several kinds of offerings.

Q. What is the subject matter of Chapter 8?

A. The robes and ceremonies appropriate to the ordination of the high priest.

Q. What is the subject matter of Chapter 9?

A. Aaron's presiding over the presentation of sacrifices on behalf of the people: sin offering, burnt offering, peace offering.

Q. What is the subject matter of Chapter 10?

A. The proper conduct of priests (10:1-15); the report (10:16-20) of an incident that appears to have evoked the regulations governing sins done unwittingly as set down in Chapter 4.

Q. What is the purpose of Chapter 11?

A. "To make a distinction between the unclean and the clean and between the living creatures that may be eaten and the living creatures that may not be eaten" (11:47). "Whatever parts the hoof and is cloven-footed and chews the cud, among the animals, you may eat" (11:3). Whatever "has fins and scales, whether in the seas or in the rivers, you may eat" (11:9). "Among the winged insects that go on all fours you may eat those which have legs above their feet" (11:21). Creatures not meeting these specifications are not only unclean but are to be carefully avoided.

Q. What ceremony in the Christian church today is based upon Leviticus 12?

A. The purification of women following childbirth.

Q. What health regulations are set forth in Chapters 13 and 14?

A. The diagnosis, treatment, isolation, control, and, when cured, the ceremonial cleansing of a variety of bodily afflictions grouped together as "leprosy."

Q. What health regulations are set forth in Chapter 15?

A. The treatment and control of bodily discharges associated with the reproductive organs.

Q. What annual religious observance is described in Chapter 16?

A. The Day of Atonement, "that atonement may be made for the people of Israel once in the year because of all their sins" (16:34).

Q. How does the New Testament relate Christ's death to the Day of Atonement?

A. On this day alone the high priest—and only he—bearing sacrificial symbols, could enter "the holy place within the veil" (16:2). Hebrews 9:12 says that "Jesus entered once for all into the Holy Place, taking not the blood of goats and calves but his own blood, thus securing an eternal redemption."

Q. What contemporary health slogan is based upon 17:11-14?

A. The American Red Cross, in its search for blood donors, announces that "Blood Means Life"; 17:11 says "the life of the flesh is in the blood"; 17:14 that "the life of every creature is the blood of it."

Q. What standard of holiness is proposed for Israel in Chapter 18?

A. The nation is to do, not "as they do in the land of Egypt" or "as they do in the land of Canaan" (18:3), but according to God's "statutes" and "ordinances, by doing which a man shall live" (18:5).

Q. How will this type of righteousness manifest itself?

A. In honorable sex relations (18:6-23; 20:10-21); in respect for the Ten Commandments (19:3,4,11,12,16); in consideration for the poor (19:9f); in the impartial administration of justice (19:15); in fairness to strangers (19:33f); in honest weights and measures (19:35f); in, abstention from such pagan rites as human sacrifice (20:1-6) and consulting "mediums and wizards" (20:6,27).

Q. What directions are given for the conduct of priests?

A. They are not to mutilate their bodies as the heathen priests do (21:5). They are to enter into honorable marriage (21:13-15). They are to keep themselves from ceremonial defilement (22:1-16).

Q. What yearly festivals are described?

A. Passover (23:5-8); first fruits (23:9-21); harvest (23:22); atonement (23:27-32); booths or tabernacles (23:33-36).

Q. What does the festival of booths commemorate?

A. "I made the people of Israel dwell in booths when I brought them out of the land of Egypt" (23:43).

Q. What punishment is prescribed for blasphemy?

A. "He who blasphemes the name of the Lord shall be put to death" (24:16).

Q. What general provision is made for punishing those who commit crimes against the person?

A. "When a man causes a disfigurement in his neighbor, as he has done, it shall be done to him" (24:19).

Q. What are the rules governing the use of the land?

A. Chapter 25:4 provides that, in an agricultural society, the seventh year "shall be a year of solemn rest for the land." This is the origin of the term "sabbatical year."

Q. What is the origin of the term *jubilee*?

A. Deriving its name from the Hebrew term for "trumpet blast" (which accompanied its beginning), the year of Jubilee was the concluding year in each fifty-year cycle. During this period property was to revert to its previous owners and slaves were to be freed (25:10-55).

Q. What "historical" event gave liberty to the Israelites and warranted their obedience?

A. "I am the Lord your God, who brought you forth out of the land of Egypt" (26:13).

Q. What passage from Leviticus provided material for Revelation?

A. Revelation 21:3 echoes 26:11f: "and I will make my abode among you, and my soul shall not abhor you, and I will walk among you, and will be your God, and you shall be my people."

Q. What words from Leviticus are inscribed upon the Liberty Bell?

A. "Proclaim liberty throughout all the land to all its inhabitants" (25:10).

Q. What prospect is held out for a nation that rejects the righteousness of God?

A. Plagues (26:21f), pestilence (26:25), desolation (26:27-32), exile (26:33).

Q. Why is the section from Chapter 17 through Chapter 26 called the Law of Holiness?

A. Because of the repeated insistence that the perfection of God should be the standard for the conduct of man (19:2; 20:7f, etc.).

THE FOURTH BOOK OF MOSES COMMONLY CALLED
NUMBERS

Q. What is the significance of the title, "Numbers"?

A. The Greek version of the Old Testament gives this book a title from which is derived the English word "Arithmetic." Translated into English as "Numbers," it refers to the census or numbering of the people. The Hebrew title, derived from *bemidhbar,* the fourth word in the Hebrew version, means "In the Desert Of."

Q. What are the main divisions of the book?

A. Chapters 1-12 tell about events at or near Mt. Sinai; 13 to 21 about Paran, and 22-36 about Moab.

Q. How was the census taken?

A. One man from each tribe assisted Moses and Aaron in numbering the males "from twenty years old and upward, all in Israel who are able to go forth to war" (1:3). The roll was kept by tribes (1:20-46), except that the Levites, whose duty it was to preside over the community's institutions of religion, "were not numbered" (1:47). Once the tribes were numbered, it was arranged that they should "encamp facing the tent of meeting on every side" (2:2). Another numbering, near the end of the desert wanderings, is reported in 26:1-51.

Q. Why was special treatment accorded the sons of Levi?

A. The numbering of them included not only adults but "every male from a month old and upward" (3:15). The Levites represent the firstborn, "for all the first-born are mine; on the day that I slew all the firstborn in the land of Egypt, I consecrated for my own all the first-born in Israel" (3:13).

Q. What exemption was provided for the sons of Levi?

A. The purpose of the census was to enroll "all in Israel who are able to go forth to war" (1:3). The Levites were to give themselves to the service of the tabernacle (1:47-53).

Q. What tasks were assigned to the Levites?

A. The sons of Gershom had charge of the tent of meeting and its appurtenances (3:21-26); the sons of Kohath had charge of the ark, the altar, and "the vessels of the sanctuary" (3:27-32); the sons of Merari had charge of "the frames of the tabernacle, the bars, the pillars, the bases, and all their accessories" (3:33-37). Those members of the three Levitical families who were "from thirty years old up to fifty years old" were assigned routine duties "to do the work in the tent of meeting" (4:3; cf. 4:1-49).

Q. What New Testament passage echoes the lists of tribes reported in 1:20-42?

A. Revelation 7:4-8, with its number of the redeemed "out of every tribe of the sons of Israel."

Q. What directions are given for encampment in battle?

A. The "tent of meeting," attended by the Levites, is to be "in the midst of the camps" (2:17); the other tribes are to be grouped around this, "each in position, standard by standard" (2:17).

Q. What provision is made for testing a wife suspected of adultery?

A. The ordeal by means of the "water of bitterness" (5:11-31).

Q. What other regulations were provided for the good of the community while in the wilderness?

A. Persons with loathsome disease were put "outside the camp" (5:1-4); Nazirites, puritans within the community, were to "eat nothing that is produced by the grapevine" (6:4; cf. 6:1-21); miscellaneous other laws were promulgated in Moab (Chapters 28 and 29).

Q. Who were the Nazirites?

A. Persons who had taken a vow to abstain from strong drink, from shaving, and from contact with dead bodies (6:1-21).

Q. What well-known benediction comes from Numbers?

A. "The Lord bless you and keep you:
The Lord make his face to shine upon you, and be gracious to you;
The Lord lift up his countenance upon you and give you peace" (6:24-26).

Q. What early stewardship records are found in Numbers?

A. Chapter 7 lists the offerings brought by the nation's leaders for constructing and equipping a place of worship.

Q. What provision is made for setting apart the Levites to their work?

A. Chapter 8:5-22 prescribes the way in which they are to be cleansed; 8:23-26 indicates how assignments are to be made according to age.

Q. What instructions are given for the observance of the Passover?

A. On the appointed day, all are to cleanse themselves of ritual defilement (9:2-13), and foreigners who wished to join in must be allowed to do so (9:14).

Q. What function did the tabernacle serve when the nation was on the march?

A. A cloud covered it by day, "and the appearance of fire by night" (9:16). When the cloud moved, it was the signal for the people to move (9:18-23).

Q. What means were used to communicate with the people?

A. Two silver trumpets were employed "for summoning the congregation, and for breaking camp" (10:2).

Q. How does God lighten Moses' load?

A. Moses picked seventy elders as his assistants (11:25).

Q. What is the significance of the fact that God "took some of the spirit that was upon" Moses and "put it upon the seventy elders; and . . . they prophesied" (11:25)?

A. It represents a beginning, during the wilderness wanderings, of the institution of prophecy that was to be so marked a feature of the religious life of Israel. Moses said: "Would that all the Lord's people were prophets, that the Lord would put his spirit upon them" (11:29).

Q. What caused the feeling among some that it would have been better not to leave Egypt?

A. "We remember the fish we ate in Egypt for nothing, the cucumbers, the melons, the leeks, the onions, and the garlic; but now our strength is dried up, and there is nothing at all but this manna to look at" (11:5ff).

Q. How did Moses acquaint himself with conditions in the Land of Promise, to which the people were bound?

A. He sent twelve men "to spy out the land of Canaan" (13:17). Their report was: ". . . it flows with milk and honey. . . . Yet the people who dwell in the land are strong, and the cities are fortified and very large" (13:27,28).

Q. Were the spies unanimous in their recommendations?

A. No. One spy, Caleb, said: "Let us go up at once, and occupy it" (13:30), but others: "We are not able to go up against the people; for they are stronger than we . . . it is a land that devours its inhabitants" (13:31f).

Q. What happened to the pessimists among the spies?

A. "The men who brought up an evil report of the land died by plague before the Lord" (14:37). Only Joshua and Caleb remained alive.

Q. Who led an insurrection against Moses and Aaron?

A. "Korah and all his company" (16:6), charging, "You have gone too far!" (16:3).

Q. What was the cause of the controversy?

A. The claim of the priests to be holier than the rest. The Levites insisted that "all the congregation are holy, every one of them, and the Lord is among them; why then do you exalt yourselves above the assembly of the Lord?" (16:3).

Q. What is Moses' reply to this?

A. "In the morning the Lord will show who is his, and who is holy" (16:5).

Q. What happened to the insurrectionists?

A. "The earth opened its mouth and swallowed them up" (16:32); others who were disgruntled were attacked by the plague until Aaron "stood between the dead and the living; and the plague was stopped" (16:48).

Q. What opposition from other tribes did the people encounter?

A. The king of Arad "fought against Israel" (21:1). Sihon, king of the Amorites, "would not allow Israel to pass through his territory" (21:23); "Og the king of Bashan came out against them" (21:33); Balak, king of Moab, sent for Balaam to curse Israel, but Balaam wound up blessing Israel three times (22-25); the Hebrews also "warred against Midian . . . and slew every male" (31:7).

Q. What tribal song celebrated the discovery of a water supply in the desert?

A. "Spring up, O well!—Sing to it!—
   the well which the princes dug,
   which the nobles of the people delved,
   with the scepter and with their staves" (21:17f).

Q. Who was appointed successor to Moses?

A. Moses took Joshua "and laid his hands upon him and commissioned him as the Lord directed" (27:23).

Q. What incident gave rise to the saying, "Be sure your sin will find you out" (32:23)?

A. Tribesmen of Reuben and Gad coveted Jazer and Gilead for their cattle, but wanted it given to them without a struggle. Moses said: "If you will take up arms . . . this land shall be your possession. . . . But if you will not do so, behold, you have sinned against the Lord; and be sure your sin will find you out" (32:20-23).

Q. What provision was made for "the manslayer who kills any person without intent" (35:11)?

A. Six cities of refuge were appointed, to which an uncertain homicide might go for protection "until he stands before the congregation for judgment" (35:12).

Q. What provision was made regarding the marriage of heiresses?

A. "Every daughter who possesses an inheritance in any tribe of the people of Israel, shall be wife to one of the family of the tribe of her father . . . so no inheritance shall be transferred from one tribe to another" (36:8).

Q. How long did the wilderness wanderings last, and why?

A. "And the Lord's anger was kindled against Israel, and he made them wander in the wilderness forty years, until all the generation that had done evil in the sight of the Lord was consumed" (32:13).

Q. What use does the New Testament make of the provision that lepers were to be driven "outside the camp" (5:4)?

A. It indicates that Jesus' identity with all forms of human misery was so complete that he suffered "outside the gate" (Hebrews 13:12).

Q. What different provisions are given regarding the age at which Levites are eligible "to do the work in the tent of meeting"?

A. Numbers 4:23 says: "from thirty years old up to fifty years old"; 8:24 says "from twenty-five years old."

Q. What explanation is given in the Apocrypha as to why life was to be had by one who "would look at the bronze serpent" (2:19)?

A. Wisdom 16:7 says:
> "he who turned toward it was saved,
>   not by what he saw,
>   but by thee, the Savior of all."

Q. How does the New Testament report of those that died in the plague differ from that given in Numbers?

A. Numbers 25:9 places the figure at 24,000; I Corinthians 10:8 at 23,000.

THE FIFTH BOOK OF MOSES COMMONLY CALLED
DEUTERONOMY

Q. What is the meaning of the word *Deuteronomy*?

A. *Deuteronomy* means "Second Law," the English transliteration of the title in the Greek Bible. The term occurs in the Septuagint at 17:18, "a copy of this law." The title in the Hebrew Bible, derived from the opening phrase *eleh d'barim,* is simply "These are the Words."

Q. What is the purpose of Deuteronomy?

A. To set the ministry of Moses in the context of the Deuteronomic reform, initiated in 621 B.C.

Q. What New Testament literary relationship is seen to parallel that between Deuteronomy and the other books of the Pentateuch?

A. That between the Gospel according to John and the Synoptics.

Q. What are the divisions of the book of Deuteronomy?

A. The historical situation portrays Israel as about to enter the Promised Land and Moses delivering a series of addresses to his people: 1-4:43 contains his first address; 4:44-28:68, his second; 29:1-30:20, his third; 31:1-34:12 consists of footnotes and appendices.

Q. What points does Moses make in his first address?

A. He recounts his choice of associates, "wise and experienced men" (1:15) and his advice to them: "You shall not be partial in judgment; you shall hear the small and the great alike; you shall not be afraid of the face of man" (1:17); God's guidance during the wilderness wanderings ("the Lord your God bore you, as a man bears his son"—1:31; "these forty years the Lord your God has been with you; you have lacked nothing"—2:7); the victories God had granted over opponents who attempted to block the way ("This day I will begin to put the dread and fear of you upon the peoples that are under the whole heaven"—2:25f; "you shall not fear them, for it is the Lord your God who fights for you"—3:22); his own inability to enter the Land of Promise ("The Lord said to me . . . Go up to the top of Pisgah, and lift up your eyes . . . for you shall not go over this Jordan"—3:27); the uniqueness of Israel's God: "has any god ever attempted to go and take a nation for himself from the midst of another nation" (4:34)?

Q. What detail is given to show how great were some of the enemies Israel had overcome?

A. Concerning Og, the king of Bashan, it is said: ". . . behold, his bedstead was a bedstead of iron . . . nine cubits was its length, and four cubits its breadth" (3:11).

Q. What are the main items in Moses' second address?

A. He repeats the Ten Commandments (5:6-21, with slight variations from the version in Exodus 20); enjoins the people to obey them "that your days may be prolonged" (6:2); reminds them that a life of gratitude and service to God should arise from the fact that in Canaan they would inhabit "great and goodly cities, which you did not build," together with houses, cisterns, vineyards, and olive trees (6:10f); urges them not to be afraid of the peoples whom they must dispossess (7:17-26) nor to boast of their own achievements ("Beware lest you say in your heart, 'My power and the might of my hand have gotten me this wealth.' You shall remember the Lord your God, for it is he who gives you power to get wealth"—8:17f; "the Lord your God is not giving you this good land to possess because of your righteousness; for you are a stubborn people"—9:6); enjoins consideration of the foreign-born ("Love the sojourner therefore; for you were sojourners in the land of Egypt—10:19); warns against the worship of false gods (13:6-18) and the imitation of pagan priests (14:1f); distinguishes between foods that may and may not be eaten (14:3-21); urges appropriate observance of the appointed feasts (16:1-17); prescribes for the administration of justice (16:18-17:20), including cities of refuge (19:1-13); regulates the conduct of war (20:1-21:14); promulgates various laws for a well-ordered community (21:15-25:19) and a suitable public worship (26:1-15); and concludes with curses upon those who reject the Law (27:15-26), blessings upon those who obey it (28:1-14), and a description of the consequences of disobedience (28:15-68).

Q. Which among the commandments is the great commandment?

A. "Hear, O Israel: the Lord our God is one Lord; and you shall love the Lord your God with all your heart, and with all your soul, and with all your might" (6:4f).

Q. What answer did Jesus give to the question, "Which commandment is the first of all?"

A. He quoted this verse (cf. Mark 12:28-30).

Q. What provision does Deuteronomy make for the instruction of the young?

A. "And these words which I command you this day shall be upon your heart; and you shall teach them diligently to your children, and shall talk of them when you sit in your house, and when you walk by the way, and when you lie down, and when you rise" (6:7).

Q. What provision was made for keeping the Law daily at the center of attention?

A. "And you shall bind them as a sign upon your hand, and they shall be as frontlets between your eyes. And you shall write them on the doorposts of your house and on your gates" (6:9).

Q. How did Deuteronomy figure in the early ministry of Jesus?

A. In his temptation experience (Matthew 4:1-11; Luke 4:1-13), he cited Deuteronomy 8:3 ("man does not live by bread alone"); 6:16 ("you shall not put the Lord your God to the test"); and 6:13 ("You shall fear the Lord your God; you shall serve him").

Q. What reason is given for God's choice of the Hebrew people?

A. "It was not because you were more in number than any other people that the Lord set his love upon you and chose you . . . but it is because the Lord loves you" (7:7f).

Q. How does the author express the uniqueness of God's choice of Israel?

A. "For you are a people holy to the Lord your God, and the Lord has chosen you to be a people for his own possession, out of all the peoples that are on the face of the earth" (14:2).

Q. What is the ark mentioned in 10:5?

A. A sacred chest or shrine for the tables of the Law.

Q. How does the writer distinguish between the way the earth is watered in Egypt and the way it is watered in the Promised Land?

A. Egypt is a land that you watered "with your feet" (11:10)— that is, in which the farmer, by kicking the edge of the irrigation ditch, diverts some of the flow into his field. The Promised Land, on the other hand, is "a land of hills and valleys, which drinks water by the rain from heaven" (11:11).

Q. Why should a book of this character contain detailed instructions for wiping out enemies, such as are found in Chapter 20?

A. A military expedition undertaken not for conquest or aggrandizement but to exterminate groups whose religious practices threatened to destroy or corrupt the religion of Israel was considered a holy war, comparable now to the Moslem *jihad*. It is the conduct of the holy war that is here outlined.

Q. Who are the cult prostitutes mentioned in 23:17?

A. Persons who engaged in "sacred marriage" in connection with the fertility rites annually carried out at Canaanite shrines (cf. Leviticus 19:29; Exodus 38:8; I Samuel 2:22; Hosea 4:14).

Q. What is notable about Chapter 26?

A. It provides a typical summary of what Psalm 106:2 calls "the mighty doings of the Lord."

Q. What is distinctive about Chapter 27?

A. It contains a dodecalogue, or Twelve Commandments.

Q. What form of punishment was provided for lesser offenses?

A. "If the guilty man deserves to be beaten, the judge shall cause him to lie down and be beaten in his presence with a number of stripes in proportion to his offense" (25:2).

Q. Why was the maximum number of stripes set at forty?

A. To avoid humiliating punishments, lest "your brother be degraded in your sight" (25:3).

Q. Was the maximum number of stripes always given?

A. No. To avoid the possibility of exceeding the appointed limit, it was usual that only thirty-nine stripes should be administered. Paul reports, "Five times I have received at the hands of the Jews the forty lashes less one" (II Corinthians 11:24).

Q. What exemptions were provided from military service?

A. According to 20:5-7, the following types of persons are exempt: the "man who has built a new house and has not dedicated it"; the man who "has planted a vineyard and not enjoyed its fruit"; the man who "has betrothed a wife and has not taken her." 24:5 says: "When a man is newly married, he shall not go out with the army or be charged with any business; he shall be free at home one year, to be happy with his wife whom he has taken."

Q. What law was designed for the prevention of cruelty to animals?

A. "You shall not muzzle an ox when it treads out the grain" (25:4); cf. 22:6: "If you chance to come upon a bird's nest, in any tree or on the ground, with young ones or eggs and the mother sitting upon the young or upon the eggs, you shall not take the mother with the young."

Q. What regulation provided the community with a building code?

A. "When you build a new house, you shall make a parapet for your roof, that you may not bring the guilt of blood upon your house, if any one fall from it" (22:8).

Q. What are the principal points of Moses' third address?

A. That obedience is the way to national happiness ("be careful to do the words of this covenant, that you may prosper in all you do"— 29:9); that God's command "is not too hard for you, neither is it far off" —30:11); and that Israel, about to enter the Land of Promise, must make choice: "I have set before you life and death, blessing and curse; therefore choose life, that you and your descendants may live" (30:19).

Q. What power and effectiveness are attributed to God's word?

A. "The word is very near you; it is in your mouth and in your heart, so that you can do it" (30:14).

Q. What does this book include in addition to Moses' three addresses?

A. The song of Moses (31:30-32:43):
"Remember the days of old,
    consider the years of many generations" (32:7);
and the "blessing with which Moses, the man of God, blessed the children of Israel before his death" (33:1-29); an account of Moses' lonely death on Mt. Pisgah ("no one knows the place of his burial to this day"—34:6).

Q. What place in history is attributed to Moses?

A. "There has not arisen a prophet since in Israel like Moses, whom the Lord knew face to face" (34:10).

Q. What section gives a good summary of the entire book of Deuteronomy?

A. Deuteronomy 10:12-22.

Q. What passage led the Samaritans, who have no Scripture other than the Pentateuch, to believe in the second coming of Moses?

A. "The Lord your God will raise up for you a prophet like me" (18:15).

Q. What passage represents an elaboration and updating of the older regulation in Exodus 21:12ff regarding one who killed unintentionally?

A. Deuteronomy 19:1-13.

Q. What section contains an early confession of Israel's faith?

A. Deuteronomy 26:5-10.

Q. Who is Jeshurun (32:15; 33:5,26; cf. Isaiah 44:2)?

A. Jeshurun is a poetic designation of Israel.

THE BOOK OF JOSHUA

Q. Who wrote the book of Joshua?

A. An unnamed historian, or historians, wrote of events in the national history that had occurred some centuries earlier. The person for whom the book is named was Moses' successor in the conquest of the Land of Promise.

Q. What passages within the book itself indicate a time later than that of Joshua?

A. References to "the treasury of the house of the Lord" (6:24; cf. 6:19) and to the "land where the Lord's tabernacle stands" (22:19) suggest a time when the temple at Jerusalem had been built, while references to "the remnant of these nations left here among you" and "marriages with them" (23:12f) seem to refer to the situation prevailing immediately after the exile. Also, the repeated use of the phrase "to this day" (4:9; 7:26; 8:28).

Q. What evidences are there within the book that the compiler used source material?

A. Chapter 10:13 states that the song just quoted comes from "the Book of Jashar." Since Jashar means "Upright," this was probably a collection celebrating the deeds of the Righteous. The allotment of territory, described in Chapters 13 to 19, probably makes use of an earlier geographical list or lists.

Q. When did Joshua take command?

A. At the death of Moses (1:1), Joshua is appointed his successor and is bidden, "Be strong and of good courage; be not frightened, neither be dismayed; for the Lord your God is with you wherever you go" (1:9).

Q. What pledge of allegiance is given by the people?

A. "Just as we obeyed Moses in all things, so will we obey you; only may the Lord your God be with you, as he was with Moses!" (1:17).

Q. How did Joshua make ready for the invasion of the Land of Promise?

A. He "sent two men secretly from Shittim as spies" (2:1).

Q. What treatment did the spies receive?

A. In Jericho they lodged in "the house of a harlot whose name was Rahab" (2:1), who hid them from the counterspies (2:6) and "let them down by a rope through a window" (2:15) so that they could escape.

Q. What was the subsequent history of Rahab?

A. When Jericho was sacked, "Rahab and her father and mother and brothers and all who belonged to her" were "saved alive" (6:23-25). Rahab is mentioned in the New Testament too (Matthew 1:5), among the ancestors of Jesus.

Q. What great deeds of God took place during the conquest of Canaan under Joshua?

A. The waters of the Jordan were stopped, so that the people "passed over on dry ground" (3:16); after a week of psychological warfare at Jericho, with the children of Israel marching daily around the city, the trumpets were blown on the seventh day and "the wall fell down flat" (6:20); at the battle of Gibeon, "The sun stayed in the midst of heaven, and did not hasten to go down for about a whole day" (10:13).

Q. How were the significant events of the conquest memorialized?

A. By the erection of stone heaps or pillars (4:2-7; 7:26; 8:29; 24:26f).

Q. What ceremonial acts were performed immediately after the Jordan had been crossed?

A. Males born during the wilderness wanderings were circumcised (5:2-9) and the Passover was celebrated (5:10).

Q. Who failed in his responsibility to the community after the attack on Ai?

A. Achan appropriated some of the spoil for himself; as a result, he and his family had to forfeit their lives (7:1-26).

Q. What military strategy was used to bring about the conquest of Ai?

A. Ambush (8:1-29).

Q. What religious acts were carried out immediately after the conquest of Ai?

A. "Then Joshua built an altar in Mt. Ebal to the Lord" (8:30), and read to the assembled community "all the words of the Law" (8:34).

Q. What was the relationship between the Israelites and the Gibeonites?

A. By a ruse, the Gibeonites led Joshua to think that they were not near neighbors, and asked for a mutual security pact (9:3-13). "And Joshua made peace with them, and made a covenant with them, to let them live" (9:15). The five kings of the Amorites (Jerusalem, Hebron, Jarmuth, Lachish, and Eglon—10:3) made an attack upon Gibeon; Joshua then came to the aid of Gibeon against the armies of the five kings, "and the Lord threw them into a panic before Israel" (10:10). The result was that the southern part of Canaan thus came under the domination of Joshua.

Q. How did Joshua win the northern hill country of Canaan?

A. By a great battle beside "the waters of Merom" (11:5), where he defeated the kings of Hazor, Madon, Shimron, and Achshaph (11:1), "with all their troops, a great host, in number like the sand that is upon the seashore, with very many horses and chariots" (11:4; cf. 11:1-23).

Q. How many kings did Joshua defeat?

A. Thirty-one, all of whom are listed in 12:1-23.

Q. What disposition of the land was made at the completion of the conquest?

A. It was apportioned by lot among the several tribes of Israel (Chapters 13-19).

Q. Why was no land allotted to the tribe of Levi?

A. "The priesthood of the Lord is their heritage" (18:7).

Q. What living space was assigned the Levites?

A. "Forty-eight cities with their pasture lands" (21:41).

Q. What were "the cities of refuge"?

A. Communities in which "the manslayer who kills any person without intent or unwittingly" (20:3) could find protection from "the avenger of blood" until the case had come to trial and been adjudicated (20:6).

Q. What two farewell messages of Joshua are reported?

A. Chapter 23 gives one address, in which occurs the phrase, "I am about to go the way of all the earth" (23:14); the other, reported in Chapter 24, rehearses the history of God's dealing with his people, from the time of Abraham, through the Egyptian bondage and deliverance, to the settlement in Canaan.

Q. What was the response of the people to Joshua's parting words?

A. "We will serve the Lord" (24:21).

Q. What evidences are there within the book that the conquest of Canaan was not so complete as one might have supposed?

A. Such statements as: "However they did not drive out the Canaanites that dwelt in Gezer: so the Canaanites have dwelt in the midst of Ephraim to this day" (16:10); and, "the Canaanites persisted in dwelling in that land. But when the people of Israel grew strong, they put the Canaanites to forced labor, and did not utterly drive them out" (17:12f).

Q. What special facilities did the Canaanites have for enabling them to resist?

A. They apparently guarded the secrets of the smelting process, and had "chariots of iron" (17:16).

Q. What place name here is symbolically transformed in the book of the prophet Hosea?

A. The Valley of Achor (7:26) means "Dale of Trouble." Hosea 2:15 promises that the Valley of Achor shall become "a door of hope."

THE BOOK OF JUDGES

Q. Who are the judges referred to in the title?

A. Charismatic leaders of Israel who recalled the nation to its heritage and served as champions of the people of Israel against their pagan neighbors.

Q. How many judges are dealt with in the book?

A. Thirteen.

Q. When did the judges live?

A. During the era of the conquest of Canaan by the Hebrews. I Kings 6:1 relates that Solomon "began to build the house of the Lord" in the fourth year of his reign, which was "the four hundred and eightieth year after the people of Israel came out of the land of Egypt." The periods of the several judges, if taken continuously, add up to more than that, but it is evident that none ruled over the entire land, and some may have been contemporaneous.

Q. What is the purpose of the book of Judges?

A. To show God's work in the history of the Hebrew people, especially in the interval between Moses and the kings.

Q. What happens in the introductory section of Judges?

A. The conquest of Canaan is still under way; the Hebrews have been unable to "drive out the inhabitants of the plain, because they had chariots of iron" (1:19). Meanwhile, in a number of communities, they have been able to "put the Canaanites to forced labor, but did not utterly drive them out" (1:28; cf. 1:30,33,35).

Q. How does the compiler account for the moral decline that he sees in the nation following the death of Joshua?

A. "And all that generation [i.e., Joshua's] were gathered to their fathers; and there arose another generation after them, who did not know the Lord or the work which he had done for Israel" (2:10).

Q. What did they do that was evil?

A. "They went after other gods. . . . So the anger of the Lord was kindled, and he gave them over to plunderers" (2:12,14).

Q. Why did the Lord "raise up" judges, or deliverers, for them?

A. "The Lord was moved to pity by their groaning because of those who afflicted and oppressed them" and "Whenever the Lord raised up judges for them, the Lord was with the judge, and he saved them from the hand of their enemies all the days of the judge" (2:18).

Q. What philosophy explains Joshua's inability to subdue the land?

A. "So the Lord left those nations, not driving them out at once . . . to test Israel by them" (2:23; 3:1).

Q. What deliverer was raised up when the people were in subjection to Cushan-rishathaim, king of Mesopotamia?

A. Othniel, the son of Kenaz, "Caleb's younger brother" (3:9).

Q. What deliverer was raised up when the "people of Israel served Eglon the king of Moab" (3:14)?

A. "Ehud, the son of Gera the Benjaminite, a left-handed man" (3:15).

Q. What weapon did Ehud use?

A. "A sword with two edges" (3:16), which he sank into the belly of Eglon, "a very fat man" (3:17), "and the fat closed over the blade" (3:22).

Q. What weapon was employed by Shamgar?

A. He "killed six hundred of the Philistines with an oxgoad" (3:31).

Q. What deliverers rescued Israel from "Jabin king of Canaan, who reigned in Hazor; the commander of his army was Sisera" (4:2)?

A. "Deborah, a prophetess" (4:4) and "Barak the son of Abinoam" (4:6).

Q. How did Sisera meet his death?

A. At the hands of a woman; seeking refuge in "the tent of Jael, the wife of Heber the Kenite" (4:17), he fell asleep; Jael "took a tent peg . . . and drove the peg into his temple" (4:21).

Q. What insight into ancient times is suggested by the fact that "Jael the wife of Heber took a tent peg" and drove it into Sisera's skull (4:21)?

A. Among the Bedouin, it was woman's work to pitch the tent.

Q. What classical denunciation is here given of those who prefer to enjoy the comforts of life rather than respond to the needs of the nation?

A. While the people of the tribe of Zebulun "jeoparded their lives to the death" (5:18), Reuben tarried "among the sheepfolds" (5:16) and "Asher sat still" (5:17).

Q. What literary classic is associated with the victory over Sisera?

A. The Song of Deborah (5:1-31).

Q. What military surprise did the Midianites spring upon the Hebrews?

A. "They would come up with their cattle and their tents, coming like locusts for number; both they and their camels could not be counted" (6:5); camel raids were a new phenomenon.

Q. Whom did God "raise up" for deliverance from the Midianites?

A. Gideon, a timid man (6:27), who required outward and visible signs of the conviction that he was to deliver the nation.

Q. What external signs were given?

A. "Fire from the rock" (6:21); dew on the fleece when "it is dry on all the ground" (6:37); a dry fleece when all the ground "was covered with dew" (6:39).

Q. What surprise message came to Gideon?

A. Usually no military commander has ever had as many troops as he wanted, but Gideon is informed that his small army is too big (7:2).

Q. How did he go about reducing the number of his troops?

A. When the "fearful and trembling" were given an opportunity to "return home . . . twenty-two thousand returned, and ten thousand remained" (7:3); the ten thousand were then reduced to three hundred.

Q. How were the three hundred chosen?

A. By a test of alertness. The troops were all ordered to drink from a stream. "Every one that laps the water with his tongue, as a dog laps," putting his hands up to his mouth, was deemed suitable; all who "knelt down to drink water" were rejected (7:5f).

Q. How did the three hundred vanquish the Midianites?

A. In a surprise raid at night, Gideon's men blew trumpets, smashed jars, and held aloft torches (7:19f); "all the army" of the enemy "ran; they cried out and fled" (7:21). Gideon and his men, pursuing, "threw all the army into a panic" (8:12).

Q. Who assumed authority at the death of Gideon?

A. His son, Abimelech, by murdering all his half brothers except Jotham (9:1-6).

Q. What fable does Jotham relate to expose the weakness of Abimelech?

A. The fable of the trees that searched for a king (9:7-15); the olive tree, the fig tree, and the vine all decline; the worthless bramble jumps at the opportunity.

Q. What end befell Abimelech?

A. "A certain woman threw an upper millstone upon Abimelech's head, and crushed his skull. Then he called hastily to his armor-bearer . . . , 'Draw your sword and kill me, lest men say of me, A woman killed him' " (9:53f).

Q. Who succeeded Abimelech?

A. "Tola the son of Puah, son of Dodo . . . judged Israel twenty-three years" (10:1f); then "Jair the Gileadite . . . judged Israel twenty-two years" (10:3).

Q. Who led Israel against the Ammonites?

A. "Jephthah the Gileadite . . . a mighty warrior" (11:1).

Q. What was Jephthah's vow?

A. "If thou wilt give the Ammonites into my hand, then whoever comes forth from the doors of my tent to meet me, when I return victorious from the Ammonites, shall be the Lord's, and I will offer him up for a burnt offering" (11:31).

Q. What was the tragic outcome of this vow?

A. His daughter and only child came out to greet him, and he "did with her according to his vow which he had made" (11:39); the story is cited to explain an annual observance in which "the daughters of Israel went year by year to lament the daughter of Jephthah the Gileadite four days in the year" (11:40).

Q. Who were Jephthah's successors?

A. Ibzan of Bethlehem (12:8); Elon the Zebulunite (12:11); Abdon the son of Hillel the Pirathonite (12:13).

Q. Into what environment was Samson born?

A. Manoah and his wife, childless, prayed for a son; an angel of the Lord promised that a son would be born, and gave instructions that he was to grow up as a Nazirite (13:1-25).

Q. What was the secret of his strength?

A. The Nazirite vow, symbolized by uncut hair.

Q. Why did Samson take a wife from among his nation's enemies?

A. "He was seeking an occasion against the Philistines" (14:4).

Q. By what exploits did Samson establish his great strength?

A. By tearing a "lion asunder as one tears a kid" (14:6); by killing thirty men of Ashkelon (14:19); having caught three hundred foxes, "he turned them tail to tail, and put a torch between each pair of tails. And when he had set fire to the torches, he let the foxes go into the standing grain of the Philistines, and burned up the shocks and the standing grain, as well as the olive orchards" (15:4f); by slaying a thousand men with a "fresh jawbone of an ass" (15:15); by removing the Gaza gate and the two posts and carrying them to Hebron (16:3), some thirty-eight miles away; finally, by pulling down the temple of Dagon. "So the dead whom he slew at his death were more than those whom he had slain during his life" (16:30).

Q. What was the riddle with which Samson taunted his enemies?

A. Reflecting the ancient belief that bees came from decaying flesh, he said of the lion he had killed:

"Out of the eater came something to eat.

Out of the strong came something sweet" (14:14).

Q. Who was responsible for Samson's downfall?

A. A designing woman, Delilah, who betrays him into the hands of the Philistines (16:4-30).

Q. Who, in the days of the judges, felt that he could obtain security by hiring a private chaplain?

A. Micah, "a man of the hill country of Ephraim" (17:1), who employed a Levite, confident "that the Lord will prosper me" (17:12).

Q. What became of Micah's chaplain?

A. Allowing the Danites to take the equipment for worship, he himself deserted to the tribe of Dan, persuaded that it was better to be "priest to a tribe" rather than to one man (18:20).

Q. What outrage befell a Levite and his concubine at Gibeah?

A. Sexual abuse (19:22-30).

Q. What reference is made to this in the Prophets?

A. In Hosea 9:9 and 10:9 mention is made of the sin committed in Gibeah.

Q. What grim act of symbolism did the Levite perform?

A. The body of the slain concubine he cut "into twelve pieces, and sent her throughout all the territory of Israel" (19:29; cf. 20:6), hoping thus to arouse his fellow Israelites to action against those who had committed the crime.

Q. What resistance did the men of Gibeah offer when the Israelites sought vengeance?

A. "Seven hundred picked men who were left-handed: every one could sling a stone at a hair, and not miss" (20:16). The Benjaminites joined in the fray, "but the men of Israel . . . smote them with the sword, men and beasts and all that they found" (20:48).

Q. How did the depleted tribe of Benjamin find wives for the men who had none?

A. At a yearly feast they lay in wait and seized "the daughters of Shiloh" (21:16-23).

Q. What festivals are mentioned in Judges?

A. The "feast of the Lord" (21:19), a celebration held annually at Shiloh when young women came out to dance in the vineyards (perhaps a specialized version of the feast of Ingathering), and a vintage festival celebrated at Shechem (9:27).

Q. What geographical description of the length and breadth of Israel is found in Judges?

A. "From Dan to Beersheba" (20:1).

Q. What concise picture is given of social conditions in the days of the judges?

A. "In those days there was no king in Israel; every man did what was right in his own eyes" (21:25).

THE BOOK OF RUTH

Q. Who is the author of the book of Ruth?

A. The work, strictly anonymous, contains no clue regarding authorship; there is no evidence to support the statement in the Talmud that it was written by Samuel.

Q. When was the book of Ruth written?

A. Although the story revolves about the era dated around 1100 B.C., the narrative probably dates from the fourth century B.C. It was written at a time when the ancient customs had to be explained (4:7).

Q. What is the purpose of the book of Ruth?

A. Probably to protest the narrowness of those who condemned all marriages with foreigners (cf. Ezra 10; Nehemiah 13:25-27).

Q. How does it make this protest?

A. By showing that David himself had Moabite blood in his veins (4:17-22).

Q. Why is it especially significant that attention is drawn to David's Moabite ancestry?

A. Because of the strict provision in the Law forbidding any Moabite to become a Jew: "No Ammonite or Moabite shall enter the assembly of the Lord; even to the tenth generation none belonging to them shall enter the assembly of the Lord forever" (Deuteronomy 23:3). Genesis 19:37 represents Moab as the result of incestuous union between Lot and his older daughter.

Q. What is the literary form of the book of Ruth?

A. It is a short story, described by Goethe as "the loveliest little whole that has been preserved to us among the epics and idyls."

Q. What is the meaning of the personal names in the story?

A. *Elimelech* means "my God is king"; *Naomi*, "my sweetness"; *Marah*, "bitter one"; *Mahlon*, "weakening"; *Chilion*, "Pining"; *Orpah*, "stiff-necked." *Ruth* could be derived from the Hebrew word for friendship, and *Boaz* from "in him is strength."

Q. If the book is of this character, why is it placed amid those historical books that the Hebrews called Former Prophets?

A. Its setting is "in the days when the judges ruled" (1.1); as a sequel to the book of Judges, its picture of quiet romance and idyllic domestic scenes is in striking contrast with the warlike exploits of Deborah and Gideon and Samson. It is a reminder that, in the history of a nation, events that center in the home may be quite as significant as those that occur in the marketplace or on the field of battle.

Q. What Hebrew marriage custom is basic to an understanding of the story?

A. The levirate marriage, by which a surviving brother is required to take as his wife the deceased brother's widow (Deuteronomy 25:5).

Q. In what relation does Boaz initially stand to Naomi and Ruth?

A. Kinship made him their legal guardian.

Q. How does he discharge his responsibility in this connection?

A. By buying from the next of kin the right of family inheritance (4:1-6).

Q. What ancient custom is followed in sealing the bargain?

A. "To confirm a transaction, the one drew off his shoe and gave it to the other" (4:7f).

Q. What is the reference to "Perez, whom Tamar bore to Judah" (4:12)?

A. Genesis 38 relates how Tamar's father-in-law, who had refused to allow the usual levirate marriage, himself became the father of the widowed Tamar's child.

Q. What use is made by the Jews of the book of Ruth?

A. It is read every year at Pentecost.

Q. Why is it appropriate for Pentecost?

A. Pentecost is the harvest festival; Ruth and Naomi are represented as returning "to Bethlehem at the beginning of barley harvest" (1:22).

Q. How is the book of Ruth echoed in the New Testament?

A. Jesus is the climax of the genealogy that relates that Boaz became "the father of Obed by Ruth, and Obed the father of Jesse, and Jesse the father of David the king" (Matthew 1:5f).

Q. What custom of agricultural lands, pictured here, has been a favorite with artists?

A. Ruth goes to the field "to glean among the ears of grain" (2:2), the prototype of many gleaners.

Q. What are some literary uses made of the book of Ruth?

A. Keats, in "Ode to a Nightingale," speaks of

> *"The self-same song that found a path*
> *Through the sad heart of Ruth, when, sick for home,*
> *She stood in tears amid the alien corn."*

Irving Fineman expanded the short story into a novel that he called *Ruth;* Father E. F. Murphy uses the Biblical Ruth as the basis of his novel, *The Song of the Cave;* Thomas Hood has a poem entitled "Ruth."

Q. What is the most frequently quoted passage from Ruth?

A. The words of a daughter-in-law to her mother-in-law: "Entreat me not to leave you or to return from following you; for where you go I will go, and where you lodge I will lodge; your people shall be my people, and your God my God; where you die I will die, and there will I be buried. May the Lord do so to me and more also if even death parts me from you" (1:16f).

Q. What ancient custom is suggested by Ruth's injunction to her daughters-in-law: ". . . return each of you to her mother's house" (1:8)?

A. This reflects the institution of polygamous marriage in which the daughter dwells in her mother's abode.

Q. What Canaanite practice is suggested by "winnowing barley tonight at the threshing-floor" (3:2)?

A. Fertility rites practiced at the harvest season.

THE FIRST BOOK OF
SAMUEL

Q. Who is the author of I Samuel?

A. David's court historian, who set down the traditions of an earlier time.

Q. When was the book written?

A. The court records began to be kept about 1000 B.C. Between that time and 850 B.C. an extensive collection of written narratives had been assembled.

Q. Why is the book named for Samuel?

A. Because he is the principal figure in Chapters 1-12.

Q. Who was Samuel?

A. Prophet and seer, last of the judges, first of the kingmakers, Samuel summed up in his own person and career the belief of the Hebrew community that God spoke through certain charismatic individuals and that the government of the community, if it were to prosper, must give heed to their direction and advice.

Q. What relationship have the books of Samuel to the preceding era in Israel's history?

A. I Samuel 4:18, reporting the death of Eli, says, "He had judged Israel forty years"; this is similar to the formula used in Judges (cf. 10:2; 12:7,11; 16:31). I Samuel 7:15 says that "Samuel judged Israel all the days of his life." I Samuel appears therefore to be a continuation of the narrative begun in Judges, and represents a transition from the era of the judges to that of the kings.

Q. What is told of Samuel's family background?

A. He was the child of Elkanah "an Ephraimite" (1:1) by Hannah, his hitherto childless wife, whose prayers (1:9-12) were rewarded by the birth of this son (1:19f); Hannah, in gratitude, dedicates the child to the Lord "as long as he lives" (1:27).

Q. In what other way does Hannah express her piety?

A. In a song (2:1-10) that became the prototype of Mary's song, the Magnificat (Luke 1:46-55).

Q. What was the situation with respect to organized religion in Samuel's day?

A. In a time when the priesthood was hereditary, Eli the priest had sons who used their office as a means of exploitation (2:12-17) and corruption (2:22-25).

Q. How is God's judgment executed in this situation?

A. The ark of God, symbol of his presence, is carried away by the Philistines; in a battle fought to recover it, the sons of Eli are slain; the father, hearing that the ark remains in the hands of the enemy, falls dead; Eli's grandson, born during these tumultuous events, is given the name Ichabod, meaning, "The glory has departed from Israel" (4:1-22).

Q. What subsequently happens to the ark?

A. It brings misfortune upon the Philistines (tumors—5:6; and "deathly panic"—5:11). This was true wherever it was carried: Ashdod, Ekron, Gaza, Gath. Finally, Philistines deposited it at Beth-shemesh, thus returning it to its rightful owners (6:1-7:2).

Q. Meanwhile, how has God been preparing Samuel for leadership in the nation?

A. As Eli's youthful assistant, he becomes familiar with the forms of worship at Shiloh (2:18,26; 3:1); in a vision of the night (3:2-18) Samuel learns of the punishment about to befall the house of Eli; as Samuel "continued to grow both in stature and in favor with the Lord and with men" (2:26; compare Luke 2:52), "all Israel from Dan to Beersheba knew that Samuel was established as a prophet of the Lord" (3:20).

Q. When did Samuel assume leadership?

A. When the ark was returned by the Philistines, he led the people in an act of sacrifice and rededication (7:3-14); thereafter "Samuel judged Israel all the days of his life. And he went on a circuit year by year" (7:15).

Q. What were the factors that led the nation to be dissatisfied with rule by judges?

A. The inadequacy of Samuel's sons ("they took bribes and perverted justice"—8:3) and the fact that the surrounding peoples were governed by kings ("now appoint for us a king to govern us like all the nations"—8:5).

Q. What is Samuel's attitude toward the establishment of a monarchy?

A. In Chapter 8 he regards this as a repudiation of the sovereignty of God (8:7) and as the beginning of forms of conscription, forced labor, and taxation that will lead soon to national ruin (8:10-20); in Chapters 9 and 10 he is represented as searching out and finding Saul, whom God has chosen to be king; Samuel anoints Saul (10:1) and presents him to the people, who respond in words that admiring throngs ever since have used about monarchs: "Long live the king!" (10:24)

Q. In what circumstances does Saul assert his authority?

A. When the followers of Nahash besieged Jabesh-gilead, Saul took command of the troops, "put the people in three companies," and "cut down the Ammonites" (11:11).

Q. What of Samuel's farewell?

A. In words later echoed by Paul (cf. Acts 20:33), he recounted his manner of life among them ("whom have I defrauded?"—12:3); recalled "the saving deeds of the Lord" (12:7), who "brought your fathers up out of the land of Egypt" (12:6); and outlined the prophetic view of history: "Only fear the Lord, and serve him faithfully. . . . But if you still do wickedly, you shall be swept away" (12:24).

Q. How does Saul exercise his kingship?

A. "He fought against all his enemies on every side" (14:47) in disregard of Samuel's warning ("now your kingdom shall not continue" —13:14; 15:10,26,35).

Q. What aid did Saul have in one battle with the Philistines?

A. Just as the Philistines attacked, "the Lord thundered with a mighty voice that day against the Philistines and threw them into confusion; and they were routed before Israel" (7:10).

Q. How did Saul displease the Lord in his encounter with the Amalekites?

A. He spared their king Agag, "and the best of the sheep and of the oxen and of the fatlings, and the lambs, and all that was good" (15:9).

Q. Why was this displeasing to God?

A. Because Agag and the Amalekites represented a religion considered dangerous to that of Israel, Saul had been commanded: "Now go and smite Amalek, and utterly destroy all that they have" (15:3).

Q. What oracle does Samuel offer in the situation?

A. "Behold, to obey is better than sacrifice,
        and to hearken than the fat of rams" (15:22).

Q. What advantage did the Philistines have in their continuing conflict with the Hebrews?

A. "There was no smith to be found throughout all the land of Israel" (13:19); the Israelites had to go to the Philistines to sharpen their tools (13:20-22).

Q. What forces arose to portend the downfall of Saul?

A. His son Jonathan proved himself an able warrior (14:1-15); David, a handsome, ruddy youth with "beautiful eyes" (16:12), skilled in playing the harp but disciplined by work in the field, fresh from slaying a giant (17:57), became Saul's armor-bearer (16:21). David attained great popularity (18:6-9; 29:5) and he and Jonathan became fast friends ("the soul of Jonathan was knit to the soul of David" —18:1).

Q. Why did Samuel think David a likely prospect for the kingship?

A. Jesse of Bethlehem thought the youngest of his sons unworthy; ("man looks on the outward appearance, but the Lord looks on the heart"—16:7); David turned out to be "skilful in playing, a man of valor, a man of war, prudent in speech, a man of good presence" (16:18); David became Saul's son-in-law (18:17-29).

Q. How does the relationship between Saul and David develop?

A. "When Saul saw and knew that the Lord was with David, and that all Israel loved him, Saul . . . was David's enemy continually" (18:28f). Saul repeatedly seeks to kill David (19:10-18), who is saved by Michal (19:11-17) and Jonathan (20:1-42); yet David, now an outlaw with headquarters in the cave of Adullam (22:1), repeatedly spares Saul's life (24:1-15; 26:1-24).

Q. Where does Saul turn for help?

A. Having failed to receive help either by dreams, or by Urim, or by prophets (28:6), he then, through a witch at Endor, seeks to consult with the spirit of the departed Samuel, but receives only the message: "Why have you disturbed me?" (28:15). Jealous and alone, hard-pressed by the Philistines, "Saul took his own sword, and fell upon it" (31:4).

Q. What principle of equality did David establish for the military?

A. "For as his share is who goes down into the battle, so shall his share be who stays by the baggage; they shall share alike" (30:24).

Q. In what way does the Septuagint present a more consistent story regarding Saul's growing jealousy of David?

A. By omitting from Chapter 18 verses 10, 11, 17-19, 27-30.

THE SECOND BOOK OF

SAMUEL

Q. Who is the author of II Samuel?

A. The court historian continues the narrative begun in I Samuel; the two books were originally one, the Hebrew manuscripts making no division between them. The official court history of David, beginning at 9:1, extends on through I Kings 2:46; Chapters 9-20 are so vivid that they are thought to rest upon the reports of eyewitnesses.

Q. Who is the principal character in II Samuel?

A. David the king.

Q. Why then is the volume called II Samuel?

A. Because it continues the prophetic interpretation of history promulgated by Samuel.

Q. How does David greet the news of Saul's death?

A. With a lament (1:19-27) containing the refrain, "How are the mighty fallen."

Q. What follows David's accession to the throne?

A. Insurrection and civil war. Ishbosheth, Saul's son, claimed the kingship over Israel ("But the house of Judah followed David—2:10); the forces of Abner, fighting for Ishbosheth, clash repeatedly with those of Joab, David's lieutenant (2:8-32; 3:6-30). "There was a long war between the house of Saul and the house of David" (3:1).

Q. How does David begin his kingship?

A. Having received a pledge of loyalty from "all the elders of Israel" (5:3), he led a force to capture Jerusalem from the Jebusites (5:6-10). He removes the ark to Jerusalem (6:1-16), which he makes his capital.

Q. What proposal is made by Nathan the prophet?

A. That in Jerusalem David build a house in which God may dwell (7:1-17); David responds with an appropriate prayer (7:18-29), but is ultimately denied the privilege of constructing the temple because of his pride in carrying out a census (24:1-10) and must settle for an altar erected on a threshing-floor purchased from Araunah (24:18-25).

Q. What of David's military exploits?

A. "David won a name for himself. . . . And the Lord gave victory to David wherever he went" (8:13f).

Q. How did David organize his government?

A. Perhaps using Egyptian administration as his model, he appointed Joab "over the army," Jehoshaphat as recorder, Zadok and Ahimelech as priests, Seraiah as secretary, and Benaiah as "overseer of the foreign bodyguards" (8:15-18; cf. 20:23-26).

Q. What personal qualities did David exhibit as king?

A. Saul's crippled grandson, Mephibosheth, was invited to live in Jerusalem, "and he ate always at the king's table" (9:13); seeing a woman whom he desired, David not only committed adultery with her (11:2-5) but ordered his general to have her husband so placed in battle that he would be killed (11:14-27); the conquered Ammonites he required "to labor with saws and iron picks and iron axes, and . . . at the brickkilns" (12:31); when David defeated the rebellion under Absalom, the victory "was turned into mourning" (19:2); restored to the throne, David "swayed the heart of all the men of Judah as one man" (19:14).

Q. Who rebuked the king for his adultery?

A. Nathan the prophet, in a parable ending with the words, "You are the man" (12:1-7).

Q. What of David's own family?

A. The child Bathsheba first bore to him died (12:15-23); Bathsheba's second child was Solomon (12:24f); another son, Amnon, committed incest with his half sister Tamar (13:1-22); Absalom, another son, slew Amnon in revenge (13:30-39).

Q. Which of David's sons led a revolt?

A. Absalom "stole the hearts of the men of Israel" (15:6) and led an insurrection, forcing David to flee from his capital; defeated by David's men in battle, Absalom met his death when his head "caught fast in an oak, and he was left hanging" (18:9).

Q. Who were "the giants in Gath" (21:22)?

A. The word translated "giants" is the same as that transliterated *Rephaim* in Genesis 14:5. There was a tradition that there had once been a race of aboriginal giants who inhabited various parts of the earth.

Q. What Psalm is found in II Samuel?

A. 22:2-51 is almost identical with Psalm 18:2-50; verses 2-31 are a general thanksgiving; verses 32-51 appear to be a king's rejoicing in the triumphs granted to him.

Q. What other hymn is included here?

A. 23:1-7 is a song in praise of God's goodness to David, "the sweet psalmist of Israel" (23:1).

Q. What military distinctions are awarded David's men?

A. Some were given the title "mighty men" (23:8-12); others, "the thirty chief men"—apparently a kind of legion of honor.

Q. How does this book differ from I Samuel in its account of the death of Goliath?

A. I Samuel 17:50f describes how David, having stunned Goliath with a stone from his slingshot, proceeded to kill him with a sword. II Samuel 21:19 says that "Elhanan . . . slew Goliath the Gittite."

Q. What psychological phenomenon, often noted in casebooks, is exhibited by Amnon?

A. Having wronged Tamar, Amnon "hated her with very great hatred; so that the hatred with which he hated her was greater than the love with which he had loved her" (13:15).

Q. What ancient belief is reflected in David's Song of Deliverance, which says of God:

"He rode on a cherub, and flew;
  he was seen upon the wings of the wind" (22:11)?

A. The Hebrews seem to have shared with their Near Eastern neighbors the belief that God had winged assistants who assisted in getting him from place to place. The imagery, however, may be simply a personification of natural phenomena.

THE FIRST BOOK OF
KINGS

Q. Who is the author of I Kings?

A. The Babylonian Talmud says that "Jeremiah wrote his own book, the book of Kings and Lamentations." The work itself gives no hint of the author's name but does indicate that a compiler made use of such sources as "the Book of the Chronicles of the Kings of Israel" (14:19; 15:31, etc.) and "the Book of the Chronicles of the Kings of Judah" (15:7,23); he appears also to have had at his disposal biographical material concerning the prophet Elijah (17-19).

Q. When was I Kings written?

A. The sources used by the author were evidently court records kept in the days of the kings whose reigns are recorded, namely from about 970 B.C. to about 850 B.C. The use that is made of the material reflects the philosophy of history introduced by the Deuteronomic reform about 621 B.C.

Q. What is the philosophy of history reflected in I Kings?

A. That kings who are faithful to Israel's God have prosperous reigns, while those who forget or forsake Israel's God meet with disaster.

Q. What pattern is used by the author in appraising the several kings?

A. He states the date of the king's accession and his age at the time; the length of his reign; the name of his mother; and whether or not he had been faithful to the pure worship of Israel's God; he concludes with mention of the king's death, place of burial, and successor.

Q. Why are Chapters 1 and 2 thought of as a continuation of II Samuel?

A. Because they give the concluding chapters in the life of David, most of whose reign is dealt with in II Samuel.

Q. What does I Kings have to say about David?

A. During the last days of his life, there was intrigue as to which of his sons should be his successor: Adonijah, who had the support of David's military leader, Joab, and Abiathar the priest (1:5-7), or Solomon, who had the support of Bathsheba and the prophet Nathan (1:11-34).

Q. Who emerges victorious from this struggle?

A. Solomon, and David enjoins him to "keep the charge of the Lord your God" (2:3). The promise is that "the throne of David shall be established before the Lord for ever" (2:45).

Q. How many wives did David have?

A. The names of eight are mentioned: Michal (I Samuel 18:27); Abigail (I Samuel 25:42); Ahinoam (I Samuel 25:43); Maacah (I Chronicles 3:2); Haggith (I Chronicles 3:2); Abital (I Chronicles 3:3); Eglah (I Chronicles 3:3); and Bathsheba.

Q. What is the meaning of I Kings 15:5: "David did right in the eyes of the Lord, and did not turn aside from anything that he commanded him all the days of his life, except in the matter of Uriah the Hittite"?

A. A polygamous society saw nothing wrong in a multiplicity of wives; in the case of Bathsheba, David's sin consisted in murdering her husband (II Samuel 11:2-27) in order to take her as his wife. It was this that "displeased the Lord."

Q. What of the beginnings of King Solomon's reign?

A. To safeguard his throne, he began by ordering the execution of Adonijah (2:23) and the banishment of Abiathar (2:27); he "made a marriage alliance with Pharaoh king of Egypt," installing Pharaoh's daughter in "the city of David" (3:1).

Q. What prayer of Solomon figured in recent United States history?

A. When Harry Truman found himself catapulted into the presidency, he quoted from 3:9: "Give thy servant therefore an understanding mind to govern thy people, that I may discern between good and evil; for who is able to govern this thy great people?"

Q. How did Solomon organize his government?

A. By appointing a high priest and associates, secretaries, recorder, commander of the army, adjutant, supervisor of the palace, and superintendent "in charge of the forced labor" (4:1-6).

Q. What provision was made for sustaining the royal establishment?

A. In addition to the king's cabinet, he appointed twelve regional officers, each of whom had to provide "food for the king and his household . . . for one month in the year" (4:7-29).

Q. What evidences are given of Solomon's wisdom?

A. His decision when two mothers claimed a single child (3:16-28). "He also uttered three thousand proverbs; and his songs were a thousand and five. He spoke of trees, from the cedar that is in Lebanon to the hyssop that grows out of the wall; he spoke also of beasts and birds, and of reptiles, and of fish. And men came from all peoples to hear the wisdom of Solomon" (4:32-34).

Q. Who came the greatest distance?

A. "Now when the queen of Sheba heard of the fame of Solomon . . . she came to test him with hard questions" (10:1); greatly impressed, her conclusion was "the half was not told me" (10:7).

Q. What was Solomon's program of public works?

A. To construct a temple, he purchased timber from Hiram, king of Tyre; "raised a levy of forced labor" (5:13) to work under the direction of foreign builders (5:18); he built also "the house of the Forest of Lebanon" (7:2-5) and "the hall of Pillars" (7:6), "the hall of the Throne" or "hall of Judgment" (7:7), a palace for himself and one for Pharaoh's daughter (7:8); outside Jerusalem he built "store-cities" and "cities for his chariots, and the cities for his horsemen" (9:19).

Q. Which of these has been recently unearthed?

A. His stables at Megiddo.

Q. What facilities for foreign trade did Solomon create?

A. "A fleet of ships" (which had to be entrusted to Tyrian "seamen who were familiar with the sea"—9:27) that "went to Ophir, and brought from there gold to the amount of four hundred and twenty talents" (9:28).

Q. What description is given of the Lord's house built by Solomon?

A. "When the house was built, it was with stone prepared at the quarry; so that neither hammer nor axe nor any tool of iron was heard in the temple, while it was being built" (6:7); it was lined with cedar, overlaid with gold, and elaborately furnished (6:8-37; 7:15-51); it was dedicated with an appropriate prayer (8:1-53) and sacrifice (8:62-64).

Q. What was the reaction of the people to Solomon's building program?

A. When the temple was finished, "they blessed the king and went to their homes joyful and glad of heart" (8:66); later, however, they became aware that the palace and other extravagances imposed upon them an intolerable burden of taxation (12:4).

Q. What effect did polygamy have upon the reign of Solomon?

A. "He had seven hundred wives, princesses, and three hundred concubines; and his wives turned away his heart" (11:3), so that he built shrines for the worship of the gods of some of his foreign wives, and "did what was evil in the sight of the Lord" (11:6); the result was that God "raised up an adversary," Hadad the Edomite (11:14), and another, Rezon, who "became leader of a marauding band" (11:23-25).

Q. Who were the kings of the Hittites (10:29) with whom Solomon carried on trade?

A. Rulers of peoples living between Syria and North Mesopotamia, sharing elements of culture with the Hittites who had extended their influence over Palestine at an earlier time, 1900 to 1200 B.C.

Q. What is told us regarding the relations between Israel and Egypt?

A. The Egyptian king "captured Gezer and burnt it with fire" and gave it "as dowry to his daughter, Solomon's wife" (9:16). To escape the violence of Joab, commander of David's army, Hadad, king of the Edomites, had fled to Egypt, where he remained until the death of David and Joab (11:14-22). Shishak, known to history as Sheshonk I (950-929 B.C.), on the alert to regain Egypt's former position in Asia, gave asylum to Jeroboam when he fled from Solomon (11:40). After the division of Israel into southern and northern kingdoms, Shishak entered Jerusalem, raided the temple treasury as well as the king's palace, and "took everything" (14:25ff).

Q. What prophet makes his appearance at the end of Solomon's reign?

A. Ahijah, who tore a new garment "into twelve pieces" (11:30), indicating that Solomon's kingdom was to be divided. Ahijah was the first to use this device of the acted parable, a device often employed by the later prophets.

Q. Who succeeded Solomon on the throne?

A. His son Rehoboam, who, refusing to heed the advice of older men, took counsel of the younger. Instead of easing the tax burden, he announced: "My father chastised you with whips, but I will chastise you with scorpions" (12:11).

Q. What effect did Rehoboam's policy have?

A. Rebellion and a divided kingdom, with Rehoboam ruling over Judah or the southern kingdom, Jeroboam, the son of Nebat (12:2), over Israel or the northern kingdom. "And there was war between Rehoboam and Jeroboam continually" (14:30).

Q. Who were Rehoboam's successors?

A. Abijam (whose "heart was not wholly true to the Lord his God"—15:3); Asa ("He put away all the male cult prostitutes out of the land, and removed all the idols that his fathers had made"—15:12); Jehoshaphat (He "walked in the way of Asa his father"—22:43, and "also made peace with the king of Israel"—22:44).

Q. Who were Jeroboam's successors?

A. Nadab ("he did what was evil"—15:26); Baasha (who gained the throne by violence: "he killed all the house of Jeroboam"—15:29); Elah (who, like his father, "made Israel to sin"—16:13); Zimri (whose reign lasted only seven days—16:15); Omri (with Tibni for a time as rival claimant to the throne, "Omri did more evil than all those who were before him"—16:25); Ahab (who outdid his father in evil—16:30: he married Jezebel, daughter of the Sidonian king, and "erected an altar for Baal"—16:31f); Ahaziah (who "provoked the Lord, the God of Israel, to anger in every way that his father had done"—22:53).

Q. Who came forward to combat the Baal worship under Ahab and Jezebel?

A. "Elijah the Tishbite" (17:1), whose presence brought sustenance and healing into the homes of the poor and bereaved (17:8-24); whose insights enabled him to predict drought (17:1-7) and rainfall (18:1,44f); whose moral witness led the king to dub him "you troubler of Israel" (18:18).

Q. How did Elijah settle the conflict between him and Baal?

A. By a contest between himself and the four hundred and fifty prophets of the false god (the "God who answers by fire, he is God"—18:24; cf. 18:20-40).

Q. What were the sequels to Elijah's victory?

A. A period of despondency on his part (19:4-18) and of determined opposition to him on the part of the queen (19:1-3).

Q. How was Elijah lifted above his despondency?

A. In a vision, accompanied by a "still small voice" (19:12), he is bidden to anoint Hazael king over Damascus, Jehu king over Israel, and Elisha as his own successor (19:15f).

Q. What enemy rose up to combat Ahab?

A. "Benhadad mustered the Syrians, and went . . . to fight against Israel" (20:26).

Q. What was the attitude of Ahab and Jezebel toward their own people?

A. Ahab coveted the property of Naboth, a small landholder, and Jezebel arranged to have the owner murdered (21:1-16).

Q. What was Elijah's judgment on this act?

A. "In the place where dogs licked up the blood of Naboth shall dogs lick your own blood" (21:19).

Q. In what endeavor did the kings of Judah and Israel unite?

A. In an effort to wrest Ramoth-gilead from the Syrians (22:1-4).

Q. What part did the prophets play in this undertaking?

A. When the "yes-men" among the prophets encouraged it, the two kings thought they should consult another; Ahab was unwilling to consult the one proposed: "I hate him, for he never prophesies good concerning me but evil" (22:8); in defiance of Micaiah, Ahab went into battle and was slain, "and the dogs licked up his blood" (22:38).

Q. How does Solomon interpret the "knowing good and evil" of Genesis 3:5?

A. For him it is "an understanding mind" enabling him to govern the people wisely and well (3:9).

Q. What mathematical error is evident?

A. The diameter of the molten sea (7:23) is given as ten cubits, its circumference as thirty cubits. Mathematicians know that the circumference of a circle is obtained by multiplying the diameter by 3.1416.

Q. What example of early liturgy is preserved here?

A. The prayer of David recorded in 8:23ff.

Q. What twentieth-century discovery confirms Solomon's commercial activities at Eziongeber (9:26)?

A. Nelson Glueck found there a great smelting refinery, the largest ever found in the Near East.

Q. What incident here is confirmed by inscriptions on the temple walls at Karnak, in Egypt?

A. Shishak's victory over Rehoboam (14:25-28).

THE SECOND BOOK OF
KINGS

Q. Who is the author of II Kings?

A. This is a continuation of an unnamed writer's historical narrative, begun in I Kings.

Q. What sources were used by the compiler of II Kings?

A. A biography of the prophet Isaiah (18:13-20:19), which was also incorporated in the book of the prophet Isaiah (Isaiah 36:1-39:8); II Kings continues also to make use of "the Book of the Chronicles of the Kings of Judah" (8:23; 12:19; 14:18; 24:5) and "the Book of the Chronicles of the Kings of Israel" (1:18; 10:34; 13:8,12; 14:15,28).

Q. When was II Kings written?

A. The sources include court records kept in the days of the kings whose reigns are recorded, namely from about 850 B.C. to 586 B.C. As in the case of I Kings, the use that is made of the material reflects the philosophy of history introduced about 621 B.C.

Q. Why are Chapters 1 and 2 thought of as extensions of I Kings?

A. Because they continue the accounts, begun in the earlier work, of the prophets Elijah and Elisha.

Q. What additional information is given about these men?

A. Elijah rebukes Ahaziah for consulting, in his illness, "Baalzebub, the god of Ekron" (1:1-16); Elijah disappears from the scene (he "went up by a whirlwind into heaven"—2:11); Elisha takes up Elijah's mantle (2:14) and uses salt to make wholesome water out of unwholesome (2:19-22); disaster befalls children who taunt Elisha by saying, "Go up, you baldhead!" (2:23).

Q. What is told of the ministry of Elisha after Elijah's departure?

A. The compiler tells of Elisha's providing for the needs of the poor (4:1-7); of the prophet's chamber kept in readiness for him in a well-to-do home (4:8-10); of his restoring a lifeless child to his mother (4:11-37); of his saving a company of men from the effects of poisonous food (4:38-41); of his directing Naaman the Syrian to a cure for his leprosy (5:1-27); of his making an axe-head float (6:1-7); of his prediction of inflation and famine for Samaria (7:1-20); of his arranging to have Jehu anointed as king (9:1-10).

Q. What monarchs of Israel are dealt with in II Kings?

A. Jehoram (or Joram: "he clung close to the sin of Jeroboam"— 3:3); Jehu ("he drives furiously"—9:20; he slew the seventy sons of Ahab "and put their heads in baskets"—10:7; he slew the worshipers of false gods, and "wiped out Baal from Israel"—10:28); Jehoahaz ("He did what was evil in the sight of the Lord"—13:2): Jehoash ("He also did what was evil"—13:11); Jeroboam II ("He restored the border of Israel from the entrance of Hamath as far as the Sea of the Arabah" —14:25); Zechariah (who ruled only six months—15:8); Shallum (who ruled only one month—15:13); Menahem (who paid tribute to Pul, king of Assyrians, "that he might help him to confirm his hold of the royal power"—15:19); Pekahiah ("he did what was evil"—15:24); Pekah (who gained the throne by slaying Pekahiah—15:25; during his reign Tiglath Pileser, king of Assyria, "carried the people captive to Assyria" —15:29); Hoshea (under whom, in 721 B.C., the kingdom of Israel came to an end when the king became a vassal of Shalmaneser, king of Assyria—17:3).

Q. What monarchs of Judah are dealt with in II Kings?

A. Jehoram ("In his days Edom revolted from the rule of Judah, and set up a king of their own"—8:20); Ahaziah ("he was son-in-law to the house of Ahab"—8:27); Athaliah (who secured the throne for herself by killing all the male members of her father's house—11:1-3; and was herself slain—11:13-16); Joash (who required the priests who had been neglecting the temple to repair it, with a "chest" to receive the offerings of the people—12:4-19); Amaziah ("he did what was right—14:3; but suffered defeat at the hands of Israel under Jehoash— 14:8-15); Azariah (who became king when he was sixteen and ruled fifty-two years—15:2); Jotham (who served for a while as regent for his aged father—15:5; and "did what was right"—15:34); Ahaz ("He even burned his son as an offering, according to the abominable practices of the nations"—16:3; and became a vassal of Assyria—16:17f); Hezekiah ("He did what was right in the eyes of the Lord, according to all that David his father had done"—18:3; "He smote the Philistines as far as Gaza and its territory, from watchtower to fortified city"—18:8); Manasseh ("he erected altars for Baal"—21:3; "he burned his son as an offering, and practiced soothsaying and augury, and dealt with mediums and with wizards"—21:6); Amon ("he did what was evil . . . as Manasseh his father had done"—21:20); Josiah (who "did what was right . . . and he did not turn aside to the right hand or to the left"—22:2; but who lost his life at the hands of the Egyptians when he sought to intercept their march on the Assyrians—23:29f); Jehoahaz (whose reign lasted only three months "when Pharaoh Neco put him in bonds"—23:33); Jehoiakim (placed on the throne as Neco's puppet—23:34-36, he became a vassal of Nebuchadnezzar—24:1); Jehoiachin (whose reign also lasted only three months; he "gave himself up to the king of Babylon"—24:12); Zedekiah (Nebuchadnezzar's puppet, under whom final disaster overtook the kingdom of Judah—25:21).

Q. How did the kingdom of Judah come to its end?

A. Under Zedekiah, the leaders of the people were carried away by the Babylonians into exile (24:18-25:21); eventually another king of Babylon freed Zedekiah, and "he dined regularly at the king's table" (25:29).

Q. What prophet's work presents vivid pictures of the end of Judah?

A. Jeremiah, who witnessed the scenes with his own eyes.

Q. Why did the Babylonians not carry the entire nation into exile?

A. The leaders were deported. "But the captain of the guard left some of the poorest of the land to be vinedressers and plowmen" (25:12).

Q. Where did those who were left turn for help?

A. To Egypt (25:26).

Q. What else does II Kings say about the dealings between Israel and Egypt?

A. When Sennacherib, sending an army westward, laid siege to Jerusalem, his commander taunted the Israelites with seeking security where none was to be found: "Behold, you are now relying on Egypt, that broken reed of a staff, which will pierce the hand of any man who leans on it" (18:21). Pharaoh Neco (609-594 B.C.), hoping to restore Egyptian sovereignty in Asia, marched against Josiah, a supporter of Babylon, slew him at Megiddo, and exacted heavy tribute from Jerusalem (23:29-35).

Q. What deliverance was wrought in the days of King Hezekiah?

A. The Assyrians, under Sennacherib, had Jerusalem surrounded; "that night the angel of the Lord . . . slew a hundred and eighty-five thousand in the camp of the Assyrians" (19:35).

Q. What early nineteenth-century literary work celebrates this occasion?

A. Lord Byron's "The Destruction of Sennacherib":
"The Assyrian came down like the wolf on the fold,
And his cohorts were gleaming in purple and gold."

Q. What significant event occurred during the reign of Josiah?

A. The long-neglected "book of the law" (perhaps a part of our Deuteronomy) was rediscovered in the temple (22:3-13); all the people joined the king in a pledge "with all his heart and all his soul, to perform the words of this covenant" (23:3).

Q. What incident recorded here is commemorated on the Moabite stone?

A. Mesha's rebellion against Israel (3:4ff).

Q. What is the meaning of the military titles enumerated in 18:17?

A. *Tartan* is equivalent of "field marshal"; *Rabsaris,* of "chamberlain"; *Rabshakeh,* of "chief officer."

Q. What place for the accumulation of refuse, significant in later Biblical thought, was established by King Josiah?

A. He "defiled Topheth, which is in the valley of the sons of Hinnom, that no one might burn his son or daughter as an offering to Molech" (23:10). This became the Gehenna of the New Testament.

THE FIRST BOOK OF THE

CHRONICLES

Q. Who is the author of I Chronicles?

A. I Chronicles, together with II Chronicles, Ezra, and Nehemiah, originally constituted a single narrative reviewing Israel's history from creation to the return from exile. In I and II Chronicles the unnamed compiler, designated the Chronicler, used material drawn from several other sections of the Hebrew Scriptures. Hebrew tradition held that this continuous narrative was begun by Ezra and completed by Nehemiah.

Q. What is the meaning of the title?

A. The English title is derived from Jerome's comment that the book could well be named "the chronicle of the whole of sacred history"; the title in the Latin Bible, *Paralipomena,* is derived from the Greek for "things omitted"—omitted, that is, from the earlier records and here supplied.

Q. When was I Chronicles written?

A. The genealogy in 3:19-24 includes six generations after the return from exile, and so would date not earlier than about 350 B.C.

Q. What is the purpose of I Chronicles?

A. To retell the history of the Hebrew people in such a way as to bring out the divine purpose that had caused the nation's adversities to be used for good.

Q. What Old Testament sources are used for the genealogies found in Chapters 1-9?

A. The tribal ancestries are traced in materials drawn from Genesis, Numbers, and Joshua.

Q. Who is the principal character in I Chronicles?

A. Chapters 10-29 deal with David the king, with the purpose of emphasizing that God had chosen him, and with the glory of David's throne.

Q. What other Old Testament materials deal with this theme?

A. Accounts of the reign of David are found in II Samuel and I Kings.

Q. How does the Chronicler's treatment of David differ from that in the other sources?

A. The Chonicler is concerned with showing that Israel's spiritual life centers in Jerusalem, a city that David established as the capital of the national life; in the process, the circumstances he relates about David are often somewhat grander than in the other narratives.

Q. What are some examples of the way in which the Chronicler magnifies David's reign?

A. 11:17-19 shows David's magnanimity and understanding in dealing with associates; 21:1 blames Satan for inciting David "to number Israel," rather than, as implied in II Samuel, David's pride in his military strength; 22:2-19 represents David's plans for building the temple (even if he did have to leave the construction to someone else), his plans for the temple worship, and his assignment of duties to the priests (23:1-29:9) and singers (25:1-31) as the crowning achievement of David's career.

Q. What are some other points at which the Chronicler outdoes his predecessor in attributing grandeur to David?

A. The organization of the government and the army (27:1-34) are on a scale which that earlier era could hardly have sustained; David's farewell to the people (28:1-29:19) and the account of David's end ("he died in a good old age, full of days, riches, and honor; and Solomon his son reigned in his stead"—29:28) contain no mention of the weakness of David's declining years, nor of the domestic intrigue regarding succession to his throne such as is contained in I Kings 1:1; the price paid for Araunah's threshing-floor ("six hundred shekels of gold by weight"—21:24) has gone up from the fifty shekels of silver (including the oxen) reported in II Samuel 24:24.

Q. What are some evidences of the Chronicler's own interest in worship?

A. The genealogies pay particular attention to Levi, the tribe of priests (6); the religious significance of the bringing of the ark to Jerusalem is emphasized (15:1-24; 16:7-42), in contrast to II Samuel 6:12-20, where it is mainly an event of political significance: "David and all the house of Israel brought up the ark of the Lord with shouting" (II Samuel 6:15). 16:7-36 is a thanksgiving hymn composed of Psalm 96:1-13; 105:1-15; 106:1,47f.

Q. What phrases from this book have found a special place in Christian worship?

A. The Lord's Prayer (Matthew 6:9-13) in the ancient manuscripts ends with the words "deliver us from evil." From the prayer that David is reported to have composed for the dedication of the temple he was not privileged to build, believers added to Jesus' words the phrases, "for thine is the kingdom and the power and the glory forever"; these terms are found in I Chronicles 29:10-13.

Q. How does this narrative differ from that of II Samuel regarding the initiating of the census?

A. II Samuel 24:1 represents God as saying to David: "Go, number Israel and Judah." I Chronicles 21:1, however, says that "Satan . . . incited David to number Israel."

Q. What is the author's philosophy of history?

A. "Judah was taken into exile in Babylon because of their unfaithfulness" (9:1).

Q. What is the author's explanation of why God did not permit David to build the temple?

A. "You may not build a house for my name, for you are a warrior and have shed blood" (28:3).

THE SECOND BOOK OF THE
CHRONICLES

Q. Who is the author of II Chronicles?

A. The unnamed historian who recounts God's dealing with the Hebrew people here continues the narrative begun in I Chronicles.

Q. What sources did the historian use?

A. Much of his material is taken from the canonical books of the Kings; in addition, he refers to "the Book of the Kings of Judah and Israel" (28:26; 32:32) and to certain materials taken from the work of "Isaiah the prophet the son of Amoz" (26:22); for the events of Solomon's reign he refers to "the history of Nathan the prophet," "the prophecy of Ahijah the Shilonite," and "the visions of Iddo the seer" (9:29; cf. 12:15); mention is made, too, of "the Chronicles of Shemaiah the prophet" (12:15), "the story of the prophet Iddo" (13:22), and "the Commentary on the Book of the Kings" (24:27); the nation's grief over Josiah's death is said to be "written in the Laments" (35:25); brief liturgical passages also rest on the Psalms (20:21, for example, is based on Psalm 106:1).

Q. What does II Chronicles do with material taken from other parts of the canonical Scripture?

A. Concerned with illustrating the Deuteronomic philosophy of history ("the men of Judah prevailed, because they relied upon the Lord, the God of their fathers"—13:18; "Jotham became mighty, because he ordered his ways before the Lord his God"—27:6), the Chronicler changes the emphasis, adds significant details, and omits deprecatory matter.

Q. What are some illustrations of the way in which II Chronicles treats its sources?

A. I Kings 10:27 says that Solomon "made silver as common in Jerusalem as stone"; II Chronicles 1:15 says this "king made silver and gold as common in Jerusalem as stone"; 9:20 adds: "silver was not considered as anything in the days of Solomon." I Kings 5:13-18 describes Solomon's "levy of forced labor"; II Chronicles 2:17ff indicates that these were "aliens." I Kings 9:11 says "Solomon gave to Hiram twenty cities in the land of Galilee"; II Chronicles 8:2 says "Solomon rebuilt the cities which Huram [also spelled "Hiram"] had given to him." In portraying the wisdom and wealth of Solomon (9:1-31), the Chronicler omits the reports of Solomon's idolatry that appear in I Kings 11:1-8. The account of Asa's reign (14:1-16:14) extends the account given in I Kings 15:8-23 to explain that for thirty-five years the king had success because he was faithful to Israel's God, but his last six years were a period of decline because he "relied on the king of Syria, and did not rely on the Lord" (16:7).

Q. What story in II Chronicles anticipates the attitude toward Samaritans stressed in Luke 10:25-37?

A. When the Samaritans "took captive two hundred thousand" people of Judah, intending to make slaves of them, Oded the prophet appeared and said: ". . . send back the captives" (28:11); in as remarkable an incident as there is in military annals, the Samaritans thereupon "took the captives, and with the spoil they clothed all that were naked among them; they clothed them, gave them sandals, provided them with food and drink . . . and carrying all the feeble among them on asses, they brought them to their kinsfolk at Jericho" (28:15).

Q. What judgment of God befell a king who tried to usurp the priestly functions?

A. King Uzziah "had a censer in his hand to burn incense, and when he became angry with the priests leprosy broke out on his forehead . . . and King Uzziah was a leper to the day of his death" (26:19,21).

Q. What echo of the prophetic teaching about dependence upon the military appears in II Chronicles?

A. When Amaziah raised an army of "three hundred thousand picked men, fit for war, able to handle spear and shield . . . a man of

God came to him and said, 'O king . . . if you suppose that in this way you will be strong for war, God will cast you down before the enemy' " (25:5-8).

Q. What devastatingly frank obituary is given for King Jehoram?

A. "He was thirty-two years old when he began to reign, and he reigned eight years in Jerusalem; and he departed with no one's regret" (21:20).

Q. What literary form, much used in the New Testament, is introduced in II Chronicles?

A. 21:12-15 reports the receipt by King Jehoram of a letter sent to him by Elijah the prophet.

Q. Why does II Chronicles play down the history of the northern kingdom?

A. Because of its rebellion from what the author believes to be the true succession: "The Lord God of Israel gave the kingship over Israel for ever to David and his sons by a covenant of salt. Yet Jeroboam the son of Nebat, a servant of Solomon the son of David, rose up and rebelled against his lord; and certain worthless scoundrels gathered about him and defied Rehoboam the son of Solomon, when Rehoboam was young and irresolute and could not withstand them" (13:5-7).

Q. What incident in the life of Jesus has its prototype in II Chronicles?

A. Following the corruptions wrought by Ahaz (28:22-25), "The priests went into the inner part of the house of the Lord to cleanse it, and they brought out all the uncleanness that they found in the temple of the Lord" (29:16); Jesus also found it necessary to cleanse the temple (Mark 11:15-19; Matthew 21:12-13; Luke 19:45-48).

Q. Revelation 22:17 extends the doctrine of the chosen people to include all who are willing to respond to the invitation of God: "let him who desires take the water of life without price"; how is this anticipated in II Chronicles?

A. Re-establishing the institution of the Passover, King Hezekiah invited the people of Israel to join the people of Judah in its celebration, and prayed: "The good Lord pardon every one who sets his heart to seek God" (30:18f).

Q. What is the Chronicler's explanation of why the people were carried away captives by the Babylonians?

A. "They kept mocking the messengers of God, despising his words, and scoffing at his prophets, till the wrath of the Lord rose against his people, till there was no remedy" (36:16).

Q. How does II Chronicles differ from I Kings in its account of the size of Solomon's cavalry?

A. I Kings 4:26 says that Solomon "had forty thousand stalls of horses for his chariots, and twelve thousand horsemen." II Chronicles 9:25 says he "had four thousand stalls for horses and chariots, and twelve thousand horsemen."

Q. How does II Chronicles differ from II Kings in its account of Ahaziah's ascent to the throne?

A. II Kings 8:26 says "Ahaziah was twenty-two years old when he began to reign"; II Chronicles 22:2 says he was forty-two.

Q. What is the difference between Huram (2:3,11) and Hiram?

A. The name of the Tyrian king appears to have been spelled both ways; however, in II Chronicles 4:11,16 Huram is the artificer employed as chief architect of Solomon's temple; in II Chronicles 2:13 he is identified as Huramabi.

Q. What prophet here deals with neighboring people in a way that foreshadows Jesus' beatitude, "Blessed are the merciful"?

A. Oded, in his dealings with the Samaritans (28:9-15).

Q. What phrase has this book given to Christian hymnody?

A. "Arm of flesh" (32:8) is found in the third stanza of Duffield's hymn, "Stand up for Jesus."

THE BOOK OF EZRA

Q. Who is the author of the book of Ezra?

A. Reference is made in 7:12 to "Ezra the priest, the scribe of the law of the God of heaven." This appears to have been the official description at the Persian court of the Commissioner for Religious Affairs. The man who occupied this position was a Hebrew of the exile; a part of the book (7:27 to 9:15) appears to consist of this man's autobiographical notes; the remainder of the book (part of a larger work covering the whole of Hebrew history from the time of Adam to the conquest by Alexander the Great) was assembled by an anonymous compiler who has come to be known, from the title of another and lengthier section of his work, as the Chronicler.

Q. When was Ezra written?

A. Ezra was one who "had set his heart to study the law of the Lord, and to do it, and to teach his statutes and ordinances in Israel" (7:10); he appears to have returned from exile about 400 B.C., and his memoirs would date from that era; the compilation as a whole was made about a century later.

Q. Why was Ezra written?

A. The other sections of the Great Compilation were intended to retell Hebrew history from the point of view of the priestly community; Ezra and Nehemiah were added in order to include the post-exilic era.

Q. What are some evidences that Ezra is a compilation rather than history written *de novo*?

A. At 7:1 Ezra is identified as "the son of Seraiah" who, in I Chronicles 6:4-15, is reported to have lived in the time of Nebuchadnezzar—something like a century and a half earlier; Ezra 2:1-67 gives a list of "the people of the province who came up out of the captivity" and who returned at the same time as Ezra; Nehemiah 7:6-69 gives practically the same list as representing those who came at an earlier time. Ezra 1:11 and 2:2 speak as if Sheshbazzar and Zerubbabel were one and the same person; a comparison of Zechariah 4:9 with Ezra 5:9,14 shows them to have been different people. Some parts of Ezra are in Aramaic, some in Hebrew. In addition, the chronology of the Persian kings appears to be confused.

Q. What literary device is used to indicate that Ezra is a continuation of the books of the Chronicles?

A. Ezra 1:1-3 picks up and repeats the closing words of II Chronicles.

Q. What political event made possible the return of the Hebrews from their exile in Babylon?

A. The conquest of Babylonia by the Persians and the decree of the Persian king, Cyrus, announcing that Jews were free to return to their homeland (1:2-4).

Q. How did Cyrus aid the return?

A. He requested his people to assist the departing exiles with money and transport (1:4-6); he also returned the gold and silver "vessels of the house of the Lord which Nebuchadnezzar had carried away from Jerusalem" (1:7).

Q. Why did the repatriated exiles focus their attention immediately upon the institutions of religion?

A. "They set the altar in its place, for fear was upon them because of the peoples of the lands" (3:3).

Q. Who led in the work of reconstruction?

A. "Zerubbabel the son of Shealtiel and Jeshua the son of Jozadak made a beginning" (3:8).

Q. How was joy blended with grief at the reconstruction of the temple?

A. ". . . old men who had seen the first house, wept with a loud voice when they saw the foundation of this house being laid, though many shouted aloud for joy" (3:12).

Q. What unexpected opposition developed?

A. Some of the Jews who had remained behind, envious of the new beginning, sent word to Artaxerxes that the returned exiles were engaged in un-Persian activities (4:1-16); the work was for a time suspended (4:17-24).

Q. Under what circumstances was it renewed?

A. Darius, the new king, finding the decree of his predecessor, ordered that no one should interfere with the rebuilding, and "if any one alters this edict, a beam shall be pulled out of his house, and he shall be impaled upon it, and his house shall be made a dunghill" (6:11).

Q. How was the completion of the rebuilding celebrated?

A. "With joy" (6:16) and appropriate sacrifices (6:17).

Q. Who was commissioned to supervise the restoration of the facilities for worship?

A. Ezra was empowered to do this; the king's decree included the provision: "Whatever is commanded by the God of heaven, let it be done in full for the house of the God of heaven, lest his wrath be against the realm of the king and his sons" (7:23).

Q. In what spirit did Ezra undertake his mission?

A. "I took courage, for the hand of the Lord was upon me, and I gathered leading men from Israel to go up with me" (7:28).

Q. What ethnic crisis faced Ezra?

A. In defiance of the ancient provisions of the Hebrew Law, some of the returning exiles had married foreign women (9:1-15).

Q. How was this crisis resolved?

A. By prayer and penitence and a resolve to "make a covenant with our God to put away all these wives and their children" (10:3; cf. 10:1-44).

Q. What form of worship, described in Ezra, is still in use in church today?

A. "They sang responsively" (3:11).

THE BOOK OF NEHEMIAH

Q. Who is the author of the book of Nehemiah?

A. A Jew, living in exile in Babylon, having risen to be "cupbearer to the king" (1:11), received permission to go "to Judah, to the city of my fathers' sepulchres, that I may rebuild it" (2:5). Some of this man's own notes are incorporated in a work that is, in effect, like Ezra, a continuation of the Chronicles.

Q. What was the nature of Nehemiah's achievement?

A. His talents and deeds were administrative rather than prophetic.

Q. When did Nehemiah return to Jerusalem?

A. During the reign of Artaxerxes I, about 445 B.C.

Q. What promise made to Moses did Nehemiah claim as his own?

A. "Though your dispersed be under the farthest skies, I will . . . bring them to the place which I have chosen" (1:9).

Q. What assistance did Artaxerxes provide?

A. Instructions to the king's forester to furnish wood needed for the rebuilding (2:8); letters "to the governors of the province Beyond the River" (2:9); a safety patrol to guard the way (2:9).

Q. What Jerusalem place names are mentioned?

A. "Valley Gate," "Dung Gate," "Fountain Gate," "Jackal's Well," "King's Pool" (2:13ff); "Sheep Gate" (3:1), "Fish Gate" (3:3), "Old Gate" (3:6); "Tower of the Hundred" (3:1), "Tower of Hananel" (3:2); "Broad Wall" (3:8), "Tower of the Ovens" (3:11), "Pool of

Shelah" (3:15), the "Angle" (3:20), "Water Gate" (3:26), "Horse Gate" (3:28), "East Gate" (3:29), "Muster Gate" (3:31).

Q. What opposition did Nehemiah encounter?

A. Neighboring tribes, led by "Sanballat the Horonite and Tobiah the servant, the Ammonite, and Geshem the Arab" (2:19) sought to interfere with the building operations.

Q. What device did the opponents employ?

A. Ridicule: "if a fox go up on it he will break down their stone wall!" (4:3).

Q. How did the opponents rationalize their activities?

A. "We are forcing our sons and our daughters to be slaves" (5:5).

Q. What disappointment was there from within?

A. The Tekoite "nobles did not put their necks to the work" (3:5).

Q. How was the work apportioned?

A. Men of one village or family would be assigned to a particular section (3:1-32).

Q. What was the secret of achievement in spite of opposition?

A. "The people had a mind to work" (4:6); "we prayed to our God, and set a guard as a protection against them day and night" (4:9); "each kept his weapon in his hand" (4:23).

Q. What Oriental gesture did Nehemiah use to bolster the determination of his people?

A. "I also shook out my lap and said, 'So may God shake out every man from his house and from his labor who does not perform this promise' " (5:13).

Q. What government subsidy did Nehemiah decline?

A. "The former governors . . . laid heavy burdens upon the people . . . yet with all this I did not demand the food allowance of the governor, because the servitude was heavy upon this people" (5:15,18).

Q. What kind of record is given of those who assisted in the rebuilding?

A. In Chapter 7 the people are listed "by genealogy."

Q. What act of public worship was carried out?

A. The "people gathered as one man into the square before the Water Gate" (8:1); Ezra "brought the law before the assembly" (8:2) and "read from it . . . from early morning until midday" (8:3).

Q. What provision was made for those who could not understand the reading of the Law in its original language?

A. Interpreters "gave the sense, so that the people understood the reading" (8:8).

Q. What was the reaction of the people?

A. They "went their way to eat and drink and to send portions and to make great rejoicing" (8:12).

Q. What ancient festival is restored?

A. The festival of booths (8:14-18).

Q. What historical memories does Ezra evoke?

A. He recalls God's gracious dealing with the people from the call of Abraham to the deliverance from Egypt, settlement in the land of Promise, and the exile and return (9:6-37). "Because of all this," the people said (9:38), "we make a firm covenant."

Q. What were the terms of this covenant?

A. The people would abstain from heathen marriages (10:30f); they would keep the ceremonial law (10:32-34); they would observe the annual festivals (10:35); they would bring the tithes (10:36-39); in short, "We will not neglect the house of our God" (10:39).

Q. Into what two classes were the returning exiles divided?

A. One tenth lived in the city; nine tenths lived in the towns of Judah (11:1,3). "And the people blessed all the men who willingly offered to live in Jerusalem" (11:2).

Q. How was the finished wall dedicated?

A. By a procession around the wall, half the people going in one direction, half in the other—all this "with gladness, with thanksgivings and with singing, with cymbals, harps, and lyres" (12:27).

Q. What reforms did Nehemiah carry out?

A. He invoked the law of separation from foreigners (13:1-3); arranged for the strict payment and collection of the tithe (13:10-14); enforced the law of the Sabbath (13:15-22); required the dissolution of mixed marriages (13:23-27).

Q. What elements of public worship still in use can be traced to Nehemiah?

A. 12:9 describes antiphonal singing by the two halves of the choir; 9:5 records a call to worship used in the synagogue: "Stand up and bless the Lord your God from everlasting to everlasting. Blessed be thy glorious name which is exalted above all blessing and praise." Synagogue worship had begun during the exile to sustain the community while far away from the site of the destroyed temple; it is possible that Nehemiah 8:2-8 represents the introduction of synagogue worship into Palestine.

THE BOOK OF ESTHER

Q. Who is the author of this work?

A. It is completely anonymous, with no hint of the author's identity; some have thought it to be the work of Ezra or of Nehemiah (Nehemiah 12:10,26).

Q. When was Esther written?

A. It belongs to the later period of Hebrew literature; 8:17, which describes how foreigners "declared themselves Jews, for the fear of the Jews had fallen upon them," may refer to the era of forced proselytism carried out between 135 and 104 B.C. by John Hyrcanus and his son Aristobulus; the events that the book reports are set in an earlier era, namely, the fifth century B.C.

Q. What is the purpose of the book?

A. To give an appropriate historical setting for the origin of the Jewish festival of Purim: in 3:7 and 9:24 there are references to selection by casting "Pur, that is the lot," similar to throwing dice; "they called these days Purim, after the term Pur" (9:26).

Q. To what use is the book now put by the Jews?

A. It is read annually at the Feast of Purim.

Q. What features of present-day observance of Purim are derived from the book?

A. "The Jews had light and gladness and joy and honor" (8:16) in a time turned "from sorrow into gladness and from mourning into a holiday; that they should make them days of feasting and gladness, days for sending choice portions to one another and gifts to the poor" (9:22).

Q. How is the name of Haman perpetuated in present-day celebrations of Purim?

A. When, in reading the book, the name of Haman is mentioned, all cry aloud, "Let his name be blotted out"; also, the specially baked cakes eaten on this occasion are called *Haman taschen*.

Q. What interesting and accurate historical description is given of the extent of Xerxes' empire?

A. That he "reigned from India to Ethiopia" (1:1; cf. 8:9).

Q. What is the setting of the story?

A. "Susa the capital" (1:2) of Persia and Media.

Q. Who is the Ahasuerus who ruled there?

A. The Persian ruler (485-465 B.C.), more generally known to history under his Greek name, Xerxes.

Q. To what type of literature does this book belong?

A. It has been described as "an historical romance" and "a novel with a purpose."

Q. What details suggest that the narrative is historical romance?

A. There is evidence of careful thought in developing the story, for example, the planning of a massacre eleven months in advance; the notice regarding it sent "to every province in its own script and every people in its own language" (3:12); the subsequent permission granted the Jews to resist the forthcoming massacre (8:11-14); the vast numbers of Persians (seventy-five thousand—9:16) slain by a tiny minority on a single day ("on the thirteenth day of the month Adar"—9:17).

Q. Why has it been said that "Patriotism rather than religion is the prevailing sentiment of the book"?

A. It is the one Biblical book in which the name of God does not occur; it is so wanting in the spirit of tenderness and forgiveness that Luther described it as containing "a great deal of heathenish naughtiness"; lacking the universal sympathy characteristic of other Biblical books, it glorifies and rationalizes a narrow Jewish nationalism.

Q. What aspects of life at a Persian court are reflected in the book?

A. Luxurious accommodations (1:4-6); lavish provision of food (a "banquet lasting for seven days"—1:5) and liquor ("the royal wine was lavished according to the bounty of the king"—1:7); separation of the women ("the harem in Susa . . . under the custody of Hegai the king's eunuch who is in charge of the women"—2:3); the exploitation of women ("to bring Queen Vashti before the king . . . in order to show the peoples and the princes her beauty"—1:11); the superiority of the male ("that every man be lord in his own house"—1:22); palace intrigue (2:21-23).

Q. What picture is given here of Jewish life in the Dispersion?

A. Though the victims of intrigue (3:8-11) and the objects of plotting and persecution (3:6), some of them could rise to positions of prominence and power in foreign lands (2:5-11; 3:2; 9:4; 10:3).

Q. What names in Esther are similar to some in Babylonian religion?

A. Mordecai is similar to Marduk, chief among Babylonian gods; Esther resembles Ishtar, queen of Babylonian goddesses.

Q. What memorable psychological portrait is drawn of Haman?

A. "Yet all this does me no good, so long as I see Mordecai the Jew sitting at the king's gate" (5:13). When the king, thinking of Mordecai, asks Haman, "What shall be done to the man whom the king delights to honor?" Haman said to himself, "Whom would the king delight to honor more than me?" (6:6).

Q. What evidence is there of the author's belief in divine providence?

A. "For if you keep silence at such a time as this, relief and deliverance will arise for the Jews from another quarter . . . who knows whether you have not come to the kingdom for such a time as this?" (4:14).

Q. What distinctive treatment has been accorded manuscripts of the book of Esther?

A. Before the invention of printing, the names of the ten sons of Haman were written in three columns of three, three, and four names, to indicate that the ten were hanged on three parallel cords; more handwritten copies of the book were circulated than of any other Old Testament work. These were often exquisitely adorned and encased in gold and silver; for this reason it is all the more curious that Esther is the one book in the Old Testament of which no copy or fragment has been found among the Dead Sea Scrolls.

Q. What act of just retribution is dramatically portrayed?

A. Mordecai receives the honors Haman coveted for himself (6:6-11); Haman is hanged on the very gallows he prepared for Mordecai (5:14; 6:4; 7:8-10).

Q. Why is Queen Esther sometimes spoken of as the Jewish Cinderella?

A. Because of her rise from humble beginnings to a place of great importance, and from deepest sorrow to highest joy—and all of this brought about in unexpected ways.

Q. What artists have painted memorable scenes from Esther?

A. Notable among many are Tintoretto, Coypel, and Rembrandt.

Q. How does a German translator begin his rendering of Esther in such a way as to suggest that it is a romantic tale?

A. Haller's translation begins, "Once upon a time."

Q. What phrase has the story given to contemporary life regarding a certain kind of leadership?

A. "The man on horseback" (6:9).

THE BOOK OF JOB

Q. Who is the author of the book of Job?

A. An unknown dramatist who used the story, well known throughout the East, of the sufferings of a righteous man, to pose the problem of human pain and bereavement in the light of Israel's belief in an upright God.

Q. When was Job written?

A. Some of its materials—notably, its basic narrative—are very ancient; probably the book came into its present form in the fourth century B.C. The character of Job was known to the author of Ezekiel (14:14,20).

Q. What is the meaning of the name Job?

A. It appears to be derived from a Hebrew verb meaning "to be an enemy," but the name is so old that its original connotation cannot be determined with certainty.

Q. Where did Job live?

A. "In the land of Uz" (1:1)—but other Old Testament references to Uz both as a land (Jeremiah 25:20) and as a personal name (Genesis 10:23; 22:21; 36:28) do not clearly establish its identity; it appears to have been peopled by Arameans and to have lain somewhere east of the Lebanons. The Septuagint identifies Job as the king of Edom.

Q. What is the literary structure of the book of Job?

A. It consists of a Prologue (Chapters 1 and 2); Dialogue (Chapters 3-31); Speeches of Elihu (Chapters 32-37); Speeches of God (38:1 to 42:6); and Epilogue (42:7-17). The Prologue and Epilogue are mainly in prose, the other sections mainly in poetry.

Q. What is the purpose of the Prologue?

A. To provide the setting for the encounter pictured in the remainder of the book; this setting reveals a wealthy man ("the greatest of all the people of the east"—1:3) who, cultivating family religion, "would rise early in the morning and offer burnt offerings according to the number of them all"—1:5). God and Satan meet in the heavenly court, described (1:6-12) in terms not unlike those of I Kings 22:19-22, and agree to put Job to the test.

Q. How is this test carried out?

A. Messengers come in quick succession, announcing to Job that Sabean raiders have slain his oxen and asses and the servants who were tending them (1:13-15); that lightning had destroyed his sheep and shepherds (1:16); that the Chaldeans had wiped out his camel corps (1:17); that a tornado had taken the lives of his children (1:18ff); after that, Job's own body was afflicted "with loathsome sores from the sole of his foot to the crown of his head" (2:7); finally, his wife, failing to understand him, advised him to "Curse God, and die" (2:9).

Q. What is Job's reaction to all this?

A. The wish that he had never been born (3:1-26).

Q. What appraisal of the situation is given by Eliphaz the Temanite?

A. Since good men do not suffer ("who that was innocent ever perished?"—4:7), Job should rejoice in the discipline he is undergoing ("happy is the man whom God reproves"—5:17).

Q. What is Job's answer to Eliphaz?

A. He protests his innocence ("I have not denied the words of the Holy One"—6:10; "make me understand how I have erred"— 6:24).

Q. What interpretation is offered by Bildad the Shuhite?

A. Asserting that if Job's children have been slain, it is no doubt because they deserve it (8:3ff), he suggests that Job console himself by consulting the wisdom of the ancients ("consider what the fathers have found"—8:8; "God will not reject a blameless man"—8:20).

Q. What is Job's answer to Bildad?

A. "Though I am innocent, I cannot answer him [God];
       I must appeal for mercy to my accuser" (9:15).

Q. What judgment is pronounced by Zophar the Naamathite?

A. "God exacts of you less than your guilt deserves" (11:6).

Q. What is Job's answer to Zophar?

A. "In the thought of one who is at ease there is contempt for misfortune" (12:5); "you whitewash with lies" (13:4).

Q. What second thoughts are offered by Eliphaz?

A. "The wicked man writhes in pain all his days" (15:20); "the company of the godless is barren" (15:34).

Q. What is Job's reply to this?

A. "Miserable comforters are you all" (16:2); "I shall not find a wise man among you" (17:10).

Q. What considered judgment is offered by Bildad the Shuhite?

A. Examination of Job's situation leads him to exclaim (18:21),
       "Surely such are the dwellings of the ungodly,
          such is the place of him who knows not God."

Q. How does Job reply to this?

A. "I know that my Redeemer lives" (19:25).

Q. What thoughts does Zophar present in the Dialogue's second round?

A. The "wicked man's portion from God" is that "The possessions of his house will be carried away" (20:29,28).

Q. How does Job counter this?

A. "How then will you comfort me with empty nothings?
       There is nothing left of your answers but falsehood"
          (21:34).

Q. What "solace" does Eliphaz offer in his third attempt?

A. "God abases the proud,
       but he saves the lowly" (22:29).

Q. What is Job's answer?

A. "Oh that I knew where I might find him" (23:3). "But he knows the way that I take" (23:10).

Q. What is Bildad's third observation?

A. "How then can man be righteous before God?" (25:4).

Q. What is Job's reply?

A. "How you have helped him who has no power!

How you have saved the arm that has no strength!" (26:2).

Q. Why is it thought that 28:1-28 is a poem separate from the main work?

A. Unrelated to the principal theme, it deals with a favorite topic of Hebrew wise men:

"But where shall wisdom be found?

And where is the place of understanding?" (28:12).

Q. What is the answer to this question?

A. "Behold, the fear of the Lord, that is wisdom;

and to depart from evil is understanding" (28:28).

Q. How does Job summarize his past happiness?

A. "I was eyes to the blind,

and feet to the lame.

I was a father to the poor,

and I searched out the cause of him whom I did not know"
(29:15ff).

Q. In asserting his integrity, what sins does Job repudiate?

A. Deceit, fraud, theft, adultery, callousness, pride, covetousness, hypocrisy, impurity (31:1-40).

Q. What is significant about the speeches of Elihu?

A. He is a young man who has no other reason for speaking than that he is "full of words" (32:18): "I must speak, that I may find relief" (32:20). He reveals himself when he accuses Job:

"Job opens his mouth in empty talk,

he multiplies words without knowledge" (35:16).

Q. How does God speak of himself in the first speech attributed to him?

A. As the great architect of the universe ("Where were you when I laid the foundation of the earth?"—38:4); as the guardian of the mysteries of life ("have you seen the gates of deep darkness?"—38:17); as sustainer and provider for his creation ("Who provides for the raven its prey,/ when its young ones cry to God . . . ?"—38:41); as the originator of primeval harmony and gladness:

". . . when the morning stars sang together,

and all the sons of God shouted for joy" (38:7).

Q. How does Job react to this?

A. "Behold, I am of small account; what shall I answer thee?" (40:4).

Q. What aspects of the divine are brought out in the second speech attributed to God?

A. His great power; his ability to control the river-horse (40:15-24) and the crocodile (41:1-34).

Q. What is Job's response?

A. "I had heard of thee by the hearing of the ear,
　　　but now my eye sees thee" (42:5).

Q. How does the Epilogue depict the end of the matter?

A. "And the Lord restored the fortunes of Job, when he had prayed for his friends" (42:10).

Q. How is the divine nature pictured in Job?

A. God is spoken of as he
　　"who made the Bear and Orion,
　　　　the Pleiades and the chambers of the south;
　　who does great things beyond understanding,
　　　　and marvelous things without number" (9:9ff);
and as the unknowable maker and guardian of men: "If I sin, what do I do to thee, thou watcher of men?" (7:20). "In his hand is the life of every living thing" (12:10); "God is great, and we know him not" (36:26).

Q. How is the human situation pictured in Job?

A. "Those who dwell in houses of clay" (4:19); "the terrors of God are arrayed against me" (6:4); "the speech of a despairing man is wind" (6:26). "Can you find out the deep things of God?" (11:7). "He has walled up my way, so that I cannot pass" (19:8).

　　"There is no gloom or deep darkness
　　　　where evildoers may hide themselves" (34:22).

Q. What are some passages from Job that have become a classical part of our literary heritage?

A. ". . . man is born to trouble
　　　as the sparks fly upward" (5:7).
"My days are swifter than a weaver's shuttle" (7:6); "his trust is a spider's web" (8:14); "the king of terrors" (18:14). "The root of the matter is found in him" (19:28).

"Lo, these are but the outskirts of his way;
and how small a whisper do we hear of him!" (26:14).

Q. What recent literature has the book of Job as its inspiration?

A. One of Thornton Wilder's plays takes its title from 19:20: "I have escaped by the skin of my teeth"; Archibald MacLeish's *The Fall of the City* illustrates 3:25:

*"For the thing that I fear comes upon me,
and what I dread befalls me."*

McLeish's study of contemporary man, facing a situation like that of Job, is entitled *J.B.*

Q. Of which beatitude is the book of Job an illustration?

A. "Blessed are the pure in heart, for they shall see God" (Matthew 5:8).

Q. What is "the fire of God" (1:16)?

A. Lightning.

Q. Of all Job's afflictions, which was the hardest to bear?

A. His wife's inability to understand that life has both its better and its worse, its richer and its poorer sides: "Shall we receive good at the hand of God, and shall we not receive evil?" (2:10).

Q. What text from Job did Jonathan Edwards make the basis of his sermon the Sunday after his daughter's death?

A. "He comes forth like a flower, and withers;
he flees like a shadow, and continues not" (14:2).

Q. What passage provides a classical description of a community in ancient Israel?

A. Chapter 29.

Q. How does the book of Job rise above the common morality of its time?

A. The sins acknowledged in Chapter 31 are not simply those conventionally recognized—deceit, fraud, theft, adultery—but also the subtler sins of covetousness, pride, and hypocrisy.

Q. Why is the hippopotamus described as "the first of the works of God" (40:19)?

A. Because its size and bulk seem to embody so much of power and strength.

Q. Why are the eyes of the crocodile said to be "like the eyelids of the dawn" (41:18)?

A. The reddish eyes, shining under water, can be seen before the head reaches the surface; the Egyptians regarded the crocodile as the symbol of the dawn.

Q. How does James Moffatt seek to bring out the significance of the names given to Job's daughters?

A. By translating, rather than by merely transliterating, them: "Ringdove, Cassia, and Applescent" (42:14).

THE PSALMS

Q. Who is the author of the Psalms?

A. As Law books are attributed to Moses and Wisdom books to Solomon, so the Psalms are attributed to David, who in II Samuel 23:1 is spoken of as "the sweet psalmist of Israel." However, some of the titles in the Psalms attribute their composition to others. Psalm 72, which lists Solomon as its author, concludes: "The prayers of David, the son of Jesse, are ended" (72:20). Psalms 42-49 are "of the sons of Korah"; 50, 73-83 are "of Asaph."

Q. Who were Asaph and the sons of Korah?

A. In I Chronicles 6:31-39 Asaph is listed among "the men whom David put in charge of the service of song in the house of the Lord." The sons of Korah formed a guild of temple singers, descended from Korah, of the tribe of Levi (I Chronicles 6:31ff; Numbers 16).

Q. When were the Psalms written?

A. They reflect the public events and personal experiences of many ages; many of them cannot be dated precisely: they are timeless in their summation of human emotion; in them, as has been said, is "the whole of the heart of man." It is probable that the Psalter was completed by the end of the third century B.C.

Q. What are the divisions of the Psalter?

A. Book I: Psalms 1-41; Book II: Psalms 42-72; Book III: Psalms 73-89; Book IV: Psalms 90-106; Book V: Psalms 107-150. Each of these collections ends with a doxology, and it is probable that the fivefold arrangement is in imitation of the five books of Moses.

Q. What duplicates are there within these several collections?

A. 14 and 53 are almost identical; 57:7-11 and 60:6-12 together duplicate 108.

Q. What are the meanings of the words *Miktam* (16); *Maskil* (32); *Shiggaion* (7)?

A. Terms not wholly clear, they probably designate the type of song—whether prayer, meditation, or lament.

Q. What are the meanings of the terms *Sheminith* (6,12), *Gittith* (8), *Alamoth* (46), *Selah, Higgaion* (9:16)?

A. Also terms not wholly clear, they have something to do with musical instruments or notations.

Q. What are the Songs of Ascents (120-134)?

A. Probably processional hymns sung as the people went up to Jerusalem for the great occasions of worship and festal celebration.

Q. What other types of Psalms can be distinguished?

A. The hymn or song of praise (100); the individual lament (3,5,6,7,42,51); the communal lament (44,74,79,80); the individual song of thanksgiving, in which the individual may be the king or other representative of the community (30,32,34,62,116); royal psalms, appropriate to the king's accession (2,110), marriage festival (45), or the beginning (20) or triumphal end (18) of a military campaign.

Q. What Psalms have been compared to "God Save the King" or "My Country, 'Tis of Thee"?

A. 106 and 122.

Q. What Psalm reflects the homesickness felt by the Hebrew exiles?

A. 137.

Q. What Psalm did John Calvin refer to as "an accurate summary of all God's perfections"?

A. 145.

Q. What Psalms appear to have been adapted for the successive days of the week?

A. 24,48,82,94,101,81,93,92.

Q. What Psalms are for particular parts of the day?

A. Psalm 4 for the evening, 5 for the morning.

Q. What Psalms resemble Isaiah 53 in that they treat of the servant of the Lord as the righteous sufferer?

A. 22,27,31,38,42,69,80,88,118.

Q. What Psalms celebrate the wonder and power of God as manifest in creation?

A. 8,19,29,104,107,148.

Q. What Psalms are acrostics?

A. Psalm 2 conceals the name of Alexander Jannaeus; Psalm 110, that of Simon Maccabaeus; the successive stanzas of 119 begin with the succession of letters in the Hebrew alphabet.

Q. What Psalm was chosen by President Eisenhower for his pre-inauguration service on January 20, 1957?

A. 46.

Q. What Psalm is regularly sung at Harvard ceremonies?

A. 78.

Q. What Psalm is made up exclusively of thanksgiving, containing no petition or request of any kind?

A. 103.

Q. What Psalm has been called the best commentary on Genesis 1?

A. 8.

Q. What Psalm enlarges on the themes of the eternal covenant with David, described in II Samuel 7:11?

A. 8ᶜ.

Q. What Psalm celebrates the Hebrew deliverance from Egypt?

A. 114.

Q. What Psalm constitutes the longest chapter in the Bible?

A. Psalm 119; significantly, it is a Psalm in praise of God's law and those who keep it.

Q. What Psalm summarizes the history of Israel?

A. 136.

Q. What did Ibn Ezra call the crown of the Psalter?

A. 139, which celebrates God's presence throughout his creation, making it impossible for man ever to escape him.

Q. What Psalms are known as the Hallel group?

A. 113 through 118, from the recurring invitation to Praise (Hebrew, *hallel*) the Lord.

Q. What reference is made in the New Testament to this group?

A. Matthew 26:30 says of Jesus and his friends at the Last Supper: "And when they had sung a hymn, they went out to the Mount of Olives."

In Hebrew usage, Psalms 113 and 114 precede the Passover meal, Psalms 115-118 follow it.

Q. What Psalm did Satan use in tempting Jesus?

A. Verses 11 and 12 of Psalm 91 (see Matthew 4:6; Luke 4:10).

Q. What Psalm is quoted at the outset of Jesus' ministry?

A. Psalm 2:7 ("You are my son, today I have begotten you") provides the words heard at Jesus' baptism (see Mark 1:11).

Q. What Psalm was in Jesus' mind at his death?

A. The word from the cross, "My God, My God, why hast thou forsaken me?" (Mark 15:34) is found at the opening of Psalm 22. It was customary Hebrew usage to designate a portion of Scripture by its opening words.

Q. What Psalm celebrates the universal character of God?

A. 150.

Q. Are many Psalms found in the Old Testament outside the Psalter?

A. Psalms are found in many other places, such as Judges 5; II Samuel 23:1-7; Hosea 6:1-3; Isaiah 2:1-4; Habakkuk 3; Jonah 2:2-9.

Q. What are some Psalms that have been adapted for Christian worship?

A. 3,6,12,36,42,84,86,100,107,110,118,130,134,135,136. More than a century ago, one Presbyterian group affirmed: "It is the will of God that, to the end of time, the Psalms be sung to the exclusion of the compositions of uninspired men."

Q. How does the Psalmist's picture of creation sometimes differ from that in Genesis?

A. Whereas in Genesis the process extended over a period of six days, in Psalm 33:9 ("he spoke and it came to be") and Psalm 148:5 ("he commanded and they were created"), creation is thought of as effected instantaneously by utterance of God's creative word.

Q. What Psalm celebrates the experiences of Joseph?

A. Psalm 105:17-22.

Q. What Psalm begins with an echo of Moses' words to Pharaoh?

A. The opening words of Psalm 24 are: "The earth is the Lord's," a quotation from Exodus 9:29.

Q. What Psalm seems to echo the events in the book of Esther?

A. Psalm 9:16 describes how

"The Lord has made himself known, he has executed judgment;
the wicked are snared in the work of their own hands."

Q. How did the community at Qumran (the source of the Dead Sea
Scrolls) carry out the description of the good man in Psalm 1:2: "on
his [God's] law he meditates day and night"?

A. It was a requirement of the sect's discipline that the reading and
interpretation of the Scriptures should be carried on continuously.

Q. What Psalm has been called "Genesis set to music"?

A. Psalm 8.

Q. What Psalms represent God's blessing as coming, as Plato said
the beatific vision came, only to one who was willing to pay the price
of toil, renunciation, and sacrifice?

A. Psalms 15 and 24:3-6.

Q. What Psalm echoes II Samuel 22:51?

A. Psalm 18:50.

Q. Why can Psalm 80 be spoken of as complementing Psalm 23?

A. Psalm 23 speaks in terms of the individual: "The Lord is my
shepherd"; Psalm 80 speaks in terms of the entire community, addressing the "Shepherd of Israel" as one "who leadest Joseph like a flock."

Q. What Psalm has been called "The Song of Thunders"?

A. Psalm 29.

Q. What Psalm suggests how a troubled conscience manifests itself
in a distraught body?

A. Psalm 32.

Q. What Psalms deal philosophically with the question of why the
righteous suffer?

A. Psalms 37, 40, 73.

Q. What Psalm probably reflects the deliverance wrought in Israel
at the time of Sennacherib's invasion?

A. Psalm 46.

Q. What Psalm anticipates the expression, "You can't take it with
you"?

A. Psalm 49:16:
"Be not afraid when one becomes rich,
    when the glory of his house increases.
For when he dies he will carry nothing away."

Q. What Psalm dramatizes the difference between Israel's God and the gods of the nations?

A. The duty of the pagans was to provide gifts of food and drink to meet the needs of the deity. Psalm 50:12f makes it clear that God has no such needs.

Q. What Psalm has been described as "the battle cry of the warrior and the watchword of the oppressed"?

A. Psalm 68.

Q. What passage from the Psalms was seized upon by the early church as providing the theological reason for Jesus' cleansing of the temple?

A. Psalm 69:9; cf. John 2:17 and Romans 15:3.

Q. What has been spoken of as "the saddest Psalm"?

A. Psalm 88, because it appears to mirror a situation in which people felt God had deserted the nation.

Q. What Psalm describes God's creation not simply as a house solidly built but also an exquisite work of art?

A. Psalm 104.

Q. What Psalm is used by the Christian church at Easter to link Resurrection with Exodus?

A. Psalm 114.

Q. What Psalm is used by Christians in the thanksgiving of women after childbirth?

A. Psalm 116.

Q. What verse of the Psalter is, by those who count such things, reckoned the middle verse in the Bible?

A. Psalm 118:9.

Q. What Psalm may have been sung at the dedication of Solomon's temple?

A. Psalm 136.

Q. Which can be described as "the most haunting of all the Psalms"?

A. Psalm 137.

Q. What Psalm, because it speaks of the immanence, rather than the transcendence, of God, is by some considered "the crown of the Psalter"?

A. Psalm 139.

Q. What Psalm phrases Israel's sense of its uniqueness?

A. "He has not dealt thus with any other nation" (147:20).

Q. What Psalm calls upon all nature to praise its Creator?

A. Psalm 148.

THE PROVERBS

Q. Who is the author of Proverbs?

A. I Kings 4:32 relates that Solomon "uttered three thousand proverbs"; because of this, the book of Proverbs has been attributed to him, and 1:1 says: "The proverbs of Solomon, son of David, king of Israel." This title, however, appears to apply only to chapters 1 through 9; at 10:1 there is a new title: "The Proverbs of Solomon," suggesting that our book represents a collection of collections. This is borne out by 25:1: "These also are the proverbs of Solomon which the men of Hezekiah king of Judah copied." 30:1 names yet another compiler: "The words of Agur, son of Jakeh of Massa," as does 31:1: "The words of Lemuel, king of Massa, which his mother taught him." Proverbs often represent the distilled wisdom of generations rather than the solemn utterance of an individual.

Q. What proverbs appear to be of Egyptian origin?

A. 22:17-24:34 appear to be a separate collection, quite like the wisdom sayings of King Amem-em-ope.

Q. When was the book of Proverbs written?

A. Though it is impossible to date the separate sayings, the present collection was made about 300 B.C.

Q. What characteristic feature of Hebrew life is represented by the Proverbs?

A. In addition to Law and Prophecy, Wisdom was a recognized source of authority. The scribes devoted themselves to codifying and transmitting this wisdom. The sages have here compiled a code of honor and a standard of conduct for sensible men.

Q. What account of creation is given in Proverbs?

A. 8:22-31 represents wisdom as the first created thing and as assisting at the rest of the creation.

Q. What Christian identification is made with this passage?

A. The New Testament version of the creative power of Wisdom is found in John 1:1: "In the beginning was the Word, and the Word was with God, and the Word was God."

Q. How does Proverbs differ from other books of the Old Testament?

A. It is the least distinctively Hebraic among them, mentioning none of the significant events in Hebrew history, none of the nation's religious observances, none of "the mighty deeds of God."

Q. What is the nature of the religion set forth in Proverbs?

A. It consists in following the way of knowledge, rather than dependence upon the grace and forgiveness of God. The way of knowledge enjoins industry, thrift, truthfulness, discretion, chastity.

Q. How does the setting of Proverbs differ from that of most Old Testament books?

A. While most reflect an agricultural or pastoral background, Proverbs speaks often of city life. The sins against which it warns flourish in cities: greed, gangsterism, robbery, murder, prostitution.

Q. How does Proverbs differ from other Old Testament books in its attitude toward the Law of Moses?

A. In Deuteronomy 21:18-21, a "stubborn and rebellious son" is to be stoned by the responsible authorities of the community; in Proverbs, a foolish child is to be reproved by "the rod of discipline" (22:15), and the duty of parents is to "Discipline your son while there is hope" (19:18).

Q. What New Testament use is made of Proverbs' idea of discipline?

A. Hebrews 12:5f quotes Proverbs 3:11f:
"My son, do not regard lightly the discipline of the Lord,
nor lose courage when you are punished by him.
For the Lord disciplines him whom he loves,
and chastises every son whom he receives."

Q. What position is assigned to woman in the book of Proverbs?

A. 9:13-18 pictures "Lady Folly" sitting at the door of her house, seeking to entice men; 19:13 says that "a wife's quarreling is a continual dripping of rain"; yet 12:4 says that "A good wife is the crown of her husband," and 31:10-31 pictures the good wife and mother whose "husband is known in the gates" (31:23), whose "children rise up and call her blessed" (31:28): "a woman who fears the Lord is to be praised" (31:30).

Q. What position is assigned to Wisdom?

A. Personified, she is represented as going up and down the streets seeking for followers (1:20-33; 8:1-9:6); Wisdom protects one from wicked men (2:12-15) and immoral women (2:16-19).

Q. What are the rewards of following Wisdom?

A. "Length of days and abundant welfare" (3:2).

"Long life is in her right hand;
in her left hand are riches and honor" (3:16).

Her ways are ways of pleasantness,
and all her paths are peace" (3:17).

Q. How does the picture of kingship given in this book differ from that in the time of Solomon?

A. Manuals of instruction designed for the king (16:10-15; 25:2-5; 31:2-9), comments on the nature of kingship (16:14f; 8:15f; 20:8,26; 28:16), and directions provided for those who are to be guests of the king (23:1f; 25:6f) suggest a court far less despotic than that which marked Solomon's reign.

Q. What is the author's doctrine of work?

A. "A slack hand causes poverty,
but the hand of the diligent makes rich,
A son who gathers in summer is prudent,
but a son who sleeps in harvest brings shame" (10:4f).

"He who is slack in his work
is a brother to him who destroys" (18:9).

Q. What creature from the world of nature is cited as a model of industry?

A. "Go to the ant, O sluggard;
consider her ways, and be wise.
Without having any chief, officer or ruler,
she prepares her food in summer,
and gathers her sustenance in harvest" (6:6-8).

Q. What tribute is paid to self-discipline?

A. "He who is slow to anger is better than the mighty,
and he who rules his spirit than he who takes a city" (16:32).

Q. What advice is given with regard to strong drink?

A. "Do not look at wine when it is red,
    when it sparkles in the cup
    and goes down smoothly.
At the last it bites like a serpent,
    and stings like an adder" (23:31f).

Q. What objects awaken the sense of wonder?

A. "Three things are too wonderful for me;
    four I do not understand:
the way of an eagle in the sky,
    the way of a serpent on a rock,
the way of a ship on the high seas,
    and the way of a man with a maiden" (30:18f).

Q. What part of Proverbs follows the acrostic pattern?

A. 31:10-31.

Q. What elements seem to indicate the presence of more than one collection?

A. Verses 4 and 5 of Chapter 26 seem to contradict each other, 21:9 and 25:24, 22:3 and 27:12, 6:10 and 24:33 represent duplicates.

Q. What psychosomatic insights are found in Proverbs?

A. "Anxiety in a man's heart weighs him down" (12:25); "jealousy makes a man furious" (6:34).

"Hatred stirs up strife,
    but love covers all offenses" (10:12).

"A tranquil mind gives life to the flesh,
    but passion makes the bones rot" (14:30).

"A glad heart makes a cheerful countenance" (15:13).

"A cheerful heart is a good medicine" (17:22).

Q. What are some often-quoted passages from Proverbs?

A. "But the path of the righteous is like the light of dawn,
    which shines brighter and brighter until full day" (4:18);

"as an ox goes to the slaughter" (7:22);

"Like a gold ring in a swine's snout
    is a beautiful woman without discretion" (11:22);

"The heart knows its own bitterness,
    and no stranger shares its joy" (14:10);

"a word in season, how good it is!" (15:23);

"A word fitly spoken

is like apples of gold in a setting of silver" (25:11);
"A good name is to be chosen
> rather than great riches,
and favor is better than silver or gold" (22:1);
"Righteousness exalts a nation,
> but sin is a reproach to any people" (14:34).

Q. What idea, occurring several times within the book, can be thought of as the motto of the collection?

A. "The fear of the Lord is the beginning of knowledge" (1:7; 9:10; 15:33).

Q. What is meant by the fear of the Lord?

A. Not dread or trepidation but awe and wholesome respect: in 2:5, wisdom's highest gift is defined as understanding "the fear of the Lord" and finding "the knowledge of God." 10:27 adds:
"The fear of the Lord prolongs life,
> but the years of the wicked will be short."

Q. What passage, suggesting the blessedness of happy marriage, rests upon the importance assumed by water in lands where it is scarce?

A. "Drink water from your own cistern,
> flowing water from your own well" (5:15).

Q. What passages emphasize a doctrine of individual responsibility?

A. "If you are wise, you are wise for yourself;
> if you scoff you alone will bear it" (9:12).
"A man who is kind benefits himself,
> but a cruel man hurts himself" (11:17).

Q. What passages emphasize the inadequacy of a doctrine of individual responsibility?

A. "He who mocks the poor insults his Maker" (17:5).
". . . he who makes his door high seeks destruction" (17:19).
"He who is kind to the poor lends to the Lord" (19:17).
"Iron sharpens iron,
> and one man sharpens another" (27:17).

Q. What description is given of the ideal king?

A. Proverbs 16:10-15.

Q. What appeal to chance is held to be a means of discovering God's will?

A. "The lot is cast into the lap,

but the decision is wholly from the Lord" (16:33).

Q. What New Testament decision was made on this basis?

A. Lots were cast to see who should be successor to Judas in the apostolic company (Acts 1:26).

Q. How does the New Testament doctrine of God's grace serve to put in different perspective the apothegm in 17:15:

"He who justifies the wicked and he who condemns the righteous

are both alike an abomination to the Lord"?

A. Paul teaches in Romans 4:5 that "to one who . . . trusts him who justifies the ungodly, his faith is reckoned as righteousness."

Q. What passage describes conscience, for which the Old Testament has no word?

A. "The spirit of man is the lamp of the Lord,

searching all his innermost parts" (20:27).

Q. What is "the ancient landmark" that the good citizen is told not to remove (22:28; 23:10)?

A. Not, as among us, a building of historic significance, but rather a tree or boulder by means of which one man's property was marked off from another's.

Q. What saying of Jesus rests upon this book's advice about how to behave at court?

A. The saying about taking the lowest place at feasts (Luke 14:8f) seems to be based upon Proverbs 25:6f.

Q. Why should the good homemaker's husband be known "in the gates"?

A. It was at the city gate that the tribal leaders held court and judged cases.

ECCLESIASTES
OR THE PREACHER

Q. Who is the author of Ecclesiastes?

A. The author styles himself "The Preacher, the son of David, king in Jerusalem" (1:1). Many have taken this to be Solomon's self-identification. It is likely, however, that this is simply a literary device, associating this collection of Wisdom literature with Solomon the wise, and that the real author or compiler thus does two things: gains authority for his work and preserves his own anonymity.

Q. Why is this book known to Jews as *Qoheleth* or *Koheleth*?

A. From the Hebrew word *koheleth,* occurring at 1:1,12; 12:8, and translated "Preacher"; the term appears to mean "orator" or "debater."

Q. When was Ecclesiastes written?

A. Both content and vocabulary suggest a time much later than Solomon's, in the Hellenistic age. 1:9f, for example, contains a remarkable summary of the Greek view of history as a never-ending series of ever-recurring cycles.

Q. What is the nature of the contents of Ecclesiastes?

A. A teacher (cf. 7:5; 10:2-4) had evidently been notably effective in imparting wisdom to his classes; he chooses by means of the written word to convey instruction to a wider audience (12:9f).

Q. What other historical allusions suggest a time later than Solomon's?

A. Solomon had only two predecessors in the kingly office, Saul and David; this writer refers to "all who were over Jerusalem before me" (1:16; cf. 2:9). The writer identifies himself with those who suffer injustice (3:16f) rather than inflict it, with the oppressed rather than with the oppressors (4:1). The reference (4:13) to "an old and foolish king, who will no longer take advice" would suggest an era other than Solomon's.

Q. How account for this book's strange blending of the secular and the sacred, its mingling of traditional piety with the spirit of critical inquiry, its emphasis upon things which appear contradictory (e.g., 4:2 and 9:4), inconsistencies, and frequent shifts in subject?

A. These have been variously explained as resulting from a compiler's bringing together of unrelated materials; from reworking by subsequent editorial hands of the author's original document; or from the changing moods of one who depicts his own inner struggle, or one whose outlook unaccountably shifts from optimism to pessimism and back again.

Q. What line early sets the tone of the book?

A. "Vanity of vanities! All is vanity" (1:2).

Q. What is the meaning of "vanity"?

A. The Hebrew word (which occurs some forty times in this book, only thirty-five times in all the rest of the Old Testament) means "breath" or "vapor"; it stands for illusion, unreality, what is beyond man's comprehension. The idiom "vanity of vanities" is the Hebrew way of expressing the superlative. Ronald Knox translates the phrase, "A shadow's shadow."

Q. What is the author's first illustration of life's futility?

A. Meaningless things go on repeating themselves endlessly (1:3-11).

Q. What is the considered result of the author's far-reaching inquiry?

A. Having applied his "mind to seek and to search out by wisdom all that is done under heaven" (1:12), he concludes that knowledge and wisdom lead to vexation and sorrow (1:18); that luxury and extravagance are "a striving after wind" (2:11); that, while "wisdom excels folly as light excels darkness" (2:13), "the wise man dies just like the fool" (2:16); that hard work does nothing but accumulate wealth that must be left to "a man who did not toil for it" (2:21).

Q. What value does the author place upon human activity?

A. God has inexorably ordained a succession of times and seasons (3:1-8), and "has made everything beautiful in its time" (3:11); God's gift to man therefore is "that every one should eat and drink and take pleasure in all his toil" (3:13).

Q. How does man's condition resemble that of the beasts?

A. "As one dies, so dies the other. They all have the same breath, and man has no advantage" (3:19).

Q. What does the author make of the injustices he observes upon earth?

A. "I thought the dead were more fortunate than the living" (4:2).

Q. What is the author's opinion of economic competition?

A. "Better is a handful of quietness than two hands full of toil and striving after wind" (4:6).

Q. Does cooperation offer a better way?

A. Yes. "Two are better than one" (4:9). "A threefold cord is not quickly broken" (4:12).

Q. What suggestions does the author have regarding public worship?

A. The worshiper should be attentive (5:1,2); prompt in the payment of vows (5:4f); reluctant to question the judgments of God (5:6).

Q. What does the author say of corruption in public life?

A. "Do not be amazed at the matter; for the high official is watched by a higher, and there are yet higher ones over them" (5:8).

Q. What of the "man to whom God gives wealth, possessions, and honor"?

A. This, too, is vanity, since "God does not give him power to enjoy them" (6:2).

Q. What contrast does the author draw between wisdom and folly?

A. Solemn utterance and willingness "to hear the rebuke of the wise" are preferable to foolish laughter (7:2-6).

Q. What advice does the author give regarding the golden mean?

A. "Be not righteous overmuch, and do not make yourself overwise. . . . Be not wicked overmuch, neither be a fool" (7:16f).

Q. What judgment, later echoed by Paul, does Koheleth pass upon his fellows?

A. "Surely there is not a righteous man on earth who does good and never sins" (7:20; compare Romans 3:23).

Q. How, in the author's opinion, do women compare with men on this score?

A. "One man among a thousand I found, but a woman among all these I have not found" (7:28).

Q. What attitudes does the writer express on the subject of authority?

A. The "word of the king is supreme" (8:4) and "He who obeys a command will meet no harm" (8:5); yet "No man has power to retain the spirit, or authority over the day of death" (8:8).

Q. How is man's sinful attitude intensified by the patience of God?

A. "Because sentence against an evil deed is not executed speedily, the heart of the sons of men is fully set to do evil" (8:11).

Q. Is the author's pessimism lightened by hope of an afterlife?

A. No. "One fate comes to all, to the . . . good and the evil" (9:2); " a living dog is better than a dead lion" (9:4); "there is no work or thought or knowledge or wisdom in Sheol, to which you are going" (9:10); "in the place where the tree falls, there it will lie" (11:3).

Q. How are life's inequalities sometimes evened out?

A. "The race is not to the swift, nor the battle to the strong" (9:11).

Q. What reward does humanity bestow upon its benefactors?

A. In a besieged city there was "a poor wise man, and he by his wisdom delivered the city. Yet no one remembered that poor man" (9:15).

Q. Why must one be careful in opinions expressed about others?

A. "A bird of the air will carry your voice" (10:20; cf. 7:21).

Q. Do life's vanity and uncertainty mean that one should withdraw?

A. On the contrary,
"Cast your bread upon the waters,
for you will find it after many days" (11:1).

Q. How does the author picture old age?

A. In a picturesque allegory, wherein the several parts of the body deteriorate (12:1-7).

Q. How does the book round out its reflections?

A. By insisting that "the whole duty of man" is to "fear God and keep his commandments" (12:13)—all this in light of the fact that "God will bring every deed into judgment, with every secret thing, whether good or evil" (12:14).

Q. What use is made of Ecclesiastes by the Jews of today?

A. It is read in the synagogues on the third day of the Feast of Tabernacles.

Q. What is the appropriateness of this usage?

A. Since the Feast of Tabernacles celebrates the joy of harvest, the reading of this book would appear somewhat incongruous except on the ground that it adds a serious note to the occasion. It is a reminder that life's joys fade quickly, that man's best efforts often end in frustration, and that he who would acquire wisdom must, as Paul later expressed it (Colossians 4:5), conduct himself "wisely toward outsiders, making the most of the time."

Q. What nineteenth-century poems have been termed the most suggestive of all commentaries on Ecclesiastes?

A. Tennyson's "The Vision of Sin," "The Palace of Art," and "The Two Voices."

Q. What passage summarizes the Greek view of history, that things simply go round in cycles?

A. "What has been is what will be,

and what has been done is what will be done;
and there is nothing new under the sun" (1:9).

Q. What idea here regarding daily duty is picked up and transformed by Paul?

A. Ecclesiastes 9:10 says: "Whatever your hand finds to do, do it with your might; for there is no work or thought or knowledge or wisdom in Sheol, to which you are going." Paul writes to the Colossians (3:23f): "Whatever your task, work heartily, as serving the Lord and not men, knowing that from the Lord you will receive the inheritance as your reward."

THE SONG OF SOLOMON

Q. Who is the author of the Song of Solomon?

A. The first-line title reads, "The Song of Songs [that is, the best of songs], which is Solomon's" (1:1). I Kings 4:32 says of King Solomon, "He also uttered three thousand proverbs; and his songs were a thousand and five." Tradition identifies this as one of that number. The work appears to be a collection of love lyrics such as were sung at week-long marriage festivals in Bible lands. They would thus belong to that popular literature of which it can hardly be said that any individual is the author.

Q. When were the songs written?

A. There are no allusions to history, and so there can be no certainty about the date. The references to Solomon (1:5; 3:7,9,11; 8:11,12) indicate a time when David's son had been glorified in popular imagination. The use of Greek and Persian loan-words suggests a date in the third century B.C.

Q. What allegorical interpretations have been given of the book?

A. That it represents (a) the longing of the ten tribes for a reunion with King Hezekiah; (b) the picture of a nation well governed; (c) Christ's love for his church.

Q. Why is it difficult to justify the allegorical interpretations?

A. Elsewhere, when Scripture allegorizes, there are obvious indications of the fact; there is no suggestion of that here. Further, it is necessary to wrench the details to fit any presumed scheme of allegorical significance.

Q. What is the obvious significance of the work?

A. That it celebrates the wonders of romantic love.

Q. Why should such a book find a place in the Scripture?

A. Genesis 1:27f represents love and marriage as part of God's purpose for man; the descriptions of love and longing in The Song of Solomon are such as could be fulfilled in a monogamous marriage. Thus it provides at once the test by which all marital relationships are to be judged, and a symbol of God's affection for his people.

Q. What are some of the best-known songs that have been found within the collection?

A. Those describing love in the spring (2:8-14) and the deathless power of love (8:6f).

Q. What other songs have been identified?

A. The bride's exultation in the affection of her lover (1:2-4), and her declaration of devotion to him (2:3-3:5); the bridegroom's delight in the beauty of the bride (4:1-15; 6:4-10), and the bride's in the physical perfections of her lover (5:10-16); the villagers hailing the bridegroom, enthroned on the threshing sledge (3:6-11); the bride dancing the sword dance as the villagers note her charms (6:13-7:6).

Q. What interpretation of the book makes it a drama?

A. Some would regard it as the story of a simple country maiden resisting the allurements of a proffered royal marriage in favor of her rustic lover, a Palestinian shepherd.

Q. What are the difficulties of this interpretation?

A. Drama, while characteristic of the Greeks, was not known among the Hebrews; also, the materials do not naturally fit into the dramatic mold or pattern, and have to be forced.

Q. Why is Sharon (2:1) an appropriate setting for some of the songs?

A. The fertile plain near Mt. Carmel is proverbial for the beauty of its flowers in the springtime.

Q. What use of the Song of Solomon was made in the early days?

A. Rabbi Akiba, in the second century, declared that "he who sings from the Song of Songs in the wine houses and makes a secular song of it, has no part in the world to come"; perhaps on this account the rule was that no one was to read it until he was thirty years of age (cf. Numbers 4:3).

Q. What use does the Jewish community make of the Song of Songs?

A. It is read on the eighth day of the Passover season.

Q. Why is it appropriate on this occasion?

A. Early rabbis interpreted it as an allegory celebrating Solomon's love of wisdom, or Israel's history from the Exodus to the coming of the Messiah, or the romance between God and Israel.

Q. What use of this work is made in the New Testament?

A. That "love is strong as death itself" (8:6) seems to be echoed in Romans 8:35; "until the day dawns," in II Peter 1:19, seems an allusion to 2:17.

Q. What Broadway productions have had titles derived from the Song of Solomon?

A. "The Voice of the Turtle" (2:12) and "The Little Foxes" (2:15).

Q. How has the Song of Solomon figured in the recent history of Bible translation in South Africa?

A. 1:5, reading, "I am very dark, but comely," has, in the new Afrikaans version, been translated, "I am comely, and burnt brown by the sun."

THE BOOK OF ISAIAH

Q. Who was Isaiah?

A. A prophet, on familiar terms with the king and the court, whose ministry spanned the reigns of "Uzziah, Jotham, Ahaz, and Hezekiah, kings of Judah" (1:1).

Q. When did Isaiah live?

A. He reports that his call to the prophetic office came "in the year that King Uzziah died"—about 740 B.C. Hezekiah reigned from about 716 to 687 B.C.

Q. What reasons are there for concluding that the work of more than one man is contained in the present book of Isaiah?

A. Three reasons—historical, linguistic, and theological—lead to the belief that this is a library of prophetical oracles, and that "Isaiah" designates not only an individual but also a school of prophets.

Q. What reason is there within the book itself for speaking of a school of prophets under the leadership of Isaiah?

A. "Bind up the testimony, seal the teaching among my disciples" (8:16).

Q. What title is given to the second part of the book?

A. Deutero-Isaiah, or II Isaiah, has come to be the conventional designation for Chapters 40-66. Some students discern further refinements, confining II Isaiah to Chapters 40-48, with Chapters 49-55 regarded as a post-exilic appendix, and Chapters 56-66, sometimes called Trito-Isaiah, or III Isaiah, as belonging to the age of Ezra and Nehemiah.

Q. What is the date of II Isaiah?

A. 549-537 B.C.

Q. What are the historical reasons for believing that not all parts of the book date from the same era?

A. In the first part of the book, Jerusalem is the center of the nation's life; in the second part, Jerusalem lies desolate and deserted ("I will raise up their ruins"—44:26; cf. 58:12; 61:4; 63:18; 64:10f). In the second part of the book, the Hebrews are suffering not at the hands of the Assyrians, who invaded their land during the lifetime of Isaiah of Jerusalem, but at the hands of the Chaldeans, who carried them into exile in the sixth century (Cyrus, the Chaldean king, is mentioned by name in 44:28 and 45:1). The people addressed in the second part of the book are in Babylon, from which they are about to be liberated ("In the wilderness prepare the way of the Lord"—40:3; "I bring near my deliverance, it is not far off"—46:13; "Go forth from Babylon, flee from Chaldea"—48:20).

Q. What linguistic arguments are there for believing that the work of more than one man is bound up in this roll?

A. The style of I Isaiah has been described as "condensed, lapidary, and plastic," while that of II Isaiah is referred to as "gentle" and "rhapsodic"; I Isaiah employs "force and grandeur," II Isaiah relies upon "persuasion and pathos." This difference in style can be observed even in translation. In addition, II Isaiah has a distinctive vocabulary, with a considerable number of frequently recurring words not found at all in I Isaiah. Among these are "to choose" (41:8f; 43:10; 44:2) and "my chosen" (43:20; 45:4; 65:9,15,22); "praise" (42:8,10,12; 43:21;

48:9; 60:18; 61:3,11; 62:7,9; 63:7; 64:11); "shoot" or "spring up," like grass (44:4; 55:10; 61:11 [twice]; 45:8; 58:8; 42:9; 43:19); "break forth into singing" (44:23; 49:13; 52:9; 54:1; 55:12); "favor," in the sense of "good will" or "acceptance" (49:8; 56:7; 58:5; 60:10; 61:2).

Q. What theological differences are there between I Isaiah and II Isaiah?

A. I Isaiah emphasizes the holiness of God ("Holy, holy, holy is the Lord of hosts"—6:3); II. Isaiah stresses his everlastingness:
"Who has performed and done this,
    calling the generations from the beginning?
I, the Lord, the first,
    and with the last; I am He" (41:4).
I Isaiah pictures the coming of the Messianic King:
". . . and the government will be upon his shoulder,
    and his name will be called
'Wonderful Counselor, Mighty God,
    Everlasting Father, Prince of Peace' " (9:6).
II Isaiah revolves about the idea of the Suffering Servant:
"He was despised and rejected by men;
    a man of sorrows, and acquainted with grief;
and as one from whom men hide their faces
    he was despised, and we esteemed him not" (53:3).
The author of I Isaiah was himself called to be a prophet ("Whom shall I send . . . ? Send me"—6:8); in II Isaiah it is the community of Israel that is called to be a prophet "to the nations" (42:1), whose function it is to establish "justice in the earth" (42:4) and be "a light to the nations" (42:6; 49:6).

Q. At what points has the text of Isaiah been corrected by reference to the Isaiah scroll, which was among the first of the finds in the Dead Sea caves?

A. A thousand years older than any copies of Isaiah that had hitherto been known, this has necessitated minor correction at thirteen points: 3:24 (insertion of the word "shame"); 14:4 ("insolent fury" replaces "golden city"); 14:30 ("I" replaces "he"); 15:9 ("Dibon" twice replaces "Dimon"); 21:8 ("he who saw" replaces "a lion"); 23:2 ("your messengers passed over the sea" replaces "who passed over the sea, they replenished you"); 33:8 ("witnesses" replaces "cities"); 45:2 ("the mountains" replaces "the swellings"); 45:8 ("that salvation may sprout forth" replaces "that they may bring forth salvation"); 49:24 ("tyrant" replaces "righteous man"); 51:19 ("who will comfort you?" replaces "how may I comfort you?"); 56:12 ("us" replaces "me"); 60:19 (addition of "by night"). In each case the corruption had resulted from a copyist's error in the days when all books had to be written out by hand. In each case, the corrected text makes better sense than the version previously known.

Q. How is the prophet summoned to begin his work?

A. Through a vision in which the heavenly court is pictured very much in terms of the court of King Uzziah ("a throne high and lifted up"—6:1), the youthful Isaiah, impressed with his own unworthiness in view of the holiness of God ("I am a man of unclean lips, and I dwell in the midst of a people of unclean lips"—6:5), receives assurance of pardon ("your guilt is taken away, and your sin forgiven"—6:7) and responds ("Here I am!") to the summons from the Eternal ("Whom shall I send . . . ?"—6:8).

Q. Under the terms of his contract, how long does Isaiah have to remain at his task?

A. "Until cities lie waste
    without inhabitant,
and houses without men,
    and the land is utterly desolate" (6:11).

Q. What was the internal situation in the nation at the time Isaiah began his ministry?

A. "Jerusalem has stumbled,
    and Judah has fallen;
because their speech and their deeds are against the Lord" (3:8).

Q. What extremity will this lead to, according to the prophet?

A. "Seven women shall take hold of one man . . . saying, 'We will eat our own bread and wear our own clothes, only let us be called by your name' " (4:1).
    "Their houses will be plundered
        and their wives ravished" (13:16);
    "And I will make boys their princes,
        and babes shall rule over them" (3:4).

Q. What is Isaiah's demand for social justice?

A. "Seek justice,
    correct oppression;
defend the fatherless,
    plead for the widow" (1:17).

Q. What is the prophet's opinion of the religious practices of his time?

A. He hears God say:
"Your new moons and your appointed feasts
    my soul hates . . .
even though you make many prayers,
    I will not listen;
    your hands are full of blood" (1:14f).

Q. What judgment awaits this situation?

A. "The Lord has taken his place to contend,
    he stands to judge his people" (3:13);
"Through the wrath of the Lord of hosts
    the land is burned" (9:19).

Q. How does Isaiah describe the city women of his time?

A. ". . . the daughters of Zion are haughty
    and walk with outstretched necks,
    glancing wantonly with their eyes,
    mincing along as they go,
    tinkling with their feet" (3:16).

Q. What judgment does the prophet envision here?

A. ". . . the Lord will take away the finery . . .
Instead of perfume there will be rottenness; . . .
    and instead of well-set hair, baldness;
    and instead of a rich robe, a girding of sackcloth;
    instead of beauty, shame" (3:18-24; cf. 32:9-13).

Q. What role did Isaiah assume at the time of the Syro-Ephraim-itish invasion ("When the house of David was told, 'Syria is in league with Ephraim,' his heart and the heart of his people shook as the trees of the forest shake before the wind"—7:2)?

A. Assuming the role of statesman, he said to king Ahaz: ". . . do not let your heart be faint because of these two smoldering stumps of firebrands" (7:4); he thought the conspiracy could not last:
"It shall not stand,
    and it shall not come to pass" (7:7).

Q. What assurance did Isaiah give to Ahaz that deliverance was near?

A. "Behold, a young woman shall conceive and bear a son . . . before the child knows how to refuse the evil and choose the good, the land before whose two kings you are in dread will be deserted" (7:14,16).

Q. What attitude did Isaiah assume toward the fall of the northern kingdom?

A. He saw it coming: "the wealth of Damascus and the spoil of Samaria will be carried away before the king of Assyria" (8:4); he warned that a like fate might await the southern kingdom, and heard God say:

". . . shall I not do to Jerusalem and her idols
as I have done to Samaria and her images?" (10:11).

Q. What was the international situation in the time of Isaiah?

A. The Assyrian conquerors were drawing ever nearer, taking successively Damascus, Samaria, Carchemish, Gaza, and Ashdod.

Q. How did the people of Israel propose to avoid becoming the victims of Assyria?

A. By military alliance with Egypt.

Q. What was the prophet's attitude toward this alliance?

A. "Behold, you are relying on Egypt, that broken reed of a staff, which will pierce the hand of any man who leans on it" (36:6).

Q. What prescription had the prophet for the nation's security?

A. "In returning and rest you shall be saved;
in quietness and in trust shall be your strength" (30:15).

Q. How does Isaiah describe Israel's relationship to God?

A. "But the Lord of hosts, him you shall regard as holy; let him be your fear, and let him be your dread" (8:13); "thus says the Lord, who redeemed Abraham . . . :

'Jacob shall no more be ashamed,
no more shall his face grow pale.
For when he sees his children,
the work of my hands, in his midst,
they will sanctify my name . . .
and will stand in awe of the God of Israel' " (29:22f).

Q. How does the prophet spell out his nation's sins?

A. ". . . their speech and their deeds are against the Lord" (3:8).

"Ah, sinful nation,
    a people laden with iniquity,
offspring of evildoers,
    sons who deal corruptly!" (1:4);

"Sons have I reared and brought up,
    but they have rebelled against me.
The ox knows its owner,
    and the ass its master's crib;
but Israel does not know,
    my people does not understand" (1:2f);

They say "to the prophets, 'Prophesy
    not to us what is right;
speak to us smooth things,
    prophesy illusions' " (30:10);

"Because this people draw near with their mouth . . .
    while their hearts are far from me,
and their fear of me is a commandment of men learned by
    rote . . .
and the wisdom of their wise men shall perish,
    and the discernment of their discerning men shall be hid"
    (29:13f).

Q. How does Isaiah's God manifest himself in nature?

A. ". . . a flame of devouring fire, with a cloudburst and tempest and hailstones" (30:30).

"I will make the heavens tremble,
    and the earth will be shaken out of its place" (13:13);
"And the waters of the Nile will be dried up,
    and the river will be parched and dry" (19:5).

Q. What analogies from human life does Isaiah use to illustrate the power and skill of God?

A. "Shall the axe vaunt itself over him who hews with it, or the saw magnify itself against him who wields it?" (10:15; cf. 10:33f).

"Shall the potter be regarded as the clay;
that the thing made should say of its maker,
'He did not make me . . . ?' " (29:16).

Q. How does God manifest himself in human life?

A. "Holy, holy, holy is the Lord of hosts;
      the whole earth is full of his glory" (6:3; cf. 5:16; 5:19,
      24; 30:11).

Q. What is Isaiah's idea of God's lordship over history?

A. "This is the purpose that is purposed
            concerning the whole earth;
      and this is the hand that is stretched out
            over all the nations.
      For the Lord of hosts has purposed,
            and who will annul it?
      His hand is stretched out,
            and who will turn it back?" (14:26f);
      "The nations roar like the roaring of many waters,
            but he will rebuke them, and they will flee far away"
            (17:13);
      "The Lord is exalted, for he dwells on high;
            he will fill Zion with justice and righteousness;
      and he will be the stability of your times,
            abundance of salvation, wisdom and knowledge;
            the fear of the Lord is his treasure" (33:5f).

Q. How is God's lordship over history demonstrated in the case
of Assyria?

A. At one time God can say:
      "Ah, Assyria, the rod of my anger,
            the staff of my fury!
      Against a godless nation I send him" (10:5f);
at another time God says, "I will break the Assyrian" (14:25). In summary: "When the Lord has finished all his work on Mount Zion and on
Jerusalem he will punish the arrogant boasting of the king of Assyria
and his haughty pride" (10:12).

Q. How does Isaiah deal with the nature worship of his time?

A. Derision is his weapon:
      "For you shall be ashamed of the oaks
            in which you delighted;
      and you shall blush for the gardens
            which you have chosen.
      For you shall be like an oak

> whose leaf withers,
> and like a garden without water" (1:29f);
> ". . . therefore, though you plant pleasant plants
> and set out slips of an alien god,
> though you make them grow on the day that you plant them,
> and make them blossom in the morning that you sow;
> yet the harvest will flee away
> in a day of grief and incurable pain" (17:10f).

Q. How does Isaiah deal with idolatry?

A. Derision is his weapon here, too:

> "Their land is filled with idols;
> they bow down to the work of their hands,
> to what their own fingers have made" (2:8; cf. 2.20; 17:8; 31:7).

Q. How will the majesty of God manifest itself?

A. "For the Lord of hosts has a day
> against all that is proud and lofty,
> against all that is lifted up and high" (2:12);
> "And the haughtiness of man shall be humbled,
> and the pride of men shall be brought low;
> and the Lord alone will be exalted in that day" (2:17; cf. 5:15).

Q. What use does Isaiah make of symbolic names?

A. He called his own children *Shear-jashub* (that is, "A remnant shall return"—7:3), signifying the prophet's belief, before the invasion by Syria and Ephraim, that the people of Israel would not be wholly blotted out; and *Maher-shalal-hashbaz* (that is, "The spoil speeds, the prey hastes"), indicating his conviction that "before the child knows how to cry 'My father' or 'My mother,' the wealth of Damascus and the spoil of Samaria will be carried away before the king of Assyria" (8:3). Picturing the desolate city that is to be, Isaiah says: "They shall name it No Kingdom There" (34:12).

Q. What symbolic acts did Isaiah perform?

A. He appears to have assumed the role of a troubador to acquaint his people with the song of the vineyard (Chapter 5), which, though planted with choice vines, "yielded wild grapes" (5:2,4). He walked "naked and barefoot for three years as a sign and portent against

Egypt and Ethiopia" (20:3), suggesting that this is what these two nations would look like when the Assyrians got through with them. To a nation "confused with wine" (28:7), he thought the talk of a child might be needed (line upon line, line upon line"—28:10,13).

Q. What was the symbolic reference in the song of the vineyard?

A. "For the vineyard of the Lord of hosts
  is the house of Israel,
and the men of Judah
  are his pleasant planting;
and he looked for justice,
  but behold, bloodshed" (5:7).

The prophet goes on from there to denounce his people's insatiable greed ("Woe to those who join house to house"—5:8), drinking bouts ("Woe to those who . . . run after strong drink"—5:11), moral perversity and confusion ("Woe to those who call evil good and good evil" —5:20), and public corruption ("Woe to those who . . . acquit the guilty for a bribe"—5:22f).

Q. What is the prophet's picture of the day of the Lord?

A. "In that day men will . . .
  enter the caverns of the rocks
    and the clefts of cliffs,
  from before the terror of the Lord,
    and from the glory of his majesty,
    when he rises to terrify the earth" (2:12,20f);
"For the Lord of hosts has a day
  of tumult and trampling and confusion
  in the valley of vision,
a battering down of walls
  and a shouting to the mountains" (22:5).

Q. What is Isaiah's doctrine of the Remnant ?

A. That, no matter what befalls the nation, a kernel of good folk will survive: "A remnant will return, the remnant of Jacob, to the mighty God. For though your people Israel be as the sand of the sea, only a remnant of them will return" (10:21f; cf. 28:5f).

Q. What is the prophet's vision of the Messianic King?

A. "The people who walked in darkness
  have seen a great light;

those who dwelt in a land of deep darkness,
 on them has light shined" (9:2).
"For to us a child is born,
 to us a son is given;
and the government will be upon his shoulder,
 and his name will be called
'Wonderful Counselor, Mighty God,
 Everlasting Father, Prince of Peace.'
Of the increase of his government and of peace
 there will be no end,
upon the throne of David, and over his kingdom,
 to establish it, and to uphold it
with justice and with righteousness
 from this time forth and for evermore" (9:6f).

Q. What will characterize the reign of the Messianic King?

A. "The wolf shall dwell with the lamb,
 and the leopard shall lie down with the kid,
and the calf and the lion and the fatling together,
 and a little child shall lead them.
The cow and the bear shall feed;
 their young shall lie down together;
and the lion shall eat straw like the ox" (11:6f).
"Behold, a king will reign in righteousness,
 and princes will rule in justice.
Each will be like a hiding-place from the wind,
 a covert from the tempest,
like streams of water in a dry place,
 like the shade of a great rock in a weary lånd" (32:1,2).

Q. What future is envisioned for Mount Zion?

A. "It shall come to pass in the latter days
 that the mountain of the house of the Lord
shall be established as the highest of the mountains,
 and shall be raised above the hills;
and all the nations shall flow to it;
 and many peoples shall come and say:
'Come, let us go up to the mountain of the Lord,
 to the house of the God of Jacob;

that he may teach us of his ways
> and that we may walk in his paths" (2:2f).

Q. What is the prophet's dream of the future for mankind?

A. God "shall judge between the nations,
> and shall decide for many peoples;

and they shall beat their swords into plowshares,
> and their spears into pruning hooks;

nation shall not lift up sword against nation,
> neither shall they learn war any more" (2:4).

Q. What is the prophet's idea of the power of faith?

A. "If you will not believe,
> surely you shall not be established" (7:9);

"I will wait for the Lord, who is hiding his face from the house of Jacob, and I will hope in him" (8:17); "He who believes will not be in haste" (28:16).

Q. What hope of immortality does the book hold out?

A. The Lord "will swallow up death for ever, and the Lord God will wipe away tears from all faces" (25:8);

"Thy dead shall live, their bodies shall rise.
> O dwellers in the dust, awake and sing for joy!

For thy dew is a dew of light,
> and on the land of the shades thou wilt let it fall" (26:19).

Q. For what nations other than Israel does the prophet have a word?

A. Babylon (13:1-22); Philistia (14:29-32); Moab (15:1-16:14); Damascus (17:1-14); Egypt (19:1-24).

Q. How does II Isaiah set forth God's concern for his creation?

A. "Who has measured the waters in the hollow of his hand
> and marked off the heavens with a span,

enclosed the dust of the earth in a measure
> and weighed the mountains in scales
> and the hills in a balance? . . .

Behold, the nations are like a drop from a bucket,
> and are accounted as the dust on the scales;
> behold, he takes up the isles like fine dust" (40:12,15);

"I have spoken, and I will bring it to pass;
> I have purposed, and I will do it" (46:11);

"Before me no god was formed,
　　nor shall there be any after me" (43:10; cf. 44:6; 46:9);
"I form light and darkness,
　　I make weal and create woe,
　　I am the Lord, who do all these things" (45:7);
"I made the earth,
　　and created man upon it;
it was my hands that stretched out the heavens,
　　and I commanded all their host" (45:12).

Q. How are God and man contrasted?

A. "For my thoughts are not your thoughts,
　　neither are your ways my ways, says the Lord.
For as the heavens are higher than the earth,
　　so are my ways higher than your ways
　　and my thoughts than your thoughts" (55:8f).

Q. How does II Isaiah deal with idols?

A. He ridicules the man who cuts down a tree to make his own: ". . . he takes a part of it and warms himself, he kindles a fire and bakes bread; also he makes a god and worships it, he makes a graven image and falls down before it. Half of it he burns in the fire; over the half he eats flesh, he roasts meat and is satisfied; also he warms himself and says, 'Aha, I am warm, I have seen the fire!' And the rest of it he makes into a god . . . he prays to it and says, 'Deliver me, for thou art my God!' " (44:14-17; cf. 40:18-20; 46:6f).

Q. How does II Isaiah picture the love and tenderness of God?

A. "He will feed his flock like a shepherd,
　　he will gather the lambs in his arms,
he will carry them in his bosom,
　　and gently lead those that are with young" (40:11).
"Can a woman forget her sucking child,
　　that she should have no compassion on the son of her
　　womb?
　Even these may forget,
　　yet I will not forget you" (49:15);
"In all their affliction he was afflicted,
　　and the angel of his presence saved them;
in his love and in his pity he redeemed them,

he lifted them up and carried them all the days of old"
(63:9).
"As one whom his mother comforts,
so I will comfort you" (66:13).

Q. What other figures of speech does the author use about God?
A. "The Lord goes forth like a mighty man,
like a man of war he stirs up his fury;
he cries out, he shouts aloud,
he shows himself mighty against his foes" (42:13).
"He put on righteousness as a breastplate,
and a helmet of salvation upon his head;
he put on garments of vengeance for clothing,
and wrapped himself in fury as a mantle" (59:17).
"I have trodden the winepress alone,
and from the peoples no one was with me" (63:3).

Q. What sections of II Isaiah are known as the Servant Songs?
A. 42:1-4; 49:1-6; 50:4-9; 52:13-53:12.

Q. What is told of the Servant in 42:1-4?
A. This passage speaks of the Servant's mission:
"He will not fail or be discouraged
till he has established justice in the earth" (42:4).

Q. What is told of the Servant in 49:1-6?
A. This passage speaks of the Servant as prophet:
"He made my mouth like a sharp sword,
in the shadow of his hand he hid me" (49:2).

Q. What is told of the Servant in 50:4-9?
A. This passage speaks of the opposition that the Servant will
encounter and of his spirit in meeting it:
"I gave my back to the smiters,
and my cheeks to those who pulled out the beard;
I hid not my face
from shame and spitting" (50:6).

Q. What is told of the Servant in 52:13-53:12?
A. The passage speaks of the power of suffering voluntarily undertaken on behalf of others:
"But he was wounded for our transgressions,
he was bruised for our iniquities;

upon him was the chastisement that made us whole,
>and with his stripes we are healed . . .
he poured out his soul to death,
>and was numbered with the transgressors;
yet he bore the sin of many,
>and made intercession for the transgressors" (53:5,12).

Q. What passages reveal II Isaiah's interpretation of history?

A. Cyrus, founder of the Persian empire and conqueror of the Chaldeans, also gave permission for the Hebrews to leave their Babylonian exile and return to their homeland. Cyrus was a foreigner who had little interest in Israel as a nation and little knowledge of Israel's God. Yet God, in the ordering of history, uses Cyrus as the instrument of his purpose:

"Thus says the Lord to his anointed, to Cyrus,
>whose right hand I have grasped,
to subdue nations before him
>and ungird the loins of kings,
to open doors before him
>that gates may not be closed" (45:1).

Q. How does II Isaiah bid his people make ready for return from exile?

A. "In the wilderness prepare the way of the Lord,
>make straight in the desert a highway for our God.
Every valley shall be lifted up,
>and every mountain and hill shall be made low;
the uneven ground shall become level,
>and the rough places a plain" (40:3f);
". . . fear not, for I am with you,
>be not dismayed, for I am your God;
I will strengthen you, I will help you,
>I will uphold you with my victorious right hand" (41:10);
"For you shall not go out in haste,
>and you shall not go in flight,
for the Lord will go before you,
>and the God of Israel will be your rear guard" (52:12).

Q. What opportunity for repentance is offered to the people of God?

A. "I was ready to be sought by those who did not ask for me;
I was ready to be found by those who did not seek me" (65:1);
"Ho, every one who thirsts,
come to the waters;
and he who has no money,
come, buy and eat!
Come, buy wine and milk
without money and without price" (55:1);
"Seek the Lord while he may be found,
call upon him while he is near;
let the wicked forsake his way,
and the unrighteous man his thoughts;
let him return to the Lord, that he may have mercy on him,
and to our God, for he will abundantly pardon" (55:6f).

Q. What future does II Isaiah envision for humanity?

A. ". . . a law will go forth from me,
and my justice for a light to the peoples.
My deliverance draws near speedily,
my salvation has gone forth,
and my arms will rule the peoples;
the coastlands wait for me,
and for my arm they hope" (51:4,5);
". . . my salvation will be for ever
and my deliverance will never be ended" (51:6; cf. 51:8);
"Keep justice, and do righteousness,
for soon my salvation will come,
and my deliverance will be revealed" (56:1);
"And the foreigners who join themselves to the Lord . . .
their burnt offerings and their sacrifices
will be accepted on my altar;
for my house shall be called a house of prayer
for all peoples" (56:6f).
"So they shall fear the name of the Lord from the west,
and his glory from the rising of the sun" (59:19).

Q. What future does II Isaiah envision for Israel?

A. "I bring near my deliverance, it is not far off,
and my salvation will not tarry;

I will put my salvation in Zion,
  for Israel my glory" (46:13).
"For behold, I create new heavens
  and a new earth;
and the former things shall not be remembered
  or come into mind. . . .
I will rejoice in Jerusalem,
  and be glad in my people" (65:17,19);
"the Lord will arise upon you,
  and his glory will be seen upon you.
And nations shall come to your light,
  and kings to the brightness of your rising" (60:2f).

Q. What power is attributed to God's Word?

A. "For as the rain and the snow come down from heaven,
  and return not thither but water the earth,
making it bring forth and sprout,
  giving seed to the sower and bread to the eater,
so shall my word be that goes forth from my mouth;
  it shall not return to me empty,
but it shall accomplish that which I purpose,
  and prosper in the thing for which I sent it" (55:10f).
"The grass withers, the flower fades;
  but the word of our God will stand for ever" (40:8);
"my spirit which is upon you, and my words which I have put in your mouth, shall not depart out of your mouth, or out of the mouth of your children, or out of the mouth of your children's children, says the Lord, from this time forth and for evermore" (59:21).

Q. How did Isaiah meet his death?

A. History contains no record, but tradition has it that Isaiah of Jerusalem was among those alluded to in Hebrews 11:37, which tells how some ancient worthies were "sawn in two."

Q. What classical expressions has Isaiah given to our speech?

A. "Come now, let us reason together" (1:18);
". . . stay and staff,
  the whole stay of bread" (3:1).
"Happy are you who sow beside all waters" (32:20);
"How beautiful upon the mountains

are the feet of him who brings good tidings,
who publishes peace, who brings good tidings of good,
who publishes salvation,
who says to Zion, 'Your God reigns' " (52:7).

Q. What phrases from Isaiah have provided modern literary titles?

A. *Rivers in the Desert* (43:20) is the title of Nelson Glueck's work on Palestinian archaeology; other phrases that have been used are *the valley of vision* (22:5) and *awake and sing* (26:19).

Q. What passage from II Isaiah was the basis of a famous sermon by William Carey, founder of the modern missionary enterprise?

A. "Enlarge the place of your tent,
and let the curtains of your habitation be stretched out;
hold not back, lengthen your cords
and strengthen your stakes" (54:2).

Q. In what ways was Jesus influenced by the book of the prophet Isaiah?

A. His first sermon in the Nazareth synagogue (Luke 4:16-22) had for its text Isaiah 61:1f; the strange reason Jesus gives for parables (Matthew 13:14f) is quoted from the commission given to Isaiah (6:9f). When the people were critical of his message, Jesus said: "Well did Isaiah prophesy of you hypocrites" (Mark 7:6; cf. Matthew 15:8), and then quoted Isaiah 29:13. At the Last Supper, Jesus said to his friends: "For I tell you that this scripture must be fulfilled in me, 'And he was reckoned with transgressors' " (Luke 22:37). The quotation is from Isaiah 53:12.

Q. What familiar phrase regarding gluttony is found?

A. "Let us eat and drink,
for tomorrow we die" (22:13; compare 56:12).

Q. What taunt song is included?

A. A song about Tyre, reproaching her as a "forgotten harlot" (23:16).

Q. What passage is echoed in Revelation?

A. Isaiah 25:8 says: "He will swallow up death for ever, and the Lord God will wipe away tears from all faces." Revelation 21:4 (cf. 7:17) says of God that "he will wipe away every tear from their eyes, and death shall be no more."

Q. What passage is echoed in the letter to Philippians?

A. Isaiah 26:3 looks for a time when Judah will sing:

"Thou dost keep him in perfect peace,
　　whose mind is stayed on thee."

Paul writes to the Philippians that it has already happened: "And the peace of God, which passes all understanding, will keep your hearts and your minds in Christ Jesus."

Q. What illustration from the life of his own time does the author use to suggest that, although God does not always act in the same way, he always acts with purpose?

A. Of this, the "rules of good husbandry" are a parable (28:24-29).

Q. What passage gives a vivid picture of life in a desert country?

A. "Each will be like a hiding-place from the wind,

　　a covert from the tempest,

　　like streams of water in a dry place

　　　　like the shade of a great rock in a weary land" (32:2).

Q. What passage, descriptive of the homeward way of the exiled Jewish community, has often been cited as describing humanity's way of the future?

A. Chapter 35.

Q. What passage pictures the universal sovereignty of God?

A. Isaiah 40:12-17.

Q. What passage poses the philosopher's problem?

A. "To whom then will you liken God?" (40:18).

Q. What song of thanksgiving is attributed to King Hezekiah, recuperating from illness?

A. Isaiah 38:10-20.

Q. What political taunt song personifies a nation as a woman of ill repute?

A. Chapter 47 deals with Babylon in that fashion.

Q. What phrases are incorporated in the description of the well-accoutered warrior given in Ephesians 6:14ff?

A. "Righteousness as a breastplate" and "helmet of salvation" (59:17).

Q. Jeremiah 29:13f represents God as saying: "When you seek me with all your heart, I will be found by you." How does Isaiah phrase the complementary truth?

A. "I was ready to be found by those who did not seek me" (65:1).

THE BOOK OF JEREMIAH

Q. Who was Jeremiah?

A. A prophet who foresaw and witnessed the destruction of Jerusalem by the Babylonians in 586 B.C.

Q. How does Jeremiah date his ministry?

A. To him "the word of the Lord came in the days of Josiah, the son of Amon, king of Judah, in the thirteenth year of his reign. It came also in the days of Jehoiakim the son of Josiah, king of Judah, and until the end of the eleventh year of Zedekiah, the son of Josiah, king of Judah, until the captivity of Jerusalem" (1:3). Since Josiah became king in 640 or 639 B.C., the thirteenth year of his reign would have been about 628 B.C.

Q. What is known of Jeremiah's childhood and youth?

A. He identifies himself (1:1) as "the son of Hilkiah, of the priests who were in Anathoth in the land of Benjamin"; 1:4f suggests predestination: "The word of the Lord came to me saying,

'Before I formed you in the womb I knew you,
and before you were born I consecrated you.'"

Q. Why do we know more of Jeremiah and his inner life than of any other prophet?

A. Because we have not only his own sermons and memoirs, sometimes called "The Confessions of Jeremiah," but also biographical material assembled and set down by his secretary, Baruch.

Q. How did Jeremiah work with his secretary?

A. "Baruch wrote upon a scroll at the dictation of Jeremiah all the words of the Lord which he had spoken to him" (36:4; cf. 45:1). Jeremiah said: "I am debarred from going to the house of the Lord; so you are to go, and . . . in the hearing of all the people . . . you shall read the words of the Lord from the scroll which you have written at my dictation" (36:6).

Q. What personal advice did Jeremiah give to Baruch?

A. "And do you seek great things for yourself? Seek them not" (45:5).

Q. Was Jeremiah's mission to Israel alone?

A. God's word came to him: "I appointed you a prophet to the nations" (1:5; cf. 46:1). God said to him also: "Take from my hand this cup of the wine of wrath, and make all nations to whom I send you drink it" (25:15).

Q. Did Jeremiah welcome his assignment to such a mission?

A. His response was: "Ah, Lord God! Behold, I do not know how to speak, for I am only a youth" (1:6).

Q. What promise did God make?

A. "I am with you to deliver you. . . . Behold I have put my words in your mouth" (1:8,9).

Q. What imagery does the prophet draw from the realm of nature?

A. "Even the stork in the heavens
        knows her times;
    and the turtledove, swallow and crane
        keep the time of their coming;
    but my people know not the ordinance of the Lord" (8:7);
    "Like the partridge that gathers a brood
        which she did not hatch,
    so is he who gets riches but not by right" (17:11).

Q. By which of his predecessors in the prophetic tradition was Jeremiah most profoundly influenced?

A. By Hosea, as the following comparisons will indicate:

Compare Jeremiah	with Hosea
3:22	14:1,4
4:3	10:12
5:30	6:10
18:13	6:10
23:14	6:10
7:9	4:2
9:12	14:9
14:10	9:9
30:9	3:5
30:22	2:23

Q. What is the poignancy of Jeremiah's having been so strongly influenced by Hosea?

A. Hosea's distinctive contribution to theology was arrived at through marriage and the relationships of home; marriage was denied to Jeremiah: "You shall not take a wife, nor shall you have sons or daughters in this place" (16:2); the reason for this was the disease and destruction soon to come upon the land (16:3f).

Q. What methods did Jeremiah use to proclaim the truth?

A. Not only preaching ("The word that came to Jeremiah from the Lord: 'Stand in the gate of the Lord's house, and proclaim there this word' "—7:2; cf. 17:19; 19:14; 22:1; 26:2; 35:2ff; 36:5,10) but also object lessons presented through the performance of symbolic acts.

Q. What were some of these symbolic acts?

A. A waistcloth hidden "in the cleft of a rock" (13:4) was later found "spoiled; it was good for nothing" (13:7): "Thus says the Lord: Even so will I spoil the pride of Judah" (13:9). A potter, working at his wheel, spoiled a vessel of clay and "reworked it into another vessel" (18:4): "Behold, like the clay in the potter's hand, so are you in my hand, O house of Israel" (18:6). The prophet bought "a potter's earthen flask" (19:1) and smashed it in the sight of the people: "Thus says the Lord. . . . So will I break this people and this city" (19:11). The prophet fashioned "thongs and yoke-bars" and put them on his neck (27:2); so the nations were to be brought "under the yoke of the king of Babylon" (27:11; cf. 28:10-13).

Q. What circumstances in the national life brought about a reform in the days of Jeremiah?

A. During Josiah's reign, the long-neglected "book of the law" was found "in the house of the Lord" (II Kings 22:8). The king led the people in an act of rededication ("to keep his commandments"—II Kings 23:3), and this initiated a reformation of the nation's religious practices and commitments.

Q. What was Jeremiah's attitude toward the reform?

A. 11:1-13 ("And the Lord said to me, 'Proclaim all these words in the cities of Judah and in the streets of Jerusalem: Hear the words of this covenant and do them' "—11:6) has sometimes been interpreted as describing a preaching tour made by Jeremiah for the purpose of encouraging acceptance of the reform. Other students believe that Jeremiah's insights into the inwardness of true religion would have made it impossible for him to support a government-sponsored reform, or any attempt to further it by compulsory changes in forms of worship. Still others believe that Jeremiah's early hopes for the reform were disappointed and that it was through this experience that he was led to speak of a religion not dependent upon forms of cult or state.

Q. With what visions was Jeremiah's ministry begun?

A. He saw "a rod of almond"; a play on the Hebrew words suggests the meaning, "I am watching over my word to perform it" (1:12); and "a boiling pot, facing away from the north" (1:13), disclosing that "Out of the north evil shall break forth. . . . They will fight against you; but they shall not prevail against you" (1:14,19).

Q. What picture does Jeremiah paint of Israel's apostasy?

A. He looks back to the ideal past from which the nation has fallen away ("I remember the devotion of your youth"—2:2); recounts God's goodness to the nation ("I brought you into a plentiful land"—2:7), but notes sorrowfully,

> "My people have changed their glory
>   for that which does not profit" (2:11).

The nation, turning desperately for help to Egypt and Assyria (2:18), has in fact become "a wild ass . . . in her heat sniffing the wind" (2:24); adopting heathen ways, the nation now has as many gods as cities (2:26-28): "You have played the harlot with many lovers" (3:1). Injustice follows inevitably upon this iniquity:

> "Also on your skirts is found
>   the lifeblood of guiltless poor" (2:34).

Q. How does the southern kingdom compare with the northern in this respect?

A. "Faithless Israel has shown herself less guilty than false Judah" (3:11).

Q. What hope of reunion between the two kingdoms is held out?

A. "And I will give you shepherds after my own heart. . . . Jerusalem shall be called the throne of the Lord, and all nations shall gather to it. . . . In those days the house of Judah shall join the house of Israel" (3:15-18).

Q. What hope is there that disaster can be averted?

A. Only if the nation repents and lives "in truth, in justice, and in uprightness" (4:2);

> "Stand by the roads, and look,
>   and ask for the ancient paths,

where the good way is; and walk in it,
     and find rest for your souls" (6:16).

Q. What new form of circumcision is envisioned as a symbol of this repentance?

A. "Remove the foreskin of your hearts" (4:4).

Q. How does the prophet picture the threatened invasion?

A. "A hot wind from the bare heights. . . . Disaster follows hard on disaster . . . anguish as of one bringing forth her first child" (4:11, 20,31).

Q. How does the prophet describe his nation's ingratitude and faithlessness to its God?

A. "When I fed them to the full,
    they committed adultery
    and trooped to the house of harlots" (5:7).
"They have spoken falsely of the Lord,
    and have cried, 'He will do nothing' " (5:12);
"They do not say in their hearts,
    'Let us fear the Lord our God,
who gives the rain in its season' " (5:24).

Q. What crowns the prophet's picture of his nation's iniquity?

A. "An appalling and horrible thing
    has happened in the land:
the prophets prophesy falsely,
    and the priests rule at their direction;
my people love to have it so" (5:30f).

Q. What does the prophet envision as the ideal relationship between God and Israel?

A. Israel is God's son (3:4,19):
"Therefore my heart yearns for him;
I will surely have mercy on him, says the Lord" (31:20).
Israel is God's wife:
"I remember the devotion of your youth,
    your love as a bride" (2:2);
Israel is God's "green olive tree, fair with goodly fruit" (11:16).

Q. What is the actual relationship between God and Israel?

A. The vine has "turned degenerate, and become a wild vine"

(2:21). The nation is guilty of unfaithfulness ("You have played the harlot with many lovers"—3:1; cf, 3:3,6-11) and idolatry ("they have burned incense to other gods" (1:16; 32:29-35). The temple itself has been polluted ("they have set their abominations in the house which is called by my name, to defile it"—7:30). Child sacrifice has been adopted ("to burn their sons and daughters in the fire"—7:31). Social evils abound:

> "They know no bounds in deeds of wickedness;
>   they judge not with justice
> the cause of the fatherless, to make it prosper,
>   and they do not defend the rights of the needy" (5:28).
> "For from the least to the greatest of them,
>   every one is greedy for unjust gain;
> and from prophet to priest,
>   every one deals falsely" (6:13; cf. 7:55ff);
> "with his mouth each speaks peaceably to his neighbor,
>   but in his heart he plans an ambush for him" (9:8).

Q. What does Jeremiah teach about God's supremacy in nature?
A. "I placed the sand as the bound for the sea" (5:22);
"At his wrath the earth quakes" (10:10);
"Are there any among the false gods of the nations that can bring rain?" (14:22).

Q. What of God's relationship to history?
A. "The nations cannot endure his indignation" (10:10);
> "I will make a full end of all the nations,
>   among whom I scattered you,
>   but of you I will not make a full end" (30:11).
"Who would not fear thee, O King of the nations?" (10:7).

Q. What of God's relationship to one nation?
A. "O thou hope of Israel,
its savior in time of trouble" (14:8).
"For I am with you to save you, says the Lord . . .
I will chasten you in just measure,
    and I will by no means leave you unpunished" (30:11);
"The Lord has saved his people,
the remnant of Israel" (31:7).

Q. What other characteristics of God does the prophet speak of?

A. "I am the Lord who practice kindness, justice, and righteousness in the earth" (9:24);

> "I the Lord search the mind
>> and try the heart" (17:10);

> "Am I a God at hand, says the Lord, and not a God afar off?
>> Can a man hide himself in secret places so that I cannot see him? says the Lord. Do I not fill heaven and earth?" (23:23f).

Q. What was Jeremiah's distinctive contribution to theology?

A. The doctrine of the New Covenant: "I will put my law within them, and I will write it upon their hearts; and I will be their God, and they shall be my people" (31:33).

Q. What were the characteristics of the New Covenant?

A. It was to be not only redemptive ("I will forgive their iniquity, and I will remember their sin no more"—31:34) but also personal and inward rather than tribal and official ("not like the covenant which I made with their fathers"—31:32). What is personal and inward is in and of itself universal ("they shall all know me, from the least of them to the greatest"—31:34) and everlasting ("I will give them one heart and one way, that they may fear me for ever"—32:39).

Q. What were some manifestations of the false religions that flourished in Jeremiah's time?

A. "The children gather wood, the fathers kindle fire, and the women knead dough, to make cakes for the queen of heaven; and they pour out drink offerings to other gods" (7:18).

Q. What is the prophet's judgment upon false religion?

A. "Will you steal, murder, commit adultery, swear falsely, burn incense to Baal, and go after other gods . . . and then come to stand before me in this house, which is called by my name?" (7:9f);

> "Their idols are like scarecrows
>> in a cucumber field,
>> and they cannot speak;
> they have to be carried,
>> for they cannot walk.
> Be not afraid of them,
>> for they cannot do evil,
>> neither is it in them to do good" (10:5).

Q. What hope is there for devotees of the popular religion?

A. To people trusting "in these deceptive words: 'This is the temple of the Lord, the temple of the Lord, the temple of the Lord' " (7:4), Jeremiah said: "Amend your ways and your doings" (7:3).

Q. What was Jeremiah's original thought regarding the quarter from which doom would descend upon his nation?

A. "Out of the north evil shall break forth upon all the inhabitants of the land" (1:14). The Scythians, a group of tribes living on the steppe from the Carpathians to the Don, were a source of constant dread.

Q. What picture does Jeremiah draw of the way in which the Scythians might be expected to attack?

A. "Behold, he comes up like clouds,
      his chariots like the whirlwind;
his horses are swifter than eagles" (4:13).

Q. What was Jeremiah's later opinion regarding the nation that would inflict punishment upon his own?

A. The Babylonians, whom he can also speak of as Chaldeans, were to be the instrument of God's judgment. In Nebuchadnezzar's rise to power, the distinction between Babylonians and Chaldeans—formerly considered to be kindred branches of the original Semite stock—ceased to exist.

Q. What was the attitude of his peers toward Jeremiah?

A. "I have become a laughingstock all the day;
      everyone mocks me" (20:7).

Q. What were Jeremiah's inner feelings in face of the popular opposition to his message?

A. "Cursed be the day on which I was born! . . .
Why did I come forth from the womb
    to see toil and sorrow,
    and spend my days in shame" (20:14,18).
"Woe is me, my mother, that you bore me, a man of strife and contention to the whole land" (15:10);
    "O that I had in the desert
      a wayfarers' lodging place,
    that I might leave my people
      and go away from them!" (9:2).

Q. What were Jeremiah's feelings regarding those who opposed him?

A. "Forgive not their iniquity,
> nor blot out their sins from thy sight.

Let them be overthrown before thee;
> deal with them in the time of thine anger" (18:23).

Q. What picture does Jeremiah draw of the desolation that awaits a land that has turned its back upon God?

A. "The dead bodies of this people will be food for the birds of the air, and for the beasts of the earth. . . . And I will make to cease from the cities of Judah and from the streets of Jerusalem the voice of mirth and the voice of gladness, the voice of the bridegroom and the voice of the bride" (7:33f).

Q. Why is it especially touching that he should have seized upon these details?

A. Because devotion to his mission had made it impossible for him personally ever to share in "the voice of gladness, the voice of the bridegroom and the voice of the bride" (cf. 16:2).

Q. What specifically did Jeremiah predict about Jerusalem?

A. "Thus says the Lord: If you will not listen to me, to walk in my law which I have set before you . . . then I will make this house like Shiloh, and I will make this city a curse for all the nations of the earth" (26:4,6).

Q. Was the position taken by Jeremiah supported by other prophets of his time?

A. Hananiah said: "Thus says the Lord of hosts, the God of Israel: I have broken the yoke of the king of Babylon" (28:2).

Q. What was Jeremiah's reply to the easy optimism of the false prophets?

A. "Do not let your prophets and your diviners who are among you deceive you, and do not listen to the dreams which they dream, for it is a lie which they are prophesying to you" (29:8f).

Q. When the disaster foreseen by Jeremiah finally came upon the nation, what was the prophet's attitude toward the destroying power, Babylon?

A. He commanded his people not to resist the threatened invasion; when King Zedekiah asked, "Is there any word from the Lord?" (37:17),

Jeremiah replied, "You shall be delivered into the hand of the king of Babylon" (37:17). "He who stays in this city shall die by the sword, by famine, and by pestilence; but he who goes out to the Chaldeans shall live" (38:2). "But if you do not surrender to the princes of the king of Babylon, then this city shall be given into the hand of the Chaldeans, and they shall burn it with fire, and you shall not escape from their hand" (38:18).

Q. What was the popular reaction to Jeremiah on this point?

A. He was accused of un-Judean activities: "he is weakening the hands of the soldiers . . . and the hands of all the people, by speaking such words" (38:4).

Q. What was the government's reaction?

A. "So King Zedekiah gave orders, and they committed Jeremiah to the court of the guard" (37:21). "So they took Jeremiah and cast him into the cistern of Malchiah . . . letting Jeremiah down by ropes . . . and Jeremiah sank in the mire" (38:6).

Q. Who rescued Jeremiah from this plight?

A. Ebed-melech the Ethiopian (38:7-13).

Q. What was Ebed-melech's reward?

A. "You shall not fall by the sword" (39:18).

Q. What choice was offered Jeremiah by the Babylonian conquerors?

A. Either to accompany the exiles or to remain behind; he chose to dwell "among the people who were left in the land" (40:6).

Q. How was Jeremiah's prophecy fulfilled in the case of King Zedekiah?

A. "The king of Babylon slew the sons of Zedekiah before his eyes, and also slew all the princes of Judah. . . . He put out the eyes of Zedekiah, and bound him in fetters, and the king of Babylon took him to Babylon, and put him in prison till the day of his death" (52:10f).

Q. How did Jeremiah proclaim his faith that, after the disaster inflicted by the Babylonians, life would be revived in the land of Judah?

A. He purchased a field and sealed up the deed of purchase in an earthenware vessel: "For thus says the Lord of hosts. . . . Houses and fields and vineyards shall again be bought in this land" (32:15).

Q. When neighboring tribes harassed the Hebrews left behind, where did they turn for help?

A. To Egypt, but Jeremiah warned against it: "All the men who set their faces to go to Egypt to live there shall die by the sword, by famine, and by pestilence, they shall have no remnant or survivor" (42:17).

Q. What effect did this warning have?

A. Insisting that Jeremiah was telling a lie (43:2), the people, taking Jeremiah and Baruch with them, "came into the land of Egypt, for they did not obey the voice of the Lord" (43:7).

Q. How did Jeremiah himself meet death?

A. Tradition has it that his fellow citizens who had dragged him with them into exile in Egypt stoned him to death there.

Q. For what nations other than his own did Jeremiah have a prophetic word from the Lord?

A. Egypt (46:2-28: "there is no healing for you"—46:11); Philistia (47:2-7: "the Lord is destroying the Philistines"—47:4); Moab (48:1-47: "the renown of Moab is no more"—48:2); the Ammonites (49:1-6: "Behold, I will bring terror upon you"—49:5); Edom (49:7-32: "Edom shall become a horror"—49:17); Damascus (49:23-27: "panic seized her"—49:24); "Kedar and the kingdoms of Hazor" (49: 28-33: "Hazor shall become a haunt of jackals"—49:33); Elam (49:34-39: "I will break the bow of Elam"—49:35); Babylon (50:1-51:58: "I am bringing against Babylon a company of great nations" —50:9; "the broad wall of Babylon shall be leveled to the ground"— 51:58).

Q. What dirges of Jeremiah led some to attribute to him the authorship of the book of Lamentations?

A. 9:9,16-21:

"Hear, O women, the word of the Lord,
　　and let your ear receive the word of his mouth;
teach to your daughters a lament,
　　and each to her neighbor a dirge" (9:20);

and Chapter 14:

"O thou hope of Israel,
　　its savior in time of trouble,
why shouldst thou be like a stranger in the land,
　　like a wayfarer who turns aside to tarry for a night?"
　　(14:8).

Q. What three groups of religious leaders in Israel are referred to in Jeremiah?

A. "The law shall not perish from the priest, nor counsel from the wise, nor the word from the prophet" (18:18).

Q. How does the work of Jeremiah illustrate the truth that prophecy is morally conditioned?

A. He hears God say to his people: ". . . if that nation, concerning which I have spoken, turns from its evil, I will repent of the evil that I intended to do to it . . . and if it does evil in my sight, not listening to my voice, then I will repent of the good which I had intended to do to it" (18:8-10).

Q. What passages in Jeremiah appear to be direct references to Deuteronomy?

A. 11:1-8 (cf. Deuteronomy 27:26; 4:20; 7:12) and 8:8.

Q. What imagery did the author of Jonah borrow from Jeremiah?

A. "Nebuchadrezzar the king of Babylon has devoured me . . .
    he has swallowed me like a monster;
he has filled his belly with my delicacies,
    he has rinsed me out" (51:34).

Q. What classical expressions has Jeremiah given to our language?

A. "They have healed the wound of my people lightly,
    saying, 'Peace, peace,'
    when there is no peace" (8:11);
"Can the Ethiopian change his skin
    or the leopard his spots?" (13:23);
"I was like a gentle lamb
    led to the slaughter" (11:19);
"The fathers have eaten sour grapes,
    and the children's teeth are set on edge" (31:29);
"Is there no balm in Gilead?" (8:22).
"The dead bodies of men shall fall . . .
    like sheaves after the reaper" (9:22).

Q. In what ways did Jeremiah influence Jesus?

A. Jesus' denunciation of the temple abuses was very much in the language of Jeremiah 7:11: "Has this house, which is called by my name, become a den of robbers in your eyes? Behold, I myself have seen it, says the Lord" (cf. Mark 11:17; Matthew 21:13; Luke 19:46).

Jesus' announcement regarding the significance of the poured-out wine ("This cup is the new covenant in my blood," reported by Paul in I Corinthians 11:25) is in the language of Jeremiah 31:31. Jesus' saying that "A prophet is not without honor, except in his own country, and among his own kin, and in his own house" (Mark 6:4; cf. Matthew 13:57; John 4:24) may well be an allusion to the situation of Jeremiah (12:6). Jesus' assertion that "He who receives a prophet because he is a prophet shall receive a prophet's reward" (Matthew 10:41) may well refer to Ebed-melech, who received and delivered the prophet Jeremiah (38:7-13; 39:15-18). In Luke 12:55f Jesus draws a parallel, similar to that in Jeremiah 8:7, between the "signs" in nature and the "signs" in history.

Q. How does Jeremiah refer to what he regards as the ideal past from which his contemporaries have fallen away?

A. He hears God say:

"I remember the devotion of your youth,
      your love as a bride,
how you followed me in the wilderness,
      in a land not sown" (2:2).

The prophet says to the people:

". . . ask for the ancient paths,
      where the good way is, and walk in it" (6:16).

Q. What was the age at which Jeremiah was called to be a prophet?

A. His initial response to the divine call is: "I am only a youth" (1:6). The Hebrew term, however, may denote any age from infancy up toward the prime of life. It is variously translated "child," "too young," "only a boy."

Q. What historical allusion may appear in the reference to one who enlarges her eyes with paint (4:30)?

A. In II Kings 9:30, Jezebel, who came to personify the vices of a godless life, is said to have "painted her eyes."

Q. What command to Jeremiah brings to mind the case of Diogenes walking the streets of Athens with a lantern in broad daylight, looking for an honest man?

A. "Run to and fro through the streets of Jerusalem,
      look and take note!
Search her squares to see

> if you can find a man,
> one who does justice
> and seeks truth" (5:1).

Q. Why does Jeremiah warn against putting too much trust in "the temple of the Lord, the temple of the Lord, the temple of the Lord" (7:4)?

A. Perhaps the deliverance described in II Kings 18:13-19:36 and celebrated in Psalm 46 had led to the popular belief that Jerusalem could never be taken.

Q. What historical character may have been in Jeremiah's mind as he longed for "a wayfarers' lodging place" in the desert (9:2)?

A. Elijah did find such a retreat (I Kings 19:4-9).

Q. What ethical standards does God hold before his people?

A. His own practice of "kindness, justice, and righteousness in the earth" (9:24).

Q. What passage describes the forms of idolatry seen by the Jews of the Diaspora?

A. Jeremiah 10:2-11.

Q. What passage is a classical description of the conditional nature of prophecy?

A. "If at any time I declare concerning a nation or a kingdom, that I will pluck up and break down and destroy it, and if that nation, concerning which I have spoken, turns from its evil, I will repent of the evil that I intended to do to it" (18:8).

Q. How does Jeremiah set forth the universal character of God?

A. "Am I a God at hand, says the Lord, and not a God afar off? Can a man hide himself in secret places so that I cannot see him?" (23:23).

Q. What prayer from early liturgy is included here?

A. Jeremiah 32:16-25.

Q. What section found in the Hebrew Bible is lacking in the Septuagint?

A. Jeremiah 33:14-26.

Q. What historical narrative is the source of 52:1-27?

A. It is in large part taken from II Kings 24:18-25:21.

THE LAMENTATIONS
OF JEREMIAH

Q. What is the meaning of "Lamentations"?

A. The book consists of dirges for the fallen city of Jerusalem. The title in Hebrew is simply *Ekhah,* meaning "How," the opening word of the text and the word commonly used to introduce a lament for the dead.

Q. Who is the author of Lamentations?

A. Because he suffered deeply in the fall of Jerusalem, Jeremiah has traditionally been thought of as the author. There is no signature in the book, and it is believed by many that the poems, perhaps by different authors, were composed by priests for the liturgical use of the surviving members of the Jerusalem community.

Q. When were the poems written?

A. The events they describe are plainly those attendant upon the fall of Jerusalem in 586 B.C. The memory of the tragic scene was still vivid, and probably they were composed within a few decades of the event.

Q. What is the literary nature of the poems?

A. Four of them are in the acrostic form; perhaps this was an aid to memory in their public use; this is "the largest single group of acrostic poems in Hebrew literature."

Q. To what other parts of the Old Testament do these laments show affinities?

A. Such communal laments as Psalms 77, 79, 102 and such personal laments as David's over Abner (II Samuel 3:33) and over Saul and Jonathan (II Samuel 1:19-27).

Q. To what does the first lament in our book compare the desolate city?

A. "How like a widow has she become" (1:1); "there is none to comfort me" (1:21).

Q. What has become of the friends who once brought solace and strength?

A. "All her friends have dealt treacherously with her,
    they have become her enemies" (1:2).

Q. Does the author regard the sack of Jerusalem as undeserved punishment?

A. No, it is accompanied by a confession of sin: "Jerusalem sinned grievously" (1:8).

"The Lord is in the right,
    for I have rebelled against his word" (1:18).

Q. Does this mean the author can look with equanimity upon the invader?

A. No. "Let all their evildoing come before thee,
    and deal with them
as thou hast dealt with me" (1:22).

Q. What figure of speech does the author use to picture the way in which the nation has been crushed?

A. "The Lord has trodden as in a wine press
    the virgin daughter of Judah" (1:15).

Q. What features mark the second lament (Chapter 2)?

A. The king in Israel was looked upon as a representative of the nation as a whole, and grief is expressed that God

"has brought down to the ground in dishonor
    the kingdom and its rulers" (2:2).

Verses 11-17 appear to be the fallen leader's own lament; this is followed by a prayer on behalf of the starving survivors (2:19-22).

Q. What is distinctive of the third lament (Chapter 3)?

A. A lament over the writer's own suffering, it is a kind of mosaic of quotations from the Psalms (51:8; 88:5f; 22:2; 7:12f; 42:5f, 11; 16:5; 33:18; 37:7; 40:1; 94:12,14; 140:12; 33:9; etc.).

Q. Does the author feel that one who has been spared has any real right to complain?

A. "Why should a living man complain,
    a man, about the punishment of his sins?
Let us test and examine our ways,
    and return to the Lord!" (3:39f).

Q. What is distinctive of the fourth lament (Chapter 4)?

A. Condemnation of the community's religious leaders:
"This was for the sins of her prophets

and the iniquities of her priests" (4:13).

Q. What is distinctive of the fifth lament (Chapter 5)?

A. It appears to be a prayer in which the congregation expresses the misery and shame of exile and pleads for God's pity.

Q. Is there hope of renewal?

A. "Restore us to thyself, O Lord, that we may be restored!
     Renew our days as of old!" (5:21).

Q. What use of Lamentations is made by the Hebrew people?

A. On the ninth of Ab, remembered as the anniversary of the date on which the destruction of Jerusalem had occurred, these poems are publicly read in the synagogue, recounting not the number of the slain, nor details of the battle, but the grief felt by the Hebrews at the desolation of their beloved city.

Q. What passage from Lamentations has been immortalized in Handel's oratorio, *The Messiah*?

A. "Is it nothing to you, all you who pass by?
     Look and see
     if there is any sorrow like my sorrow" (1:12).

Q. What passage from Lamentations was used by the Mau-Mau in the 1950's to describe the situation of the people of Kenya?

A. "Remember, O Lord, what has befallen us;
     behold, and see our disgrace!
   Our inheritance has been turned over to strangers,
     our homes to aliens.
   We have become orphans, fatherless;
     our mothers are like widows.
   We must pay for the water we drink,
     the wood we get must be bought.
   With a yoke on our necks we are hard driven;
     we are weary, we are given no rest" (5:1-5).

Q. What historical reference probably led to Jeremiah's being thought of as the author?

A. II Chronicles 35:24f tells how, at the death of a good king, "All Judah and Jerusalem mourned for Josiah. Jeremiah also uttered a lament for Josiah."

THE BOOK OF EZEKIEL

Q. Who was Ezekiel?

A. A prophet who lived at the time of the destruction of Jerusalem and was deported to Babylon following the first conquest of Judah, in 597 B.C.: "I was among the exiles by the river Chebar" (1:1; cf. II Kings 24:14-16).

Q. How is his career dated?

A. Some of the prophecies are variously dated in "the thirtieth year" 1:1), "the tenth year" (29:1), "the twenty-seventh year" (29:17), but the point of reference is not clear; in 1:2 a scribe has inserted a comment identifying the thirtieth year as "the fifth year of the exile of King Jehoiachin," which would be 593 B.C.

Q. What was Ezekiel's family background?

A. "The word of the Lord came to Ezekiel the priest" (1:3); the work throughout shows the concern for the place and manner of worship and the other institutions of religion that would be natural to one who was a member of the hereditary priesthood.

Q. What picturesque language does the prophet use in reporting how he traveled from one place to another?

A. "The Spirit lifted me up and took me away" (3:14). "He put forth the form of a hand, and took me by a lock of my head; and the Spirit lifted me up between earth and heaven, and brought me in visions of God to Jerusalem" (8:3). "The hand of the Lord was upon me, and brought me in the visions of God into the land of Israel, and set me down upon a very high mountain" (40:1f).

Q. What function did Ezekiel perform for his fellow deportees?

A. He was in a real sense their pastor, solacing and strengthening individuals, and keeping alive in them the hope for the rebirth of a nation through the survival of a righteous remnant, and planting in their minds dreams of a Jerusalem restored and redeemed.

Q. How does Ezekiel describe his techniques as pastor?

A. "I came to the exiles at Telabib, who dwelt by the river Chebar. And I sat there overwhelmed among them seven days" (3:15). It also appears that his home was a rendezvous for the exiles: "as I sat in my house, with the elders of Judah sitting before me, the hand of the Lord God fell there upon me" (8:1; cf. 14:1; 20:1).

Q. What are the major divisions of the book of Ezekiel?

A. Chapters 1-24 contain oracles of judgment evidently uttered between the first deportation (597 B.C.) and the final destruction (586 B.C.) of Jerusalem. Chapters 25-32 contain oracles on the surrounding nations that were gloating over Judah's downfall. Chapters 33-39 speak of a renewed Judah and one reunited with Israel. Chapters 40-48 deal with the renewal of the national life in conformity with the temple cult.

Q. What is the basic theme of the book?

A. Present judgment is a preparation for future renewal (14:12-23).

Q. What was Ezekiel's concept of the prophetic office?

A. "Son of man, I have made you a watchman for the house of Israel; whenever you hear a word from my mouth, you shall give them warning from me" (3:17). "Son of man, I send you to the people of Israel, to a nation of rebels. . . . The people also are impudent and stubborn. . . . And whether they hear or refuse to hear . . . they will know that there has been a prophet among them" (2:3-5).

Q. What response was he to expect?

A. "But the house of Israel will not listen to you; for they are not willing to listen to me; because all the house of Israel are of a hard forehead and of a stubborn heart" (3:7). "And lo, you are to them like one who sings love songs with a beautiful voice and plays well on an instrument, for they hear what you say, but they will not do it" (33:32).

Q. How is the prophet to conduct himself in the face of such odds?

A. "Whenever you hear a word from my mouth, you shall give them warning from me. If I say to the wicked, O wicked man, you shall surely die, and you do not speak to warn the wicked to turn from his way, that wicked man shall die in his iniquity, but his blood I will require at your hand. But if you warn the wicked to turn from his way, and he does not turn from his way; he shall die in his iniquity, but you will have saved your life" (33:7-9).

Q. What use does the prophet make of symbolic acts?

A. He constructed a replica of a besieged city (4:1-13: "This is a sign for the house of Israel"); for three hundred and ninety days he lay immobilized on his left side and for forty days on his right side, indicating, respectively, the number of years of punishment in store for Israel and Judah; the diet to which he was limited during that period further symbolized the fact that "I will break the staff of bread in Jerusalem; they shall eat bread by weight and with fearfulness; and they shall drink water by measure and in dismay" (4:16). In the presence of people who would recognize a shorn head as a mark of captivity (as prisoners' heads still are sometimes shaved), the prophet was commanded to "take a sharp sword; use it as a barber's razor and pass it over your head and your beard; then take balances for weighing, and divide the hair" (5:1) into three parts, the symbolism of which is: "A third part of you shall die of pestilence . . . famine . . . a third part . . . by the sword . . . a third part I will scatter to all the winds" (5:12). Carrying his baggage on his shoulder, the prophet digs his way through a wall by night, symbolizing the nation's going into exile (12:1-16). The prophet holds up a sword, "polished, sharpened for slaughter" (21:8f), as a sign that the people and princes of Israel are "delivered over to the sword" (21:12). The sword also marks two ways, "For the king of Babylon stands at the parting of the way" (21:18,21). The prophet puts into a boiling cauldron "the choicest pieces of flesh" (24:5,4): "Woe to the bloody city, to the pot whose rust is in it" (24:6).

Q. How does the prophet symbolize the complete identification of himself with his message?

A. There was extended to him a scroll, with "words of lamentation and mourning and woe" (2:10); commanded to "eat this scroll" (3:1), he complied: "I ate it; and it was in my mouth as sweet as honey" (3:3).

Q. How is the prophet's domestic life made to serve his mission?

A. At the sudden death of his wife ("I am about to take the delight of your eyes away from you at a stroke"—24:16), Ezekiel was told, "You shall not mourn or weep nor shall your tears run down" (24:16). This is. for an example to the nation in exile: "Your sons and your daughters whom you left behind shall fall by the sword. And you shall do as I have done: you shall not cover your lips, nor eat the bread of mourners" (25:21f).

Q. Ezekiel has been called "a poet with a gorgeous Oriental imagination luxuriating in details"; how can this be illustrated?

A. "As for the appearance of the wheels and their construction: their appearance was like the gleaming of the chrysolite; and the four had the same likeness, their construction being as it were a wheel within a wheel . . . they went in any of their four directions without turning as they went. The four wheels had rims and they had spokes; and their rims were full of eyes round about" (1:16-18; cf. 10:6-19; 11:22).

Q. What distinctive literary device did the prophet employ?

A. The people said of him: "Is he not a maker of allegories?" (20:49).

Q. What are some examples of his allegorizing?

A. "There were two women, the daughters of one mother; they played the harlot in Egypt. . . . Oholah was the name of the elder and Oholibah the name of her sister. . . . As for their names, Oholah is Samaria, and Oholibah is Jerusalem" (23:2-4; cf. 23:2-49). In Chapter 16 the entire history of Israel is summarized through the tale of a foundling who was adopted into a well-to-do family and then became degenerate. Again, "A great eagle with great wings and long pinions, rich in plumage of many colors, came to Lebanon and took the top of the cedar; he broke off the topmost of its young twigs and carried it to a land of trade, and set it in a city of merchants . . . there was another great eagle with great wings and much plumage; and behold, this vine bent its roots toward him, and shot forth its branches toward him that he might water it" (17:3f,7); the prophet thus symbolically describes the policies of Babylon and Egypt.

Q. What use did Ezekiel make of parable?

A. "Like the wood of the vine among the trees of the forest, which I have given to the fire for fuel, so will I give up the inhabitants of Jerusalem" (15:6). "Your mother was like a vine in a vineyard" (19:10; cf. 19:10-14).

Q. Who are Gog and Magog (38:1; cf. 38:1-39:29)?

A. Symbolic representations epitomizing heathen powers ("Behold, I am against you, O Gog"—38:3).

Q. What is the larger significance of Gog and Magog?

A. Their appearance here, in Chapters 38 and 39, is the first appearance within the book of Ezekiel of apocalyptic, that form of literature later elaborated in Daniel and Revelation; Gog and Magog reappear in Revelation 20:8.

Q. What human characteristics does Ezekiel refer to in his attempt to picture God in terms that men know?

A. "A likeness as it were of a human form" (1:26). "As I live, says the Lord God, surely with a mighty hand and an outstretched arm, and with wrath poured out, I will be king over you" (20:33). "I will turn my face from them" (7:22; cf. 14:8); "my eye will not spare, nor will I have pity; and though they cry in my ears with a loud voice, I will not hear them" (8:18); "this is the place of my throne and the place of the soles of my feet, where I will dwell in the midst of the people of Israel for ever" (43:7).

Q. What moral qualities does Ezekiel attribute to God?

A. Pity (16:6); compassion ("As a shepherd seeks out his flock when some of his sheep have been scattered abroad, so will I seek out my sheep"—34:12); revulsion from wickedness ("When she carried on her harlotry so openly and flaunted her nakedness, I turned in disgust from her"—23:18; cf. 36:17).

Q. How does God act to vindicate his own character?

A. "You shall know that I am the Lord" (6:7). "I will manifest my holiness among you in the sight of the nations" (20:41). "O Sidon . . . I will manifest my glory in the midst of you" (28:22). "I will vindicate the holiness of my great name, which has been profaned among the nations" (36:23). "I will bring you against my land, that the nations may know me, when through you, O Gog, I vindicate my holiness before their eyes" (38:16; cf. 20:9,14,22,44). "So I will show my greatness and my holiness and make myself known in the eyes of many nations. Then they will know that I am the Lord" (38:23).

Q. What kinds of religious abuses had been going on in Jerusalem?

A. When the prophet entered the temple, "there, portrayed upon the wall round about, were all kinds of creeping things, and loathsome beasts, and all the idols of the house of Israel" (8:10); there, too, "sat women weeping for Tammuz" (8:14) [Tammuz was "the Sumerian deity of spring vegetation"] and men, "with their backs to the temple of the Lord . . . worshiping the sun toward the east" (8:16). "Woe to the women who sew magic bands upon all wrists, and make veils for the heads of persons of every stature" (13:18) [a reference to women who practiced divination].

Q. What moral wrongs does Ezekiel expose?

A. "If he begets a son who is a robber, a shedder of blood, who does none of these duties, but eats upon the mountains, defiles his neighbor's wife, oppresses the poor and needy, commits robbery, does not restore the pledge, lifts up his eyes to the idols, commits abomination, lends at interest, and takes increase; shall he then live?" (18:10-12). "Father and mother are treated with contempt in you; the sojourner suffers extortion in your midst; the fatherless and the widow are wronged in you" (22:7). "And I sought for a man among them who should build up the wall and stand in the breach before me for the land, that I should not destroy it; but I found none" (22:30).

Q. What does Ezekiel say about the religious leaders of his people?

A. He describes them as faithless shepherds who look after themselves rather than after the flock (34:1-6).

Q. What is Ezekiel's outlook on Israel's history?

A. Other prophets looked back to what they regarded as an ideal past from which the nation had fallen away. Ezekiel holds that Israel has been rebellious from the outset: "they and their fathers have transgressed against me to this very day" (2:3); "nor did they forsake the idols of Egypt" (20:8).

Q. Did the prophets who were his contemporaries agree with his assessment of the situation?

A. "Say to those who prophesy out of their own minds: 'Hear the word of the Lord!' . . . Woe to the foolish prophets who follow their own spirit, and have seen nothing! . . . My hand will be against the prophets who see delusive visions and who give lying divinations" (13: 2f,9). "And her prophets have daubed for them with whitewash, seeing false visions and divining lies for them, saying, 'Thus says the Lord God,' when the Lord has not spoken" (22:28).

Q. What advice did Ezekiel have for King Zedekiah, who thought an alliance with Egypt might mean liberation from Babylon?

A. That his only reasonable policy was to acknowledge his obligation to the Babylonians: "in Babylon he shall die. Pharaoh and his mighty army and great company will not help him in war" (17:16f).

Q. What future does Ezekiel envision for the nation he loved?

A. "And the land that was desolate shall be tilled, instead of being the desolation that it was. . . . And they will say, 'This land that was desolate has become like the garden of Eden' " (36:34,36). Chapters 40-

48, sometimes referred to as Ezekiel's Utopia, picture a restored Jerusalem in which the idea of the holiness of God is related to every facet of the common life.

Q. What does Ezekiel say about Israel's neighbor, Tyre?

A. "Your rowers have brought you out
    into the high seas.
The east wind has wrecked you
    in the heart.of the seas" (27:26; cf. 26:1-27:36).
"The merchants among the peoples hiss at you;
    you have come to a dreadful end
    and shall be no more for ever" (27:36).

Q. What does Ezekiel say to the prince of Tyre?

A. "Because your heart is proud,
    and you have said, 'I am a god' . . .
    you shall die the death of the slain . . .
    all who know you among the peoples
        are appalled at you;
    you have come to a dreadful end
        and shall be no more for ever" (28:1,8,19).

Q. Of what other value are the oracles on Tyre?

A. They form an excellent description of the wealth of an ancient city.

Q. What does Ezekiel say about Sidon?

A. "Behold, I am against you, O Sidon,
    and I will manifest my glory in the midst of you" (28:20).

Q. What does the prophet say about Pharaoh?

A. "You consider yourself a lion among the nations
    but you are like a dragon in the seas; . . .
    I will haul you up in my dragnet.
And I will cast you on the ground" (32:2-4).

Q. What was Ezekiel's distinctive contribution to religion?

A. The concept of personal responsibility: "Behold, all souls are mine; the soul of the father as well as the soul of the son is mine: the soul that sins shall die" (18:4). This means that a good father is not to be punished for a wicked son, nor an evil father spared for the sake of a good son: "The son shall not suffer for the iniquity of the father, nor the father suffer for the iniquity of the son; the righteousness of the righteous shall

be upon himself, and the wickedness of the wicked shall be upon himself"
(18:20).

Q. What changed condition is envisioned for the people?

A. "A new heart I will give you, and a new spirit I will put within
you; and I will take out of your flesh the heart of stone and give you a
heart of flesh" (36:26).

Q. What is to be the symbol of this renewal?

A. "I will sprinkle clean water upon you, and you shall be clean
from all your uncleanness" (36:25).

Q. What is Ezekiel's most famous vision?

A. "The Lord . . . set me down in the midst of the valley; it was
full of bones" (37:1). The dry bones symbolize the decimated nation:
"these bones are the whole house of Israel" (37:11). The question is,
"can these bones live?" (37:3)—that is, can the nation be revived? The
answer, happily, is: "the bones came together, bone to its bone. And as
I looked, there were sinews on them, and flesh had come upon them, and
skin had covered them . . . and the breath came into them, and they
lived" (37:7-10).

Q. Which of the prophet's visions greatly influenced the New Testament?

A. The picture of the New Jerusalem, in Revelation 21:1-22:5,
owes much to Ezekiel's vision of the restored city in Ezekiel 40:1-43:5
(note the walls, the gates, the court "foursquare," the measuring rod, and
the presence of God's glory: "the sound of his coming was like the sound
of many waters"—43:2; cf. Revelation 19:6; 14:2).

Q. What other passages from Ezekiel are borrowed by the author of
Revelation?

A. "My dwelling place shall be with them, and I will be their God,
and they shall be my people" (37:27; cf. Revelation 21:3). Revelation
2:17 promises to each believer "a new name," and Revelation 22:4 says,
"his name shall be on their foreheads"; Ezekiel's book closes with the
assurance that the entire city shall have a new name: "And the name of
the city henceforth shall be, The Lord is there" (48:35). The "four living
creatures" of Revelation 4:6-8 are borrowed from Ezekiel 1:5-14.

Q. What is symbolized by "the four living creatures"?

A. They seem to represent God's sovereignty over all created life.
Man has been commissioned to subdue the earth; the lion is the most

powerful of wild beasts; the ox is the strongest of domesticated animals; the eagle is king of the air.

Q. What worthies in other parts of the Old Testament are referred to by Ezekiel?

A. "Noah, Daniel, and Job" (14:14,20; cf. 28:3).

Q. What other section of the Old Testament is similar to Ezekiel?

A. The Holiness Code, of Leviticus 17-26, shows similarities in spirit and outlook.

Q. What proverbial expressions has Ezekiel given to our speech?

A. "All knees will be weak as water" (21:7); "a wheel within a wheel" (1:16). "The fathers have eaten sour grapes, and the children's teeth are set on edge" (18:2).

Q. What phrase, appearing often in Ezekiel, became Jesus' favorite self-designation?

A. "Son of man" (Ezekiel 2:1, etc.), always used by Jesus of himself and not used of him by others, occurs sixty-nine times in the Synoptic Gospels.

Q. What passage is a classical denunciation of false prophets?

A. Ezekiel 13:1-16.

Q. What section gives a good summary of the entire book?

A. Ezekiel 14:12-23, with its insistence that current catastrophe is a prelude to future renewal and that the latter will come through a purified remnant, "survivors to lead out sons and daughters."

Q. What passage relates the history of Israel in terms of a foundling child who, having been adopted into a well-to-do family, turned out badly?

A. Chapter 16.

Q. Where does the author set forth his philosophy of history?

A. Chapter 17 makes it clear that, however great their power, neither the Babylonian king nor the Egyptian Pharaoh holds the key to human destiny; it is God who decides among the nations.

Q. What natural imagery forms the basis for a parable of God's sovereignty?

A. A "sprig from the lofty top of the cedar" grows into a noble tree providing shade and shelter (17:22-24).

Q. What passage sets forth the faithfulness of God that continues in spite of the faithlessness of men?

A. "I have no pleasure in the death of anyone, says the Lord God; so turn and live" (18:32).

Q. In what way does Ezekiel appear to be more pessimistic than other prophets?

A. The other prophets buttressed their demands of righteousness with references to an earlier and better day, when the nation was obedient; Ezekiel, however, interprets all the national history in terms of broken covenants and "the abominations of their fathers" (20:4).

Q. To what does the prophet attribute the national failure?

A. The desire for conformity: "Let us be like the nations, like the tribes of the countries, and worship wood and stone" (20:32).

Q. What is the Song of the Sword?

A. "A sword, a sword is sharpened
            and also polished,
    sharpened for slaughter,
            polished to flash like lightning!" (21:9f).

Q. To what does the polished sword refer?

A. To God's judgment, manifest at one time in the military might of the Babylonian conqueror (21:18-22), at another in that of the Chaldean (21:28-32).

Q. What section enumerates the failures by which each supposedly responsible group in society has become irresponsible?

A. Chapter 22.

Q. How completely had the nation abandoned its righteous standards?

A. "I sought for a man among them who should build up the wall and stand in the breach before me for the land that I should not destroy it; but I found none" (22:30).

Q. How does the prophet picture the position accorded him by his contemporaries?

A. "They come to you as people come, and they sit before you as my people, and they hear what you say but they will not do it; for with their lips they show much love, but their heart is set on their gain. And lo, you are to them like one who sings love songs with a beautiful voice and plays well on an instrument, for they hear what you say, but they will not do it" (33:31f).

Q. What ruler is envisioned as returning to lend stability to the nation?

A. "My servant David shall be king over them" (37:24).

Q. What economic safeguards are envisioned for the future?

A. "The prince shall not take any of the inheritance of the people, thrusting them out of their property; he shall give his sons their inheritance out of his own property, so that none of my people shall be dispossessed of his property" (46:18).

THE BOOK OF DANIEL

Q. Who is the author of Daniel?

A. The title evidently refers to a book about Daniel, rather than to a book by Daniel; the writer is not named.

Q. When was Daniel written?

A. One of the latest Old Testament books, it probably came into being during the second century B.C.

Q. Why was Daniel written?

A. To encourage the Hebrews who were having to undergo another persecution, this one at the hands of Antiochus the Great, by recounting the deeds of national heroes who lived at an earlier time.

Q. What is the theme of the book of Daniel?

A. "The Most High rules the kingdom of men, and gives it to whom he will, and sets over it the lowliest of men" (4:17).

Q. When did Daniel live?

A. The stories about him place him in the era of the Babylonian exile; he is represented as having been among those deported by Nebuchadnezzar, king of Babylon; the first deportation carried out under Nebuchadnezzar occurred in 597 B.C.

Q. Where else is Daniel mentioned in the Bible?

A. The lists of deportees who returned from Babylon include Daniel, son of Ithamar (Ezra 8:2; cf. Nehemiah 10:6). In Ezekiel 14:14 the prophet, condemning the iniquity of the land, hears God say: ". . . even if these three men, Noah, Daniel, and Job, were in it, they would deliver but their own lives by their righteousness." Daniel is there spoken of as one who lived in some remote and heroic age of the past.

Q. What evidences are there that the author was not particularly concerned with historical precision?

A. He speaks of Belshazzar as Nebuchadnezzar's son (5:2) and immediate successor, whereas the historic Belshazzar was the son of Nabonidus. The author speaks as if the Medes were the conquerors of the Babylonians and that the conquest was carried out by Darius the Mede (5:31). Historically, Cyrus the Persian was the conqueror of Babylon, and Darius I was a Persian who began to reign about 522 B.C.

Q. What is the literary nature of the book of Daniel?

A. Chapter 1-6 are stories in which Daniel interprets the dreams of others; chapters 7-12 contain visions of Daniel himself. The book was originally in two languages: 1:1-2:4a and Chapters 8-12 in Hebrew, the remainder in Aramaic, perhaps in imitation of the bilingual character of Ezra (cf. Ezra 4:7).

Q. Who was deported at the same time as Daniel?

A. Hananiah, Mishael, and Azariah. At the Babylonian court the four of them were renamed Belteshazzar, Shadrach, Meshach, and Abednego. Of these, Daniel continues to be known mainly by his Hebrew name, but his three companions by the names bestowed by the Babylonians.

Q. What treatment was given these youths?

A. Chosen to serve in the king's palace because they were "handsome and skilful in all wisdom, endowed with knowledge, understanding learning" (1:4), they were placed in training "for three years," to learn "the letters and language of the Chaldeans" (1:5,4).

Q. What dietary problem faced the young men?

A. "The king assigned them a daily portion of the rich food which the king ate, and of the wine which he drank" (1:5). The Hebrew youths asked to be put upon a simpler regimen: "Test your servants for ten days; let us be given vegetables to eat and water to drink" (1:12).

Q. What was the outcome of the test?

A. "They were better in appearance and fatter in flesh than all the youths who ate the king's rich food" (1:15).

Q. What was the result of the education given the young men?

A. "In every matter of wisdom and understanding concerning which the king inquired of them, he found them ten times better than all the magicians and enchanters that were in all his kingdom" (1:20).

Q. How did Daniel further gain the king's favor?

A. Troubled by a dream he had had, the king demanded that his wise men tell him the meaning of his dream without his divulging the contents; Daniel assures the king that "No wise men, enchanters, magicians, or astrologers can show to the king the mystery which the king has asked, but there is a God in heaven who reveals mysteries" (2:27f). Instructed from that source, Daniel outlines the dream: a great image, frightening in appearance, made of mixed metals, its feet partly of clay, is destroyed by a stone that "became a great mountain" (2:31-36).

Q. What is the symbolism of the "great image," with head of gold, breast and arms of silver, belly and thighs of bronze, legs of iron, feet partly iron and partly clay? (2:31-33).

A. It is not a representation of anything spatial, but rather an attempt to picture the course of world history: the successive segments and metals will appear as the centuries unfold; when God destroys the last kingdom ("smote the image on its feet of iron and clay"—2:34), he simultaneously destroys all the rest. That the Hebrews dared such a mental picture suggests how little experience they had had at manufacturing images; the Greeks would never have thought of so awkward a symbol.

Q. What was the meaning of this dream?

A. Daniel interprets it to be a portent of four successive kingdoms, to be followed by "a kingdom which shall never be destroyed" (2:36-45).

Q. What promotion did this win for Daniel?

A. "Then the king gave Daniel high honors and many great gifts, and made him ruler over the whole province" (2:48).

Q. What form of worship did Nebuchadnezzar introduce?

A. He made "an image of gold, whose height was sixty cubits and its breadth six cubits" (3:1), requiring all his subjects, when the signal was given, "to fall down and worship the golden image" (3:5).

Q. How did Shadrach, Meshach, and Abednego respond to the command to worship the image?

A. "Our God whom we serve is able to deliver us . . . and he will deliver us. . . . But if not, be it known to you, O king, that we will not serve your gods or worship the golden image which you have set up" (3:17f).

Q. What punishment was meted out to the defiant ones?

A. They were cast into "the burning fiery furnace," which had been "heated seven times more than it was wont to be heated." Though the fire slew those men who "thrust them in," it had no effect upon the three young men except to destroy their bonds; the king saw them walking unhurt "in the midst of the fire," accompanied by a fourth whose appearance was "like a son of the gods" (3:25).

Q. What then becomes of the young men?

A. The king promotes them to a position of authority, and makes a decree that anyone in the future who speaks anything against them "shall be torn limb from limb" (3:29).

Q. What dream of the king is Daniel next called upon to interpret?

A. That of a great tree suddenly cut down, only "the stump of its roots" left; the man symbolized by the stump is to have his mind replaced by a beast's mind. Daniel interprets the tree as representing the king's greatness; the king, however, is to "be driven from among men . . . and made to eat grass like an ox" (4:25). Daniel concludes the interpretation with a warning: "break off your sins by practicing righteousness, and your iniquities by showing mercy to the oppressed, that there may perhaps be a lengthening of your tranquillity" (4:27). Within a year the king did lose his mind, "was driven from among men, and ate grass like an ox" (4:33); his reason, however, was restored; reinstated in his kingdom, he was moved to "praise and extol and honor the King of heaven" (4:37).

Q. What is significant about Daniel's declaration that "the Most High rules the kingdom of men" (4:17,25)?

A. He affirmed this at a time when all the facts of history seemed to deny it. This was the faith that sustained Israel in all its adversity.

Q. What vision comes to Belshazzar?

A. At "a great feast for a thousand of his lords" (5:1), he used the vessels brought from the Jerusalem temple as drinking vessels (5:2-4). "Immediately the fingers of a man's hand appeared and wrote" a strange message on the palace wall. The frightened king summons Daniel, who interprets it to mean: "You have been weighed in the balances and found wanting" (5:27).

Q. How do the people around Darius, successor to Belshazzar, seek to dislodge Daniel from his position of power?

A. They obtain a decree establishing a loyalty oath "that whoever makes petition to any god or man for thirty days," except to the king, "shall be cast into the den of lions" (6:7). Daniel defies the edict, continues to worship the God of Israel, and is thrown into the den of lions, but "God sent his angel and shut the lions' mouths," and the king issues a decree proclaiming the God of Daniel to be "the living God" (6:26).

Q. What was the vision that Daniel himself had in the first year of Belshazzar's reign?

A. Four strange beasts coming up out of the sea: a lion with the wings of an eagle; a bear with "three ribs in its mouth"; a leopard with four heads; "a fourth beast, terrible and dreadful and exceedingly strong." Recalling the experience, Daniel says: ". . . my thoughts greatly alarmed me, and my color changed; but I kept the matter in my mind" (7:28); his conclusion was that the beasts represented kings of the earth whose "dominion was taken away" (7:12). There comes, then, "one like a son of man":

". . . his dominion is an everlasting dominion,
      which shall not pass away" (7:14).

Q. What was Daniel's vision in the third year of King Belshazzar's reign?

A. A ram, with two horns, "charging westward and northward and southward" (8:4), and a he-goat with "a conspicuous horn between his eyes"; the he-goat trampled upon the ram, but when "the he-goat magnified himself exceedingly . . . the great horn was broken, and instead of it there came up four conspicuous horns" (8:8). From one of them "came forth a little horn, which grew exceedingly great" (8:9). The angel Gabriel interprets this for Daniel in terms of world history: the two horns of the ram were the kings of Media and Persia; the he-goat was the king of Greece; the great horn between his eyes represented the first king (evidently an allusion to Alexander the Great); "four kings shall rise from his nation, but not with his power" (8:22—Alexander's domain, following his death, was divided into four parts). Then "a king of bold countenance" shall arise, one who "shall cause fearful destruction" (8:23f—apparently an allusion to Antiochus, ruler of part of the domain that had been Alexander's, who sought to impose Hellenism upon the Hebrews in the second century B.C.)

Q. How is the New Testament doctrine of grace anticipated in a prayer that Daniel offers?

A. A prayer confessing the sins of his people and asking for deliverance is concluded by Daniel with these words: "we do not present our supplications before thee on the ground of our righteousness, but on the ground of thy great mercy" (9:18).

Q. What description does Gabriel give of the duration of the exile to which Daniel and his people are being subjected?

A. "Seventy weeks of years" (9:24)—that is, 490 years, divided into three eras of seven weeks (49 years), sixty-two weeks (434 years), and one week (7 years). Though this chronology does not fit the known history, the last week plainly refers to Antiochus: "upon the wing of abominations shall come one who makes desolate" (9:27).

Q. What vision came to Daniel in the third year of the reign of Cyrus, king of Persia?

A. A man, "his face like the appearance of lightning, his eyes like flaming torches" (10:6) speaks of four kings to arise in Persia (a reference seemingly to Cyrus, Cambyses, Darius, and Xerxes, the four Persian kings named in the Old Testament); further allusions refer to the events that followed the divisions of Alexander's empire and led to the tyranny of Antiochus, "a contemptible person to whom royal majesty has not been given" (11:21), who "shall exalt himself and magnify himself above every god" (11:36). This portends for the Hebrew people "a time of trouble, such as has never been since there was a nation" (12:1).

Q. With what word of enduring hope does the vision conclude?

A. "Your people shall be delivered . . . and many of those who sleep in the dust of the earth shall awake, some to everlasting life, and some to shame and everlasting contempt. And those who are wise shall shine like the brightness of the firmament; and those who turn many to righteousness, like the stars for ever and ever" (12:1-13).

Q. What is the conclusion of the book of Daniel?

A. "Blessed is he who waits and comes to the thousand three hundred and thirty-five days. But go your way till the end; and you shall rest, and shall stand in your allotted place at the end of the days" (12:12f).

Q. What is the larger significance of this?

A. If Daniel was, as many believe, the last book of the Old Testament, then this represents the concluding word of the Old Testament: the pattern of world history is confused, but one can wait in confidence that God will make sense of it.

Q. What parts of the Old Testament are drawn upon for the prayer attributed to Daniel in 9:4-19?

A. Ezra 9; Nehemiah 1,9; I Kings 3; Jeremiah 26,32,44.

Q. What is the author's philosophy of history?

A. At a time when all the facts seemed against it, he continually affirms his belief that "the Most High rules the kingdom of men" (4:17, 25).

THE BOOK OF HOSEA

Q. Who was Hosea?

A. He identifies himself (1:1) as "the son of Beeri," but we have no information about Beeri.

Q. Where did Hosea live?

A. He was a native of the northern kingdom (under "the house of Jehu" and "the kingdom of the house of Israel"—1:4).

Q. How does his native countryside figure in his work?

A. Mizpah (5:1), Gilead (6:8), Gilgal (12:11), Gibeah and Ramah (5:8), valley of Jezreel (1:5), Shechem (6:9), and Samaria (7:1) are the places, often mentioned, in which the prophet carries out his mission.

Q. What of Hosea's family background?

A. The references to priests (4:6ff; 5:1; 6:9) and the things with which priests are concerned (altars—8:11; "unclean food"—9:3) have led to the conjecture that he was himself a member of the hereditary priestly class.

Q. What is known of Hosea's personal life?

A. He was married to Gomer (1:2f), and the father of children (1:3).

Q. What symbolic names were given to his children?

A. Jezreel ("I will punish the house of Jehu for the blood of Jezreel"—1:4); Not pitied ("for I will no more have pity on the house of Israel"—1:6); Not my people ("for you are not my people and I am not your God"—1:9).

Q. What happened to Hosea's home?

A. His wife proved faithless ("I will go after my lovers"—2:5; cf. 1:3; 3:1).

Q. Did this mean the end of Hosea's love for her?

A. No. When her lovers had finished with her and put her up for sale as a slave, Hosea reports, "I bought her for fifteen shekels of silver and a homer and a lethech of barley" (3:2).

Q. How did this affect his work as a prophet?

A. His call to be a prophet came through this human relationship; he saw that the infidelity of his wife had its counterpart in the life of his people: idolatry is conjugal infidelity ("the land commits great harlotry by forsaking the Lord"—1:3).

Q. What punishment is deserved alike by idolatry and adultery?

A. "I will put an end to all her mirth . . .
  and I will lay waste her vines and her fig trees,
    of which she said,
  'These are my hire,
    which my lovers have given me.'
I will make them a forest,
  and the beasts of the field shall devour them" (2:11f).

Q. Will this deserved doom descend upon the guilty?

A. "And I will have pity upon Not pitied,
    and I will say to Not my people, 'You are my people' "
    (2:23).

Q. How did Hosea's personal domestic tragedy help him to interpret God's relationship to his people?

A. Hosea reasoned that if he, a mortal man, could continue to love one who had wronged him so deeply, then God must be even more patient and long-suffering with the sinful human race. Hosea is therefore the first to speak of God as love:

  "When Israel was a child, I loved him, . . .
  I led them with cords of compassion,
    with the bands of love" (11:1,4).
  "I will heal their faithlessness;
    I will love them freely,
    for my anger has turned from them" (14:4).

Q. What epithet does Hosea apply to God's affection?

A. He speaks repeatedly of "steadfast love" (2:19; 4:1; 6:4,6; 10:12; 12:6).

Q. What is to be man's response to God's steadfast love?

A. "Come, let us return to the Lord;

for he has torn, that he may heal us;

he has stricken, and he will bind us up" (6:1).

Q. What imagery from the natural world does Hosea use to describe God's affection?

A. "His going forth is sure as the dawn;

he will come to us as the showers,

as the spring rains that water the earth" (6:3).

"I will be as the dew to Israel;

he shall blossom as the lily,

he shall strike root as the poplar" (14:5).

Q. What imagery from the family does Hosea use?

A. God is the bridegroom, Israel is the bride; God is the father, Israel is the son.

Q. How is this relationship sealed?

A. Through a covenant, which Israel has broken (6:7; 8:1; 9:10).

Q. How does ignorance of the Torah result in the broken covenant?

A. "My people are destroyed for lack of knowledge" (4:6).

Q. How does the broken covenant manifest itself in the nation's life?

A. "There is swearing, lying, killing, stealing, and committing adultery;

they break all bounds and murder follows murder" (4:2).

"You have loved a harlot's hire

upon all threshing floors" (9:1; cf. 4:12ff, 17ff; 5:3f; 9:1; 13:ff).

Q. To what forms of corruption in public worship did the broken covenant lead?

A. "They kept sacrificing to the Baals,

and burning incense to idols" (11:2).

"I have spurned your calf, O Samaria" (8:5); "gold which they used for Baal" (2:8; cf. 10:5).

Q. How did the broken covenant manifest itself in the political sphere?

A. In separation between northern and southern kingdoms ("They made kings, but not through me"—8:4; cf. 13:9-11).

Q. What does Hosea have to say regarding foreign policy?

A. "Assyria shall not save us" (14:3).

"For they have gone up to Assyria,
> a wild ass wandering alone" (8:9).

"Ephraim is like a dove,
> silly and without sense,

calling to Egypt, going to Assyria" (7:11).

Q. What picture does Hosea draw of the doom that awaits a people that turns its back upon God?

A. He sees a land ravaged by drought, parched by the wind, decimated by war (13:15f).

Q. What course of action is open to the faithless nation?

A. Repentance, with the prophet providing a litany for the penitent:

"I will return again to my place,
> until they acknowledge their guilt and seek my face,
> and in their distress they seek me, saying,
'Come, let us return to the Lord' " (5:15; 6:1).

"Return, O Israel, to the Lord your God,
for you have stumbled because of your iniquity" (14:1);

". . . for the ways of the Lord are right
> and the upright walk in them,
> but the transgressors stumble in them" (14:9).

Q. How will God's grace manifest itself to the penitent nation?

A. The land ravaged by drought "shall blossom as the lily" (14:5); the land parched by wind "shall flourish as a garden" (14:7); the faithlessness of the people will be healed (14:4), and in love God's anger will be turned away (14:4).

Q. What is Hosea's idea of the true God?

A. In contrast with the gods of their Canaanite neighbors, dying and rising with the cycle of vegetation, Israel's God is a "living God" (1:10).

Q. What allusions does Hosea make to the earlier history of his people?

A. God's word, "I would redeem them" (7:13), rests upon the deliverance wrought at the time of the Exodus;

"Samaria's king shall perish,
> like a chip on the face of the waters" (10:7)

may echo Exodus 32:20; the reference to God as healer (11:3) recalls Exodus 15:26; 9:10-14 celebrates the wonder that God should have chosen Israel; 12:13 recalls that "By a prophet the Lord brought Israel up from Egypt."

Q. What picturesque term does Hosea use regarding a man-made idol?

A. He calls it "not God" (8:6).

Q. How is Jesus' word in Luke 11:21f anticipated in Hosea?

A. The prophet warns (8:14) that palaces and fortified cities offer no security to a nation that has forgotten its Maker (cf. 1:7).

Q. What use of Hosea's work is made in the New Testament?

A. The reference to changing "Not my people" to "You are my people" (2:23) is cited in Romans 9:25 and I Peter 2:10. In I Corinthians 15:55 Paul quotes Hosea 13:14. The saying in 11:1, "Out of Egypt I called my son," is, in Matthew 2:15, given a new setting, making it applicable to the holy family's escape from Herod's wrath.

Q. What title given to Christ is derived from Hosea?

A. One New Testament term for Christ is "the bridegroom" (Mark 2:19f; John 3:29; cf. Matthew 22:1-14; 25:1-13; Ephesians 5:25; II Corinthians 11:2; Revelation 19:7; 21:9; 22:17). Hosea often employs the marriage bond to symbolize the relationship between God and Israel ("I will betroth you to me in faithfulness"—2:20).

Q. What classical expression has Hosea given to our language?

A. "For they sow the wind,
　　　and they shall reap the whirlwind" (8:7).

Q. To what period in Hebrew history did Hosea look back as one in which the people did God's will?

A. The era of the wilderness wanderings, after the nation "came out of the land of Egypt" (2:15).

Q. To what saying of Hosea did Jesus direct the attention of his hearers?

A. When he said, "Go and learn what this means, 'I desire mercy, and not sacrifice' " (Matthew 9:13), he was citing Hosea 6:6.

Q. How does Hosea summarize his nation's history during the period of the monarchy?

A. He hears God say:

"I have given you kings in my anger,
and I have taken them away in my wrath" (13:11).

Q. Moses is commonly thought of as a lawgiver; how does Hosea refer to him?

A. "By a prophet the Lord brought Israel up from Egypt" (12:13; cf. Deuteronomy 34:10).

THE BOOK OF JOEL

Q. Who was Joel?

A. In 1:1 he gives his own name and his father's name: "Joel, the son of Pethuel"; beyond this, nothing else is known; Pethuel is a name that does not occur elsewhere.

Q. When did Joel live?

A. Probably in the early part of the fourth century B.C.

Q. What reasons are there for dating the book then?

A. For his contemporaries, the book is dated with reference to a plague of locusts so devastating that the daily sacrifices were discontinued (1:13); it was evidently this disaster that summoned the prophet to his work. Although locust plagues returned with some regularity, this one appears to have been of unprecedented proportions—yet we have no way of dating it. The prophet writes, however, at a time when the people of Israel have been "scattered among the nations" (3:2); this implies a date after the return from exile. When the prophet writes, too, the Phoenicians are engaged in the slave trade, having "sold the people of Judah and Jerusalem to the Greeks" (3:6); Greek contact with the Phoenicians appears to nave begun in the fourth century B.C.

Q. What use does Joel make of other prophets?

A. 3:10 is a parody on the well-known dream of peace, pictured in Isaiah 2:2-4 and Micah 4:1-3. The picture of a fountain coming "forth from the house of the Lord" (3:18) is probably an echo of Ezekiel 47:1f. Joel's closing words, "the Lord dwells in Zion" (3:21) appear to be taken from Ezekiel 48:35; 2:2 quotes Zephaniah 1:15. 3:16 and 3:18 may be compared with Amos 1:2 and Amos 9:13.

Q. What kinds of locusts made up the plague?

A. Four kinds are enumerated: the "cutting locust" (mentioned also in Amos 4:9); the "swarming locust"; the "hopping locust" (mentioned also in Psalm 105:34; Jeremiah 51:14; Nahum 3:16); and the "destroying locust" (mentioned also in I Kings 8:37; Psalm 78:46; Isaiah 33:4); while different Hebrew words are used for the several kinds of locust, they may apply to different stages in the life cycle of the devourer.

Q. What figure of speech is used with regard to the locusts?

A. 1:6 describes them as "a nation . . . powerful and without number," just as ants and badgers are spoken of in Proverbs 30:25f as "a people"; in 2:5 the locusts are spoken of as "like a powerful army drawn up for battle"—an army that leaves in its wake nothing but a scorched earth.

Q. What use is made in the New Testament of the work of the prophet Joel?

A. Peter's sermon on the Day of Pentecost (Acts 2:16-21) is an interpretation of Joel 2:28-32, applying it to the events of Peter's own time.

Q. What devastation is wrought by the locusts?

A. Trees and vines are withered; fields are dried up; cattle and sheep can find no pasture. The gloom and misery left by the hordes of swarming creatures are summed up in 1:12:

"The vine withers,
　　the fig tree languishes.
Pomegranate, palm, and apple,
　　all the trees of the field are withered;
and gladness fails
　　from the sons of men."

Q. What historical analogy do the locusts bring to the prophet's mind?

A. The Day of the Lord, to which the people looked forward as a time of national triumph and supremacy, will rather be a time of judgment upon all the wicked, in Israel as well as elsewhere:

"Before them peoples are in anguish,
　　all faces grow pale" (2:6).

Q. What judgment does Joel pronounce upon nations other than his own?

A. "What are you to me, Tyre and Sidon, and all the regions of
Philistia?" (3:4).
"Egypt shall become a desolation
and Edom a desolate wilderness" (3:19).

Q. What elements of hope are there in the book?

A. God's wrath may be averted by a penitent nation,
"for he is gracious and merciful,
slow to anger, and abounding in steadfast love" (2:13);
there is promised also an outpouring of God's Spirit, as a result of which
". . . your sons and your daughters shall prophesy,
your old men shall dream dreams,
and your young men shall see visions" (2:28).

Q. To what still more ancient prophecy does this hark back?

A. Moses looked for the time when "all the Lord's people" would
be "prophets, that the Lord would put his spirit upon them" (Numbers
11:29).

Q. What future felicity does Joel envision for his people?

A. "In that day
the mountains shall drip sweet wine,
and the hills shall flow with milk,
and all the stream beds of Judah
shall flow with water;
and a fountain shall come forth from the house of the Lord
and water the valley of Shittim" (3:18).

Q. What phrases from Joel have been used as literary titles in the
modern world?

A. "The valley of decision," which occurs twice in 3:14, and "the
years which the . . . locust has eaten" (2:25).

THE BOOK OF AMOS

Q. Who was Amos?

A. One of "the shepherds of Tekoa" (1:1), Tekoa being a Judean
village six miles south of Bethlehem.

Q. When did Amos live?

A. "In the days of Uzziah king of Judah and in the days of Jeroboam . . . king of Israel" (1:1). Uzziah reigned from 767 to 740 B.C., and Jeroboam II from 782 to 753 B.C.

Q. Did Amos belong to the class of professional religious leaders?

A. "I am no prophet, nor a prophet's son; but I am a herdsman, and a dresser of sycamore trees" (7:14).

Q. How does the work of Amos differ from that of prophets before his time?

A. He is the first to commit his oracles to writing.

Q. Where and how did Amos receive his call to be a prophet?

A. "The Lord took me from following the flock, and . . . said . . . 'Go, prophesy to my people Israel' " (7:15).

Q. What figures of speech derived from his peasant origin serve Amos as vehicles of truth?

A. "Does a lion roar in the forest,
> when he has no prey?
Does a young lion cry out from his den,
> if he has taken nothing?
Does a bird fall in a snare on the earth
> when there is no trap for it?" (3:3-5).
"Behold, I will press you down in your place,
> as a cart full of sheaves presses down" (2:13);
". . . as if a man fled from a lion,
> and a bear met him;
or went into the house and leaned with his hand against the wall,
> and a serpent bit him" (5:19).
"As the shepherd rescues from the mouth of a lion two legs, or a piece of an ear, so shall the people of Israel who dwell in Samaria be rescued" (3:12).

Q. How does nature provide imagery for a description of Amos' own call?

A. "Surely the Lord does nothing,
> without revealing his secret
> to his servants the prophets.
The lion has roared;
> who will not fear?

The Lord has spoken;
    who can but prophesy?" (3:7f).

Q. What was the political condition of his people in the time Amos lived?

A. "Woe to those who are at ease in Zion,
and to those who feel secure on the mountain of Samaria . . .
who drink wine in bowls,
    and anoint themselves with the finest oils,
        but are not grieved over the ruin of Joseph!" (6:1,6).

Q. What were the social conditions of the time?

A. "I will smite the winter house with the summer house;
    and the houses of ivory shall perish,
and the great houses shall come to an end" (3:15);
". . . you trample upon the poor
and take from him exactions of wheat" (5:11).
"Woe to those who lie upon beds of ivory,
    and stretch themselves upon their couches,
and eat lambs from the flock,
    and calves from the midst of the stall;
who sing idle songs to the sound of the harp" (6:4f).
"Hear this, you who trample upon the needy,
    and bring the poor of the land to an end,
saying, 'When will the new moon be over,
    that we may sell grain?
And the sabbath,
    that we may offer wheat for sale,
that we may make the ephah small and the shekel great,
    and deal deceitfully with false balances,
that we may buy the poor for silver
    and the needy for a pair of sandals,
    and sell the refuse of the wheat?' " (8:4-6).
"For three transgressions of Israel,
    and for four, I will not revoke the punishment;
because they sell the righteous for silver,
    and the needy for a pair of shoes—
they that trample the head of the poor into the dust of the earth,
    and turn aside the way of the afflicted" (2:6f).

Q. What were the cult practices of the time?

A. "Come to Bethel, and transgress;
    to Gilgal, and multiply transgression;
bring your sacrifices every morning,
    your tithes every three days" (4:4).
"Those who swear by Ashimah of Samaria,
    and say, 'As thy god lives, O Dan,'
and, 'As the way of Beersheba lives,'
    they shall fall and never rise again" (8:14).

Q. What were the moral conditions of the time?

A. "A man and his father go in to the same maiden,
    so that my holy name is profaned;
they lay themselves down beside every altar
    upon garments taken in pledge;
and in the house of their God they drink
    the wine of those who have been fined" (2:7f).

Q. What were the religious conditions of the time?

A. Some were depending upon sacrifices to save them ("Did you bring to me sacrifices and offerings the forty years in the wilderness, O house of Israel?"—5:25); others had actually turned to idolatry ("your star-god, your images, which you made for yourselves"—5:26); none would listen to reproof:

"They hate him who reproves in the gate,
    and they abhor him who speaks the truth" (5:10).

Q. What was the most ominous circumstance of all?

A. "Therefore he who is prudent will keep silent in such a time;
    for it is an evil time" (5:13).

Q. What does Amos teach regarding the sovereignty of God in nature?

A. "And I also withheld the rain from you
    when there were yet three months to the harvest;
I would send rain upon one city,
    and send no rain upon another city;
one field would be rained upon,
    and the field on which it did not rain withered . . .
I smote you with blight and mildew;
    I laid waste your gardens and your vineyards;

your fig trees and your olive trees the locust devoured;
yet you did not return to me, says the Lord . . .
For lo, he who forms the mountains, and creates the wind,
and declares to man what is his thought;
who makes the morning darkness,
and treads on the heights of the earth—
the Lord, the God of hosts, is his name!" (4:7,9,13).

Q. What does Amos teach regarding God's sovereignty over the nations?

A. "I sent among you a pestilence after the manner of Egypt . . .
I overthrew some of you,
as when God overthrew Sodom and Gomorrah,
and you were as a brand plucked out of the burning" (4: 10f).

"Did I not bring up Israel from the land of Egypt,
and the Philistines from Caphtor and the Syrians from Kir?" (9:7).

Q. What does Amos teach regarding God's relationship to Israel?

A. God has given to Israel and Judah a law (2:4), raised up some of their "young men for Nazirites" (2:11), and does nothing without revealing it to the prophets (3:7).

Q. How does Amos interpret the doctrine of the chosen people?

A. God thinks no more, no less, of Israel than of Ethiopia:
"Are you not like the Ethiopians to me,
O people of Israel?" (9:7).

God's choice of Israel is not a special privilege but a special responsibility:
"You only have I known
of all the families of the earth;
therefore I will punish you
for all your iniquities" (3:2).

Q. For what other nations does Amos have a word?

A. Damascus ("I will send a fire upon the house of Hazael"—1:4), Gaza ("I will not revoke the punishment"—1:6), Tyre ("I will send a fire upon the wall of Tyre"—1:10); Edom ("I will not revoke the punishment"—1:11), Ammonites ("I will not revoke the punishment"—1:13), Moab ("I will send a fire upon Moab"—2:2).

Q. How does Amos climax this judgment of the nations?

A. By turning to his own people of Judah and Israel with similar messages: "I will not revoke the punishment" (2:4,6).

Q. How did a Judean shepherd know so much about what was going on in the world?

A. His annual sheep-shearing, with subsequent trips to market, enabled him to learn what had transpired in the world beyond. In fact, one of his most famous sermons was delivered at Bethel, the national shrine, on a feast day (7:13).

Q. What was the reaction to this sermon?

A. "Then Amaziah the priest of Bethel sent to Jeroboam king of Israel, saying, 'Amos has conspired against you in the midst of the house of Israel.' . . . And Amaziah said to Amos, 'O seer, go, flee away . . . never again prophesy at Bethel' " (7:10-13).

Q. What are some of the visions in which Amos perceived the truth?

A. The prophet saw a plumb line, and heard God say:
"Behold, I am setting a plumb line
    in the midst of my people Israel" (7:8).
The prophet saw a basket of ripe summer fruit, and heard God say:
"The end has come upon my people Israel" (8:2).

Q. What does Amos have to say about the looked-for Day of the Lord?

A. "Woe to you who desire the day of the Lord!
    Why would you have the day of the Lord?
It is darkness, and not light" (5:18).

Q. What message does Amos have for the women of his nation?

A. "Hear this word, you cows of Bashan,
who are in the mountains of Samaria,
who oppress the poor, who crush the needy,
    who say to their husbands, 'Bring, that we may drink!' "
        (4:1).

Q. What is the prophet's verdict upon the popular religion of his time?

A. "I hate, I despise your feasts,
    and I take no delight in your solemn assemblies.

Even though you offer me your burnt offerings and cereal offerings,

    I will not accept them,

and the peace offerings of your fatted beasts

    I will not look upon.

Take away from me the noise of your songs;

    to the melody of your harps I will not listen" (5:21-23).

Q. How will God's judgment manifest itself in such a situation?

A. " 'Therefore I will take you away into exile beyond Damascus,'
says the Lord" (5:27).

    " 'For behold, I will raise up against you a nation,

        O house of Israel,' says the Lord, the God of hosts;

    'and they shall oppress you from the entrance of Hamath

        to the Brook of the Arabah' " (6:14).

Q. What is there left for the nation to do?

A. "But let justice roll down like waters,

    and righteousness like an ever-flowing stream" (5:24).

"Hate evil, and love good,

    and establish justice in the gate;

it may be that the Lord, the God of hosts,

    will be gracious to the remnant of Joseph" (5:15).

Q. What future does Amos envision for his people?

A. " 'Behold, the days are coming,' says the Lord,

    'when the plowman shall overtake the reaper

    and the treader of grapes him who sows the seed;

the mountains shall drip sweet wine,

    and all the hills shall flow with it.

I will restore the fortunes of my people Israel,

    and they shall rebuild the ruined cities and inhabit them;

they shall plant vineyards and drink their wine,

    and they shall make gardens and eat their fruit.

I will plant them upon their land,

    and they shall never again be plucked up

        out of the land which I have given them,' says the
        Lord your God" (9:13-15).

THE BOOK OF OBADIAH

Q. What is the meaning of the name *Obadiah*?

A. "Servant of Yahweh."

Q. When did Obadiah live?

A. 1:11-14 tells of how Israel's old enemy, Edom, gloated over the destruction of Jerusalem; the book therefore was written after that event, which occurred in 586 B.C.

Q. With respect to size, what distinction has Obadiah?

A. Its original two-word title, "Obadiah's vision," is unique, and the book itself is the shortest in the Old Testament.

Q. To what other prophets is Obadiah indebted?

A. Approximately one-third of his brief work appears to have been taken over from Jeremiah (compare Obadiah 1-8 with Jeremiah 49:7-16), or else both were taken from a common source. Obadiah's picture of the day of the Lord (verses 15-18) seems to owe something to Amos 5:18 ("darkness, not light"), Isaiah 34:8 ("a day of vengeance"), and Isaiah 63.4 (vengeance on Edom).

Q. What does Obadiah envision for Edom's future?

A. He looks forward to the time when Edom's exultation over fallen Israel will return to haunt it; the nation that has gloated over fallen Israel will itself be brought low:

"As you have done, it shall be done to you,

your deeds shall return on your own head" (verse 15).

Q. How did Edom's contempt manifest itself?

A. On the day when Jacob was carried off, Edom "stood aloof" (verse 11); it "gloated" over its brother's misfortune (verse 12); it joined in the looting (verse 13); it blocked up the fugitives' way of escape (verse 14).

Q. Who are the "Saviors" referred to in verse 21 as going "up to Mount Zion to rule Mount Esau"?

A. Judges 3:9 and 5:15 describe the nation's rulers as deliverers; perhaps these are meant. The Septuagint, however, suggests not "Saviors," but "those who are saved." This would mean that Israelites, returning from exile, shall regain political sovereignty.

Q. Who are those who "live in the clefts of the rock" (verse 3)?

A. The capital city of Edom was Sela, the Rock, known to later history as Petra, "the rose-red city half as old as time." The prophet says, in verse 4:

"Though you soar aloft like the eagle,

though your nest is set among the stars,

thence I will bring you down, says the Lord."

Q. Who are "the wise men out of Edom" (verse 8)?

A. Although Edom was not generally noted for its wisdom, Eliphaz (Job 2:11) is identified as "the Temanite"—that is, resident in a district of Edom.

Q. How will the day of God's triumph manifest itself?

A. The nations will stagger like drunken men (verse 16); "the house of Jacob shall possess their own possessions" (verse 17); "and the kingdom shall be the Lord's" (verse 21).

Q. Is any use made of the book of Obadiah in the New Testament?

A. No. It is neither quoted nor referred to.

THE BOOK OF JONAH

Q. What is the meaning of the name *Jonah*?

A. *Jonah* is the Hebrew word for "dove"; since "dove" was a pet name for Israel (Psalm 74:19; Hosea 7:11), the name may well personify the nation as a whole.

Q. Was Jonah an historical person?

A. II Kings 14:25 speaks of God's "servant Jonah the son of Amittai, the prophet, who was from Gath-hepher."

Q. Who was Amittai?

A. He is identified in 1:1 as the father of Jonah; the word, however, means "truth," and may also have here a symbolic significance.

Q. Where was Gath-hepher?

A. It was a town in Galilee whose very existence refutes the snobbish notion of the citified people of Jerusalem: "Search and you will see that no prophet is to rise from Galilee" (John 7:52).

Q. When was the book of Jonah written?

A. The exact date is unknown, but Nineveh was destroyed in 612 B.C. and enough time elapsed for Nineveh to have become a representative type, standing for the most depraved of all non-Jewish communities (cf. Nahum 2:1-12). The universalism of the book, insisting that God cares even for Ninevites, is in distinct contrast to the exclusivity of Ezra and Nehemiah, who ordered the returning exiles to divorce their foreign wives.

Q. What other protests against narrowness are there in the book?

A. The sailors, though worshipers of false gods, show solicitous concern (1:8) for their strange passenger who "was fleeing from the presence of the Lord" (1:10).

Q. What device is used for determining who, among those on board, is responsible for bringing trouble to the ship?

A. "They cast lots" (1:7); like many people still in tribal societies, the Hebrews looked upon this as a valid way of finding out the will of God:

> "The lot is cast into the lap,
>> but the decision is wholly from the Lord" (Proverbs 16:33;
>> cf. Acts 1:23-26).

Q. What literary forms are found in the book of Jonah?

A. Jonah 2:2-9 is a poem or psalm similar to the psalms found elsewhere in the Bible; if one reads it without reference to the remainder of the book, it appears to be a self-contained unit suitable for expressing gratitude for deliverance from drowning or any distress; the whole of the book is thought by some to be a sermon based upon Jeremiah 18:8: ". . . if that nation, concerning which I have spoken, turns from its evil, I will repent of the evil that I intended to do to it."

Q. Had the figure of a nation being swallowed by a fish been used before in Hebrew literature?

A. Jeremiah 51:34 uses precisely this imagery:

> "Nebuchadrezzar the king of Babylon has devoured me,
>> he has crushed me;
> he has made me an empty vessel,
>> he has swallowed me like a monster;
> he has filled his belly with my delicacies,
>> he has rinsed me out."

Q. What other evidences are there within the book of Jonah that the whole is to be taken symbolically?

A. Reference is made in 3:7 to the king of Nineveh; since Nineveh was a city, the capital of Assyria, it had no king of its own. Nineveh is spoken of as "an exceeding great city, three days' journey in breadth" (3:3); archaeology indicates that the city wall was about seven and one-half miles long and that the distance across the city was less than three miles. Also, the mourning in Nineveh is not confined to human beings; beasts, too, were to be covered with sackcloth, to cry aloud to God, and to turn from their evil ways (3:8).

Q. Where was Tarshish, the city to which Jonah set out?

A. Tartessus, in Spain; Jonah was thus starting in the opposite direction from Nineveh and, since Spain was thought to be at the end of the world, was going as far in the opposite direction as he possibly could.

Q. What is the theological message of Jonah?

A. "Thou art a gracious God and merciful, slow to anger, and abounding in steadfast love" (4:2).

Q. What was the effect upon the Ninevites of this proclamation?

A. "They turned from their evil way" (3:10).

Q. What effect did the repentance of the Ninevites have upon Jonah?

A. He was angry and despondent (4:1).

Q. How did his despondency express itself?

A. In terms reminiscent of Elijah's sitting "down under a broom tree" and asking that his life be taken away (I Kings 19:4), Jonah, too, went out of the city to sulk in the shade (4:3,5ff).

Q. What was the plant that grew to shelter Jonah?

A. Probably the castor-oil plant, with its hand-shaped leaves causing it to be called Palma Christi.

Q. What happened to the plant?

A. A worm attacked it and it withered (4:7).

Q. What is the conclusion of the story?

A. If Jonah pities the shrunken plant that he did not make, should not the Creator God "pity Nineveh, that great city" (4:10)?

Q. How does the story indicate the inclusiveness of God's love?

A. He looks with tenderness upon a community of poor and ignorant persons and their animals: ". . . in which there are more than a hundred and twenty thousand persons who do not know their right hand from their left, and also much cattle" (4:11).

Q. What interpretations are given in the New Testament of "the sign of the prophet Jonah"?

A. Matthew 12:40 says: "For as Jonah was three days and three nights in the belly of the whale, so will the Son of man be three days and three nights in the heart of the earth." Since Jesus was entombed from Friday afternoon to Sunday morning, he was not in the earth three nights, and Luke 11:30 interprets the sign of Jonah as the proclamation of God's love to foreigners: "For as Jonah became a sign to the men of Nineveh, so will the Son of man be to this generation."

Q. What use has been made of the book of Jonah by dramatists in the modern world?

A. Gunter Rutenborn's *Sign of Jonah* draws a parallel between Jonah and the captain of a Nazi submarine.

THE BOOK OF MICAH

Q. What is the meaning of the name *Micah*?

A. It is an abbreviated form of *Micaiah,* "Who is like Yah?"

Q. When did Micah live?

A. 1:1 tells us that the word of the Lord came to Micah "in the days of Jotham, Ahaz, and Hezekiah, kings of Judah"; that would date him between 739 and 693 B.C. Perhaps the reformation under Hezekiah (II Kings 18:3-6) was the result of Micah's preaching.

Q. Where did Micah live?

A. 1:1 identifies him as coming from Moresheth; 1:14 refers to this as Moresheth-gath, indicating proximity to the Philistine Gath; this is on the coastal plain known as the Shephelah.

Q. What was Micah's background?

A. Nothing definite is related about this; we can only infer from his writings that he was a countryman of humble origin in whom the oppressed poor of the nation found a champion.

Q. What were the social conditions against which Micah protested?

A. The exploitation carried out by the well-to-do who are like wild creatures: they

". . . eat the flesh of my people,
and flay their skin from off them" (3:3).

They lie awake at night plotting evil (2:1), and "When the morning dawns, they perform it. . . . They covet fields, and seize them" (2:2).

Q. What of the administration of justice in the time of Micah?

A. The nation's rulers, he says,

"abhor justice
and pervert all equity . . .
Its heads give judgment for a bribe" (3:9,11).

Q. What were the domestic conditions?

A. A man cannot trust his wife (7:5);

". . . the son treats the father with contempt,
the daughter rises up against her mother,
the daughter-in-law against her mother-in-law;
a man's enemies are the men of his own house" (7:6).

Q. What use did Jesus make of this?

A. The moral demands of the Gospel will cause divisions within families, "and a man's foes will be those of his own household" (Matthew 10:36).

Q. What were the business conditions in Micah's time?

A. Vendors use "wicked scales" and "a bag of deceitful weights" (6:11).

Q. What were the moral conditions?

A. In direct contravention of Deuteronomy 23:18, the wages of the prostitute had not only been brought into the temple but used to purchase idols (1:7).

Q. What ceremonial practices were substituted for the moral attributes required in the Law?

A. Burnt offerings innumerable, "calves a year old" (6:6), "thousands of rams," "ten thousands of rivers of oil" (6:7).

Q. What of religious conditions?

A. "Its priests teach for hire,
its prophets divine for money" (3:11).

Suggesting the type of religion the people really wanted, Micah says:

"If a man should go about and utter wind and lies,
saying, 'I will preach to you of wine and strong drink,'
he would be the preacher for this people!" (2:11).

Q. What future does Micah foresee for this kind of religion?

A. "The sun shall go down upon the prophets,
    and the day shall be black over them;
the seers shall be disgraced,
    and the diviners put to shame" (3:6,7).

Q. What passage in Micah has been described as the high-water mark of the Hebrew Srciptures?

A. A Scottish scholar has said that to Micah 6:8 no subsequent generation has been able to add anything either of grandeur or of tenderness; it sums up the messages of three of Micah's predecessors in the prophetic tradition: Amos (5:24), Hosea (6:6; 11:1,8), and Isaiah (6:5; 29:19).

Q. What other prophet echoes a saying of Micah?

A. Jeremiah 26:18f recalls how Micah of Moresheth prophesied (3:12) that

"Zion shall be plowed as a field:
Jerusalem shall become a heap of ruins."

Q. Will God's judgment be confined to Judah?

A. Samaria, too, will be "a heap in the open country" (1:6).

Q. What natural phenomena will accompany the judgmental activity of God?

A. "The mountains will melt under him
    and the valleys will be cleft" (1:4).

Q. What forms will disarmament take in Israel?

A. "I will cut off your horses from among you
and will destroy your chariots . . .
and throw down all your strongholds" (5:10f).

Q. What will become of the inhabitants of the land?

A. "You shall go forth from the city
and dwell in the open country;
you shall go to Babylon" (4:10).

Q. Is this the prophet's final word?

A. Like others of the prophets, Micah is confident that the nation's decline and fall will be followed by a glorious restoration:

". . . the mountain of the house of the Lord
shall be established as the highest of the mountains,
and shall be raised up above the hills;
and peoples shall flow to it" (4:1).

Q. Will the restoration be confined to Israel?

A. Its blessings will overflow upon "many nations":
"For out of Zion shall go forth the law,
and the word of the Lord from Jerusalem" (4:2).

Q. What dream of peace has Micah given to the world?

A. Inscribed on a wall near the United Nations building is the quote:
"They shall beat their swords into plowshares,
and their spears into pruning hooks" (4:3).

Q. What kind of economic situation will characterize the glorious age to come?

A. "They shall sit every man
under his vine and under his fig tree,
and none shall make them afraid" (4:4).

Q. What is Micah's doctrine of the Remnant?

A. He is sure that the surviving nucleus of his countrymen will, "in the midst of many peoples," be
"like dew from the Lord,
like showers upon the grass . . .
like a lion among the beasts of the forest" (5:7f).

Q. What historical circumstances make it, from the human point of view, unpardonable that Israel should have turned its back upon God?

A. The "saving acts of the Lord," including the deliverance from Egypt, victory over Moab, safe passage crossing the Jordan (6:3f; cf. 7:15).

Q. To what other historical circumstance is reference made in the book of Micah?

A. 2:13 may allude to Sennacherib's invasion of Judah in 701 B.C. (cf. II Kings 18:13ff).

Q. What classical expression regarding defeat has Micah given to the world?

A. "They shall lick the dust like a serpent" (7:17).

Q. What theological concept gives Micah confidence for the future?

A. "Who is a God like thee, pardoning iniquity
and passing over transgression
for the remnant of his inheritance?
He does not retain his anger for ever
because he delights in steadfast love" (7:18).

Q. What figure of speech does Micah draw from the law court?

A. 6:1-5 pictures a court in which Israel is defendant and God is both prosecutor and judge; the mountains, being old and acquainted with the righteousness of God, serve as witnesses.

Q. What contribution did Micah make to the Christmas story?

A. Judah's deliverer, this countryman imagines, will come not from one of the great centers of population but from Bethlehem, "little to be among the clans of Judah" (5:2). Matthew 2:5 sees in this a prediction of the place where Jesus should be born.

THE BOOK OF NAHUM

Q. What is the meaning of *Nahum*?

A. The name means "comforter"; it may have been given to the author because he brought comfort to the land of Judah.

Q. Where did Nahum live?

A. He is called (1:1) Nahum of Elkosh, but Elkosh has not been identified.

Q. When did Nahum live?

A. His book is a series of poems exulting in the overthrow of Nineveh. Since the Assyrian capital fell to the Babylonians and Medes in 612 B.C., the prophet must have written about that time. The concluding verses (3:18f) look back upon the destruction of Nineveh as a *fait accompli:* "All who hear the news of you clap their hands over you."

Q. What is distinctive about the book of Nahum?

A. Unlike the work of other prophets, it contains no indictment of sinful Israel, no call to repentance; it consists only of delight over a fallen foe. It has been said that the book contains little more "than the cry 'Hurray!' from a poet who voiced the feelings of his outraged countrymen."

Q. What literary devices are used by the author?

A. Within the longer poem there is an acrostic in which approximately fifteen letters of the Hebrew alphabet are used.

Q. What is Nahum's standing as a poet?

A. As a singer of martial songs he has been ranked with the authors of the Song of Deborah (Judges 5) and David's lament over Saul and Jonathan (II Samuel 1:19-27).

Q. What is the religious value of Nahum?

A. Vivid word pictures describe how the tyrant receives the treatment he has earlier meted out to others; perhaps this illustrates the Hebrew philosophy of history:

"The wicked shall depart to Sheol,
all the nations that forget God" (Psalm 9:17).

There is nothing here of the Bible's enduring message of forgiveness to enemies.

Q. What poetic expression does Nahum borrow from Isaiah?

A. Nahum 1:15:

"Behold, on the mountains the feet of him
who brings good tidings,
who proclaims peace!"

is quite like Isaiah 52:7, a passage also quoted in Romans 10:15.

Q. What are the "good tidings" in Nahum?

A. News of Nineveh's destruction.

Q. To what Roman statesman has Nahum been compared?

A. Cato became famous for his slogan, *Carthago delenda est;* it has been said that Nahum's life work is summed up in the phrase, *Ninua delenda est.*

Q. In what terms does Nahum picture the avenging wrath of God?

A. Like storm and whirlwind that lay waste the earth (1:3-5); like fire that produces unendurable heat (1:6); like "an overflowing flood" (1:8), God will "make a full end of his adversaries" (1:8).

Q. What is the meaning of the line, "he will not take vengeance twice on his foes" (1:9)?

A. The devastation once wrought will be so great that another could not possibly be needed.

Q. What picture does Nahum draw of the besieged city?

A. With enemy chariots raging in the streets (2:3f), siege-engines set up (2:5), the officers summoned to the defense stumbling as they go (2:5),

> "The river gates are opened,
> the palace is in dismay . . .
> Nineveh is like a pool
> whose waters run away.
> 'Halt! Halt!' they cry;
> but none turns back" (2:6,8).

Q. To what does the prophet allude when he mentions a lion that has "filled his caves with prey" (2:12)?

A. As a symbol of Assyria, the lion is often found in ancient sculpture and inscriptions; here the Assyrian army is spoken of as a lion that, having torn "enough for his whelps and strangled prey for his lionesses" (2:12), returns to his lair—that is, the capital city of Nineveh.

Q. In what terms does Nahum picture the destruction that awaits Nineveh?

A. The proclamation "Woe to the bloody city" (3:1) includes a picture of heaped-up corpses (3:3), nakedness and harlotry (3:5), filth and contempt—all resulting in the proud city's becoming a "gazing-stock" (3:6).

Q. What other historical circumstances are referred to in the book?

A. Nineveh is no "better than Thebes" (the Egyptian capital, captured by the Assyrians in 663 B.C.); at the time of the fall of Thebes, Egypt was ruled by Ethiopia (3:9); she received aid from Put (perhaps Somaliland) and Libya (3:9). In spite of all these resources and allies, Thebes was taken; Nineveh can expect no easier fate.

Q. What terms does Nahum use in picturing Nineveh's doom?

A. Its fortresses are "like fig trees with first-ripe figs"—ready to fall (3:12); its troops are helpless as women, and the city's gates are already wide open (3:13); its princes and wise men are

> ". . . like clouds of locusts
> settling on the fences
> in a day of cold—
> when the sun rises they fly away" (3:17).

THE BOOK OF HABAKKUK

Q. What is the origin of the name *Habakkuk*?

A. It is apparently derived from an Akkadian word applied to a garden plot or fruit tree.

Q. When did Habakkuk live?

A. His book seems to reflect the Chaldeans' rise to power about 600 B.C. and the Chaldean invasion of Jerusalem in 597 B.C.

Q. What else do we know about Habakkuk?

A. Nothing, except that one of the apocryphal additions to the book of Daniel represents him as about to take bread and gruel to reapers in a field when an angel commanded him to take this food to Daniel in the lions' den. Habakkuk replied that he had never been in Babylon and did not know the lions' den. Whereupon the angel of the Lord seized him by the head and carried him by his hair to Babylon, where he breathlessly placed the food on the edge of the pit and called Daniel to come and get it. Daniel gave thanks that God had remembered him, and the angel took Habakkuk back to his own country.

Q. Why has Habakkuk been called "the skeptic among the prophets"?

A. Because he raises the basic problem of the righteousness and justice of God: why do "guilty men, whose own might is their god" (1:11) obtain power in the world?

Q. What is Habakkuk's answer to the question he raises?

A. At first he sees the wicked nations as destroying one another; if the Assyrians have been oppressive, God is "rousing the Chaldeans, that bitter and hasty nation," to "seize habitations not their own" (1:6). Habakkuk later sees the Chaldeans as oppressors and God is silent "when the wicked swallows up the man more righteous than he" (1:13). There is no answer to this except that the final outcome does not yet appear:

> "For still the vision awaits its time;
>> it hastens to the end—it will not lie.
> If it seem slow, wait for it" (2:3).

Q. How does Habakkuk portray the Chaldean warriors?

A. "Dread and terrible are they. . . .
Their horses are swifter than leopards,
    more fierce than the evening wolves;
    their horsemen press proudly on. . . .
They gather captives like sand. . . .
They laugh at every fortress . . .
    they sweep by like the wind and go on" (1:8-11).

Q. What light do the Dead Sea Scrolls throw on Habakkuk?

A. Among the early finds at Qumran was a commentary on Habakkuk, applying the word of the prophet to the situation of the Qumran community near the beginning of the Christian era. The Dead Sea ascetics, like Palestine as a whole, faced the danger of invasion by the Romans. The words written by Habakkuk at the time of the Chaldean invasion are applied existentially to the later situation. Also, the Dead Sea commentary on Habakkuk knows only what we call Chapters 1 and 2, confirming for some the belief that what we call Chapter 3 is a psalm added to the earlier portion of the book.

Q. What phrases has Habakkuk contributed to the language of prayer?

A. He speaks of God in terms now often used in address to the Deity:

"Thou who art of purer eyes than to behold evil
    and canst not look on wrong" (1:13).

He has provided a frequently used call to worship:

"But the Lord is in his holy temple;
    let all the earth keep silence before him" (2:20).

He speaks also of the time when

"the earth will be filled
    with the knowledge of the glory of the Lord,
        as the waters cover the sea" (2:14).

Prayers for forgiveness often quote 3:2: "In wrath remember mercy." 3:17f is "indispensable for a harvest thanksgiving after a wet English summer."

Q. What figure of speech does Habakkuk use regarding the treatment that the wicked man accords good men?

A. He regards men as like fish or "crawling things that have no ruler" (1:14), and so

"He brings all of them up with a hook . . .
he gathers them in his seine" (1:15).

Q. What figure of speech does Habakkuk use regarding himself as a prophet?

A. Like other men in the prophetic tradition, he speaks of himself as a man in the watchtower, anxiously scanning the horizon to see "what God will say" (2:1).

Q. What is Habakkuk's philosophy of the manner in which a religious leader ought to communicate with his people?

A. "Write the vision;
make it plain upon tablets,
so he may run who reads it" (2:2).

Q. What future does Habakkuk see for the wicked?

A. He pronounces woe upon "him who gets evil gain" (2:9); "him who builds a town with blood" (2:12); him who makes his neighbor drunk (2:15).

Q. What is Habakkuk's judgment upon idol-makers?

A. "Woe to him who says to a wooden thing, Awake;
to a dumb stone, Arise!" (2:19).

Q. What is the literary style of Chapter 3?

A. It is in the form of a psalm, with musical notations similar to those found in the Psalter.

Q. What does the Psalm celebrate?

A. God's greatness in creation ("he veiled his power"—3:4); God's terror in punishment ("thou didst trample the nations in anger"—3:12); God's kindness to his own ("I will joy in the God of my salvation—3:18).

Q. What is the origin of the figure of speech in 3:8:
". . . when thou didst ride upon thy horses,
upon thy chariot of victory"?

A. This appears to have been taken over from the nature religions. The Greeks had the story of Phaethon, who obtained permission to drive the chariot of the sun across the heavens for one day. When Elijah bade farewell to Elisha, "a chariot of fire and horses of fire separated the two of them" (II Kings 2:11; cf. Psalm 68:17).

Q. What passage in Habakkuk is basic to the theology of the New Testament?

A. At a time when the Hebrews were threatened with invasion and destruction by the Chaldeans, the prophet, sure that his people could not deliver themselves by violence, heard God say: "the righteous shall live by his faith" (2:4). Paul uses these words in Galatians 3:11 as a summary of his message to the churches of Galatia; he quotes them also in Romans 1:17 as the basis of what he wishes to say to Christians in the capital of the empire. Further, the author of Hebrews 10:38f quotes these words of Habakkuk as a kind of preface to his catalog of the heroes of faith. Historically, the quotation from Habakkuk has been the watchword of the Reformation.

THE BOOK OF ZEPHANIAH

Q. What is the meaning of the name *Zephaniah*?

A. "Yah has sheltered" or "Yah has treasured."

Q. When did Zephaniah live?

A. In the latter part of the seventh century B.C. He himself tells us that "the word of the Lord" came to him "in the days of Josiah the son of Amon, king of Judah" (1:1); this would date him about 621 B.C.

Q. What else do we know about Zephaniah?

A. He tells us (1:1) that he was "the son of Cushi, son of Gedaliah, son of Amariah, son of Hezekiah." The last-named is perhaps the king who ruled over Judah from 715 to 687 B.C. Zephaniah would thus be of royal descent. No other prophet names so many of his ancestors, but the others mentioned by Zephaniah are unknown. His work shows what his lineage suggests, namely, that he was at home in court circles.

Q. What were the conditions prevailing at the time Zephaniah prophesied?

A. It was at a time when foreign influences were strong: in religion this manifested itself in worship of "the hosts of heaven"—that is, astral deities of the Assyrians, and swearing by Milcom, god of the Ammonites (I Kings 11:5,33; II Kings 23:13). In political life this manifested itself in the wearing of "foreign attire" (1:8); in a sense of self-sufficiency on the part of "the oppressing city" (3:1); and in a general decline of public and private morals:

". . . her judges are evening wolves
 that leave nothing till the morning.
Her prophets are wanton, faithless men;
 her priests profane what is sacred,
  they do violence to the law" (3:4).

Q. Amid the deterioration of the national life, what picture is given of the steadfastness of God?

A. ". . . every morning he shows forth his justice,
 each dawn he does not fail" (3:5).

Q. What does "every one who leaps over the threshold" mean in 1:9?

A. I Samuel 5:1-5 explains "why the priests of Dagon and all who enter the house of Dagon do not tread on the threshold of Dagon in Ashdod to this day." Because of the calamity there described, that spot became taboo. Perhaps the practice in Zephaniah 1:9 represents a superstition requiring one to avoid contact with the threshold. Another theory is that the reference is to some form of social injustice that disregarded the sanctity of poor homes.

Q. What does Zephaniah regard as the grimmest feature of life in his time?

A. The complete indifference of those who say in their hearts, "The Lord will not do good, nor will he do ill" (1:12).

Q. What is the meaning of "thickening upon their lees" (1:12)?

A. The prophet suggests that a smug, self-satisfied community has become like the dregs in a wine barrel.

Q. By what other prophet was Zephaniah influenced?

A. From Amos 5:18-20 he takes over the concept of "the day of the Lord" (1:7), "the great day of the Lord" (1:14), "the day of the wrath of the Lord" (2:2).

Q. What prospect does Zephaniah hold out for the day of the Lord?

A. "A day of wrath is that day,
 a day of distress and anguish,
a day of ruin and devastation,
 a day of darkness and gloom" (1:15).

Q. Cries of desolation "will be heard from the Fish Gate, a wail from the Second Quarter," a wail also from the "inhabitants of the Mortar" (1:10f); what do these terms designate?

A. Different geographical areas in the city of Jerusalem: the Fish

Gate is mentioned in Nehemiah 12:39; the prophetess Huldah had her home in the Second Quarter (II Kings 22:14); the Mortar was a center of business activity.

Q. How far will this desolation extend?

A. Within the city, men "shall walk like the blind . . . their blood shall be poured out like dust" (1:17); destruction, too, will come upon Gaza, Ashkelon, Ashdod, Ekron, and other cities of the Philistines; upon the inhabitants of Moab and Ammon, who had gloated over Judah's plight; upon Assyria and its capital city Nineveh—the latter is to become a lodge for vultures and hedgehogs, with hoot owls in the windows and ravens croaking on the threshold (2:14). The time of trouble will, in fact, extend to the whole creation:

> "I will utterly sweep away everything . . .
> I will sweep away man and beast;
>> I will sweep away the birds of the air
>> and the fish of the sea . . .
> I will cut off mankind
>> from the face of the earth" (1:2f).

Q. What New Testament idea is foreshadowed by Zephaniah?

A. God's decision to "father the nations, to assemble kingdoms" for judgment appears to find echo in Jesus' picture of the Great Assize: "Before him will be gathered all the nations" (Matthew 25:32).

Q. What hope does Zephaniah hold out for the future?

A. Less optimistic than most of the prophets, Zephaniah nevertheless believed that there would come a time when the nations would "call on the name of the Lord" (3:9); fear (3:13) and disaster and reproach (3:18) will be banished from Israel; God will "renew you in his love" (3:17) and "restore your fortunes" (3:20). This picture of a saved and righteous remnant is so different from the remainder of the book that many suppose it to come from the hand of an editor later than the time of Zephaniah.

Q. What favorite hymn of the Middle Ages was based upon Zephaniah?

A. Thomas of Celano's "Dies Irae," many times translated into English. One translation begins:

> "Day of wrath, O dreadful day,
> When this world shall pass away."

THE BOOK OF HAGGAI

Q. What is the meaning of the name *Haggai*?

A. It appears to be derived from *hagh,* the Hebrew word for "festival," and may indicate that its bearer was born at a festal season.

Q. When did Haggai live?

A. About 520 B.C. The dates in the book (1:1,15; 2:1,10,20) refer to the second year of the Persian King, Darius I, who reigned from 522 to 486 B.C.

Q. Where else in Scripture is there a reference to Haggai?

A. Ezra 5:1f tells how "the prophets Haggai and Zechariah . . . prophesied to the Jews." Ezra 6:14 relates that "the elders of the Jews built and prospered through the prophesying of Haggai the prophet and Zechariah the son of Iddo."

Q. What were the circumstances under which Haggai prophesied?

A. The Jews who had returned from exile had been more concerned with getting themselves comfortably settled than with rebuilding the house of worship.

Q. What evidence was there that the temple had been neglected?

A. Though the people were themselves living in fine paneled houses, the temple still "lies in ruins" (1:4).

Q. What disasters does the prophet envision as a result of the neglect of the house of God?

A. Drought, famine, hunger, and inflation (1:6,11).

Q. How does the prophet picture inflation?

A. "He who earns wages earns wages to put them into a bag with holes" (1:6); this has been described as "the earliest Biblical allusion to coined money."

Q. To whom does Haggai address his message?

A. To Zerubbabel the governor, Joshua the high priest (1:1), and "all the remnant of the people" (1:12).

Q. What is the reference to the remnant?

A. From the time of Isaiah (cf. Isaiah 11:11) onward, the prophets believed that the people of God, however decimated they might be, would at least survive in a faithful nucleus or remnant.

Q. Who was Zerubbabel?

A. A leader of the returning exiles, he is pictured in 2:23 as one who will become "like a signet ring" (cf. Jeremiah 22:24)—that is, God's representative, occupying a position of authority in the new age that is to follow the new temple.

Q. What historical parallel to the return from exile is cited?

A. "I am with you, says the Lord of hosts, according to the promise that I made you when you came out of Egypt" (2:4f).

Q. What was the result of the ministry of Haggai?

A. The "Lord stirred up the spirit of Zerubbabel . . . and the spirit of Joshua . . . and the spirit of all the remnant of the people; and they came and worked on the house of the Lord of hosts" (1:14).

Q. How would the rebuilt temple compare with the original?

A. "The latter glory of this house shall be greater than the former, says the Lord of hosts" (2:9).

Q. What twentieth-century use has been made of this passage?

A. The cathedral at Coventry, England, was shattered by bombs during World War II; the rebuilt cathedral has these words inscribed upon it.

Q. What picture did Haggai give to the author of Revelation?

A. Haggai 2:7 hears God say: ". . . the treasures of all nations shall come in, and I will fill this house with splendor." Revelation 21:24-26 represents the nations as bringing their honor and glory into the city of God.

Q. What aspect of the ceremonial law does Haggai cite to portray the spiritual plight of his people?

A. Holy flesh carried in the priest's garment does not import holiness to other objects, but unclean objects defile all that they touch. So, says Haggai, the rottenness of the nation's life suggests that some polluted thing must be spreading its evil throughout the land (2:11-14).

Q. In what way did Haggai anticipate the Sermon on the Mount?

A. His insistence that life cannot be properly lived until the priority of God is recognized is summed up in Matthew 6:33: "But seek first his kingdom and his righteousness, and all these things shall be yours as well."

THE BOOK OF ZECHARIAH

Q. What is the meaning of the name *Zechariah*?

A. "Yah has remembered."

Q. When did Zechariah live?

A. His writing, concerned with the new age that is to follow the rebuilding of the temple, apparently dates from the period following the return of the exiles, about 520 B.C.

Q. What else do we know about Zechariah?

A. As with Haggai, his name is mentioned in Ezra 5:1 and 6:14 as one who "prophesied to the Jews who were in Judah and Jerusalem." Ezra identifies him as "the son of Iddo." Nehemiah 12:4,16 lists Iddo among the exiles who returned with Zerubbabel and Joshua. Nothing else is known about him, unless he is to be identified with "that young man" of 2:4.

Q. Why is it believed that the book in its present form combines the work of two men?

A. The style of Chapters 9-14 is markedly different from that of 1-8, and the name of Zechariah does not occur after Chapter 8. Chapters 1-8 are prose; Chapters 9-14 are interspersed with poetic oracles.

Q. What experiences of Zechariah form the basis of the prophetic oracles?

A. He reports frequent visions, oftentimes in strange imagery. 4:1 states that "the angel who talked with me came again, and waked me, like a man that is wakened out of his sleep." The authoritative nature of the visions is suggested by the prophet's insistence that the speaker in them is "the Lord of hosts" (2:8,9,11; 4:9; etc.). Some of the passages read like sermons in which a saying of the prophet has been developed by his followers.

Q. What is the purpose of the book of Zechariah?

A. To comfort the people with the supreme lesson of the nation's history, namely, that God will return to his people when they return to him (1:2-6).

Q. What characteristic term for a section of the Hebrew Bible is used by Zechariah?

A. 1:4 speaks of "the former prophets," a term that came to be used of Joshua, Judges, I and II Samuel, I and II Kings.

Q. What is Zechariah's vision of the horsemen?

A. In 1:7-17 he sees "a man riding upon a red horse . . . and behind him were red, sorrel, and white horses . . . sent to patrol the earth" (1:8,10), like the mounted posts of the Persians. The report comes: "My cities shall again overflow with prosperity" (1:17).

Q. Where in the New Testament is use made of this imagery?

A. In Revelation 6:2-8.

Q. What is Zechariah's vision of the horns?

A. The horn is a characteristic Biblical symbol for power and authority (cf. Jeremiah 48:25; Luke 1:69). In Zechariah 1:18-21 the prophet sees four horns, symbolizing the kingdoms that have been hostile to Judah; these four horns are, in turn, to be "cast down" by "four smiths" (1:20f).

Q. What is the vision of the man with the measuring line?

A. In 2:1-5 the prophet sees a man setting out "to measure Jerusalem"; he learns that God's protection will be around about the city "like a wall of fire."

Q. What is the vision of the heavenly court?

A. In Zechariah 3:1-10, Joshua, the nation's high priest and representative before God, is arraigned before the angel of the Lord, arrayed in "filthy garments," accused by Satan; when the people clothe their priest with clean garments and a clean turban, God promises to "remove the guilt of this land in a single day" (3:9). In this connection, the symbolism of the turban is to be interpreted by reference to Exodus 28:36ff, where a priest appropriately turbaned takes upon himself the people's guilt.

Q. What is the vision of the lampstand and the olive trees?

A. In 4:1-14˙ the prophet sees a lampstand with seven lamps between two olive trees; the lamps represent "the eyes of the Lord, which range through the whole earth" (4:10); the olive trees represent Zerubbabel and Joshua, the political and religious leaders "who stand by the Lord of the whole earth" (4:14).

Q. What, according to this vision, is the secret of greatness upon earth?

A. "Not by might, nor by power, but by my Spirit, says the Lord of hosts" (4:6).

Q. What classical expression has been lifted from this vision?

A. 4:10 assures us that "whoever has despised the day of small things shall rejoice."

Q. What is the vision of the flying scroll?

A. In 5:1-4 the prophet sees a huge scroll flying about over the face of the earth proclaiming the doom of "every one who steals . . . and every one who swears falsely" (5:3).

Q. What is the vision of the ephah and the woman?

A. In 5:5-11 the prophet sees an ephah (roughly equivalent to our bushel basket); when the leaden cover is removed, a woman symbolizing Wickedness was "sitting in the ephah" (5:7). Two other women, with "wings like the wings of a stork," carry the ephah and its contents "to the land of Shinar," where a house is prepared for it—that is, wickedness is banished to Babylon, where it can be appropriately worshiped.

Q. What is the vision of the four chariots?

A. In 6:1-8 the prophet sees four chariots setting out in different directions "to . . . patrol the earth" (6:7); their purpose in doing this is to scatter the Spirit of God over the land.

Q. What symbolic action brings to its close the series of visions?

A. In 6:9-15 a gold and silver crown is placed upon the head of Joshua the high priest and he is given the name "the Branch: for he shall grow up in his place, and he shall build the temple of the Lord" (6:12). "And those who are far off shall come and help to build the temple" (6:15).

Q. Why did Hebrews have to be brought from "far off"?

A. Because they had refused to hearken to the word of the Lord, God had "scattered them with a whirlwind among all the nations which they had not known" (7:14).

Q. What conduct is demanded of those who return?

A. "Render true judgments, show kindness and mercy each to his brother, do not oppress the widow, the fatherless, the sojourner, or the poor" (7:9,10).

Q. What picture does Zechariah paint of the restored Jerusalem?

A. "Old men and old women shall again sit in the streets of Jerusalem, each with staff in hand for very age. And the streets of the city shall be full of boys and girls playing in its streets" (8:4f).

Q. What new name is given Jerusalem?

A. It is to be called "the faithful city" and its mountain, "the holy mountain" (8:3).

Q. What phrases does Revelation borrow from this word picture?

A. Revelation 21:3 echoes 8:8: "they shall be my people and I will be their God."

Q. What are some characteristics of the redeemed society pictured by Zechariah?

A. The good earth will provide for the necessaries of life (8:12); men will "speak the truth to one another" (8:16); fasts will be replaced by "seasons of joy and gladness, and cheerful feasts" (8:19); other nations will look to Israel for leadership, "for we have heard that God is with you" (8:23).

Q. What titles are found within the second part of Zechariah's work?

A. The phrase "An Oracle" at 9:1 is introductory to that section; the same phrase at 12:1 is an introduction to the remainder of the book.

Q. From what era do these oracles date?

A. The historical allusions are difficult to identify, and the oracles seem to have been preserved because the truths they represent apply to many situations.

Q. What communities besides Israel are brought under judgment?

A. Israel's neighbors: the ancient city of Damascus; Tyre and Sidon, with their political sophistication and business acumen (9:2-4); Gaza, Ekron, and Ashdod, cities of Philistia (9:5-7).

Q. What picture is given of Judah's victorious armies?

A. In 10:3 God promises to make the house of Judah like a "proud steed in battle"; gifts of leadership, too, will be bestowed; these are symbolized by "the cornerstone," "the tent peg," and "the battle bow" (10:4).

Q. What reference is there to the Dispersion?

A. "Though I scattered them among the nations,
yet in far countries they shall remember me,
and with their children they shall live and return" (10:9; cf. 10:10-12).

Q. What allegorical picture is drawn?

A. In 11:4-17 shepherds are represented as presiding over a "flock doomed to be slain"; the shepherd who replaces the faithless shepherds has two staffs: Grace and Union.

Q. How does David figure in the prophet's vision?

A. On the nation's day of triumph "the feeblest . . . shall be like David" (12:8); upon the house of David will be poured a spirit of compassion and supplication (12:10); "there shall be a fountain opened for the house of David and the inhabitants of Jerusalem to cleanse them from sin and uncleanness" (13:1).

Q. What plagues will befall those who oppose God's plan for a redeemed Jerusalem?

A. "Their flesh shall rot while they are still on their feet, their eyes shall rot in their sockets, and their tongues shall rot in their mouths" (14:12; cf. 14:15).

Q. What is the meaning of the words, "there shall be inscribed on the bells of the horses, 'Holy to the Lord' " (14:20)?

A. Bells, originally intended to ward off evil spirits, are now to be inscribed like the diadem of the high priest (Exodus 28:36); horses, the emblem of military might (as in Isaiah 31:1ff) will be made to serve the purposes of God.

Q. How else is the common life of the nation to be transformed?

A. "Every pot in Jerusalem and Judah shall be sacred to the Lord of hosts" (14:21).

Q. What are the wounds "received in the house of my friends" (13:6)?

A. Some interpret them as the kind of mutilation that the false prophets inflicted upon themselves (as in I Kings 18:28); others suppose they were marks borne by members of the temple staff to identify them as property of the Deity.

Q. What picture does Zechariah give of God's universal rule?

A. ". . . his dominion shall be from sea to sea,
            and from the River to the ends of the earth" (9:10; cf. Psalm 72:8); "and the Lord will become king over all the earth; on that day the Lord will be one and his name one" (14:9).

Q. What contribution does Zechariah make to the passion narrative of Christ?

A. Matthew 21:5 (cf. John 12:15) represents Zechariah 9:9 as having described the triumphal entry beforehand:

"Lo, your king comes to you;
    triumphant and victorious is he,
humble and riding on an ass,
    on a colt the foal of an ass."

Matthew 26:15; 27:5-10 interprets the actions of Judas in terms of Zechariah 11:12-13.

Q. What other passages from Zechariah are quoted in the New Testament?

A. John the Baptizer, in Matthew 3:4, is clothed with a garment resembling Zechariah's "hairy mantle" (13:4); Matthew 21:44 alludes to the "heavy stone" of Zechariah 12:3; John 10:12 alludes to "the worthless shepherd" of Zechariah 11:17; Revelation 21:23-25 echoes Zechariah 14:7; the "river of the water of life," of Revelation 22:1, is similar to the "living waters" of Zechariah 14:8; Matthew 9:36 brings to mind Zechariah 10:2.

THE BOOK OF MALACHI

Q. What is the meaning of *Malachi*?

A. A Hebrew word "my messenger"; the term is probably not a personal name but rather the title of an anonymous book.

Q. What use is made of this title in the New Testament?

A. The earliest gospel begins with a quotation from Malachi 3:1:

"Behold, I send my messenger before thy face,
    who shall prepare thy way" (Mark 1:2).

Q. When did "my messenger" live?

A. The contents of the book indicate that it is addressed to those who returned from exile some time after 538 B.C.

Q. Why does the book of Malachi appropriately stand at the conclusion of the Old Testament?

A. Its final paragraph phrases hope and expectation: "Behold, I will send you Elijah the prophet before the great and terrible day of the Lord comes. And he will turn the hearts of fathers to their children and the hearts of children to their fathers, lest I come and smite the land with a curse" (4:5,6).

Q. Why do the rabbis, in reading this passage, conclude by repeating verse 5 after verse 6?

A. Because of unwillingness to end a book or lesson with a harsh saying, the next-to-last verse was repeated in the synagogue reading; the same procedure was applied to Isaiah, Lamentations, and Ecclesiastes.

Q. Why was Elijah thought of as one who would return?

A. II Kings 2:11 records that as Elijah and Elisha "went on and talked, behold, a chariot of fire and horses of fire separated the two of them. And Elijah went up by a whirlwind into heaven"; as a prophet who did not die, he was the natural choice for the representative of the prophetic tradition who would return and overcome the estrangement between the generations.

Q. How is this expectation preserved in the world today?

A. In the Hebrew ritual of Passover, a place is reserved at table for Elijah; a cup is poured for Elijah; at one point, the youngest person present opens the door in the hope that Elijah may be standing there ready to enter.

Q. How does the New Testament reflect the expectation of Elijah's return or second coming?

A. John the Baptizer, the first prophet of the Elijah type in many generations, caused people to wonder whether he was Elijah (John 1:21); still others wondered whether Jesus was the expected Elijah (Mark 6:15). Jesus himself pronounced the judgment: "For all the prophets and the law prophesied until John; and if you are willing to accept it, he is Elijah who is to come" (Matthew 11:13f).

Q. What is the burden of the message brought by "my messenger"?

A. That formal worship in the rebuilt temple will not be enough. If the national life is to be restored, instruction must be given in the Law (2:7); home life must be purified ("let none be faithless to the wife of his youth"—2:15).

Q. What passage from Malachi is often used as a call to worship in Christian churches?

A. "For from the rising of the sun to its setting my name is great among the nations, and in every place incense is offered to my name, and a pure offering" (1:11).

Q. What reason does Malachi offer as to why Israelites should not despise one another?

A. "Have we not all one father? Has not one God created us?" (2:10).

Q. What passage from Malachi sets forth a philosophy of steward-ship?

A. "Bring the full tithes into the storehouse, that there may be food in my house" (3:10).

Q. What phrases from Malachi have found their way into Handel's oratorio, *The Messiah*?

A. The "Lord whom you seek will suddenly come to his temple. . . . But who can endure the day of his coming, and who can stand when he appears? For he is like a refiner's fire" (3:1f).

Q. What passage from Malachi is often cited as summarizing the world mission of the church?

A. "But for you who fear my name the sun of righteousness shall rise, with healing in its wings" (4:2).

Q. What kind of offering is despised by the Lord?

A. Any offering that represents ill-gotten gain, earned by violence (1:13) or taken by deceit (1:14) or presented to cover up blemishes (1:14).

Q. How does Malachi's philosophy of worship foreshadow that of the New Testament?

A. 3:2-5 anticipates Matthew 5:23f: "So if you are offering your gift at the altar, and there remember that your brother has something against you, leave your gift there before the altar and go; first be recon-ciled to your brother, and then come and offer your gift."

THE APOCRYPHA

Introduction

Q. What is the meaning of *Apocrypha*?

A. It is derived from a Greek word meaning "hidden" and originally applied to sacred books taken out of circulation because the manuscripts had become frayed or in some way considered unsuitable for general use. The term now refers to Old Testament books found in the Alexandrian canon but not in the Jerusalem canon. Considered authoritative in the Roman and Greek churches, and with a semi-canonical status in some Protestant churches, the Apocrypha have been included in all authorized English Bibles.

THE FIRST BOOK OF
ESDRAS

Q. What is the significance of the name "Esdras"?

A. It is the Greek form of the name Ezra.

Q. What is the meaning of the "I" in the title?

A. I Esdras is the title in the Septuagint; in Lucian's revision of the Septuagint, this work is called II Esdras, the title I Esdras there being given to what we know as Ezra-and-Nehemiah. In the Vulgate, this work, known as III Esdras, is placed after the New Testament, as if it were a kind of appendix.

Q. Why is it given this position?

A. Jerome rejected it because it was not a part of the Hebrew canon; it failed to win canonical status at the Council of Trent.

Q. What is the purpose of I Esdras?

A. To give a history of the Hebrews from the time of the good king Josiah to the time of Ezra.

Q. What other Scriptures does it parallel?

A. It relates many of the same incidents—although not always in the same order—as are to be found in the work of the Chronicler.

Q. What is the distinctive material contained here that is not found in Chronicles-Ezra-Nehemiah?

A. The story of the three youths who were members of the body-guard of King Darius (3:1-4:60).

Q. What is the origin of this story?

A. Many suppose it to have been borrowed from the Persians, who trained their young men not in the three R's, but in horsemanship, archery, and truth-telling.

Q. Who is the author of I Esdras?

A. An unknown writer whose work, originally produced in Hebrew, was translated into Greek by someone else.

Q. When was the translation made?

A. Probably in the second century B.C.

Q. How does the work begin?

A. With a description of how "Josiah kept the passover to his Lord in Jerusalem" (1:1) and urged his people to "worship the Lord your God . . . in accordance with the directions of David king of Israel and the magnificence of Solomon his son" (1:5); "from the king's possessions" Josiah provided "thirty thousand lambs and kids, and three thousand calves" (1:7).

Q. What is the historian's evaluation of that occasion?

A. "No passover like it had been kept in Israel since the times of Samuel the prophet" (1:20).

Q. What is the next historical incident reported by the author?

A. The death of Josiah "in the plain of Megiddo" (1:29), and the mourning led by "Jeremiah the prophet" (1:32).

Q. Who followed Josiah on the throne?

A. Jeconiah, Jehoiakim, and Jehoiachin (1:34-44).

Q. What happened to Jehoiachin?

A. "After a year Nebuchadnezzar sent and removed him to Babylon . . . and made Zedekiah king of Judea" (1:45f).

Q. How does the author account for the occurrence of the exile?

A. The people mocked God's "messengers, and whenever the Lord spoke, they scoffed at his prophets" (1:51).

Q. How does the author describe the Chaldean invasion?

A. They "slew the young men with the sword . . . and did not spare young man or virgin, old man or child. . . . And all the holy vessels of the Lord, great and small . . . they took and carried away to Babylon" (1:53f).

Q. What happened when Cyrus became king?

A. "The Lord stirred up the spirit of Cyrus" (2:2), so that he issued a decree allowing the Hebrews to return to their homeland (2:3-7).

Q. What opposition developed after the return?

A. Rulers in Coelesyria and Phoenicia complained to the king, "If this city is built and the walls finished, they will not only refuse to pay tribute but will even resist kings" (2:19); the work was delayed for a time (2:30).

Q. What is the setting for the Story of the Three Guardsmen?

A. "King Darius gave a great banquet," at which all "ate and drank"; Darius then "went to his bedroom, and went to sleep, and then awoke" (3:1-3); meanwhile, each of three guardsmen had placed under the king's pillow his own opinion of "what one thing is strongest" (3:5,8).

Q. What did the king do upon awaking?

A. He summoned his councilors, read the three statements, and ordered the three young men to "explain their statements" (3:16).

Q. What was the first statement?

A. "Wine is strongest" (3:10).

Q. With what arguments is this supported?

A. "It leads astray the minds of all who drink it. . . . It makes all hearts feel rich . . . and makes every one talk in millions . . . and when they recover from the wine, they do not remember what they have done" (3:18-24).

Q. What was the second statement?

A. "The king is strongest" (3:11).

Q. How is this supported?

A. If he tells men "to kill, they kill; if he tells them to release, they release. . . . All his people and his armies obey him" (4:2-12).

Q. What was the third statement?

A. "Women are strongest" (cf. 4:14).

Q. How is this supported?

A. "Women give birth to the king and to every people . . . women brought up the very men who plant the vineyards from which comes wine . . . men cannot exist without women." . . . A man "faces lions, and he walks in darkness, and when he steals and robs and plunders, he brings it back to the woman he loves" (4:14-32).

Q. With what conclusion does the third guardsman sum up the whole matter?

A. "Great is truth, and strongest of all" (4:41).

Q. How is this supported?

A. "With her there is no partiality or preference, but she does what is righteous. . . . To her belongs the strength and the kingship and the power and the majesty of all the ages" (4:39f).

Q. What reward is claimed by the winning guardsman?

A. "Then he said to the king, 'Remember the vow which you made to build Jerusalem' " (4:43).

Q. How did Darius respond?

A. With letters of safe conduct, instructions to "bring cedar timber from Lebanon to Jerusalem" (4:48), and an order "that land and wages should be provided for all who guarded the city" (4:56).

Q. How did this affect the Hebrew people?

A. "They praised the God of their fathers because he had given them release and permission to go up and build Jerusalem" (4:62).

Q. What accompaniment did Darius arrange for those returning?

A. He "sent with them a thousand horsemen to take them back to Jerusalem in safety, with the music of drums and flutes" (5:2).

Q. What census rolls are included in I Esdras?

A. 5:4-46 lists "the names of the men who went up," and 8:28-49

"the principal men . . . who went up . . . from Babylon"; 9:18-36
contains a list of those who "had married foreign women."

Q. To what did the returning exiles first devote their attention?

A. "They erected the altar in its place, for all the peoples of the
land were hostile to them and were stronger than they" (5:50).

Q. How was the temple acclaimed?

A. "They sang hymns, giving thanks to the Lord, because his goodness and his glory are for ever upon all Israel" (5:61).

Q. What did the builders say to their detractors?

A. "We are the servants of the Lord who created the heaven and
the earth" (6:13).

Q. How did Darius reply to those who opposed the work?

A. By citing the decree of Cyrus, who "ordered the building of the
house of the Lord . . . the cost to be paid from the treasury of Cyrus
the king" (6:24f).

Q. What evidence was there of more-than-human help?

A. "The holy work prospered, while the prophets Haggai and
Zechariah prophesied; and they completed it by the command of the
Lord God of Israel" (7:3f).

Q. What thank-offering was presented at the dedication?

A. "One hundred bulls, two hundred rams, four hundred lambs,
and twelve he-goats for the sins of Israel . . . they sacrificed the passover lamb for all the returned captives" (7:7,12).

Q. What Hebrew leader does the narrative next introduce?

A. "Ezra came up from Babylon as a scribe skilled in the law of
Moses" (8:3).

Q. Why were the people fortunate in Ezra's coming?

A. "Ezra possessed great knowledge, so that he omitted nothing
from the law of the Lord or the commandments, but taught all Israel all
the ordinances and judgments" (8:7).

Q. What commission did Artaxerxes give to Ezra?

A. He decreed that all "who freely choose to do so, may go with
you to Jerusalem . . . and to carry to Jerusalem the gifts for the Lord
of Israel which I and my friends have vowed. . . . And whatever else
occurs to you as necessary for the temple of your God, you may provide
out of the royal treasury" (8:8-18).

Q. How was Ezra to administer justice?

A. "And you, Ezra, according to the wisdom of God, appoint judges and justices to judge all those who know the law of your God, throughout all Syria and Phoenicia; and those who do not know it you shall teach" (8:23).

Q. How did Ezra make ready for the journey?

A. "I proclaimed a fast for the young men before our Lord, to seek from him a prosperous journey" (8:50).

Q. What was the reaction of Ezra when he discovered, upon returning to Jerusalem, that "the holy race has been mixed with the alien peoples of the land" (8:70)?

A. Grief-stricken, he said: "O Lord, I am ashamed and confounded before thy face. For our sins have risen higher than our heads" (8:74).

Q. What was the response of the people?

A. "Let us take an oath to the Lord about this, that we will put away all our foreign wives, with their children" (8:93).

Q. When this was publicly acted upon, what atmospheric conditions were recorded?

A. "And all the multitude sat in the open square before the temple, shivering because of the bad weather that prevailed" (9:6).

Q. When Ezra read the law to the people, how long did he read?

A. "He read aloud in the open square before the gate of the temple from early morning until midday" (9:41).

Q. What posture did the people assume?

A. "And when he opened the law, they all stood erect" (9:46).

Q. What assistants did Ezra have?

A. The Levites "taught the law of the Lord, at the same time explaining what was read" (9:48).

Q. How was this day concluded?

A. "Then they all went their way, to eat and drink and enjoy themselves, and to give portions to those who had none, and to make great rejoicing; because they were inspired by the words which they had been taught" (9:54f).

THE SECOND BOOK OF
ESDRAS

Q. By what other name is II Esdras known?

A. In the Roman Church it is called IV Esdras and in printed editions of the Vulgate, it is placed after the New Testament.

Q. In what language was II Esdras written?

A. The Aramaic version, which has been lost, appears to have been the original; the work survives in an old Latin version and in several Oriental versions.

Q. What is the nature of II Esdras?

A. It is an apocalyptic work.

Q. What is the mark of apocalyptic?

A. Purporting to be divine revelation, the disclosure is often represented as having been made to a Biblical character. Usually in visionary form, the meaning of the revelation is frequently interpreted by an angel; sometimes the angel conducts the seer on a tour of realms beyond the earth.

Q. To whom is the revelation in II Esdras made?

A. To "the prophet Ezra . . . of the tribe of Levi, who was a captive in the country of the Medes in the reign of Artaxerxes, king of the Persians" (1:1,3); in 3:1 Ezra is identified with Salathiel, who lived a century before.

Q. When was II Esdras written?

A. In its present form it seems to date from about 96 A.D.

Q. Is the work a unity?

A. To a characteristically Jewish apocalypse, dating from an earlier time, a redactor has added beginning and closing sections (Chapters 1 and 2, and Chapters 15 and 16) written from the point of view of a Christian.

Q. What history does the author cite as evidencing God's goodness to his people?

A. "Surely it was I who brought you through the sea, and made safe highways for you when there was no road. . . . The quails were a sign to you. . . . I . . . gave you manna for food; you ate the bread of angels" (1:13,15,19).

Q. What leaders did God provide?

A. Abraham, Isaac, Jacob, and the Twelve Prophets (1:39); also Isaiah and Jeremiah (2:18).

Q. How did the people react toward these messengers?

A. "I sent to you my servants the prophets, but you have taken and slain them and torn their bodies in pieces" (1:32).

Q. What results from Israel's rejection of God?

A. "I will turn to other nations and will give them my name" (1:24). "I will give your houses to a people that will come, who without having heard me will believe" (1:35).

Q. What family simile is used to express the broken relationship between God and the chosen people?

A. "Go, my children, because I am a widow and forsaken. I brought you up with gladness; but with mourning and sorrow I have lost you, because you have sinned before the Lord God and have done what is evil" (2:2f).

Q. What figure of speech drawn from the political realm is used to express the same idea?

A. "Tell my people that I will give them the kingdom of Jerusalem, which I was going to give to Israel. Moreover, I will take back to myself their glory, and will give to these others the everlasting habitations, which I had prepared for Israel" (2:10f).

Q. What resources await the new Israel?

A. "The tree of life shall give them fragrant perfume, and they shall neither toil nor become weary" (2:12). "I have consecrated and prepared for you twelve trees loaded with various fruits, and the same number of springs flowing with milk and honey, and seven mighty mountains on which roses and lilies grow; by these I will fill your children with joy" (2:19).

Q. How is the new Israel to live?

A. "Guard the rights of the widow, secure justice for the fatherless, give to the needy, defend the orphan, clothe the naked, care for the injured and the weak, do not ridicule a lame man, protect the maimed, and let the blind man have a vision of my splendor" (2:20ff).

Q. What is the duty of the new Israel?

A. "Receive what the Lord has entrusted to you and be joyful, giving thanks to him who has called you to heavenly kingdoms" (2:37).

Q. What prospect awaits?

A. "He who will come at the close of the age is close at hand. Be ready for the rewards of the kingdom, because the eternal light will shine upon you for evermore" (2:35).

Q. What did the spirit of Ezra see on Mount Zion?

A. "A great multitude, which I could not number, and they were all praising the Lord with songs" (2:42).

Q. Who was placing crowns upon their heads and palms in their hands?

A. "The Son of God, whom they confessed in the world" (2:47).

Q. What caused the spirit of Ezra to be greatly agitated? (3:3)?

A. "The desolation of Zion and the wealth of those who lived in Babylon" (3:2).

Q. How does the author summarize all prior history?

A. God ("and that without help"—3:4) created Adam who, "burdened with an evil heart, transgressed. . . . Thus the disease became permanent" (3:21f). The flood destroyed the sinful inhabitants of the world, except for "Noah with his household, and all the righteous who have descended from him" (3:11). When subsequent generations began to be even "more ungodly than were their ancestors" (3:12), God chose Abraham, made "with him an everlasting covenant," and gave to him Isaac and Jacob (3:13-16); when the descendants of Jacob came out of Egypt, God led them to Sinai and there gave his "commandment to the posterity of Israel" (3:19). "So the times passed and the years were completed" and God raised up "a servant, named David" (3:23), who built a city, "but the inhabitants of the city transgressed" (3:24f) and were delivered into the hands of the enemy (3:27).

Q. What philosophical problem was posed when Babylon "gained dominion over Zion" (3:28)?

A. "I have seen how thou dost endure those who sin, and hast spared those who act wickedly, and hast destroyed thy people, and hast preserved thy enemies" (3:30).

Q. How did experience in other lands deepen this perplexity?

A. "I have traveled widely among the nations and have seen that they abound in wealth, though they are unmindful of thy commandments" (3:33).

Q. What rebuke comes to the seer?

A. "Your understanding has utterly failed regarding this world, and do you think you can comprehend the way of the Most High?" (4:2).

Q. What three challenges are set before the seer?

A. "Go, weigh for me the weight of fire, or measure for me a measure of wind, or call back for me the day that is past" (4:5).

Q. What conclusion is drawn from the seer's inability to perform any of these?

A. "You cannot understand the things with which you have grown up; how then can your mind comprehend the way of the Most High?" (4:10f).

Q. What is the seer's reaction to this?

A. "It would be better for us not to be here than to come here and live in ungodliness, and to suffer and not understand why" (4:12).

Q. How does the problem of theodicy in this book differ from that in Job?

A. The book of Job is concerned with the sufferings of the individual; II Esdras is concerned with the sufferings of a nation: why has Israel "been given over to the Gentiles as a reproach" (4:23)?

Q. What partial explanations are offered?

A. "The age is hastening swiftly to its end . . . this age is full of sadness and infirmities" (4:26f); "the age is divided into twelve parts, and nine of its parts have already passed" (14:11; cf. 14:10,17); "a grain of evil seed was sown in Adam's heart from the beginning, and how much ungodliness it has produced" (4:30).

Q. What will be the signs of the age to come?

A. "The sea of Sodom shall cast up fish . . . menstruous women shall bring forth monsters . . . then shall reason hide itself, and wisdom shall withdraw into its chamber" (5:7-9).

Q. What effect did these visions have upon the seer?

A. "My body shuddered violently, and my soul was so troubled that it fainted" (5:14).

Q. What is the angel's reply when the seer says: ". . . every hour I suffer agonies of heart, while I strive to understand the way of the Most High and to search out part of his judgment" (5:34)?

A. "Gather for me the scattered raindrops, and make the withered flowers bloom again for me . . . and then I will explain to you the travail that you ask to understand" (5:36f).

Q. What reason is there to believe that the present generation is inferior to earlier ones?

A. "Those born in the strength of youth are different from those born during the time of old age, when the womb is failing" (5:53).

Q. Is the present situation the result of chance or untoward circumstance or plan?

A. The seer hears God say: "At the beginning of the circle of the earth . . . then I planned these things" (6:1,6).

Q. What signs will appear when "the seal is placed upon the age which is about to pass away" (6:20)?

A. "Infants a year old shall speak with their voices, and women with child shall give birth to premature children at three or four months, and these shall live and dance. Sown places shall suddenly appear unsown, and full storehouses shall suddenly be found to be empty" (6:21f).

Q. With what attitude should one face such portents?

A. "Believe and do not be afraid" (6:33).

Q. What section of Genesis is presented in résumé?

A. The six days of creation, described in Genesis 1, are here recounted (6:38-53).

Q. What is distinctive about this author's account of the third day?

A. "On the third day thou didst command the waters to be gathered together in the seventh part of the earth; six parts thou didst dry up and keep so that some of them might be cultivated and planted and be of service before thee" (6:42).

Q. What historic discovery partly hinged on this?

A. Believing this to be a statement of fact, Christopher Columbus assumed there could not be too much water separating him from the land he hoped to reach.

Q. How does recounting the story of creation exacerbate the seer's problem?

A. "If the world has indeed been created for us, why do we not possess the world as an inheritance?" (6:59).

Q. What is the answer to this?

A. "The entrances of this world were made narrow and sorrowful and toilsome . . . unless the living pass through the difficult and vain experiences, they can never receive those things that have been reserved for them" (7:12,14).

Q. How is the age of Messiah pictured?

A. He will reign for four hundred years, after which "the world will be turned back to primeval silence for seven days. . . . And the earth shall give up those who are asleep in it. . . . And patience shall be withdrawn; but only judgment shall remain, truth shall stand; faithfulness shall grow strong" (7:28-34).

Q. Why has judgment not been sooner imposed?

A. "For how long the time is that the Most High has been patient with those who inhabit the world, and not for their sake, but because of the times which he has foreordained" (7:74).

Q. What is to be "the order of the souls of the righteous" (7:99)?

A. "Their face is to shine like the sun . . . they are to be made like the light of the stars, being incorruptible from then on" (7:97).

Q. Can the goodness of one avail for another on the day of judgment?

A. "Every one shall bear his own righteousness or unrighteousness" (7:105).

Q. What feeling does this induce in the seer?

A. "It would have been better if the earth had not produced Adam. . . . O Adam, what have you done? For though it was you who sinned, the fall was not yours alone, but ours also who are your descendants" (7:116,118).

Q. What prayer does Ezra offer?

A. That God "who inhabitest eternity . . . whose glory is beyond comprehension" (8:20f) will "look not upon the sins of thy people, but at those who have served thee in truth" (8:26).

Q. What is the reply to Ezra's concern about the lost?

A. "Do not ask any more questions about the multitude of those who perish. For they also received freedom, but they despised the Most High" (8:55f).

Q. How does God summarize the doctrine of the chosen people?

A. I "saved for myself one grape out of a cluster, and one plant out of a great forest" (9:21).

Q. What is the meaning of Ezra's vision of the mourning woman who, childless for thirty years, gives birth to a son who, on his wedding day, "fell down and died" (9:38-10:4)?

A. The woman is Zion (10:44); the years of her barrenness symbolized the ages when Israel had no temple; the birth of the son was the building of Solomon's temple; the death of the son was "the destruction which befell Jerusalem" (10:45-48); the destroyed city, however, is to be succeeded by a better.

Q. What is the meaning of Ezra's vision of the "eagle that had twelve feathered wings and three heads" (11:1), and the roaring lion "aroused out of the forest" (11:37)?

A. This is a picturesque summary of world history, in the manner of Daniel 7:7f,23. The eagle represented the Roman empire; the wings and heads were Roman emperors—the three heads probably referring to Vespasian, Titus, and Domitian. The lion is "the Messiah, whom the Most High kept until the end of days, who will arise from the posterity of David, and . . . deliver in mercy the remnant of my people" (12:32,34).

Q. What did Ezra mean to the people?

A. "For of all the prophets you alone are left to us, like a cluster of grapes from the vintage, and like a lamp in a dark place, and like a haven for a ship saved from a storm" (12:42).

Q. What is the meaning of the vision of "something like the figure of a man come up out of the heart of the sea" (13:3)?

A. "This is he whom the Most High has been keeping for many ages, who will himself deliver his creation" (13:26).

Q. How did Ezra preserve the visions he had seen?

A. He selected five men "trained to write rapidly" (14:24). "And the Most High gave understanding to the five men, and by turns they wrote what was dictated, in characters which they did not know" (14:42).

Q. How many books were written in this way?

A. Ninety-four, of which twenty-four (the number in the Hebrew canon) were to be made public, the remaining seventy to be reserved for "the wise among your people" (14:45f).

Q. What counsel is offered the believer in time of "sword and famine and death and destruction" (15:5)?

A. "Do not fear the plots against you, and do not be troubled by the unbelief of those who oppose you. For every unbeliever shall die in his unbelief" (15:3,4). "Behold, the word of the Lord, receive it; do not disbelieve what the Lord says" (16:36).

Q. What functions do angels perform in this book?

A. An angel serves to interpret the visions (2:44,48). The angel Uriel converses with the seer, convincing him that man who cannot understand earthly things can hardly expect "to inquire about the ways above" (4:1-25). "I fasted seven days, mourning and weeping, as Uriel the angel had commanded me" (5:20). "Jeremiel the archangel" (4:36-52) also converses with the seer, explaining, "Concerning the signs about which you ask me, I can tell you in part" (4:52). In prayer Ezra addresses God as one "before whom the hosts of angels stand trembling and whose command they are changed to wind and fire" (8:21f).

TOBIT

Q. Who is the author of Tobit?

A. An unnamed writer whose work was done perhaps in the third century B.C. Though he appears to have worked in a Semitic language, it is the Greek and Latin texts that now are known.

Q. What is the nature of the work?

A. It is a short historical novel.

Q. What is the setting of the story?

A. The time when, about 722 B.C., the Hebrews were carried away captive by the Assyrians.

Q. What errors of geography suggest the romantic quality of the narrative?

A. When the author speaks of Nineveh, it appears to have been Seleucia that he had in mind; he speaks (9:6) of Rages as but a day's camel ride from Ecbatana, whereas actually it was a journey of almost two weeks.

Q. What is the character of Tobit?

A. Before being carried away captive, he contributed of his income not merely one tithe but three tithes (1:7f), and "performed many acts of charity" (1:3). In Nineveh he refused to eat Gentile food, gave "bread to the hungry" and "clothing to the naked," and was careful to arrange decent burial for his countrymen (1:10-18).

Q. What happened as a result of the latter?

A. Returning from burying a man "strangled and thrown into the market-place," and knowing that he was ceremonially unclean, Tobit "slept by the wall of the courtyard" where sparrow droppings fell into his "eyes and white films formed" (2:3-10).

Q. What is told of Tobit's wife?

A. Anna "earned money at women's work" (2:11), but became impatient with her husband when he questioned her about a kid she brought home. "You seem to know everything!" she said (2:14).

Q. What is Tobit's reaction to this?

A. A prayer asking God to take away his life, "because I have heard false reproaches, and great is the sorrow within me" (3:6).

Q. Meanwhile, what is happening in Ecbatana?

A. "Sarah, the daughter of Raguel, was reproached by her father's maids, because she had been given to seven husbands, and the evil demon Asmodeus had slain each of them before he had been with her as his wife" (3:7f).

Q. What is Sarah's prayer?

A. "Command that I be released from the earth and that I bear reproach no more" (3:13).

Q. What effect did the two prayers have?

A. "The prayer of both was heard in the presence of the glory of the great God. And Raphael was sent to heal the two of them" (3:17).

Q. Hoping—and expecting—to die, what advice does Tobit give to his son Tobias?

A. "Do not neglect your mother. . . . Do not turn your face away from any poor man . . . do not be afraid to give according to the little you have . . . what you hate, do not do to any one. . . . You have great wealth if you fear God and refrain from every sin and do what is pleasing in his sight" (4:3-21).

Q. Upon what journey does Tobit dispatch Tobias?

A. To recover "the money which he had left in trust with Gabael at Rages in Media" (4:1).

Q. Who accompanied the untraveled Tobias?

A. "So he went to look for a man; and he found Raphael, who was an angel, but Tobias did not know it" (5:4f); "and the young man's dog was with them" (5:16).

Q. What were Anna's feelings at her son's departure?

A. "Why have you sent our child away? Is he not the staff of our hands . . . ? Do not add money to money, but consider it rubbish as compared to our child" (5:18).

Q. What happened when Tobias, encamped along the Tigris, "went down to wash himself" (6:2)?

A. "A fish leaped up from the river and would have swallowed the young man" (6:2). Upon instructions from his guide, Tobias removed "the heart and liver and gall," then "roasted and ate the fish" (6:4).

Q. What explanation did the disguised Raphael give as to why "the heart and liver and gall" had to be saved?

A. "If a demon or evil spirit gives trouble to any one, you make a smoke from these before the man or woman, and that person will never be troubled again. And as for the gall, anoint with it a man who has white films in his eyes, and he will be cured" (6:6-8).

Q. What is the reaction of Tobias when the angel predicts that he will marry Sarah?

A. "A demon is in love with her, and he harms no one except those who approach her. . . . I fear that I may die and bring the lives of my father and mother to the grave in sorrow" (6:14).

Q. What was Raphael's reply?

A. "Do not be afraid; for she was destined for you from eternity" (6:17).

Q. What happened upon arrival at the home of Raguel?

A. Tobias, already yearning deeply for Sarah, asked for a marriage contract, which Raguel and his wife Edna proceeded to draw up (7:1-14).

Q. What does Edna say to the weeping Sarah?

A. "Be brave, my child; the Lord of heaven and earth grant you joy in place of this sorrow of yours" (7:18).

Q. How did Tobias prepare himself?

A. Into the marriage chamber "he took the live ashes of incense and put the heart and liver of the fish upon them and made a smoke" (8:2).

Q. What effect did this have upon Asmodeus?

A. "When the demon smelled the odor he fled to the remotest parts of Egypt" (8:3).

Q. What prayer does Tobias offer?

A. "Grant that I may find mercy and may grow old together with her" (8:7).

Q. Meanwhile, what has Raguel been doing?

A. He "went and dug a grave, with the thought, 'Perhaps he too will die' " (8:9f).

Q. What was Raguel's response when a maid reported that she had opened the door of the bridal chamber "and found them both asleep"?

A. A prayer:

"Show them mercy, O Lord;
and bring their lives to fulfilment in health and happiness and
mercy" (8:17).

Q. How is the errand accomplished for which Tobias was sent?

A. While Tobias remains at the fourteen-day wedding feast, Raphael goes to Rages and recovers the money (9:5).

Q. Back at home, what are the feelings of Tobit and Anna?

A. Tobit was "greatly distressed" at the delay. Anna said: . . . the lad has perished' " (10:3f).

Q. What send-off did Raguel give to Tobias?

A. He gave him not only his daughter but "half of his property in slaves, cattle, and money" (10:10).

Q. When the party, returning to Nineveh, found Anna "looking intently down the road for her son" (11:5), what did Tobias do?

A. He ran on ahead, "took hold of his father," and "sprinkled the gall upon his father's eyes, saying, 'Be of good cheer, father' " (11:11).

Q. What was the effect upon Tobit?

A. "The white films scaled off from the corners of his eyes. Then he saw his son and embraced him. . . . Then Tobit went out to meet his daughter-in-law at the gate of Nineveh, rejoicing and praising God" (11:13-16).

Q. What is the reply of Raphael when Tobit and Tobias offer him half the money that has been brought back?

A. The angel said: "Praise God and give thanks to him. . . . God sent me to heal you" (12:6,14).

Q. What is Tobit's response?

A. A "prayer of rejoicing" (13:1-18).

Q. What of Tobit's last days?

A. After his blindness, he lived a hundred years. At the age of 158 he advised Tobias and his family to go to Media, "for I fully believe what Jonah the prophet said about Nineveh" (14:4). He then died, "and Tobias gave him a magnificent funeral" (14:11).

Q. What of the last days of Tobias?

A. "He grew old with honor, and he gave his father-in-law and mother-in-law magnificent funerals. He inherited their property and that of his father Tobit. He died in Ecbatana of Media at the age of a hundred and twenty-seven years" (14:13f).

Q. What use was made of this story in the Book of Common Prayer of 1549?

A. Tobias and Sarah (rather than, as now, Abraham and Sarah) were mentioned as the ideal pair.

Q. Who in the modern world has made a play out of this story?

A. James Bridie: *Tobias and the Angel.*

Q. Where in the New Testament is this story echoed?

A. Mark 12:20-23 poses the case of a woman married successively to seven husbands.

JUDITH

Q. Who is the author of Judith?

A. No indication is given.

Q. Where was Judith written?

A. It appears to be of Palestinian origin.

Q. When was Judith written?

A. Probably in the second century B.C.

Q. Why was Judith written?

A. To support the patriotic fervor of those who were staking their lives, their fortunes, and their sacred honor on the effort to rid the land of Antiochus IV and his defilement.

Q. What is the literary form of the work?

A. While some have argued that it is an historical narrative, others regard it as a romantic novel.

Q. What are some evidences within the book that the author is not primarily concerned with historical accuracy?

A. Although the story deals with a great and memorable deliverance of the Hebrew people, its setting, Bethulia, cannot be identified; it would be as if the principal battle of the American revolution had been fought at a place no one ever heard of. Again, the dates are not clear. The events purport to have occurred during the reign of "Nebuchadnezzar, who ruled over the Assyrians in the great city of Nineveh" (1:1; cf. 1:12; 2:1, etc.); yet it was at a time when the Jews "had only recently returned from the captivity" (4:3; cf. 5:19). Nebuchadnezzar, king of Babylonia, did not come to the throne until after the destruction of Nineveh. It was Nebuchadnezzar who carried the Hebrew people away captive, not who allowed them to return. The wall that Nebuchadnezzar built ("seventy cubits high and fifty cubits wide"—1:2) appears to be unnecessarily large. Again, Nebuchadnezzar is reported (1:5) to have "made war against King Arphaxad." There is an Arphaxad in Genesis 10:22, but no king by that name is known. Further, the victory celebration appears to have been unduly prolonged: Nebuchadnezzar and "a vast body of troops . . . feasted for one hundred and twenty days" (1:16); the journey from Nineveh to Cilicia, a distance of some three hundred miles, was accomplished in a march of three days (2:21). Finally, the very name of the heroine, Judith, meaning "Jewess," appears to be symbolic.

Q. What was the purpose of Nebuchadnezzar's expedition against "all who lived in the west" (1:7)?

A. "It was decided that every one who had not obeyed his command should be destroyed" (2:3; cf. 2:6).

Q. What was the size of the army?

A. "One hundred and twenty thousand foot soldiers and twelve thousand cavalry" (2:5)—that is, "archers on horseback" (2:15).

Q. What provision was made for food and transport?

A. "He collected a vast number of camels and asses and mules for transport, and innumerable sheep and oxen and goats for provision" (2:17).

Q. What message did Nebuchadnezzar send to the people he intended to attack?

A. "Tell them to prepare earth and water, for I am coming against them in my anger" (2:7); the formula, "prepare earth and water," meant unconditional surrender.

Q. What success did the armies have?

A. They marched triumphantly through Mesopotamia, plundered the Midianites, sacked the cities in the region of Damascus (2:21-27). "So fear and terror . . . fell upon all the people who lived along the seacoast, at Sidon and Tyre" (2:28). The inhabitants of these and other communities "sent messengers to sue for peace" (3:1), saying, "Our cities also and their inhabitants are your slaves; come and deal with them in any way that seems good to you" (3:4).

Q. Who was the leader of Nebuchadnezzar's troops?

A. "Holofernes, the chief general of his army, second only to himself" (2:4).

Q. What did Holofernes do to the conquered peoples?

A. "He demolished all their shrines and cut down their sacred groves . . . so that all nations should worship Nebuchadnezzar only" (3:8).

Q. What effect did all this have upon the Hebrews?

A. "They were therefore very greatly terrified at his approach, and were alarmed both for Jerusalem and for the temple of the Lord their God" (4:2).

Q. What defensive measures did they take?

A. They "seized all the high hilltops and fortified the villages on them and stored up food in preparation for war" (4:5). They seized "the passes up into the hills, since by them Judea could be invaded, and it was easy to stop any who tried to enter, for the approach was narrow, only wide enough for two men at the most" (4:7).

Q. Who took the lead in the defense of Israel?

A. "So the Israelites did as Joakim the high priest and the senate of the whole people of Israel, in session at Jerusalem, had given order" (4:8).

Q. What other steps were taken?

A. The people donned sackcloth and "fasted many days" (4:12f), while the priests "offered the continual burnt offerings and the vows and freewill offerings of the people" (4:14).

Q. What was the reaction of Holofernes to all these measures?

A. He "called together all the princes of Moab and the commanders of Ammon and all the governors of the coastland, and said to them, 'Tell me, you Canaanites, what people is this that lives in the hill country? . . . why have they alone, of all who live in the west, refused to come out and meet me?' " (5:2-4).

Q. What advice was given by "Achior, the leader of all the Ammonites"? (5:5).

A. After recounting the history of the Hebrew people and God's dealing with them (5:5-19), he said: ". . . if there is any unwitting error in this people and they sin against their God and we find out their offense, then we will go up and defeat them. But if there is no transgression in their nation . . . their God will protect them, and we shall be put to shame before the whole world" (5:20f).

Q. What is the reaction of the troops in Holofernes' army?

A. "We will not be afraid of the Israelites; they are a people with no strength or power for making war" (5:23).

Q. What is the reaction of Holofernes himself?

A. Asking "Who is God except Nebuchadnezzar?" (6:2), he "ordered his slaves, who waited on him in his tent, to seize Achior and take him to Bethulia and hand him over to the men of Israel" (6:10), in order that he might "perish along with them" (6:8).

Q. What happens when Holofernes moves upon Bethulia?

A. "When the Israelites saw their vast numbers they were greatly terrified, and every one said to his neighbor, 'These men will now lick up the face of the whole land' " (7:4).

Q. How did Holofernes begin the siege?

A. He "led out all his cavalry in full view of the Israelites in Bethulia, and examined the approaches to the city, and visited the springs that supplied their water, and seized them and set guards of soldiers over them" (7:6f), forcing the rationing of water in Bethulia (7:21).

Q. What was the reaction of the citizens of Bethulia?

A. After thirty-four days of continually decreasing water supply, they demanded of "Uzziah and the rulers of the city" (7:23), "surrender the whole city to the army of Holofernes" (7:26).

Q. What was the reply of the king?

A. "Let us hold out for five more days; by that time the Lord our

God will restore to us his mercy. . . . But if these days pass by, and no help comes for us, I will do what you say" (7:30f).

Q. Who comes forward with a plan for deliverance?

A. Judith, widow of Manasseh, "beautiful in appearance," wealthy in this world's goods, and one who "feared God with great devotion" (8:8).

Q. What is Judith's judgment upon Uzziah's proposal for a five-day waiting period?

A. "Who are you, that have put God to the test this day . . . if he does not choose to help us within these five days, he has power to protect us within any time he pleases" (8:12,15).

Q. What philosophic argument does Judith advance in support of her position?

A. "You cannot plumb the depths of the human heart, nor find out what a man is thinking; how do you expect to search out God . . . ? Do not try to bind the purposes of the Lord our God; for God is not like man, to be threatened, nor like a human being, to be won over by pleading" (8:14,16).

Q. With reference to what historical circumstances does Judith bolster her position?

A. She is sure that "God has not tried us with fire, as he did" Abraham, Isaac, and Jacob (8:24-27).

Q. What plan does Judith offer?

A. Without disclosing all that is in her mind, she asks—and receives—permission to leave the city, with her maid.

Q. How did she execute her plan?

A. She "arrayed herself in her gayest apparel . . . put on . . . all her ornaments, and made herself very beautiful" (10:3f). Giving her maid wine and oil, "parched grain and a cake of dried fruit and fine bread" to carry, she and the maid went until challenged by an Assyrian patrol.

Q. What does she reply to the sentry?

A. "I am a daughter of the Hebrews, but I am fleeing from them, for they are about to be handed over to you. . . . I am on my way to the presence of Holofernes . . . and I will show him a way by which he can go and capture the hill country without losing one of his men" (10:12f).

Q. What impression did she make upon the troops?

A. "She was in their eyes marvelously beautiful . . . and every one said to his neighbor, 'Who can despise these people, who have women like this among them?' " (10:14,19).

Q. What was the result of her ruse?

A. Holofernes received her into his tent, saying, "I have never hurt anyone who chose to serve Nebuchadnezzar" (11:1).

Q. What hope does Judith hold out to Holofernes?

A. That her people, thirsty and starving, are about to violate the laws by consuming the temple offerings; this will bring down the wrath of God, and "on that very day they will be handed over to you" (11:15).

Q. What was the response of Holofernes?

A. "You are not only beautiful in appearance, but wise in speech" (11:23); he gave her the requested permission to go back and forth through the lines of his troops in order that she might observe the Hebrew laws of ritual cleanliness.

Q. What happened at the banquet that Holofernes arranged for Judith on the fourth day of her going in and out?

A. Holofernes, "moved with a great desire to possess her . . . drank a great quantity of wine, much more than he had ever drunk in any one day since he was born" (12:16,20). His slaves withdrew, leaving Judith "alone in the tent, with Holofernes stretched out on his bed" (13:2). While he was still "overcome with wine" (13:2), she took his own sword, "struck his neck twice with all her might, and severed his head from his body" (13:8).

Q. How did Judith make her escape?

A. She "gave Holofernes' head to her maid, who placed it in her food bag" (13:9f), and then availed herself of the permission, previously obtained, to return in the evening to her own people.

Q. How did she announce her victory?

A. "Praise God, who has not withdrawn his mercy from the house of Israel, but has destroyed our enemies by my hand this very night!" (13:14).

Q. What effect did this have upon the previously skeptical Achior?

A. "He believed firmly in God, and was circumcised, and joined the house of Israel" (14:10).

Q. What happened in Holofernes' army when his headless body was discovered?

A. "Fear and trembling came over them, so that they did not wait for one another, but with one impulse all rushed out and fled by every path across the plain and through the hill country" (15:2).

Q. What acclaim was accorded Judith?

A. The high priest and senate said: "You are the exaltation of Jerusalem, you are the great glory of Israel, you are the great pride of our nation" (15:9).

Q. What was Judith's response?

A. A hymn of praise and thanksgiving (16:2-17) very like some of the Psalms.

Q. What happened to Judith afterward?

A. "Many desired to marry her, but she remained a widow all the days of her life. . . . She became more and more famous, and grew old in her husband's house, until she was one hundred and five years old" (16:22f).

Q. To what other heroines is Judith akin?

A. Jael (Judges 5:24-27; 4:17-22); Deborah (Judges 4:1-5:31); and Esther.

Q. What are some notable phrases from the prayers of Judith?

A. "The things thou didst intend came to pass" (9:5). "For thy power depends not upon numbers, nor thy might upon men of strength; for thou art God of the lowly, helper of the oppressed, upholder of the weak, protector of the forlorn, savior of those without hope" (9:11).

THE ADDITIONS TO THE
BOOK OF ESTHER

Q. What is the source of these additions?

A. The Septuagint, or Greek version, of Esther is approximately sixty per cent longer than the Hebrew version. The latter contains 163 verses, the former 270.

Q. At what points do the Greek additions enlarge upon the Hebrew text?

A. Addition *A* (11:2-12:6) comes before 1:1; *B* (13:1-7) follows

3:13; *C* (13:8-14:19) and *D* (15:1-16) follow 4:17; *E* (16:1-24) follows 8:12; *F* (10:4-11:1) follows 10:3, which is the conclusion of canonical Esther.

Q. Has this order always been preserved?

A. Jerome, translator of the Vulgate, removed all the additions from their context and grouped them together as an appendix at the end of the book. However, he left Addition *F* in place after 10:3, thus putting the interpretation of Mordecai's dream (addition *F*) before the dream itself (Addition *A*). English versions that follow Jerome's order therefore present a series of disconnected additions.

Q. What is the content of *A* (11:2-12:6)?

A. The dream of Mordecai, "a Jew, dwelling in the city of Susa, a great man, serving in the court of the king . . . one of the captives whom Nebuchadnezzar . . . had brought from Jerusalem" (11:3f).

Q. What was the nature of the dream?

A. "Two great dragons" incited the surrounding countries "to fight against the nation of the righteous" (11:6f), but "there came a great river, with abundant water; light came, and the sun rose, and the lowly were exalted and consumed those held in honor" (11:10f).

Q. What is the content of *B* (13:1-7)?

A. The edict of "The Great King, Artaxerxes, to the rulers of the hundred and twenty-seven provinces from India to Ethiopia" (13:1).

Q. What was the nature of the edict?

A. Pointing out that "among all the nations in the world there is scattered a certain hostile people," marked out by laws and customs of their own, the king appoints a day on which all Jews shall, "with their wives and children, be utterly destroyed . . . so that those who have long been and are now hostile may in one day go down in violence to Hades, and leave our government completely secure and untroubled hereafter" (13:4-7).

Q. What is the content of *C* (13:8-14:19)?

A. The prayer of Mordecai, "calling to remembrance all the works of the Lord" (13:8), and the prayer of Esther, who "took off her splendid apparel and put on the garments of distress and mourning" (14:2).

Q. What was the nature of the prayer of Mordecai?

A. Protesting that his refusal to bow down to Haman had been in order that "I might not set the glory of man above the glory of God" (13:14), he petitions the "God of Abraham" to "spare thy people; for the eyes of our foes are upon us to annihilate us" (13:15).

Q. What is the nature of Esther's prayer?

A. "Help me, who am alone and have no helper but thee, O Lord . . . hear the voice of the despairing, and save us from the hands of evildoers" (14:14,19).

Q. What is the content of *D* (15:1-16)?

A. Esther's entrance into the presence of the king.

Q. How did she make ready for this ordeal?

A. She "arrayed herself in splendid attire. . . . She was radiant with perfect beauty, and she looked happy, as if beloved, but her heart was frozen with fear" (15:1,5).

Q. What effect did her coming into his presence have upon the king?

A. "He was most terrifying. . . . Then God changed the spirit of the king to gentleness" (15:6,8).

Q. What is the content of *E* (16:1-24)?

A. The decree made by Artaxerxes on behalf of the Jews.

Q. What was the nature of the decree?

A. Reversing the position he had taken earlier, the king, having found "that the Jews, who were consigned to annihilation . . . are not evildoers" (16:15), cancels the former edict and says, ". . . permit the Jews to live under their own laws" (16:19).

Q. What is the content of *F* (10:4-11:1)?

A. The interpretation of Mordecai's dream.

Q. What did the dream signify?

A. "The tiny spring which became a river, and there was light and the sun and abundant water—the river is Esther, whom the king married and made queen. The two dragons are Haman and myself" (10:6f). God has "made two lots, one for the people of God and one for all the nations. And these two lots came to the hour and moment and day of decision. . . . And God remembered his people and vindicated his inheritance" (10:10-12).

THE WISDOM OF SOLOMON

Q. Who is the author of The Wisdom of Solomon?

A. As the name of Moses was synonymous with law and David with poetry, so that of Solomon was synonymous with wisdom, and an anonymous sage—or sages—has here set down the kind of wise counsel that might have been appropriate to a man in Solomon's position.

Q. At what points does the author try specifically to fit his book into the framework of Solomon's reign?

A. Solomon encountered the leaders of many other nations—Tyre, Egypt, Sheba—and the Wisdom of Solomon begins with words that Solomon might have addressed to his fellow sovereigns:

"Love righteousness, you rulers of the earth,
think of the Lord with uprightness,
and seek him with sincerity of heart" (1:1).

The passage in 7:7:

"Therefore I prayed, and understanding was given me;
I called upon God, and the spirit of wisdom came to me"

is no doubt an allusion to I Kings 3:9-12, which reports the prayer offered by Solomon upon his accession to the throne: "Give thy servant an understanding mind to govern thy people, that I may discern between good and evil." Personifying wisdom, the author says, "I loved her and sought her from my youth" (8:2). 9:1-18 is a prayer for the kind of wisdom by means of which

"I shall judge thy people justly,
and shall be worthy of the throne of my father" (9:12).

I Kings 4:33 says that Solomon "spoke of trees, from the cedar that is in Lebanon to the hyssop that grows out of the wall; he spoke also of beasts, and of birds, and of reptiles, and of fish." Wisdom of Solomon 7:17-20 explains that it was God

"who gave me unerring knowledge of what exists . . .
the natures of animals and the temples of wild beasts,
the powers of spirits and the reasonings of men,
the varieties of plants and the virtues of roots."

Q. How does the author set forth the philosophy of the men who reject wisdom and reason "unsoundly"?

A. "Come, therefore, let us enjoy the good things that exist. . . .
Let us crown ourselves with rosebuds before they wither. . . .
Let us oppress the righteous poor man,
let us not spare the widow
nor regard the gray hairs of the aged.
But let our might be our law of right" (2:6-11).

Q. What philosophical position is accorded Wisdom?

A. "Though she is but one, she can do all things,
and while remaining in herself, she renews all things;
in every generation she passes into holy souls
and makes friends of God, and prophets" (7:27).
"She reaches mightily from one end of the earth to the other,
and she orders all things well" (8:1);
"those who get it obtain friendship with God" (7:14).
"For wisdom is more mobile than any motion;
because of her pureness she pervades and penetrates all things.
For she is a breath of the power of God,
and a pure emanation of the glory of the Almighty. . . .
For she is a reflection of eternal light,
a spotless mirror of the working of God,
and an image of his goodness" (7:24-26).

Q. What future reckoning is envisioned?

A. The wicked
"will come with dread when their sins are reckoned up,
and their lawless deeds will convict them to their face.
Then the righteous man will stand with great confidence
in the presence of those who have afflicted him" (4:20;5:1).

Q. What figures of speech are used to describe the fleeting character
of the things for which the wicked live?

A. ". . . like a rumor that passes by;
like a ship that sails through the billowy water,
and when it has passed no trace can be found . . .
or as, when a bird flies through the air,
no evidence of its passage is found . . .
or as, when an arrow is shot at a target,
the air, thus divided, comes together at once,
so that no one knows its pathway" (5:9-12).

Q. How is "the hope of the ungodly man" described?

A. It is

"like chaff carried by the wind
and like a light hoarfrost driven away by a storm;
it is dispersed like smoke before the wind,
and it passes like the remembrance of a guest who stays but
a day" (5:14).

Q. What passages stress the equality of all men?

A. "For the Lord . . . will not stand in awe of any one,
nor show deference to greatness;
because he himself made both small and great,
and he takes thought for all alike" (6:7).
"And when I was born, I began to breathe the common air,
and fell upon the kindred earth,
and my first sound was a cry, like that of all.
I was nursed with care in swaddling cloths.
For no king has had a different beginning of existence;
there is for all mankind one entrance into life, and a common
departure" (7:3-6).

Q. What is the author's doctrine of grace?

A. "God's grace and mercy are with his elect,
and he watches over his holy ones" (4:15).
"For thou lovest all things that exist,
and hast loathing for none of the things which thou hast made,
for thou wouldst not have made anything if thou hadst hated
it" (11:24).
"But thou, our God, art kind and true,
patient, and ruling all things in mercy.
For even if we sin we are thine, knowing thy power" (15:1f).

Q. What procedures are recommended for obtaining wisdom?

A. "He who rises early to seek her will have no difficulty,
for he will find her sitting at his gates.
To fix one's thought on her is perfect understanding" (6:14f).

Q. Does the author consider wisdom to be the possession of old
men alone?

A. Here is why the youthful king seeks wisdom:
"Because of her I shall have glory among the multitudes

and honor in the presence of the elders, though I am young"
(8:10).
"For old age is not honored for length of time,
nor measured by number of years;
but understanding is gray hair for men,
and a blameless life is ripe old age" (4:8f);
"youth that is quickly perfected will condemn the prolonged
old age of the unrighteous man" (4:16).

Q. What are the practical advantages of possessing wisdom?

A. ". . . she knows the things of old, and infers the things to come;
she understands turns of speech and the solution of riddles;
she has foreknowledge of signs and wonders
and of the outcome of seasons and times" (8:8).
"When I enter my house, I shall find rest with her,
for companionship with her has no bitterness,
and life with her has no pain, but gladness and joy" (8:16).

Q. What is the author's definition of fear?

A. "For fear is nothing but the surrender of the helps that come
from reason" (17:12).

Q. How does the author account for the presence of death?

A. "God did not make death . . .
But ungodly men by their words and deeds summoned death"
(1:13,16);
"for God created man for incorruption,
and made him in the image of his own eternity,
but through the devil's envy death entered the world,
and those who belong to his party experience it" (2:23f).

Q. What is the author's doctrine of immortality?

A. Giving heed to the laws of wisdom "is assurance of immortality" (6:18), and "righteousness is immortal" (1:15).
"Because of her [i.e., wisdom] I shall have immortality,
and leave an everlasting remembrance to those who come after
me" (8:13).
"But the souls of the righteous are in the hand of God,
and no torment will ever touch them" (3:1).
"But the righteous live for ever,
and their reward is with the Lord" (5:15).

Q. What fate awaits those who do not gain the life that comes through wisdom?

A. "But the ungodly will be punished as their reasoning deserves, who disregarded the righteous man and rebelled against the Lord;

for whoever despises wisdom and instruction is miserable" (3:10f).

Q. How does Enoch illustrate the author's thesis?

A. "There was one who pleased God and was loved by him, and while living among sinners he was taken up. He was caught up lest evil change his understanding or guile deceive his soul" (4:10f).

Q. What use does the author make of the favorite Hebrew numerical device of grouping things by seven?

A. He lists seven wise men from Adam to Moses (10:1-21); seven sounds (17:18f) that terrified the Egyptians when "with one chain of darkness they all were bound" (17:17); seven points of contrast between Israel and the Egyptians (11:1-26; 16:1-19:21). In addition, the description of wisdom in 7:22f enumerates twenty-one (i.e., 3 x 7) distinctive attributes (it is "intelligent, holy, subtle . . . invulnerable," etc.)

Q. Who are the seven exemplars of wisdom in early Hebrew history?

A. Adam (who is contrasted with Cain), Noah, Abraham, Lot, Jacob, Joseph, Moses.

Q. How else was wisdom manifest in the life of the nation?

A. "She guided them along a marvelous way, and became a shelter to them by day, and a starry flame through the night. She brought them over the Red Sea" (10:17f).

After that, wisdom guided the people "through an uninhabited wilderness" (11:2; cf. 16:2; 19:12). He who is the source of wisdom, too, prepared the way in Canaan,

"that the land most precious of all to thee might receive a worthy colony of the servants of God" (12:7).

Q. To the author, what was the instrument of the deliverance that God wrought in Egypt?

A. ". . . thy all-powerful word leaped from heaven, from the royal throne,

into the midst of the land that was doomed,

a stern warrior carrying the sharp sword of thy authentic command" (18:15f).

Q. Wherein lies a nation's true security?

A. "A multitude of wise men is the salvation of the world,

and a sensible king is the stability of his people" (6:24).

Q. How does the author picture the greatness of God?

A. ". . . the whole world before thee is like a speck that tips the scales,

and like a drop of morning dew that falls upon the ground" (11:22).

"For thou hast power over life and death" (16:13).

Q. How does the author ridicule idols and idol-makers?

A. A man takes "a stick crooked and full of knots" (13:13) and fashions

"it like the image of a man,

or makes it like some worthless animal,

giving it a coat of red paint. . . .

When he prays . . .

he is not ashamed to address a lifeless thing.

For health he appeals to a thing that is weak;

for life he prays to a thing that is dead" (13:13,14,17,18).

Q. How does the author account for the origin of idolatry?

A. "For the idea of making idols was the beginning of fornication,

and the invention of them was the corruption of life,

for neither have they existed from the beginning

nor will they exist for ever.

For through the vanity of man they entered the world" (14:12-14).

Q. What does he think were the first examples of idol-making?

A. "For a father, consumed with grief at an untimely bereavement, made an image of his child, who had been suddenly taken from him. . . .

Then the ungodly custom, grown strong with time, was kept as a law, and at the command of monarchs graven images were worshiped" (14:15f).

Q. To what does idolatry lead?

A. "For the worship of idols not to be named
is the beginning and cause and end of every evil" (14:27).

Q. What well-known phrases occur in this book?

A. "Holy land" as a description of Canaan (12:3); "good hope" (12:19); "they call such great evils peace" (14:22); "misspent toil" (15:8); "cheaper than dirt" (15:10); "he is better than the objects he worships" (15:17); "the universe defends the righteous" (16:17); "the food of angels" (16:20); "great are thy judgments" (17:1); "prisoners of long night" (17:2); "sick soul" (17:8); "a prison not made of iron" (17:16); "singing the praises of the fathers" (18:9); "the fate they deserved" (19:4).

Q. What are some phrases from the Wisdom of Solomon that are echoed in the New Testament?

A. "That which hold all things together" (1:7) is echoed in Colossians 1:17; "our life will pass away like the traces of a cloud" (2:4) is echoed in Jude 12 and II Peter 2:17; "our allotted time is the passing of a shadow" (2:5) is echoed in James 1:17; "this earthy tent" (9:15) is echoed in II Corinthians 5:1. 13:1-9 provides several phrases for Paul in Romans 1:18-25; references to Noah's ark ("the hope of the world took refuge on a raft . . . blessed is the wood by which righteousness comes" —14:6f) are echoed in I Peter 3:18-21; 18:1 ("heard their voices but did not see their forms") is echoed in Acts 26:14-18; cf. Acts 22:9; 19:6 ("the whole creation in its nature was fashioned anew") is echoed in Romans 8:22 and II Corinthians 5:17.

Q. With what doxology does the author conclude his work?

A. "For in everything, O Lord, thou hast exalted and glorified thy people;
and thou hast not neglected to help them at all times and in all places" (19:22).

ECCLESIASTICUS, OR THE WISDOM OF
JESUS THE SON OF
SIRACH

Q. What is the meaning of the title?

A. *Ecclesiasticus,* derived from the Greek word for "church," has made its way into English through the Vulgate; it seems to indicate that, of all the books in the Apocrypha, this is pre-eminently the one that, as expressed in the sixth of the Thirty-Nine Articles, "the Church doth read for example of life and instruction of manners."

Q. What is the alternative title?

A. "The Wisdom of Jesus the Son of Sirach"; shortened to "Sirach," this is the title often used.

Q. What is the significance of the word "Wisdom" in the title?

A. It identifies this book with the attitude and traditions of that group of men in Hebrew society known as "The Wise." As distinguished from priests and prophets, this group cherished and transmitted the lore that had commended itself to the sages of preceding generations. "Wisdom" provided the kind of guidance that enabled a man to be successful in business, get on well with his fellows, obtain status in the community, handle prosperity with discretion, and face with courage and fortitude whatever adversities life might bring.

Q. Who was "Jesus the Son of Sirach"?

A. *Jesus* is the Greek form of the Hebrew *Joshua,* a name not uncommon among Jews. This Jesus identifies himself as the Son of Sirach, who, in 50:27, is identified as "son of Eleazar, of Jerusalem." The Son of Sirach is English for *Ben Sira,* a Hebrew phrase by which the author is often referred to.

Q. What is distinctive about this designation?

A. Except for the writings of the prophets and the memoirs of Nehemiah, it is the only writing in the Hebrew Scriptures to which the author attached his name.

Q. When was Sirach written?

A. The events of the Maccabean revolt had evidently not taken place, and 190-180 B.C. seems a likely date.

Q. What of Ben Sira's background?

A. His respectful references to the Law and the Scribes, who were students of the Law (10:5; 38:24f; 44:4), suggest that he himself may have been a scribe or member of what we should call the legal profession; Biblical literature's best description of the scribe is to be found in 39:6b-11. From 51:23 it is inferred that Ben Sira was the headmaster of an academy:

> "Draw near to me, you who are untaught,
>   and lodge in my school."

Q. Did Ben Sira spend all his time in Jerusalem?

A. Apparently not. He writes:

> "I have seen many things in my travels,
>   and I understand more than I can express" (34:11).

From 39:4 it is sometimes inferred that his own travels may have been those of an ambassador:

> "He will serve among great men
>   and appear before rulers;
> he will travel through the lands of foreign nations,
>   for he tests the good and the evil among men."

Q. What effect should learning have upon those who possess it?

A. "Those who love learning should make even greater progress in living according to the law" (Prologue).

Q. What does the author suggest regarding the responsibility of the scribe toward others?

A. "Those who love learning should be able to help the outsiders by both speaking and writing" (Prologue).

Q. What is necessary for one who would become expert in the Law?

A. "The wisdom of the scribe depends on the opportunity of leisure" (38:24).

Q. What philosophical position is assigned to wisdom?

A. "All wisdom comes from the Lord" (1:1). "Wisdom was created before all things" (1:4). "The Lord himself created wisdom" (1:9). "Whoever loves her loves life" (4:12). "Blessed is the man who meditates on wisdom" (14:20). "Pursue wisdom like a hunter" (14:22).

Q. What relationship has wisdom to the fear of the Lord?

A. To fear the Lord "is the beginning of wisdom" (1:14), "wisdom's full measure" (1:16), "the crown of wisdom" (1:18), "the root of wisdom" (1:20).

> "The man who fears the Lord. . . .
>> Will find gladness and a crown of rejoicing,
>>> and will acquire an everlasting name" (15:1,6).
> "He who fears the Lord will not be timid,
>> nor play the coward, for he is his hope" (34:14).
> "The fear of the Lord is like a garden of blessing" (40:27).

Q. What attitude does the wise man take toward adversity?

A. "Accept whatever is brought upon you,
and in changes that humble you be patient" (2:4).
"Good things and bad, life and death,
poverty and wealth, come from the Lord" (11:14).

Q. How is I Peter 1:7, a New Testament picture regarding adversity, here anticipated?

A. "For gold is tested in the fire" (2:5).

Q. How does the wise man conduct himself toward others?

A. "The greater you are, the more you must humble yourself" (3:18). "Do not be ashamed to confess your sins" (4:26).
". . . I have not labored for myself alone,
but for all who seek instruction" (33:17).

Q. How does the wise man conduct himself in the master-servant relationship?

A. "Do not be like a lion in your home,
nor be a faultfinder with your servants" (4:30).
"Do not abuse a servant who performs his work faithfully,
or a hired laborer who devotes himself to you" (7:20).
"Fodder and a stick and burdens for an ass;
bread and discipline and work for a servant.
Set your slave to work and you will find rest;
leave his hands idle, and he will seek liberty" (33:24f).

Q. What of the wise man and his friends?

A. "A pleasant voice multiplies friends,
and a gracious tongue multiplies courtesies.
Let those that are at peace with you be many,
but let your advisers be one in a thousand" (6:5f).
"A faithful friend is an elixir of life" (6:16).

"Forsake not an old friend. . . .
A new friend is like new wine" (9:10).
"And establish the counsel of your own heart,
     for no one is more faithful to you than it is.
For a man's soul sometimes keeps him better informed
     than seven watchmen sitting high on a watchtower"
          (37:13f).

Q. How does the wise man look upon work?

A. "Do not hate toilsome labor, or farm work, which were created by the Most High" (7:15). "Do not make a display of your wisdom when you do your work" (10:26).

Q. What does the author say of those who work with their hands?

A. "Without them a city cannot be established . . .
     they keep stable the fabric of the world,
     and their prayer is in the practice of their trade"
          (38:32,34).

Q. What is the wise man's attitude toward the needy?

A. "Stretch forth your hand to the poor" (7:32).
"Do not fail those who weep" (7:34).
"Do not shrink from visiting a sick man" (7:35).
"Be like a father to orphans" (4:10).

Q. What does the author say about silence?

A. "There is one who keeps silent because he has no answer,
     while another keeps silent because he knows when to speak.
A wise man will be silent until the right moment. . . .
Whoever uses too many words will be loathed,
     and whoever usurps the right to speak will be hated"
          (20:6-8).
"A sandy ascent for the feet of the aged—
     such is a garrulous wife for a quiet husband" (25:20).
"Speak concisely, say much in few words;
     be as one who knows and yet holds his tongue" (32:8).

Q. What three things does the author consider "beautiful in the sight of the Lord and of men"?

A. "Agreement between brothers,
          friendship between neighbors,
          and a wife and husband who live in harmony" (25:1).

Q. What "three kinds of men" does the author say his "soul hates"?

A. "A beggar who is proud, a rich man who is a liar,
and an adulterous old man who lacks good sense" (25:2).

Q. What is the author's doctrine of the two ways?

A. "Before a man are life and death,
and whichever he chooses will be given to him" (15:17).
"Woe to timid hearts and slack hands,
and to the sinner who walks along two ways." (2:12).

Q. What is the duty of those in public life?

A. "A wise magistrate will educate his people" (10:1).

Q. What does the author say about the medical profession?

A. "Honor the physician with the honor due him, according to your need of him;
for the Lord created him;
for healing comes from the Most High" (38:1).
"The Lord created medicines from the earth,
and a sensible man will not despise them . . .
the pharmacist makes of them a compound.
His works will never be finished;
and from him health is upon the face of the earth" (38:4,8).
"A long illness baffles the physician" (10:10).
"Before you speak, learn,
and before you fall ill, take care of your health" (18:19).
"And give the physician his place, for the Lord created him. . .
He who sins before his Maker,
may he fall into the care of a physician" (38:12,15).

Q. What event in Israel's history does the author cite as illustrating the uses of medicine?

A. "Was not water made sweet with a tree
in order that his power might be made known?" (38:5).
This is evidently an allusion to Exodus 15:23-25. When the children of Israel "came to Marah, they could not drink the water of Marah because it was bitter." God showed Moses "a tree, and he threw it into the water, and the water became sweet."

Q. What psychosomatic insights are here?

A. "A man's heart changes his countenance,
  either for good or for evil.
The mark of a happy heart is a cheerful face" (13:25f).
"Jealousy and anger shorten life,
  and anxiety brings on old age too soon.
A man of cheerful and good heart
  will give heed to the food he eats" (30:24f).
"Wakefulness over wealth wastes away one's flesh,
  and anxiety about it removes sleep.
Wakeful anxiety prevents slumber" (31:1f).
"Healthy sleep depends on moderate eating;
  he rises early and feels fit" (31:20).

Q. Who are the "famous men" (44:1) whom the author praises?

A. Enoch ("an example of repentance to all generations"—44:16),
Noah ("Everlasting covenants were made with him"—44:18), Abraham
("when he was tested he was found faithful"—44:20), Isaac (who, for
Abraham's sake, was given "the same assurance"—44:22), Jacob (God
"acknowledged him with his blessings"—44:23), Moses ("beloved by
God and man"—45:1), Aaron ("a holy man"—45:6), Phinehas ("in the
ready goodness of his soul"—45:23), Joshua ("a great savior of God's
elect"—46:1), Caleb (from whom people learned that "it is good to
follow the Lord"—46:10), the judges ("may their memory be blessed"
—46:11), Samuel ("By his faithfulness he was proved to be a prophet"
—46:15), Nathan ("rose up to prophesy"—47:1), David ("he sang
praise with all his heart"—47:8; cf. 45:25), Solomon ("you were loved
for your peace"—47:16), Rehoboam ("whose policy caused the people
to revolt"—47:23) and Jeroboam ("who caused Israel to sin"—47:23),
Elijah ("Blessed are those who saw you"—48:11), Elisha ("in all his
days he did not tremble before any ruler"—48:12), Hezekiah (who "did
what was pleasing to the Lord"—48:22), Josiah ("in the days of wicked
men he strengthened godliness"—49:3), Jeremiah ("consecrated in the
womb as prophet"—49.7), Ezekiel ("who saw the vision of glory"—
49:8), the twelve prophets ("they comforted the people of Jacob"—49:
10), Zerubbabel ("He was like a signet on the right hand"—49:11) and
Jeshua ("raised a temple holy to the Lord"—49:12), Nehemiah ("he
raised for us the walls that had fallen"—49:13), Enoch ("he was taken

up from the earth"—49:14), Joseph (no one like him "has been born"
—49:15), Shem and Seth ("honored among men"—49:16), Adam
(honored "above every living being in the creation"—49:16), Simon the
high priest ("fortified the temple"—50:1).

Q. What phrases reveal the author's idea of God?

A. "For the Lord is compassionate and merciful;

　　he forgives sin and saves in time of affliction" (2:11);

"the Lord is slow to anger" (5:4); "he has not given any one permission
to sin" (15:20); "to those who repent he grants a return" (17:24); "He
who lives for ever created the whole universe" (18:1); "the prayer of a
poor man goes from his lips to the ears of God" (21:5); "O Lord, Father
and Ruler of my life" (23:1); "the eyes of the Lord are ten thousand
times brighter than the sun" (23:19); "the Lord will never give up his
mercy" (47:22).

　　"The eyes of the Lord are upon those who love him . . .

　　　　he grants healing, life, and blessing" (34:16,17);

"the prayer of the humble pierces the clouds" (35:17); "thou art the
Lord, the God of the ages" (36:17).

　　"He has ordained the splendors of his wisdom,

　　　　and he is from everlasting and to everlasting" (42:21).

　　"Though we speak much we cannot reach the end,

　　　　and the sum of our words is, 'He is the all' " (43:27).

Q. What elements in nature show the greatness of God?

A. "The glory of the stars is the beauty of heaven. . . .

　　Look upon the rainbow, and praise him who made it. . . .

　　By his command he sends the driving snow

　　　　and speeds the lightnings of his judgment" (43:9,11,13).

Q. What is the author's idea of immortality?

A. "The father may die, and yet he is not dead,

　　　　for he has left behind him one like himself" (30:4).

　　"Children and the building of a city establish a man's name"
　　　　(40:19).

　　"The days of a good life are numbered,

　　　　but a good name endures for ever" (41:13);

　　"may the name of those who have been honored

　　live again in their sons!" (46:12).

Q. What is the author's attitude toward parental responsibility?

A. "Do you have children? Discipline them,
  and make them obedient from their youth" (7:23).
"Do not desire a multitude of useless children . . .
  to die childless is better than to have ungodly children"
  (16:1,3).

Q. What should be the father's disposition toward his children?

A. "He who loves his son will whip him often,
  in order that he may rejoice at the way he turns out"
  (30:1).
"A horse that is untamed turns out to be stubborn,
  and a son unrestrained turns out to be wilful" (30:8).

Q. What comes of a father's failure at this point?

A. "It is a disgrace to be the father of an undisciplined son" (22:3).
"Discipline your son and take pains with him,
  that you may not be offended by his shamelessness" (30:
  13).

Q. What, in turn, does the author say of filial responsibility?

A. "Whoever honors his father will be gladdened by his own children" (3:5).
"Call no one happy before his death;
  a man will be known through his children" (11:28).

Q. What observations are there regarding youth and age?

A. "All living beings become old like a garment" (14:17).
"Do not disdain a man when he is old,
  for some of us are growing old" (8:6).
"You have gathered nothing in your youth;
  how then can you find anything in your old age?" (25:3).

Q. What material things are worth striving for?

A. "The essentials for life are water and bread
  and clothing and a house to cover one's nakedness" (29:
  21).
"He who loves gold will not be justified,
  and he who pursues money will be led astray by it" (31:5).
"Health and soundness are better than all gold,
  and a robust body than countless riches" (30:15).
"Basic to all the needs of man's life
  are water and fire and iron and salt

and wheat flour and milk and honey,
the blood of the grape, and oil and clothing" (39:26).

Q. What are the duties of a guest?

A. "Eat like a human being what is set before you,
and do not chew greedily, lest you be hated" (31:16).

"If they make you master of the feast, do not exalt yourself
(32:1).

"Leave in good time and do not be the last;
go home quickly and do not linger" (32:11).

Q. What does the author say about wine?

A. "Do not aim to be valiant over wine,
for wine has destroyed many" (31:25).

"Wine drunk to excess is bitterness of soul,
with provocation and stumbling" (31:29).

Q. What is the author's position with respect to dreams?

A. ". . . dreams give wings to fools.
As one who catches at a shadow and pursues the wind,
so is he who gives heed to dreams. . . .
Unless they are sent from the Most High as a visitation,
do not give your mind to them.
For dreams have deceived many" (34:1,2,6).

Q. What is the author's attitude toward women?

A. "From a woman sin had its beginning,
and because of her we all die" (25:24).

"Better is the wickedness of a man than a woman who does
good;
and it is a woman who brings shame and disgrace" (42:14).

Q. What is ths author's attitude toward wives?

A. "Do not deprive yourself of a wise and good wife,
for her charm is worth more than gold" (7:19);

"happy is he who lives with an intelligent wife" (25:8).

"I would rather dwell with a lion and a dragon
than dwell with an evil wife" (25:16).

"Any iniquity is insignificant compared to a wife's iniquity"
25:19).

"Happy is the husband of a good wife;
the number of his days will be doubled" (26:1).

"A good wife is a great blessing" (26:3).

"An evil wife is an ox yoke which chafes" (26:7).

"A silent wife is a gift of the Lord" (26:14).

"A modest wife adds charm to charm" (26:15).

Q. To what does the author compare a good homemaker?

A. "Like the sun rising in the heights of the Lord,

so is the beauty of a good wife in her well-ordered home" (26:
16);

"he who acquires a wife gets his best possession" (36:24).

Q. What is the author's teaching about race?

A. "What race is worthy of honor? The human race. . . .

What race is unworthy of honor? Those who transgress the
commandments" (10:19).

Q. What canon of Scripture was known to the author?

A. "The law and the prophets and the other books of our fathers"
(Prologue).

Q. How does the author face the problem of translating his grandfather's work?

A. The reader is urged "to be indulgent in cases where, despite our
diligent labor in translating, we may seem to have rendered some phrases
imperfectly. For what was originally expressed in Hebrew does not have
exactly the same sense when translated into another language" (Prologue).

Q. What forms of worship are found in Ecclesiasticus?

A. Prayer of petition (36:1-17); prayer of thanksgiving (51:1-12);
adoration of the Creator (16:24-18:14; 42:15-43:33).

Q. What sayings in Sirach are paralleled by proverbs in the Western world?

A. "How can the clay pot associate with the iron kettle?" (13:2).

"Birds flock with their kind" (27:9).

"The way of sinners is smoothly paved with stones,

but at its end is the pit of Hades" (21:10);

"idleness teaches much evil" (33:27).

Q. What are some other wise and witty sayings recorded by
Sirach?

A. "Do not argue about a matter which does not concern you"
(11:9). "Who will pity a snake charmer bitten by a serpent?" (12:13).

"Whoever touches pitch will be defiled" (13:1). "Do not go to law against a judge" (8:14). "A hymn of praise is not fitting on the lips of a sinner" (15:9). "To a sensible man education is like a golden ornament" (21:21).

"Like a eunuch's desire to violate a maiden
   is a man who executes judgments by violence" (20:4).

"An ungracious man is like a story told at the wrong time,
   which is continually on the lips of the ignorant" (20:19).

Q. What are some passages from Ben Sira that are echoed in the New Testament?

A. 10:14 in Luke 1:52; 7:34 in Romans 12:15; 11:32 in James 3:5; 26:7 in II Corinthians 6:14; 28:2 in Matthew 6:12; 29:7 in Matthew 5:42; 33:31 in Philemon 16; 34:12 in II Corinthians 11:23; 43:26 in Colossians 1:17.

Q. What Christian hymn was inspired by a passage in Ecclesiasticus?

A. 50:22-24 is the basis for a hymn written about 1636 by a German pastor, Martin Rinkart (1586-1649); the first two stanzas were composed for the author's own family to use as a grace before meat; the finished hymn, traditionally associated with the conclusion of the Thirty Years' War, has been called the German *Te Deum;* it is sung in the German churches on New Year's Eve. In the translation of Catherine Winkworth, whose *Lyra Germanica* "opened a new source of light, consolation, and strength in many thousand homes," the first stanza is as follows:

"Now thank we all our God
   With heart and hands and voices,
Who wondrous things has done,
   In whom the world rejoices;
Who, from our mothers' arms,
   Hath blessed us on our way
With countless gifts of love,
   And still is ours today."

BARUCH

Q. Who is the Baruch for whom the book is named?

A. He is identified (1:1) as "the son of Neraiah, son of Mahseiah, son of Zedekiah, son of Hasadiah, son of Hilkiah"; he appears in the prophetic books of the Old Testament as secretary to Jeremiah (Jeremiah 32:12; 36:4,18; 43:3; 45:1).

Q. What is the literary form of "Baruch"?

A. The Vulgate gives its title as "The Prophecy of Baruch"; the work consists of an historical introduction followed by prayers and poems.

Q. Are these all by a single author?

A. Because of great differences in literary style, as well as in content, it is believed by many that the book combines the work of two, three, or even four men.

Q. When was the book written?

A. Although the historical setting is in 586 B.C., the work in its present form is thought to date from the third or second century B.C.

Q. What is the historical setting?

A. Following "the time when the Chaldeans took Jerusalem and burned it with fire" (1:2), Baruch delivered this message "in the hearing of all the people, small and great, all who dwelt in Babylon by the river Sud" (1:4).

Q. What was the effect upon the people?

A. "Then they wept, and fasted, and prayed before the Lord; and they collected money, each giving what he could; and they sent it to Jerusalem" (1:5-7), saying: "pray for the life of Nebuchadnezzar. . . . And pray for us" (1:11,13).

Q. What form of prayer was suggested?

A. A confession of sins: "We did not heed the voice of the Lord our God . . . but we each followed the intent of his own wicked heart" (1:21; cf. 1:15-3:8).

Q. Upon what other Scriptures is this passage modeled?

A. Daniel 9:7-10; Deuteronomy 28; Jeremiah 31:31; 32:40.

Q. What follows the prayer of confession?

A. A poem in praise of wisdom (3:9-4:4).

Q. To what does the author attribute the fact that Israel is "growing old in a foreign country" (3:10)?

A. "You have forsaken the fountain of wisdom" (3:12).

Q. What other Scriptures influence the panegyric on wisdom?

A. Job 28; Proverbs 8; Ecclesiasticus 24; Deuteronomy 30:11-13.

Q. With what statutes does the author identify wisdom?

A. "She is the book of the commandments of God,
and the law that endures for ever" (4:1).

Q. What Christian hymn is based on this poem?

A. Joseph Addison's "The spacious firmament on high" was inspired by Psalm 19:1-6 and Baruch 3:34;

". . . the stars shone in their watches, and were glad;
he called them and they said, 'Here we are!'
They shone with gladness for him who made them."

Q. What use has been made of this hymn in the age of electronic communication?

A. It was recited by Jane Cowl on the dedicatory program for the NBC building in Rockefeller Center, New York.

Q. How does Baruch's praise of wisdom warn against Greek philosophy?

A. "Do not give your glory to another,
or your advantages to an alien people" (4:3).

Q. What follows the poem in praise of wisdom?

A. A poem containing words of comfort (4:5-5:9).

Q. By what other Scriptures was this inspired?

A. Isaiah 40-55.

Q. What philosophy of suffering is here?

A. "You were handed over to your enemies,
because you angered God" (4:6).

Q. What description is given of the Chaldeans?

A. "For he brought against them [i.e., Judah] a nation from afar,
a shameless nation, of a strange language,
who had no respect for an old man,
and had no pity for a child" (4:15).

Q. How does the author sum up Israel's history subsequent to the Chaldean invasion?

A. "My tender sons have traveled rough roads" (4:26).

Q. What future does the author envision for Babylonia?

A. "For fire will come upon her from the Everlasting for many days,

and for a long time she will be inhabited by demons"
(4:35).

Q. What future is envisioned for Israel?

A. "For he who brought these calamities upon you

will bring you everlasting joy with your salvation" (4:29).

Q. How will nature manifest God's favor?

A. "The woods and every fragrant tree

have shaded Israel at God's command" (5:8).

THE LETTER OF
JEREMIAH

Q. What is the literary form of this work?

A. Although called a "letter," it has no characteristics of the epistolary form but is rather in the nature of a tract, owing something to the Stoic diatribe. In the Vulgate and in the King James Version it is simply Chapter 6 of "Baruch"; the Septuagint makes it a separate work.

Q. When was this letter written?

A. Some date it in the fourth century B.C., some in the second century B.C.

Q. What is the reason for its being called a letter of Jeremiah?

A. Jeremiah 29:1-23 records a "letter which Jeremiah the prophet sent from Jerusalem to the elders of the exile" with this warning to those who had been carried away captive: "Do not let your prophets and your diviners who are among you deceive you"; this is the inspiration for the present letter.

Q. What are the circumstances under which it was reportedly sent?

A. "A letter which Jeremiah sent to those who were to be taken to Babylon as captives by Nebuchadnezzar, king of the Babylonians" (verse 2).

Q. Against what dangers does the letter warn?

A. "Now in Babylon you will see gods make of silver and gold and wood. . . . So take care not to become at all like the foreigners or to let fear for these gods possess you" (verse 4f).

Q. What specific references are made to Babylonian religious practices?

A. The mourning for dying gods (verse 32) and the maidens' sacrifice of their virginity (verse 43).

Q. In what ways does the author ridicule idols?

A. They "cannot speak" (verse 8); they "cannot save themselves from rust and corrosion" (verse 12); "they do not notice when their faces have been blackened by the smoke of the temple" (verse 21); they have "no feeling" (verse 24); "there is no breath in them" (verse 25). "They cannot set up a king or depose one" (verse 34). "They cannot save a man from death or rescue the weak from the strong" (verse 36). "They cannot take pity on a widow or do good to an orphan" (verse 38); "they cannot set up a king over a country or give rain to men" (verse 53).

Q. How do the Chaldeans themselves acknowledge the inadequacy of their idols?

A. "When fire breaks out in a temple of wooden gods overlaid with gold or silver, their priests will flee and escape, but the gods will be burnt in two like beams" (verse 55).

Q. What is preferable to idols?

A. "So it is better to be a king who shows his courage, or a household utensil that serves its owner's need, than to be these false gods" (verse 59).

Q. What is the author's final verdict upon idols?

A. "Like a scarecrow in a cucumber bed, that guards nothing, so are their gods of wood, overlaid with gold and silver" (verse 70).

THE PRAYER OF AZARIAH AND
THE SONG OF THE THREE YOUNG MEN

Q. What relationship have these to the canonical Scriptures?

A. They are additions to the book of Daniel, inserted between Daniel 3:23 and 3:24.

Q. What is the appropriateness of this insertion?

A. Daniel 3:23 relates how "These three men, Shadrach, Meshach and Abednego, fell bound into the burning fiery furnace." This addition begins, "And they walked about in the midst of the flames, singing hymns to God and blessing the Lord. Then Azariah stood and offered this prayer . . ." (verse 1f).

Q. Who was Azariah?

A. One of Daniel's three companions, Hananiah, Mishael, and Azariah, to whom the Babylonians gave the names Shadrach, Meshach, and Abednego (Daniel 1:6f).

Q. What element of confession is included in the prayer?

A. "All that thou hast done to us,
    thou hast done in true judgment" (verse 8; cf. 4,5).

Q. What was the nature of the judgment that had befallen?

A. "Thou hast given us into the hands of lawless enemies, most hateful rebels,
    and to an unjust king, the most wicked in all the world" (verse 9).

Q. What historical circumstance is pleaded?

A. The covenant that God had made with Abraham, Isaac, and Israel (verse 12).

Q. How does the author approach the Deity?

A. "Yet with a contrite heart and a humble spirit may we be accepted" (verse 16).

Q. Does the prayer breathe forgiveness?

A. On the contrary: "Let all who do harm to thy servants be put to shame" (verse 20).

Q. To what other Scriptures is this prayer related?

A. Daniel 9:4-19; Jeremiah 26; 32; 44; Ezra 9; Nehemiah 1; 9; Psalm 51.

Q. How was the fiery furnace stoked?

A. "The king's servants . . . did not cease feeding the furnace fires with naphtha, pitch, tow, and brush. And the flame streamed out above the furnace forty-nine cubits" (verse 24).

Q. What protection had those for whom this was to have been an incinerator?

A. "But the angel of the Lord came down into the furnace to be with Azariah and his companions, and drove the fiery flame out of the furnace, and made the midst of the furnace like a moist whirling wind, so that the fire did not touch them at all" (verse 26ff).

Q. What did the men in the furnace do?

A. "Then the three, as with one mouth, praised and glorified and blessed God in the furnace" (verse 28).

Q. With what words did they do this?

A. In a hymn beginning "Blessed art thou, O Lord, God of our fathers" (verse 29), and concluding "for his mercy endures for ever" (verse 68).

Q. What subsequent use has been made of this hymn?

A. It has made its way into Christian liturgy as the *Benedicite,* the title being derived from the Latin verb used in the frequently recurring phrase, "Bless the Lord." From early times the *Benedicite* has been used by Christians as a canticle in morning worship.

Q. What things in creation are called upon to "Bless . . . the Lord"?

A. The heavens, and all powers that reside therein; sun, moon, and stars; winds and all weather; the earth, with all mountains and hills; all growing things; waters, whether springs, rivers, or seas—and the whales that move therein; birds and beasts and cattle; Israel and all the sons of men; all servants of the Lord and souls of the righteous (verses 35-65).

Q. How does the canticle reach its climax?

A. "Bless the Lord, Hananiah, Azariah and Mishael . . .
   for he has . . .
      delivered us from the midst of the burning fiery furnace"
      (verse 66).

Q. To what other sections of the Scripture is this hymn related?

A. Psalms 136, 148, 150.

SUSANNA

Q. Why was this story appended to the book of Daniel?

A. Ezekiel 28:3 speaks of the difficulty of being "wiser than

Daniel." Ezekiel 14:14,20 lists Daniel, along with Noah and Job, as an exemplar of uprightness. In point of fact, Daniel's reputation for shrewdness was almost as great as Solomon's, and in the post-exilic era it was inevitable that tales of superior judgment and insight like this one should become attached to his name.

Q. Who is the Susanna for whom the story is named?

A. "A very beautiful woman and one who feared the Lord" (verse 2), wife of Joakim, who "was very rich and had a spacious garden adjoining his house" (verses 1,4), to which the elders often came.

Q. What passion possessed two of the elders?

A. When they saw Susanna going for a walk in the garden, "they began to desire her" (verse 8).

Q. How did they plan to implement their desire?

A. Concealing themselves in the garden, they approached her when the maids had gone out (verse 19).

Q. What was Susanna's defense?

A. She screamed (verse 24).

Q. What explanation did the elders offer when brought before the authorities?

A. That they had caught her in the embrace of a young man (verse 37).

Q. Which story appeared the more credible, that of Susanna or that of the elders?

A. "The assembly believed" the two men "because they were elders of the people and judges; and they condemned her to death" (verse 41).

Q. When Susanna prayed, protesting her innocence, who came to her aid?

A. "God aroused the holy spirit of a young lad named Daniel" (verse 45).

Q. How did Daniel propose to retry the case?

A. Concerning the elders upon whose testimony Susanna had been condemned, he said: "Separate them far from each other, and I will examine them" (verse 51).

Q. When the men were examined separately, what question did Daniel put to each?

A. "Under what tree did you see them being intimate?" (verses 54,58).

Q. What answer was given by the first?

A. "Under a mastic tree" (verse 54).

Q. What answer was given by the second?

A. "Under an evergreen oak" (verse 58).

Q. Why is it difficult to express in English all that is expressed in Greek with respect to the two trees?

A. In each instance, there is a play on words. At mention of the mastic tree, Daniel says: "the angel of God . . . will immediately cut you in two" (verse 55); in Greek, the words translated "mastic tree" and "cut" are similar. At mention of the evergreen oak, Daniel says: "the angel of God is waiting with his sword to saw you in two" (verse 59); in Greek, the words translated "evergreen oak" and "saw" are similar. It has been suggested that, to translate the puns into English, some rendering such as this would be necessary: "pine tree . . . pine away, ash tree . . . turn to ashes."

Q. What is the judgment of the people upon hearing the self-incriminating answers of the elders?

A. "Out of their own mouths Daniel had convicted them of bearing false witness" (verse 61).

Q. What punishment was imposed upon the elders?

A. "They did to them as they had wickedly planned to do to their neighbor; acting in accordance with the law of Moses, they put them to death" (verse 62).

Q. How did this situation serve to enhance the position of Daniel in the community?

A. "From that day onward Daniel had a great reputation among the people" (verse 64).

Q. What are some musical compositions inspired by the story of Susanna?

A. Carlisle has a modern opera entitled *Susannah*. Handel's oratorio, *Susanna,* begins with a series of songs celebrating the domestic bliss of Susanna and Joakim; when Joakim suddenly departs on a journey, Susanna, filled with dark forebodings, is comforted by the chorus.

BEL AND THE DRAGON

Q. What position is here attributed to Daniel in the reign of Cyrus the Persian over Babylon?

A. "Daniel was a companion of the king, and was the most honored of his friends" (verse 2).

Q. Who or what was Bel?

A. "The Babylonians had an idol called Bel" (verse 3); the name is similar to that elsewhere transliterated "Baal."

Q. Who lived in the temple of Bel and supervised the worship there?

A. "Now there were seventy priests of Bel, besides their wives and children" (verse 10).

Q. Why did Daniel refuse to worship Bel?

A. "Because I do not revere man-made idols, but the living God" (verse 5).

Q. How does the king seek to prove that Bel is living?

A. By citing the huge quantities of food and drink that daily disappeared after being placed before it: "every day they spent on it twelve bushels of fine flour and forty sheep and fifty gallons of wine" (verse 3).

Q. What is Daniel's opinion?

A. "This is but clay inside and brass outside, and it never ate or drank anything" (verse 7).

Q. What test was proposed by the priests?

A. "You yourself, O king, shall set forth the food and mix and place the wine, and shut the door and seal it with your signet. And when you return in the morning, if you do not find that Bel has eaten it all, we will die; or else Daniel will, who is telling lies about us" (verse 11f).

Q. Why were the priests confident about such a test?

A. "Beneath the table they had made a hidden entrance, through which they used to go in regularly and consume the provisions" (verse 13).

Q. How did Daniel prepare for the test?

A. "Then Daniel ordered his servants to bring ashes and they sifted them throughout the whole temple in the presence of the king alone" (verse 14).

Q. What transpired during the night?

A. "The priests came with their wives and children, as they were accustomed to do, and ate and drank everything" (verse 15).

Q. What was the reaction of the king the following morning upon finding the food gone and the seals still unbroken?

A. "You are great, O Bel; and with you there is no deceit" (verse 18).

Q. What was Daniel's reaction?

A. "Then Daniel laughed . . . and said: 'Look at the floor and notice whose footprints these are' " (verse 19).

Q. What was the king's reaction now?

A. He "was enraged," and when he saw "the secret doors," he put he priests "to death and gave Bel over to Daniel, who destroyed it and its temple" (verse 22).

Q. In the history of literature, what distinction belongs to this story?

A. It is one of the earliest examples of the literary form that has come to be known as the detective story.

Q. Besides Bel, what other object of worship was there in the land of the Hebrew exile?

A. "There was also a great dragon, which the Babylonians revered" (verse 23).

Q. When the king affirmed that "this is a living god; so worship him" (verse 24), what was Daniel's reply?

A. "If you, O king, will give me permission, I will slay the dragon without sword or club" (verse 26).

Q. When permission was granted, how did Daniel proceed?

A. He "took pitch, fat, and hair, and boiled them together and made cakes, which he fed to the dragon" (verse 27).

Q. What was the result?

A. "The dragon ate them, and burst open. And Daniel said, 'See what you have been worshiping!' " (verse 27).

Q. What was the reaction of the populace?

A. They "conspired against the king, saying, 'The king has become a Jew' . . . they said, 'Hand Daniel over to us, or else we will kill you and your household' " (verse 28f).

Q. What was the result?

A. "Under compulsion he handed Daniel over to them. They threw Daniel into the lions' den, and he was there for six days" (verse 31).

Q. What was the daily diet of the seven lions?

A. "Every day they had been given two human bodies and two sheep; but these were not given to them now, so that they might devour Daniel" (verse 32).

Q. What provision was made for Daniel's dinner while in the lions' den?

A. The prophet Habakkuk, who was going into the field with bread and pottage for the reapers, was transported by an angel, who "took him by the crown of his head, and lifted him by his hair and set him down in Babylon right over the den. . . . Then Habakkuk shouted, Daniel! Daniel! Take the dinner which God has sent you" (verses 33-37).

Q. What was Daniel's response?

A. "Daniel said, 'Thou hast remembered me, O God, and hast not forsaken those who love thee.' So Daniel arose and ate" (verse 38f).

Q. What happened to Habakkuk?

A. "And the angel of God immediately returned Habakkuk to his own place" (verse 39).

Q. When the king, on the seventh day, came with the expectation of mourning for Daniel, what did he find?

A. "There sat Daniel" (verse 40).

Q. What effect did this have upon the king?

A. He "shouted with a loud voice, 'Thou art great, O Lord God of Daniel, and there is no other besides thee.' And he pulled Daniel out, and threw into the den the men who had attempted his destruction" (verse 41f).

THE PRAYER OF MANASSEH

Q. Who was Manasseh?

A. One of the kings of Judah, Hezekiah's son, who "was twelve years old when he began to reign, and he reigned fifty-five years in Jerusalem" (II Kings 21:1ff).

Q. What kind of reign did he have?

A. He "did what was evil in the sight of the Lord" (II Kings 21:2).

Q. What kinds of evil did he do?

A. "He rebuilt the high places . . . he erected altars for Baal . . . and the graven image of Asherah that he had made he set in the house" of the Lord in Jerusalem (II Kings 21:3-7).

Q. What relation has The Prayer of Manasseh to other Scriptures?

A. II Chronicles 33:12ff relates that when Manasseh "was in distress he entreated the favor of the Lord his God and humbled himself greatly before the God of his fathers. He prayed to him, and God received his entreaty and heard his supplication and brought him again to Jerusalem into his kingdom. Then Manasseh knew that the Lord was God." The canonical Scriptures thus tell of how Manasseh "humbled himself" and "prayed," but do not report the prayer that is here preserved.

Q. What does the canonical Scripture say concerning sources for the life of Manasseh?

A. "Now the rest of the acts of Manasseh, and his prayer to his God, and the words of the seers who spoke to him in the name of the Lord God of Israel, behold, they are in the Chronicles of the Kings of Israel. And his prayer, and how God received his entreaty, and all his sin and his faithlessness, and the sites on which he built high places and set up the Asherim and the images, before he humbled himself, behold, they are written in the Chronicles of the Seers" (II Chronicles 33:18f); although this work has perished, the prayer may have been salvaged from it.

Q. What is the burden of the prayer?

A. It is an expression of penitence.

Q. How does the prayer address the Deity?

A. As the God
"of Ábraham and Isaac and Jacob . . .
thou who hast made heaven and earth . . .
thou who hast shackled the sea" (verses 1-3).

Q. How is God's greatness contrasted with man's weakness?

A. "Thy glorious splendor cannot be borne,
and the wrath of thy threat to sinners is irresistible" (verse 5).

Q. What gives the sinner boldness of access?

A. "Immeasurable and unsearchable is thy promised mercy,
for thou art the Lord Most High,
of great compassion, long-suffering, and very merciful" (verse
7).

Q. What is the attitude of Deity toward repentance?

A. "In the multitude of thy mercies
thou hast appointed repentance for sinners" (verse 7; cf. verse
13).

Q. What confession is offered?

A. "The sins I have committed are more in number than the sand
of the sea. . . .
I have provoked thy wrath
and have done what is evil in thy sight" (verse 9f).

Q. What is the faith in which the prayer is offered?

A. "Unworthy as I am, thou wilt save me in thy great mercy,
and I will praise thee continually all the days of my life" (verse
15).

THE FIRST BOOK OF THE
MACCABEES

Q. What is the meaning of the word *Maccabees*?

A. *Maccabeus,* a descriptive epithet applied to Judas, leader of the Jewish revolt against Antiochus Epiphanes, is commonly thought to mean "The Hammerer"; from *Maccabeus* is derived *Maccabees,* the term applied to the brothers of Judas and their followers in the Great Revolt.

Q. What character in European history had a similar epithet?

A. Charles Martel, grandfather of Charlemagne, was called "The Hammer"; by defeating the Moors in the battle of Tours (732 A.D.), Charles the Hammer repulsed the Moslem invasion of Europe.

Q. Who is the author of I Maccabees?

A. An unnamed writer, evidently a Palestinian Jew resident in Jerusalem.

Q. When did he write?

A. The concluding verses of the book (16:23ff) report that "The rest of the acts of John [i.e., John Hyrcanus I] are written in the chronicles of his high priesthood," which la. ed from 134 to 104 B.C. This would seem to date I Maccabees about 100 B.C. The Romans, who took over Jerusalem in 63 B.C., are consistently presented as "friends and allies" of the Jews (cf. 8:29; 15:17).

Q. For what purpose did he write?

A. To set forth the glorious achievement of those Hebrews who, under God, revolted from pagan domination.

Q. In what language did he write?

A. The work, which has come down to us in the Greek language, appears to have been translated from a Hebrew original.

Q. What are some characteristic idioms that disclose a Hebrew original?

A. "Many evils have come upon us" (1:11; cf. Deuteronomy 31:21); they "sold themselves to do evil" (1:15; cf. I Kings 21:20); many "were wounded and fell" (1:18; 3:11; 8:10, etc.; cf. Judges 9:40; I Chronicles 5:22).

Q. How does I Maccabees begin?

A. With a summary of the career of Alexander the Great ("He advanced to the ends of the earth, and plundered many nations"—1:3), the division of his empire, and the wicked rule of his successors ("they caused many evils on the earth"—1:9).

Q. What is the point of beginning with Alexander?

A. Because from among his heirs and successors "came forth a sinful root, Antiochus Epiphanes" (1:10), whose domain included the land where the Hebrews lived.

Q. What was the attitude of Antiochus toward Israel?

A. He encouraged the lawless ones "to observe the ordinances of the Gentiles. So they built a gymnasium in Jerusalem, according to Gentile custom, and removed the marks of circumcision, and abandoned the holy covenant" (1:13f).

Q. How did Antiochus extend his sovereignty?

A. He "captured the fortified cities in the land of Egypt, and he plundered the land of Egypt" (1:19).

Q. To what did he next turn his attention?

A. "He went up against Israel and came to Jerusalem with a strong force. He arrogantly entered the sanctuary" and plundered it (1:20ff):

> "He committed deeds of murder
>> and spoke with great arrogance" (1:24).

Q. What effect did this have upon the Hebrews?

A. "Israel mourned deeply in every community . . .
>> and all the house of Jacob was clothed with shame" (1:25,
>> 28).

Q. What did Antiochus do two years later?

A. He "came to Jerusalem with a large force . . . plundered the city, burned it with fire, and tore down its houses and its surrounding walls" 1:31).

> "On every side of the sanctuary they shed innocent blood . . .
>> her feasts were turned into mourning,
> her sabbaths into a reproach,
>> her honor into contempt" (1:37,39).

Q. What proclamation was made throughout the land of Judah?

A. The people were ordered by Antiochus to build "shrines for idols, to sacrifice swine and unclean animals, and to leave their sons uncircumcised" (1:47f).

Q. How was the king's decree carried out in Jerusalem?

A. "They erected a desolating sacrilege upon the altar of burnt offering. . . . The books of the law . . . they tore to pieces and burned with fire . . . they put to death the women who had their children circumcised" (1:54-60).

Q. Did the entire Hebrew nation assent to this?

A. "But many in Israel stood firm. . . . They chose to die rather than to be defiled by food or to profane the holy covenant" (1:62f).

Q. Who resolved to avenge this disgrace?

A. Mattathias, "a priest of the sons of Joarib," and his five sons: John, Simon, Judas called Maccabeus, Eleazar, and Jonathan (2:1-5).

Q. What summons did Mattathias issue to the people?

A. " 'Let every one who is zealous for the law and supports the covenant come out with me!' And he and his sons fled to the hills and left all that they had in the city" (2:27f).

Q. What happened to others who "went down to the wilderness to dwell there" (2:29)?

A. They were massacred when the king's forces "attacked them on the sabbath" (2:38), a day when those who observed the Law could not resist (2:34).

Q. What decision was then taken by Mattathias and his men?

A. "Let us fight against every man who comes to attack us on the sabbath day; let us not all die as our brethren died" (2:41).

Q. What actions were carried out by Mattathias and his supporters?

A. They "tore down the altars; they forcibly circumcised all the uncircumcised boys. . . . They hunted down the arrogant men. . . . They rescued the law out of the hands of the Gentiles" (2:45-48).

Q. When "the days drew near for Mattathias to die" (2:49), what counsel did he give his sons?

A. Recounting the faithfulness of Hebrew heroes from Abraham to Daniel (2:52-60), he said: "Observe, from generation to generation, that none who put their trust in him will lack strength" (2:61).

Q. Whom did he appoint as his successors?

A. "Simeon your brother is wise in counsel; always listen to him. . . . Judas Maccabeus has been a mighty warrior . . . he shall command the army" (2:65f).

Q. How were the deeds of Judas celebrated in song?

A. "He was like a lion in his deeds. . . .
    He went through the cities of Judah;
        he destroyed the ungodly out of the land" (3:4,8).

Q. What was the symbol of the prowess of Judas?

A. When "Apollonius gathered together Gentiles and a large force from Samaria to fight against Israel . . . Judas took the sword of Apollonius, and used it in battle the rest of his life" (3:10-12).

Q. How did Judas prepare his men for victory over "Seron, the commander of the Syrian army" (3:13)?

A. By saying to his hungry, fainthearted troops: "It is not on the size of the army that victory in battle depends, but strength comes from Heaven . . . we fight for our lives and our laws" (3:19-21).

Q. When Antiochus sent Ptolemy, Nicanor, and Gorgias, "mighty men among the friends of the king," (3:38) with forty thousand infantry and seven thousand cavalry "into the land of Judah" to "destroy it," how did Judas rally his troops?

A. Those "who were building houses, or were betrothed, or were planting vineyards, or were fainthearted" (3:56) were allowed to return home; to the remainder Judas said: "It is better for us to die in battle than to see the misfortunes of our nation and our sanctuary" (3:59).

Q. What happened when Judas and his men moved against Gorgias?

A. The enemy "all fled into the land of the Philistines" (4:22).

Q. How did Judas and his men celebrate this victory?

A. "On their return they sang hymns and praises to Heaven, for he is good, for his mercy endures for ever. Thus Israel had a great deliverance that day" (4:24f).

Q. When Judas moved against Lysias, what was the result?

A. "When Lysias saw the rout of his troops and observed the boldness which inspired those of Judas, and how ready they were either to live or to die nobly, he departed to Antiochus and enlisted mercenaries, to invade Judea again with an even larger army" (4:35).

Q. How did Judas restore the true worship in Jerusalem?

A. He "detailed men to fight against those in the citadel until he had cleansed the sanctuary" (4:41). He tore down the old altar, which had been defiled by the pagan sacrifices, and "built a new altar like the former one" (4:47); "it was dedicated with songs and harps and lutes and cymbals" (4:54).

Q. What new festival was introduced?

A. It was "determined that every year at that season the days of the dedication of the altar should be observed with gladness and joy for eight days, beginning with the twenty-fifth day of the month of Chislev" (4:59).

Q. What New Testament reference is there to this annually recurring event?

A. "It was the feast of the Dedication at Jerusalem . . . and Jesus was walking in the temple" (John 10:22).

Q. What is the present-day name of this celebration?

A. Chanukah, or Hanukkah.

Q. What effect had the rededication upon Israel's neighbors?

A. "They became very angry" (5:1), so that Judas was forced to move against "the sons of Esau" (5:3), "the sons of Baean" (5:4), the

Ammonites (5:6), "Jazer and its villages" (5:8). Simon liberated the oppressed Jews of Galilee "and led them to Judea with great rejoicing" (5:23). Judas and Jonathan took Bozrah and Dathema, Alema, "Chaspho, Maked, and Bosor, and the other cities of Gilead" (5:28-36); returning triumphantly to Judah ("they went up to Mount Zion with gladness and joy"—5:54), he went south and took Hebron, then "turned aside to Azotus in the land of the Philistines" (5:65-68).

Q. How did Antiochus receive the news of Judas' victories?

A. "He was astounded and badly shaken. He took to his bed and became sick from grief, because things had not turned out for him as he had planned" (6:8). Realizing that he was dying, "he called for Philip, one of his friends" (6:14) and made him regent, in order that "he might guide Antiochus his son and bring him up to be king" (6:15); Antiochus V was named Eupator (6:17).

Q. What happened when the invader assembled a tremendous body of troops, plus "thirty-two elephants accustomed to war" (6:30)?

A. "Judas marched away from the citadel and encamped at Bethzechariah, opposite the camp of the king" (6:32).

Q. How did the king deploy his forces?

A. "With each elephant they stationed a thousand men . . . and five hundred picked horsemen. . . . And upon the elephants were wooden towers . . . and upon each were four armed men . . . and also its Indian driver" (6:35-37).

Q. How did Eleazar distinguish himself in this battle?

A. When he "saw that one of the beasts was equipped with royal armor. . . . He got under the elephant, stabbed it from beneath, and killed it, but it fell to the ground upon him and there he died" (6:43,46). "So he gave his life to save his people and to win for himself an everlasting name" (6:44).

Q. What was the outcome of this battle?

A. "When the Jews saw the royal might and the fierce attack of the forces, they turned away in flight" (6:47). The king "sent to the Jews an offer of peace, and they accepted it" (6:60).

Q. Who now replaced Antiochus V on the throne?

A. Demetrius I, son of Seleucus IV, returning from Rome where he had been held as hostage, slew Lysias and Antiochus V, and "took his seat upon the throne of his kingdom" (7:4).

Q. What led Demetrius to send Bacchides "to take vengeance on the sons of Israel" (7:9)?

A. "Alcimus, who wanted to be high priest" (7:5), reported to him that "Judas and his brothers have destroyed all your friends, and have driven us out of our land" (7:6). When Judas and his followers "took vengeance on the men who had deserted" (7:24), Alcimus "returned to the king and brought wicked charges against them" (7:25).

Q. Who next was sent against the Jews by Demetrius?

A. Nicanor, "who hated and detested Israel" (7:26).

Q. What success did Nicanor have?

A. His army "was crushed, and he himself was the first to fall in the battle" (7:43). The Jews "cut off Nicanor's head and the right hand which he had so arrogantly stretched out, and . . . displayed them just outside of Jerusalem. The people rejoiced greatly and celebrated that day as a day of great gladness" (7:47,48).

Q. What new force next emerged in Hebrew history?

A. "Judas heard of the fame of the Romans" (8:1); he sent ambassadors "to Rome to establish friendship and alliance, and to free themselves from the yoke; for they saw that the kingdom of the Greeks was completely enslaving Israel" (8:17f). The ambassadors, entering the Senate chamber, asked "that we may be enrolled as your allies and friends" (8:20).

Q. What move did Demetrius make when he heard "that Nicanor and his army had fallen in battle" (9:1)?

A. He "sent Bacchides and Alcimus into the land of Judah a second time" (9:1). "The earth was shaken by the noise of the armies" (9:13).

Q. What was the outcome?

A. "The battle became desperate, and many men on both sides were wounded and fell. Judas also fell, and the rest fled" (9:17,18).

Q. How was the news of Judas' death received?

A. "All Israel made great lamentation for him" (9:20). In words that David had used of another, they said, "How is the mighty fallen!" (9:21; cf. II Samuel 1:19).

Q. What effect did the death of Judas have?

A. "There was great distress in Israel, such as had not been since the time that prophets ceased to appear among them" (9:27).

Q. To whom did the Jews turn for leadership?

A. They chose Jonathan; he "accepted the leadership and took the place of Judas his brother" (9:31).

Q. What success did Jonathan have against Bacchides?

A. He joined battle on the banks of the Jordan, and slew one thousand of Bacchides' troops, but Jonathan and his men had to swim across the Jordan in order to save their own lives (9:48f).

Q. How did Bacchides assert his authority?

A. He "took the sons of the leading men of the land as hostages" (9:53) and gave Alcimus "orders to tear down the wall of the inner court of the sanctuary" (9:54).

Q. How did Alcimus meet his end?

A. Engaged in this irreverent action, "his mouth was stopped and he was paralyzed. . . . And Alcimus died at that time in great agony" (9:55f). Bacchides withdrew (9:57); returning, he offered terms of peace (9:70f).

Q. What was the result of the peace treaty?

A. "Thus the sword ceased from Israel. And Jonathan dwelt in Michmash. And Jonathan began to judge the people, and he destroyed the ungodly out of Israel" (9:73).

Q. What did Demetrius do when Alexander Balas laid claim to his throne?

A. He offered Jonathan concession, so that "Jonathan dwelt in Jerusalem and began to rebuild and restore the city" (10:10).

Q. How did Alexander counter this?

A. He sent word to Jonathan, ". . . we have appointed you today to be the high priest of your nation . . . you are to take our side and keep friendship with us" (10:20).

Q. What was Demetrius' reply to this?

A. "Let Jerusalem and her environs, her tithes and her revenues, be holy and free from tax" (10:31). Judea and the neighboring districts were "to be under one ruler and obey no other authority but the high priest" (10:38). The temple revenue, formerly sent to Demetrius, "is canceled, because it belongs to the priests who minister there" (10:42). "Let the cost of the rebuilding . . . be paid from the revenues of the king" (10:44f).

Q. What was the reaction of Jonathan and his people to these terms?

A. "They did not believe or accept them, because they remembered the great wrongs which Demetrius had done in Israel. . . . They favored Alexander" (10:46f).

Q. With whom did Alexander make alliance?

A. With Ptolemy, king of Egypt (10:51-58).

Q. How did Alexander treat Jonathan?

A. He "enrolled him among his chief friends, and made him general and governor of the province" (10:65).

Q. When Demetrius II, seeking to regain his father's throne, sent Apollonius against Jonathan, what was the outcome?

A. Jonathan and Simon won a great victory. "When Alexander the king heard of these things, he honored Jonathan still more; and he sent to him a golden buckle" (10:88f).

Q. What happened to Alexander?

A. He was defeated in battle by Ptolemy, his father-in-law, who "put on the crown of Asia" (11:13). Ptolemy, however, lived but three days and Demetrius II became king (11:19).

Q. How did Demetrius II treat the Jews?

A. He sent a letter saying he was "determined to do good" to the Jews "because of the good will they show toward us . . . we have granted release from the royal taxes" (11:33f).

Q. Who led the revolt against Demetrius?

A. Trypho, who "had formerly been one of Alexander's supporters" (11:39), sought to place Antiochus VI on the throne.

Q. What part did the Jews play in suppressing this rebellion?

A. Jonathan "sent three thousand stalwart men to him at Antioch, where they killed" in a single day "as many as a hundred thousand" (11:44,47).

Q. How did Demetrius reward this support?

A. "He broke his word about all that he had promised; and he became estranged from Jonathan" (11:53).

Q. When Trypho succeeded in placing young Antiochus on the throne, how did the Jews fare?

A. Antiochus confirmed Jonathan in the high priesthood and made

Simon "governor from the Ladder of Tyre to the borders of Egypt" (11: 57-59). Jonathan defeated the forces of Demetrius II at Kadesh in Galilee (11:67-74).

Q. Where did Jonathan turn for alliance and support?

A. He sent men "to Rome to confirm and renew the friendship with them" (12:1); he also wrote to the Spartans, "so that we may not become estranged from you" (12:10).

Q. What reply did the Spartans make?

A. "It has been found in writing concerning the Spartans and the Jews that they are brethren and are of the family of Abraham" (12:21).

Q. How did Jonathan meet his death?

A. At the hands of Trypho, who was determined "to become king of Asia" (12:39-50).

Q. What effect did the death of Jonathan have upon neighboring nations?

A. They said to the Jews: "They have no leader or helper. Now therefore let us make war on them and blot out the memory of them from among men" (12:53).

Q. Who succeeded Jonathan?

A. When Simon said, "I will avenge my nation and the sanctuary and your wives and children" (13:6), the people "answered in a loud voice, 'You are our leader in place of Judas and Jonathan your brother' " (13:8).

Q. How did Simon memorialize those members of his family already martyred?

A. He "erected seven pyramids, opposite one another, for his father and mother and four brothers" (13:28).

Q. When Trypho killed the young king Antiochus (13:31), what steps did Demetrius take?

A. He gave to the Hebrews immunity from taxation, and granted pardon for all past "errors and offenses"; thus, in the year 142 or 141 B.C., "the yoke of the Gentiles was removed from Israel" (13:41).

Q. How did the Jews repossess their capital city?

A. They "entered it with praise and palm branches, and with harps and cymbals and stringed instruments, and with hymns and songs, because a great enemy had been crushed" (13:51).

Q. How was the rule of Simon celebrated?

A. In song:

"The land had rest all the days of Simon.

He sought the good of his nation. . . .

He made the sanctuary glorious" (14:4-15).

Q. What was the reaction of foreign allies to the death of Jonathan and the appointment of Simon?

A. "It was heard in Rome, and as far away as Sparta, that Jonathan had died, and they were deeply grieved. When they heard that Simon his brother had become high priest . . . they wrote to him on bronze tablets to renew . . . the friendship and alliance" (14:16-18).

Q. How did the Jews memorialize the deeds of the Maccabees?

A. On Mount Zion they set up bronze tablets enumerating their deeds and proclaiming, "They brought great glory to their nation" (14:29).

Q. In what political events did Simon become embroiled?

A. Antiochus VII, brother of Demetrius II, demanded aid in overthrowing Trypho. When the proffered help was considered inadequate, Antiochus sent Cendebeus against the Jews.

Q. To whom did Simon assign the leadership of his troops?

A. Summoning his two older sons, he said, "I have grown old, and you by His mercy are mature in years. Take my place and my brother's, and go out and fight for our nation, and may the help which comes from Heaven be with you" (16:3); they routed the army of Cendebeus (16:4-10).

Q. How did Simon meet his death?

A. His son-in-law made him a great banquet, at which his men "rushed in against Simon in the banquet hall, and they killed him and his two sons [Mattathias and Judas] and some of his servants. So he committed an act of great treachery" (16:16f).

Q. Who remained of the house of the Maccabees?

A. John Hyrcanus, whose achievements "are written in the chronicles of the high priesthood" (16:23f).

Q. What was Luther's opinion of I Maccabees?

A. He considered it "not unworthy" of canonicity.

THE SECOND BOOK OF THE
MACCABEES

Q. What is the relationship of II Maccabees to I Maccabees?

A. The two books deal to some extent with the same era of Hebrew history. II Maccabees, however, is more limited in scope. I Maccabees deals with the time from 175 to 135 B.C., II Maccabees only with the period from 175 to 161 B.C. I Maccabees 1:10-7:50 parallels II Maccabees, though treating the material in a different way.

Q. Who is the author of II Maccabees?

A. An unknown translator and condenser reports that he has made use of an earlier work: "The story of Judas Maccabeus and his brothers, and the purification of the great temple . . . all this, which has been set forth by Jason of Cyrene in five volumes, we shall attempt to condense into a single book" (2:19,23).

Q. What was his purpose in making this abridgment?

A. "We have aimed to please those who wish to read, to make it easy for those who are inclined to memorize, and to profit all readers" (2:25).

Q. Did he find it easy to make this digest of another man's work?

A. "For us who have undertaken the toil of abbreviating, it is no light matter but calls for sweat and loss of sleep" (2:26).

Q. What analogy does the author draw between his work and that of the original?

A. "For as the master builder of a new house must be concerned with the whole construction, while the one who undertakes its painting and decoration has to consider only what is suitable for its adornment, such in my judgment is the case with us" (2:29).

Q. What does the author believe to be the relationship between style and content?

A. "For just as it is harmful to drink wine alone . . . while wine mixed with water is sweet and delicious and enhances one's enjoyment, so also the style of the story delights the ears of those who read the work" (15:39).

Q. What success does the author believe he has had in making his précis?

A. "If it is well told and to the point, that is what I myself desired; if it is poorly done and mediocre, that was the best I could do" (15:38).

Q. Who was Jason of Cyrene (2:23)?

A. His work survives only in the epitome that is given in II Maccabees. Like most Jews of the Diaspora, he seems to have written in Greek. Nothing else is known about him.

Q. When did the epitomist do his work?

A. Probably about 100 B.C.

Q. How does II Maccabees differ from I Maccabees when it treats of the same era in Hebrew history?

A. Somewhat in the way I and II Chronicles differ from I and II Kings.

Q. In the case of the books of the Maccabees, how is this difference illustrated with reference to the size of armies?

A. The military exploits in II Maccabees are grander. I Maccabees 4:28f reports that Lysias, with sixty thousand infantrymen and five thousand cavalrymen, came against Judas and his ten thousand men, and "there fell of the army of Lysias five thousand men" (I Maccabees 4:34). II Maccabees 11:2,4,11, reporting the same battle, says that Lysias had eighty thousand foot soldiers, thousands of horsemen, plus eighty elephants; he lost eleven thousand foot soldiers and sixteen hundred horsemen. In a later expedition, Lysias, according to I Maccabees 6:30, commanded one hundred thousand foot soldiers, twenty thousand horsemen, and "thirty-two elephants accustomed to war"; II Maccabees 13:2 gives the figures as "one hundred and ten thousand infantry, five thousand three hundred cavalry, twenty-two elephants, and three hundred chariots armed with scythes."

Q. How is the difference illustrated with respect to the persons involved?

A. Jason and Menelaus are not mentioned in I Maccabees, while Mattathias, originator of the Maccabean revolt, is not mentioned in II Maccabees.

Q. How is the difference illustrated with respect to dates?

A. I Maccabees dates the death of Antiochus before the rededication of the temple; II Maccabees places it afterward. I Maccabees 4:52 says the temple was rededicated three years after its pollution; II Maccabees 10:3 says it occurred "after a lapse of two years."

Q. How does the author of II Maccabees begin his work?

A. By quoting two letters, one sent by "the Jewish brethren in Jerusalem and . . . Judea, to their Jewish brethren in Egypt" (1:1), the other from "those in Jerusalem and those in Judea and the senate and Judas, To Aristobulus, who is of the family of the anointed priests, teacher of Ptolemy the king, and to the Jews in Egypt" (1:10).

Q. What is the purpose of the first letter?

A. Written about 124 B.C., it recalls an earlier letter, sent about 143 B.C., describing "the critical distress which came upon us . . . after Jason and his company revolted . . . and shed innocent blood" (1:7f), but the temple worship has been restored: "we lighted the lamps and we set out the loaves" (1:8).

Q. What is the purpose of the second letter?

A. Written about 164 B.C., it reports that God "drove out those who fought against the holy city" (1:12), and "we thought it necessary to notify you, in order that you also may celebrate the feast of booths and the feast of the fire given when Nehemiah, who built the temple and the altar, offered sacrifices" (1:18).

Q. What is the reference to fire in Nehemiah's time?

A. At the time of the deportation to Babylon, the priests "took some of the fire of the altar and secretly hid it in the hollow of a dry cistern" (1:19). At the return under Nehemiah, they found not "fire but thick liquid"; when this was spilled on the wood and the sun shone upon it, "a great fire blazed up" (1:22).

Q. What prayer did Nehemiah offer on that occasion?

A. "Gather together our scattered people, set free those who are slaves among the Gentiles, look upon those who are rejected or despised, and let the Gentiles know that thou art our God" (1:27).

Q. What other historical material was included in the second letter?

A. An account of how Jeremiah the prophet ordered those who were being deported to take with them some of the fire, "not to forget the commandments of the Lord, nor to be led astray" (2:1f); he also sealed up in a cave, for safekeeping, "the tent and the ark and the altar of incense" (2:5). Mention is made, too, of how Solomon, following in the tradition of Moses (2:11), "offered sacrifice for the dedication and completion of the temple" (2:9).

Q. What else does the author include in his preface?

A. A summary of what he intends to recount: "The story of Judas Maccabeus and his brothers, and the purification of the great temple, and the dedication of the altar, and further the wars against Antiochus Epiphanes and his son Eupator" (2:19f), as well as a statement that he is presenting a condensation of the work of Jason.

Q. What events preceded the revolt of the Maccabees?

A. One was intrigue over the high priesthood. Simon, a "captain of the temple," (3:4), disputing with Onias the high priest over "the administration of the city market" (3:4), reported to Apollonius, governor of a neighboring region, "that the treasury in Jerusalem was full of untold sums of money" (3:6). Apollonius, in turn, reported it to the king, who sent Heliodorus "to effect the removal of the aforesaid money" (3:7).

Q. How was the effort of Heliodorus and his bodyguard frustrated?

A. "There appeared to them a magnificently caparisoned horse, with a rider of frightening mien, and it rushed furiously at Heliodorus and struck at him with its front hoofs . . . he suddenly fell to the ground and deep darkness came over him, his men . . . put him on a stretcher and carried him away" (3:25,27f).

Q. What did Heliodorus do upon recovering his senses?

A. He "offered sacrifice to the Lord and made very great vows to the Savior of his life. . . . And he bore testimony to all men of the deeds of the supreme God, which he had seen with his own eyes" (3:35f).

Q. What advice did Heliodorus give the king regarding future attacks upon Jerusalem?

A. "If you have an enemy or plotter against your government, send him there, for you will get him back thoroughly scourged, if he escapes at all, for there certainly is about the place some power of God" (3:38).

Q. How did Simon assess the blame for what had happened?

A. He said it was Onias "who had incited Heliodorus and been the real cause of the misfortune" (4:1).

Q. How was Onias removed from his office?

A. "Jason the brother of Onias obtained the high priesthood by corruption, promising the king" large sums of money (4:7f).

Q. What did Jason do when he assumed office?

A. "He at once shifted his countrymen over to the Greek way of life" (4:10).

Q. In what way did he do this?

A. "He founded a gymnasium right under the citadel, and he induced the noblest of the young men to wear the Greek hat" (4:12). Even the priests, "no longer intent upon their service at the altar . . . hastened to take part in the unlawful proceedings" (4:14).

Q. How did Jason intend to support the quadrennial games at Tyre?

A. He "sent envoys . . . to carry three hundred silver drachmas for the sacrifice to Hercules" (4:19); the envoys chose, instead, to apply it "to the construction of triremes" (4:20).

Q. How was Jason removed from office?

A. Menelaus, brother of the previously ousted Simon, although "possessing no qualification for the high priesthood, but having the hot temper of a cruel tyrant and the rage of a savage wild beast" (4:25), "secured the high priesthood for himself, outbidding Jason by three hundred talents of silver" (4:24).

Q. How did Menelaus conduct himself in office?

A. "With no regard to justice," he had Onias "put out of the way" (4:34), "stole some of the gold vessels of the temple" (4:32), and gave them as a bribe to the king's deputy; he "remained in office, growing in wickedness, having become the chief plotter against his fellow citizens" (4:50).

Q. What happened in Jerusalem when Antiochus "made his second invasion of Egypt" (5:1)?

A. "Over all the city, for almost forty days, there appeared golden-clad horsemen charging through the air, in companies fully armed with lances and drawn swords" (5:2).

Q. When rumor falsely reported the death of Antiochus, what did Jason do?

A. "Made an assault upon the city . . . not realizing that success at the cost of one's kindred is the greatest misfortune" (5:6). Fleeing the hostility aroused by his actions, Jason fled "into the country of the Ammonites" (5:7), then to that of the Lacedaemonians, where he "died in exile" (5:9).

Q. What effect did this have upon Antiochus?

A. Supposing Judea to be in revolt, he attacked Jerusalem, "took the city by storm" (5:11), massacred eighty thousand, and sold into slavery another eighty thousand (5:14); "guided by Menelaus, who had become a traitor both to the laws and to his country," and "elated in spirit," he then plundered the temple, carrying away "the holy vessels with his polluted hands" (5:16), carrying away also funds amounting to "eighteen hundred talents"; he left behind "governors to afflict the people" (5:22).

Q. How did Judas Maccabeus survive this time of troubles?

A. He, "with about nine others, got away to the wilderness, and kept himself and his companions alive in the mountains as wild animals do" (5:27).

Q. What steps did Antiochus take to suppress Judaism?

A. The Jerusalem temple he dedicated to Olympian Zeus, and the Samaritan temple to "Zeus the Friend of Strangers" (6:2); prostitution was introduced into the sacred precincts (6:4); the people were forced to celebrate "the feast of Dionysus . . . wearing wreaths of ivy" (6:7); two women were executed "for having circumcised their children" (6: 10); refugees seeking safety in a cave "were all burned together" (6:11).

Q. What philosophy of suffering does the author give to explain why the Jews were subjected to these afflictions?

A. "These punishments were designed not to destroy but to discipline our people" (6:12).

Q. What is told regarding the martyrdom of Eleazar?

A. Eleazar, an elderly scribe "in high position," was commanded "to eat swine's flesh" (6:18). When his tormentors offered him the opportunity secretly to substitute meat of his own choosing, he refused and was killed, "leaving in his death an example of nobility and a memorial of courage" (6:31).

Q. What family martyrdom is related?

A. A mother and her seven sons were required, "under torture with whips and cords, to partake of unlawful swine's flesh" (7:1). The seven sons, one after the other, were tortured and executed before the mother's eyes. "Though she saw her seven sons perish in a single day, she bore it with good courage" (7:20).

Q. What resistance did Judas Maccabeus offer his people's oppressors?

A. He and his companions enlisted an army of six thousand loyalists (8:1). "Coming without warning, he would set fire to towns and villages. He captured strategic positions and put to flight not a few of the enemy" (8:6).

Q. What resource did Judas and his men have that the enemy did not?

A. "For they trust to arms and acts of daring," said Judas (8:18), "but we trust in the Almighty God."

Q. What historical circumstance did Judas cite by way of encouragement to his people?

A. He recounted, among other incidents, the deliverance that came in "the time of Sennacherib, when one hundred and eighty-five thousand perished" (8:19; cf. II Kings 19:35; Isaiah 37:36). "With these words he filled them with good courage and made them ready to die for their laws and their country" (8:21).

Q. How did Judas deploy his forces?

A. "He divided his army into four parts. He appointed his brothers also, Simon and Joseph and Jonathan, each to command a division" (8:21f).

Q. What befell Nicanor, appointed by Ptolemy "to wipe out the whole race of Judea" (8:9)?

A. He was forced to flee "like a runaway slave" (8:35), acknowledging "that the Jews had a Defender" (8:36).

Q. What befell Antiochus, setting out to "make Jerusalem a cemetery of Jews" (9:4)?

A. Stricken with incurable disease, he "gave up all hope for himself and wrote to the Jews" a letter commending to them his son and successor (9:18-27).

Q. What did Judas and his troops do when they "recovered the temple and the city" (10:1)?

A. "They tore down the altars which had been built in the public square by the foreigners. . . . They purified the sanctuary, and made another altar of sacrifice" (10:2f); "they offered hymns of thanksgiving to him who had given success to the purifying of his own holy place" (10:7).

Q. When the Idumeans "received those who were banished from Jerusalem, and endeavored to keep up the war" (10:15) and "took refuge in two very strong towers," what did Judas do?

A. He "immediately captured the two towers. Having success at arms in everything he undertook, he destroyed more than twenty thousand in the two strongholds" (10:23).

Q. When an attack was made by Timothy, who had "gathered a tremendous force of mercenaries and collected the cavalry from Asia in no small number" (10:24), how was the issue resolved?

A. "Twenty thousand five hundred" of his troops "were slaughtered, besides six hundred horsemen" (10:31). "Timothy himself fled," and took refuge in a cistern, and was killed (10:32,37).

Q. What aid did the Hebrews have in this encounter?

A. "When the battle became fierce, there appeared to the enemy from heaven five resplendent horsemen . . . and they were leading the Jews. Surrounding Maccabeus and protecting him with their own armor and weapons, they kept him from being wounded. And they showered arrows and thunderbolts upon the enemy, so that, confused and blinded, they were thrown into disorder and cut to pieces" (10:29f).

Q. What happened when Lysias, intending to make the city a home for Greeks (11:2), came with eighty thousand men, plus cavalry and eighty elephants (11:4), against Jerusalem?

A. Maccabeus and his men "hurled themselves like lions against the enemy. . . . Lysias himself escaped by disgraceful flight" (11:11f), and "realized that the Hebrews were invincible because the mighty God fought on their side" (11:13).

Q. What help did the Hebrews have on this occasion?

A. "A horseman appeared at their head, clothed in white and brandishing weapons of gold" (11:8).

Q. What correspondence followed this encounter?

A. Lysias sent the Jews a letter: "If you will maintain your good will toward the government, I will endeavor for the future to help promote your welfare" (11:19). Antiochus sent a letter to Lysias: "The Jews do not consent to our father's change to Greek customs . . . our decision is that their temple be restored to them and that they live according to the customs of their ancestors" (11:24f). Antiochus sent the Jews a letter: "Those who go home by the thirtieth day of Xanthicus will have our pledge of friendship and full permission for the Jews to enjoy their own food and laws, just as formerly" (11:30f). The Romans sent the Jews a letter: "With regard to what Lysias the kinsman of the king has granted you, we also give consent" (11:35).

Q. When the people of Joppa, "by a public vote of the city" (12:4), invited Jews to join in a boat ride, then "took them out to sea and drowned them" (12:4), what did Judas do?

A. "He set fire to the harbor by night, and burned the boats, and massacred those who had taken refuge there" (12:6).

Q. When a miscellaneous company of Gentiles, behaving "most insolently toward Judas and his men" (12:14), immured themselves in Caspin, what did Judas do?

A. Judas and his men "took the city . . . and slaughtered untold numbers, so that the adjoining lake . . . appeared to be running over with blood" (12:16).

Q. What help did the Jews have on this occasion?

A. They called upon "the great Sovereign of the world, who without battering rams or engines of war overthrew Jericho in the days of Joshua" (12:15).

Q. How does the author account for the casualties suffered by the Jews in a battle with Gorgias?

A. "Under the tunic of every one of the dead they found sacred tokens of the idols of Jamnia, which the law forbids the Jews to wear. And it became clear to all that this was why these men had fallen" (12:40).

Q. How did Judas expiate this infidelity?

A. He "took up a collection, man by man, to the amount of two thousand drachmas of silver, and sent it to Jerusalem to provide for a sin offering" (12:43).

Q. What use of this passage is now made by the Roman Church?

A. To justify those who "pray for the dead" (12:44).

Q. How did Menelaus meet his death?

A. Seeking to strengthen his position by allying himself with Antiochus, he was pushed by Antiochus into a tower filled with hot ashes. "And this was eminently just; because he had committed many sins against the altar whose fire and ashes were holy, he met his death in ashes" (13:8).

Q. When the younger Antiochus "was coming to show to the Jews far worse things than those that had been done in his father's time," (13:9), how did Judas meet the threat?

A. "With a picked force of the bravest young men, he attacked the king's pavilion at night and slew as many as two thousand men in the camp. He stabbed the leading elephant and its rider" (13:15).

Q. What treachery did Alcimus commit?

A. A former high priest, Alcimus presented gifts to king Demetrius and informed him that "as long as Judas lives, it is impossible for the government to find peace" (14:10).

Q. What action did the king take?

A. He appointed Nicanor "governor of Judea, and sent him off with orders to kill Judas and scatter his men, and to set up Alcimus as high priest" (14:12f). Nicanor, however, "shrank from deciding the issue by bloodshed" (14:18) and made peace with Judas; so Judas "married, settled down, and shared the common life" (14:25). Alcimus reported this to the king, who thereupon ordered Judas sent as a prisoner to Antioch (14:27), but Judas "went into hiding" (14:30).

Q. How did "Razis, one of the elders of Jerusalem" (14:37), escape "more than five hundred soldiers" whom Nicanor sent to arrest him?

A. "Being surrounded, Razis fell upon his own sword, preferring to die nobly rather than to fall into the hands of sinners and suffer outrages unworthy of his noble birth" (14:41f).

Q. How did Judas strengthen his men for battle with Nicanor?

A. "He armed each of them not so much with confidence in shields and spears as with the inspiration of brave words, and he cheered them all by relating a dream, a sort of vision, which was worthy of belief" (15:11).

Q. What was the dream?

A. "Onias, who had been high priest," introduced " 'a man who loves the brethren and prays much for the people and the holy city, Jeremiah, the prophet of God.' Jeremiah . . . gave to Judas a golden sword . . . 'a gift from God, with which you will strike down your adversaries' " (15:14-16).

Q. What was the result of the subsequent encounter?

A. Judas and his troops slew thirty-five thousand men and found "Nicanor, lying dead, in full armor" (15:28).

Q. How was this victory symbolized?

A. Judas "cut out the tongue of the ungodly Nicanor. . . . And he hung Nicanor's head from the citadel, a clear and conspicuous sign to every one of the help of the Lord" (15:33,35).

Q. What distinctive idea regarding immortality appears in II Maccabees?

A. Two martyrs die in the hope of receiving back their mutilated bodies (7:11; 14:46); this appears to be the only book in the Apocrypha that teaches the resurrection of the flesh.

Q. How did the Maccabees use the Scriptures for the encouragement of the troops?

A. Judas "appointed Eleazar to read aloud from the holy book" (8:23).

Q. What slogans served to inspire the troops?

A. Judas, on one occasion, "gave the watchword, 'God's Help'" (8:23); on another, "He gave his men the watchword, 'God's victory'" (13:15).

THE NEW TESTAMENT

Introduction

Q. What is the New Testament?

A. A collection of writings, originating in the early Christian community, proclaiming to all and sundry that he of whom the prophets spoke has now been revealed; the long-awaited age to come has already come; God in Christ has visited and redeemed his people.

Q. What is the meaning of *Testament*?

A. The same Greek word can also be translated "Covenant"; Bible title pages often bring this out in some way such as is done in the Revised Standard Version: "The New Covenant, Commonly Called the New Testament of our Lord and Savior Jesus Christ."

Q. What is the significance of the word *New* in "New Testament"?

A. It means that to the Hebrew Bible, which the Christians call the Old Testament, something new and wonderful has been added; meanings long hidden are now made clear; history has been fulfilled; expectation has become realization.

Q. What Old Testament passage speaks of a New Covenant?

A. Jeremiah 31:31-33 hears God say: "Behold, the days are coming says the LORD, when I will make a new covenant with the house of Israel and the house of Judah, not like the covenant which I made with their fathers when I took them by the hand to bring them out of the land of Egypt, my covenant which they broke, though I was their husband, says the LORD. But this is the covenant which I will make with the house of Israel after those days, says the LORD: I will put my law within them, and I will write it upon their hearts; and I will be their God, and they shall be my people."

Q. What kinds of writings are found in the New Testament?

A. Four may be distinguished. One of these, the Gospel, is unique, representing a new literary form; the others were adaptations of conventional forms: the historical narrative (the Acts of the Apostles); the letter (the Epistles); the Apocalypse (Revelation).

Q. What is the difference between Epistle and Gospel?

A. The Gospel represents the "Glad Announcement" of what God in Christ has done for the world; the Epistles represent the application of this "Good News" to situations in the early church, situations often precisely parallel to those in which modern man finds himself. Worshipers in liturgical churches are familiar with these two terms. The Roman Catholic missal and the Anglican Book of Common Prayer contain specific sections from the Epistles and Gospels for every Sunday and Holy Day throughout the year. Hearers are thus confronted with selections from two different parts of the New Testament.

Q. How was the early church organized?

A. It took over the Jewish custom of giving a special responsibility to the elders, or heads of families. Beyond that, it appears to have had no formal organizational pattern, but simply developed structures and procedures in accordance with current needs. Developments in the several communities do not appear to have been identical. Thus it comes about that all three twentieth-century forms of church government—congregational, presbyterial, and episcopal—trace their origins to the New Testament.

Q. What forms of ministry were there in the early church?

A. Ephesians 4:11 speaks of apostles, prophets, evangelists, and pastor-teachers. The first three appear to have been itinerant; the latter represented a settled ministry.

Q. How did the early Christian communities keep in touch with one another?

A. In addition to the journeying of apostles, prophets, and evangelists, ordinary believers going to a strange town would look up fellow

Christians. At a time when public hostelries were often brothels, hospitality to strangers was an important part of believers' fellowship (Romans 12:13; I Timothy 3:2; 5:10; Hebrews 13:2; I Peter 4:9; Titus 1:8). Furthermore, special messengers were sent as occasion required (Philippians 2:25; Ephesians 6:21,22; Colossians 4:7).

Q. What is the difference between *apostle* and *disciple?*

A. The term *disciple,* meaning "learner," is applicable to all who followed Jesus; *apostle,* meaning "one sent," is chiefly used of those who companied most closely with Jesus during the days of his flesh. Luke 6:13 tells how Christ "called his disciples, and chose from them twelve, whom he named apostles." The term, however, is extended to include others in the early church who were especially commissioned: Paul (Colossians 1:1, etc.), Barnabas (Acts 14:14), perhaps Andronicus and Junias (Romans 16:7), possible others (I Corinthians 15:5,7).

The Gospel

Q. What is the meaning of the word *gospel*?

A. Originally written "good spell," the term means "good news," or "glad announcement."

Q. How many gospels are there?

A. English versions count four, but in the Bible the word *gospel* does not occur in the plural; there is ONE GOSPEL, variously described as "the gospel" (Philippians 1:7), "my gospel" (Romans 2:16), "our gospel" (I Thessalonians 1:5), "the gospel of Christ" (II Corinthians 9:15), "the gospel of God" (Romans 1:1), "the glorious gospel" (I Timothy 1:1), "the gospel of peace" (Ephesians 6:15), "an eternal gospel" (Revelation 14:6). The early church knew a fourfold gospel—that is, one gospel according to four different people.

Q. When were the gospels written?

A. Probably in the last third of the first century A.D.—that is, between 64 A.D. and 100 A.D.

Q. Why were they not written sooner?

A. For several reasons: (a) the early church already had a book— it took over the Jewish Scriptures, which Christians call the Old Testament, and read them in the light of what Jesus was and did; (b) many Christians believed that the end of the world was at hand and saw no need to write; (c) the first Christians were largely artisans (cf. I Corinthians 1:26), and were not the kind of people to create literature; (d) writing materials were scarce and expensive; (e) although we like to rush into print with our good ideas, the ancients had an aversion to committing their thoughts to writing: Papias, one of the apostolic fathers, said, "I did not think that I could get so much profit from the contents of books as from the utterances of a living and abiding voice" (compare II John 12; III John 13).

Q. To what literary genre do the gospels belong?

A. Although they contain biographical elements, they are not biographies in the modern sense; although they contain poems and short stories, they are not anthologies; although they contain directions for leading a new life, they are not a set of laws; although they contain wise sayings, they are not a collection of prudent aphorisms. They are, in fact, unique; as the name implies, they are simply proclamations of good news.

Q. What was the order of the composition of the gospels?

A. It is generally held that Mark came first, then either Matthew or Luke, then John; Augustine, however, believed that Mark was "the follower and abbreviator of Matthew," and some contemporary scholars question the priority of Mark.

Q. What relationship have Matthew, Mark, Luke, and John to the gospels that bear their names?

A. The earliest written gospel is within a generation of the time of Jesus; meanwhile, the gospel stories had circulated by word of mouth; each important center of Christian life would make its own collection of those narratives and sayings; it is likely that editor or redactor, rather than writer or author, most aptly describes the function performed by Matthew, Mark, Luke, and John.

Q. Why are the gospel writers called "evangelists"?

A. From *evangelion*, the Greek word for "gospel," from which term are derived the English *evangel, evangelism,* and *evangelist;* an evangelist is a proclaimer of good news.

Q. In what language were the gospels written?

A. All four have come down to us in the Greek language; some suppose that an Aramaic original lies behind one or more of the gospels; no Aramaic gospel has ever been found.

Q. What are the "synoptic gospels"?

A. Matthew, Mark, and Luke.

Q. Why are they called "synoptic"?

A. *Synoptic* means "seen together" or "giving a common view"; in spite of individual peculiarities, Matthew, Mark, and Luke have a striking resemblance; John, on the other hand, has qualities or characteristics that put it in a class by itself.

Q. Do the gospel writers identify themselves?

A. No. Since it was Christ alone who mattered, they were content to remain anonymous.

Q. How do we determine authorship?

A. Although certainty may not be possible, we have an occasional bit of internal evidence (what the writers unconsciously tell us about themselves) and the testimony of the early church.

Q. Who among the church fathers is our earliest witness?

A. Papias, of Hierapolis, in Phrygia, who lived from about 65 to about 135 A.D., wrote an "Exposition of the Lord's Oracles," known to us through fragments preserved by later writers, chiefly Eusebius of Caesarea.

Q. What kind of relationship is thought to exist among the synoptic gospels?

A. It is believed that Matthew and Luke each used Mark; that other material common to Matthew and Luke came from another source, oral or written, called Q (from the German *Quelle,* "source"); and that Matthew and Luke each had access to a body of material not known to the other; Matthew's additional source is referred to as M, Luke's as L.

Q. How are the gospels symbolized in art?

A. The "four living creatures" of Revelation 4:7 (compare Ezekiel 10:14) have been thought to symbolize the four evangelists: "the first living creature like a lion [Mark], the second living creature an ox [Matthew], the third living creature [Luke] with the face of a man, and the fourth living creature like a flying eagle [John]."

THE GOSPEL ACCORDING TO
· MARK

Q. Why do we start with Mark?

A. For three reasons: it is thought to be the earliest of the gospels; its outline, taken over by Matthew and Luke, is basic to the Synoptic tradition; it gives us a summary of what the first Christians believed and taught about Christ.

Q. Who is the Mark whose name is associated with this gospel?

A. He is identified in Colossians 4:10 as "the cousin of Barnabas"; his mother Mary had a home in Jerusalem that appears to have been a meeting place for early Christians (Acts 12:12); associated with Paul and Barnabas in some of their missionary undertakings (Acts 12:25), Mark turned back when they started into central Asia Minor (Acts 13:5,13); Paul, for that reason, refused to allow him to accompany him again, but Barnabas took him on a second journey to Cyprus (Acts 15:37-39); II Timothy 4:11 suggests reconciliation between Paul and Mark; the author of I Peter 5:13 refers to "my son Mark," a relationship no doubt established through their common devotion to the gospel.

Q. What does Mark tell us about himself?

A. Because Mark 14:51f would otherwise have no point, it is often supposed that Mark himself was the young man who "ran away naked"; it is sometimes conjectured also that the "man carrying a jar of water" (Mark 14:13) may have been Mark; thus, by prearranged signal, the disciples of Jesus, coming into the city from the outside at a crowded time, would be able to find their way to the appointed place.

Q. What other information do we have about Mark?

A. Tradition associates him with the founding of the church in Alexandria, and the Coptic Church claims him as its first bishop.

Q. What source did Mark have for compiling a gospel?

A. Papias said: "Mark, having become the interpreter of Peter, wrote down accurately whatsoever he remembered. It was not, however, in exact order that he related the sayings or deeds of Christ. For he neither heard the Lord nor accompanied him." If ancient books had had title pages in the modern manner, Mark's might have read: "Reminiscences of the Apostle Peter, reported and translated by his assistant, John Mark."

Q. What evidences are there in Mark of special concern for Peter?

A. Jesus opens his public ministry by summoning Peter and his brother to leave their nets and "become fishers of men" (1:17); Peter's home seems to have been Jesus' base of operations in Capernaum (1:29; 2:1); the first healing is the cure of Peter's mother-in-law (1:30f); a special post-resurrection message is indicated for Peter (16:7).

Q. For whom was Mark written?

A. For Christians living outside of Palestine, with special reference to those in Rome; its message to believers there could be summed up in the words of Hebrews 12:3: "Consider him who endured from sinners such hostility against himself, so that you may not grow weary or faint-hearted."

Q. Why is it supposed that Mark was intended for readers outside Palestine?

A. The care with which the author explains Palestinian customs (7:3f; 7:11; 15:42), names (3:17; 10:46), and phrases (5:41; 7:34) presupposes that the expected readers would be unfamiliar with these.

Q. What terms are there within the book that link it with Rome?

A. Mark's distinctive contribution to the temptation narrative is: ". . . and he was with the wild beasts" (1:13)—perhaps this was inserted for the consolation of those believers in Rome who lived under threat of being thrown to the wild beasts in the arena. In addition, Mark takes over into Greek certain Latin words, such as *centurion* (15:39, 44f) and the one translated "soldier of the guard" (6:27); the word translated "pallet" (2:4,9,11f; 6:55) is a colloquial Latin term for stretcher or camp-bed; the adjective translated "of Nazareth" in 16:6 may also have been originally a Latin form.

Q. When was Mark written?

A. Probably about 65 A.D.

Q. Where was Mark written?

A. Apart from inferences that may be drawn from the evangelist's association with Peter and Peter's preaching in Rome, there is no evidence regarding the place of origin.

Q. What was the purpose of the Gospel according to Mark?

A. To show how the public ministry of Jesus exhibits him as "Son of God with power" (cf. Romans 1:4).

Q. Why is the lion used in Christian art to symbolize Mark?

A. Because his is the gospel of the "Strong Son of God."

Q. What are the three basic questions with which Mark deals?

A. (a) Who was Jesus? (b) Why was he crucified? (c) What did he expect of his followers?

Q. What four titles of Jesus are suggested in Mark?

A. Son of God (1:1,11; 13:32; 15:39), Son of man (10:45; 14;62), the Christ (8:27-30); the Suffering Servant (8:31; 10:45).

Q. What is the meaning of the term "Christ"?

A. Derived from the Greek, "The Anointed," it is the New Testament equivalent of the Old Testament "Messiah."

Q. What four memorable pictures of Jesus does Mark include?

A. He remembers Jesus (a) asleep on a cushion in a boat during a storm (4:37f); (b) taking the children in his arms (10:16); (c) gazing affectionately upon the rich young man (10:21); (d) a lonely and resolute figure striding ahead of the disciples on the road to Jerusalem (10:32).

Q. How much of Mark is reproduced by Matthew and Luke?

A. Approximately ninety-five percent; of the 661 verses in Mark, 600 are either reproduced or substantially represented in Matthew, 350 in Luke; only thirty-one of Mark's verses are not represented in either Matthew or Luke.

Q. What unique contribution does Mark make to the story of Jesus?

A. Mark alone records (a) the parable of the seed growing silently (4:26-29); (b) the healing of the deaf mute (7:31-37) and of the blind man at Beth-saida (8:22-26); (c) the three questions evoked by the dullness of the disciples (8:17f); (d) three questions about the dispute among the disciples (9:33); (e) the incident of the young man who escaped without his clothing the night of Jesus' arrest (14:51f); (f) the blows inflicted on Jesus by the guards of the high priests (14:65b); (g) Pilate's uneasiness and question to the centurion (15:44); (h) an occasional striking detail, as that the multitudes sat down on the "green" grass (6:39).

Q. What treatment does Mark accord Jesus?

A. He delights in recording his actual gestures and movements (cf. 3:5; 5:30; 6:41; 7:34; 8:33; 9:35f; 10:16,21,23; 11:11); he is frank also in setting down the human traits of Jesus: his longing for solitude (1:55; 6:30-32); his anger (3:5) and indignation (10:14—on slender textual evidence, the New English Bible at Mark 1:41 speaks of Jesus' "warm indignation"); his need for rest (4:38); his sense of hunger (11:12).

Q. What treatment does Mark accord the disciples of Jesus?

A. He is frank in setting down their weaknesses and failures: they were slow to apprehend the meaning of Jesus and his deeds (8:4); they sought preferment for themselves (10:35-37); Peter so misunderstood the meaning of Messiahship that Jesus spoke words of stern rebuke: "Get behind me, Satan! For you are not on the side of God but of man" (8:33). Although Mark records the gospel preached by Peter, he does not hush up the fact of Peter's falling asleep at a critical time (14:37), nor of Peter's denial (14:66-72); Mark does, however, omit Peter's ignominious failure to walk on the water (compare Mark 6:45-52 with Matthew 14:22-33).

Q. What evidences are there in Mark of verbatim reports of the words of Jesus?

A. Seven times Mark records the actual syllables that fell from Jesus' lips (3:17; 5:41; 7:11; 7:34; 10:46; 14:36; 15:34). It is all but unique in the history of the world that these words have come down to us in their original Aramaic along with the translation.

Q. What are the characteristics of Mark's literary style?

A. The "sketchy, disconnected character of the narrative" has often been noted; terse and vivid sentence is added to terse and vivid sentence by simple connectives such as *and, immediately, again;* the author is fond of double negatives (concealed in translation) and diminutives (references to little daughter, little son, little dog, little fish, little boat are not always preserved in translation).

Q. Why does the gospel according to Mark end abruptly with verse 8 of Chapter 16?

A. The most ancient manuscripts break off there, though the reason is not entirely clear. Did Mark intend his work to end in that way? Did persecution overtake him, his work still unfinished? Did the worn end of the papyrus roll simply drop off? The medieval church, not content with the work in its original form, added a variety of endings, three of which are known.

Q. Why was Mark referred to in the early church as "the stump-fingered one" or "the club-footed one"?

A. One guess is that, in the scuffle in the garden the night of Jesus' arrest, Mark's fingers were shorn off by the weapons of the police (cf. 14:51f); another is that, in literal obedience to Jesus' word in Mark 9:43, he mutilated himself; still another—and this is the most plausible—is that the reference is not to Mark as a person but to the clipped style of his narrative or the truncated, curtailed character of the document.

Q. When is Mark remembered in the Christian year?

A. April 25 commemorates St. Mark the Evangelist.

Q. Why has Mark's work been called a story of our Lord's passion with an introduction?

A. Because so large a proportion of the total is concerned not only with the last week in Jesus' life but also with the tensions building up toward his suffering and death.

Q. What is the literary and historical significance of Mark's work?

A. As constituting a new literary form, as describing the life and death of the Son of man who was also the Son of God, it is impossible to overestimate the importance of this work for our human story.

THE GOSPEL ACCORDING TO
MATTHEW

Q. Who is the Matthew whose name is associated with this gospel?

A. The lists of the twelve disciples (Matthew 10:2-4; Mark 3:16-19; Luke 6:14-16; Acts 1:13) include Matthew; only Matthew's listing identifies him as "Matthew the tax collector" (10:3); Matthew 9:9 relates that he was called when Jesus saw him "sitting at the tax office"; only Matthew records the problem Jesus had in paying the temple tax; Papias relates that "Matthew compiled the oracles in the Hebrew language"; perhaps these "oracles" were collections of the sayings of Jesus relating to John the Baptizer, to his own disciples, to his opponents, and to the end of the age that many were expecting.

Q. For whom was the gospel according to Matthew written?

A. Its numerous references to the Old Testament indicate that it was primarily intended for those who were familiar with those Scriptures, the Hebrew people.

Q. When was the gospel according to Matthew written?

A. Probably about 75 A.D.

Q. Where was the gospel according to Matthew written?

A. Tradition associates Matthew with Antioch, the Syrian city where Jesus' "disciples were for the first time called Christians" (Acts

11:26); perhaps his work also enshrines traditions about Jesus that were common in Jerusalem.

Q. What was the purpose of the gospel according to Matthew?

A. To show that Jesus is "he of whom the prophets speak," the Messiah of Jewish expectation.

Q. How does Matthew carry out this purpose?

A. At the outset he traces the genealogy of Jesus in such a way as to establish his right to sit on David's throne, and his position as the most distinguished in the long line of Abraham (1:1-17); as frequently as he can, he links the events of Jesus' life with words spoken long before. Thus, the holy family flees the wrath of Herod "to fulfil what the Lord had spoken by the prophet, 'Out of Egypt have I called my son' " (2:15; cf. Hosea 11:1). Remorseful Judas flung down in the temple the bribe he had accepted; the money was used to purchase a burying ground for strangers; this was done to fulfil the word of the prophet, "And they took the thirty pieces of silver . . . and they gave them for the potter's field" (27:3-10; cf. Zechariah 11:12f and Acts 1:16-20).

Q. In what other ways does Matthew link his narrative with the Hebrew Scriptures?

A. He has five great discourses, each ending with a formula beginning, "And when Jesus finished these sayings" (7:28f; 11:1; 13:53; 19:1; 26:1). This appears to be in imitation of the Old Testament, with its five books of Moses and its five collections of Psalms (i.e., Psalms 1-41; 42-72; 73-89; 90-106; 107-150).

Q. What passages in Matthew suggest a prejudice in favor of the Hebrews?

A. "Go nowhere among the Gentiles, and enter no town of the Samaritans, but go rather to the lost sheep of the house of Israel" (10:5) and "I was sent only to the lost sheep of the house of Israel" (15:24).

Q. Is this prejudice offset by passages suggesting universal concern?

A. The gospel according to Matthew concludes with the Great Commission: "Go therefore and make disciples of all nations. . . ."

Q. Matthew alone reports the visit of the Magi to the infant redeemer (2:1-12); who were the Magi?

A. Primitive scientists, seeking to learn of man's destiny from the stars; Matthew does not give their names nor their country of origin, nor does he even state how many there were. That there were three has been inferred from the three gifts that are enumerated—gold and frankincense and myrrh (2:11). That they were kings has been deduced from such Old Testament passages as Psalm 72:10; Isaiah 49:7; Isaiah 60:10. Their names, given them by tradition—Caspar, Melchior, and Balthazar —date only from the eighth century A.D.

Q. If Mark's gospel was written first, why does Matthew come first in our New Testaments?

A. Because Matthew's numerous references to the Old Testament make his work a fitting transition to the New. Eleven times he has some formula such as, "this took place to fulfil what the Lord had spoken by the prophet" (1:22; 2:5,15,17,23; 4:15f; 8:17; 12:17-21; 13:35; 21:4; 27:9f). From its position as the first gospel, Matthew has done more than any other to fashion the church's picture of Jesus.

Q. What does Matthew tell about the church?

A. His two references to the church distinguish his gospel as the only one of the four in which the word *church* occurs. To Peter's great confession, recorded by Mark (8:27-30), Matthew adds the words attributed to Jesus: ". . . on this rock I will build my church" (16:18); Matthew alone records the instructions for settling a dispute by referring it to the church (18:15-17).

Q. What collections of the sayings of Jesus are to be found in Matthew?

A. The Sermon on the Mount (5:1-7:29); the mission of the disciples (10); the nature of the kingdom (a collection of parables in Chapter 13); instructions with regard to church discipline (18); discourse on the last things (Chapters 24 and 25).

Q. What are some of Matthew's distinctive contributions to the gospel story?

A. The parable of the generous employer (20:1-16); the parable of the two sons (21:28-32); the parable of the wise and foolish maidens (25:1-13); the picture of the nations summoned to judgment (25:31-46); the death of Judas (27:3-10); the warning to Pilate from his wife (27:19); the figures emerging from the tombs (27:52f); the bribing of the soldiers (28:11-15).

Q. How does Matthew deal with the materials he takes over from Mark regarding the human traits of Jesus?

A. He gives them less emphasis: where Mark (6:3) pictures Jesus as a carpenter, Matthew (13:55) refers to him as "the carpenter's son"; where Mark (10:18) has Jesus say, "Why do you call me good? No one is good but God alone," Matthew (19:17) has it: "Why do you ask me about what is good? One there is who is good."

Q. How does Matthew deal with the materials he takes over from Mark regarding the weaknesses of the disciples?

A. Where Mark (10:35-37) has James and John asking for preferment, Matthew (20:20) represents their mother as making this request for them; Matthew omits the stern rebuke to Peter that Mark records in 8:33. It is interesting in this connection to note that Matthew 5:32 adds "except on the ground of unchastity" to the prohibition of divorce found in Mark 10:11f.

Q. How does Matthew treat other material taken over from Mark?

A. He sometimes makes alterations, of greater or lesser significance, in the details: whereas Mark 6:8 reports that Jesus, at the sending out of the disciples, "charged them to take nothing for their journey except a staff," Matthew 10:9f says: "Take no gold, nor silver, nor copper in your belts, no bag for your journey, nor two tunics, nor sandals, nor a staff." Where Mark 4:11 refers to "the secret of the kingdom of God," Matthew 13:11 speaks of "the secrets of the kingdom of heaven."

Q. Why is Matthew represented in Christian art by an ox?

A. Because Matthew delineates Jesus' life as the perfect sacrifice, fulfilling for all mankind the requirements of the ceremonial law.

Q. Why did Renan call Matthew the most important book ever written?

A. Because it was the most widely read gospel in the early church and because it is the most inclusive source for the study of Jesus' ideas and ideals; the Sermon on the Mount would alone go far to justify this estimate.

Q. What organizational features in Matthew suggest the habits of a tax collector?

A. A fondness for grouping incidents or topics in numerical combinations. There are two groups of three miracles each (8:1-15; 9:18-34), three parables of sowing (13:1-32), three prayers in Gethsemane (26:36-45); seven evil spirits (12:45), seven loaves and seven baskets of food left over (15:34,37); and seven woes (Chapter 23). Such details, as if the compiler were arranging things in columns, suggest that the tax collector's office contributed something to the telling of the Good News.

Q. When is Matthew remembered in the Christian year?

A. September 21 commemorates St. Matthew, Apostle and Evangelist.

Q. What contemporary poet has written a litany for St. Matthew's Day?

A. W. H. Auden.

Q. What designation did Pope Pius XII give to Matthew?

A. In 1956 the Roman pontiff named the Apostle Matthew as the patron saint of bookkeepers.

Q. Why is Matthew's work referred to as the gospel of judgment?

A. It alone records the parable of judgment upon the nations (25:31-46). More than any other gospel, it brings out those elements in the ministry of Jesus that emphasize the sorrowful fate of those who make of religion nothing but an outward form (6:1-18; 23:23-28); those who hear the Lord's words but refuse to do them (7:26f); those who show no mercy upon their fellow men (18:21-35).

Q. What do we know of Matthew apart from the New Testament?

A. Tradition places his later ministry both in Ethiopia and around the Black Sea. Clement of Alexandria, about 200 A.D., says that Matthew escaped martyrdom, but his martyrdom in Ethiopia is commemorated by the Christians there.

THE GOSPEL ACCORDING TO
LUKE

Q. Who was Luke?

A. His name, a shortened form of the Latin *Lucanus,* indicates a Gentile origin. The reference in II Timothy 4:11 ("Luke alone is with me") suggests that he was a traveling companion of Paul. In Philemon 24 Paul lists him among "my fellow workers." In Colossians 4:14 the apostle describes him as "the beloved physician." Since Philippi was not universally recognized as "the leading city of Macedonia," it is often assumed that the historian who makes that claim in Acts 16:12 was boasting of his home town; thus it is inferred both that he was from Philippi and that, in God's providence, he was "the man of Macedonia" who, in a dream of the night, was seen imploring Paul, "Come over to Macedonia and help us" (Acts 16:9). Tradition holds that he was a native of Antioch. Origen and Jerome said he was a brother of Titus.

Q. What part did Luke play in creating the New Testament?

A. He is associated not only with the gospel that bears his name but also with the Acts of the Apostles, designed as a sequel to his first volume.

Q. What sources did Luke have for writing a gospel?

A. Acts 24:14 states that Paul, under detention by the Roman government, remained in Caesarea "many days"; it is believed that during this time Luke took advantage of the opportunity to gather together the traditions about Jesus then current in that city.

Q. What does Luke tell us about his method as historian?

A. He states in the preface to his gospel (1:1-4) that he has engaged in careful research in order to set the record straight.

Q. What allusions in this gospel support the belief that Luke was a physician?

A. Where Mark (1:30) and Matthew state simply that Peter's mother-in-law "lay sick with a fever," Luke (4:38) makes a more precise diagnosis: "was ill with a high fever." Where Mark 14:47 and Matthew 26:51 report that, in the scuffle the night of Jesus' arrest, the high priest's slave got an ear cut off, Luke 22:50 says it was "his right ear." Luke (4:23) alone reports the popular adage repeated by Jesus, "Physician, heal yourself." Where Mark (5:26) says, concerning the woman who had been hemorrhaging for twelve years, that she "had suffered much under many physicians, and had spent all that she had, and was no better but rather grew worse," Luke omits this remark about the medical profession and says simply that "she could not be healed by anyone" (8:43).

Q. For whom was the gospel according to Luke written?

A. As a Gentile himself—and perhaps the only Gentile writer in the New Testament—Luke writes for Gentile Christians.

Q. Who is the Theophilus to whom Luke (1:3) dedicates his work?

A. *Theophilus* is a Greek word meaning "lover of God"; possibly it is a symbolic representation for anyone who would believe and accept the gospel. The epithet "most excellent," however, suggests a particular person, perhaps a Roman official, the kind whom we should address as "right honorable." The precise identity of Theophilus is unknown.

Q. When was the gospel according to Luke written?

A. Probably between 80 and 85 A.D.

Q. Where was the gospel according to Luke written?

A. The ancient "Anti-Marcionite Prologue" to Luke identifies the place of writing as "Achaia."

Q. What was the purpose of the gospel according to Luke?

A. To show that Christianity is a universal religion, by demonstrating Jesus' compassion upon the poor and the oppressed and his sympathy for foreigners; Luke's gospel manifests the truth of Paul's declaration in Galatians 3:28: "There is neither Jew nor Greek, there is neither slave nor free, there is neither male nor female; for you are all one in Christ Jesus."

Q. How does Luke carry out this purpose?

A. He traces the genealogy of Jesus not simply through David to Abraham, as Matthew does, but clear back to Adam, thus dramatically emphasizing his thesis that Jesus is not a Jew only but universally human, and blood brother to all mankind. Rather than showing prejudice against Samaritans, Luke tells of a visit by Jesus to a Samaritan village (9:51-56); of a good Samaritan (10:30-37), and of a grateful Samaritan, the only one of the ten lepers, cured by Jesus, who came back to give thanks (17:12-18). Luke alone (4:18) reports the words of Jesus at the outset of his ministry:

> "The Spirit of the Lord is upon me,
> because he has anointed me to preach good news to the poor.
> He has sent me to proclaim release to the captives
> and recovering of sight to the blind,
> to set at liberty those who are oppressed,
>   to proclaim the acceptable year of the Lord."

Q. Did Jesus deliberately choose this passage for his inaugural, or was it the assigned lesson for the day in the synagogue?

A. It is not clear which was the case; lectionaries were sometimes followed in the synagogue, but there was also freedom of choice. In any case, Jesus found in the words of Isaiah 61:1f a description of the kind of Messiahship upon which he was entering.

Q. How does Luke show the fulfilment of Jesus' promise of "good news to the poor"?

A. "Good news to the poor" is emphasized in Luke's version of the Beatitudes: where Matthew (5:3) has "Blessed are the poor in spirit," Luke (6:20) has "Blessed are you poor." Where Matthew (5:6) has "Blessed are those who hunger and thirst for righteousness," Luke (6:21) has "Blessed are you that hunger now." Luke is the only evangelist to report the poverty of the holy family: the two birds offered by Mary and Joseph at the presentation in the temple were recognized as an appropriate sacrifice for those who could not afford a lamb (compare Luke 2:24 with Leviticus 12:6-8); the parable of the poor man at the rich man's gate (16:19-31); the grim story of the man who had fertile lands, bountiful crops, and bulging barns but was "not rich toward God" (12:16-21); the woes Jesus pronounced upon the inconsiderate rich (6:24f).

Q. How does Luke show the fulfilment of Jesus' promise of "recovering of sight to the blind"?

A. Luke 18:35-43 describes the cure of a blind man near Jericho who "was sitting by the roadside begging" and crying out, "Lord, let me receive my sight."

Q. How does Luke show the exemplification by Jesus of "the acceptable year of the Lord"?

A. For Luke the ministry of Jesus appears to have been but one year long; moreover, the passage from which this is taken goes on to add: "and the day of vengeance of our God" (Isaiah 61:2). Luke notes that Jesus, in the exercise of "a great discrimination," "closed the book" before reading those words. Jesus' ministry is itself a year of grace and favor for all sorts and conditions of people.

Q. Why has Luke been called the St. Francis of Assisi among the evangelists?

A. Because of his emphasis upon Jesus' compassion for the poor.

Q. Why has Luke been called the philanthropist among the evangelists?

A. Because he remembers Jesus' words to people of wealth.

Q. What does Luke tell about the inner life of Jesus?

A. More than the other synoptic writers, Luke portrays the kneeling Christ; he alone gives Jesus' teaching about prayer as contained in the parable of the friend at midnight (11:5-8) and the parable of the woman who would not take no for an answer (18:1-8). Luke alone tells that it was as Jesus "was praying in a certain place" that his disciples asked him to provide them with a pattern of prayer (11:1-4).

Q. Why does Luke's version of the Lord's Prayer differ from Matthew's (6:9-13)?

A. Perhaps on so important a subject similar teaching was given on more than one occasion; perhaps different communities preserved slightly different versions of the prayer Jesus had taught.

Q. Why in the Lord's Prayer do some churches say "debts" and "debtors," others "trespasses" and "those who trespass against us"?

A. The "trespasses" version is from a sixteenth-century English translation adopted for the Prayer Book of the Church of England; the King James and Revised Standard Versions use "debts."

Q. Why do some people conclude the Lord's Prayer with "Thine is the kingdom and the power and the glory forever," while others omit this?

A. The earliest manuscripts of Matthew do not have this doxology, and it has never been in Luke; the phrases are derived from a prayer of David recorded in I Chronicles 29:11. To the prayer as taught by Jesus, the church added phrases familiar from Jewish liturgy.

Q. What is distinctive about Jesus' birth narratives as recorded in Luke?

A. All are set in poetic vein; Luke alone records the annunciation to Mary (1:26-38); the song of Mary (the *Magnificat*—1:46-55); the song of Zechariah (the *Benedictus*—1:68-79); the song of the heavenly host (2:14); the song of Simeon (the *Nunc Dimittis*—2:29-35); because of all this, Luke has been called "the man who gave us Christmas."

Q. Why are Luke's Christmas songs known as the *Magnificat,* the *Benedictus,* and the *Nunc Dimittis*?

A. From the opening words of these songs in the Vulgate, the Latin version of the Bible that has influenced much of liturgy. The English translations of the opening phrases are, respectively: "My soul magnifies the Lord"; "Blessed be the Lord God of Israel"; and "Lord, now lettest thou thy servant depart in peace."

Q. What evidences are there that Luke was especially concerned with family life, paying notable attention to women and children?

A. He alone records: (a) the incident of the boy Jesus in the temple at the age of twelve (2:41-52); (b) the anointing of Jesus in the home of Simon the Pharisee by "a woman of the city" (7:36-50); (c) the women who ministered to Jesus (8:1-3); (d) Jesus' visit to the home of Mary and Martha (10:38-42); (e) the exclamation of a woman in the crowd regarding the happiness of the mother of Jesus (11:27f); (f) the healing of the woman who "could not fully straighten herself" (13:10-17).

Q. What is Luke's distinctive theological emphasis?

A. His is the gospel of the Holy Spirit. Mark 1:14 says: "Jesus came into Galilee"; Luke says (4:14): "Jesus returned in the power of the Spirit into Galilee." Mark 6:2 and Matthew 13:54 report that Jesus paid a visit to the Nazareth synagogue; Luke alone (4:18) reports the sermon beginning, "The Spirit of the Lord is upon me." Luke emphasizes, too, that "joy and gladness" accompany the activities of the Spirit (cf. 1:14).

Q. What are other distinctive features of Luke's gospel?

A. He alone reports: (a) the word *daily* in connection with Jesus' outline of the conditions of discipleship (compare 9:23 with Mark 8:34; Matthew 16:24); (b) two of Jesus' sayings from the cross: "Father, forgive them; for they know not what they do" (23:34) and "Today you will be with me in Paradise" (23:43); (c) Jesus' post-resurrection appearance to the two disciples of Emmaus (24:13-35); (d) the ascension of Jesus (24:50-53); (e) the saying about Satan "falling like lightning from heaven" (10:17-20); (f) the saying about Herod "that fox" (13:31-33); (g) the saying, "the kingdom of God is in the midst of you" (9:17-21); (h) the saying about the two swords (22:35-38); (i) the three parables dealing with lost things (15:3-32); (j) John the Baptizer's specific directions to various groups (3:10-14).

Q. Why is Luke represented in Christian art as a man?

A. Because the Christ he pictures is humanity as it might be, humanity as it ought to be, humanity as God intended it to be.

Q. Why did a medieval tradition identify Luke as a painter?

A. No doubt because his vivid word pictures made it easy to think of him as a superb artist.

Q. Where can one see a picture reputedly painted by Luke?

A. "The Black Madonna [so called because the pigments have blackened with age] of Czestochowa," located in the Chapel of Our Lady in the Polish town of that name, is said to have been painted by Luke.

Q. Why did Renan call Luke "the most beautiful book in the world"?

A. It represents a perfect blending of matter and style; it pictures the compassion of Jesus in words that are simple and moving.

Q. What extended sections represent some of Luke's unique contributions to the gospel?

A. Luke 1:5-2:52 narrates the infancy and childhood of Jesus; the narrative material is interspersed with poetic fragments resembling the Psalms of the Old Testament; this material is presented as from the point of view of Mary, the mother of Jesus. Luke 9:51-19:27 contains a collection of teachings, in the parabolic and other forms, hung on a sketchy narrative. Luke 9:51 represents Jesus as having "set his face to go to Jerusalem"; by the end of this section he has still not arrived.

Q. Why can Luke be described as the New Testament writer most concerned with what happened on the open road?

A. Not only is he the only writer who lingers long over the journey to Jerusalem, but he alone tells of the man who fell among thieves along the Jericho road (10:30-37). He alone has preserved the story of the Emmaus road (24:13-35). Turning to his second volume, we note his account of how an Ethiopian eunuch was converted on "the road that goes down from Jerusalem to Gaza" (Acts 8:26) and of how Saul of Tarsus was converted on the road to Damascus (Acts 9:1-9).

Q. What does Luke do with the materials he has in common with Matthew?

A. He sometimes heightens the dramatic effect by adding a few words, as when in the temptation narrative he adds (4:5) the phrase, "in a moment of time," to Matthew's "the devil showed him all the kingdoms of the world"; he concludes the temptation narrative by saying (4:13) the devil "departed from him till an opportune time." In the account of the cure of Peter's mother-in-law, Luke adds the word "immediately" (4:39) to Matthew's "she rose and served" (Matthew 8:15; Mark 1:31). Where Matthew 10:29 quotes Jesus as having said: "Are not two sparrows sold for a penny?" Luke 12:6 shows that an even greater bargain could be had if the birds were purchased in quantities: "Are not five sparrows sold for two pennies?" Matthew 12:40 interprets the sign of Jonah in this way: "For as Jonah was three days and three nights in the belly of the whale, so will the Son of man be three days and three nights in the heart of the earth." Luke 11:30 gives a very different interpretation: "For as Jonah became a sign to the men of Nineveh, so will the Son of man be to this generation."

Q. What attitude does Luke have toward the Pharisees?

A. He alone tells of how some Pharisees warned Jesus of Herod's plot to kill him (13:31f). Three times (7:36-50; 11:37f; 14:1-25) Luke pictures Jesus in the homes and at the tables of Pharisees.

Q. Does Luke's concern to show Jesus' friendliness for Pharisees have anything to do with Luke's association with Paul?

A. It is an attractive suggestion that Luke learned to emphasize this through his association with the apostle who, liberated from Pharisaism, continued to remember his origins: "as to the law a Pharisee" (Philippians 3:5), "a Pharisee, a son of Pharisees (Acts 23:6).

Q. On what day is Luke remembered in the Christian year?

A. October 18 commemorates St. Luke the Evangelist.

THE GOSPEL ACCORDING TO
JOHN

Q. Who is the John whose name is associated with this gospel?

A. Because John was a name used almost as frequently in the ancient world as among us, it is impossible to tell with certainty: John the son of Zebedee, among the first to be called as a disciple (Mark 1:19), was one of the inner circle present with Jesus in some of the high moments of his ministry (Mark 9:2; 14:33); some suppose that the Apostle John is the author and that he is referring to himself when he mentions "the disciple whom he [i.e., Jesus] loved" (19:26) and the disciple who "was lying close to the breast of Jesus" (13:23). Papias, however, refers to an Elder (Greek presbyter) John (compare II John 1, III John 1). Some suppose that the Elder John was a disciple and protégé of the Apostle John. In any case, the link with apostolic times seems secure.

Q. For whom was the gospel according to John written?

A. Its use of terms common in Graeco-Roman thought (*word, life,* *light, truth*) suggest that it is an interpretation of Christianity for those not trained in Judaism; it is, however, for all men everywhere who stand in need of life that is life to the full.

Q. When was the gospel according to John written?

A. Probably the last among the four, between 90 and 100 A.D.

Q. Where was the gospel according to John written?

A. Tradition lists Ephesus as the place of writing; the claims of Alexandria have also been put forward.

Q. What is the purpose of the gospel according to John?

A. The author himself tells us plainly: "Now Jesus did many other signs in the presence of the disciples, which are not written in this book; but these are written that you may believe that Jesus is the Christ, the Son of God, and that believing you may have life in his name" (John 20:30f).

Q. Is there special significance in the author's use of the word *signs* in describing his purpose?

A. He regards Jesus' mighty deeds not as marvels designed to evoke wonder but as evidence that God is at work among men.

Q. What signs are there in the gospel?

A. Seven are commonly distinguished: the wine in the water jars at the marriage feast in Cana (2:1-11); the cleansing of the temple (2:13-32); the healing of the lame man at the pool of Bethzatha (5:2-18); the healing of the man born blind (9:1-12); the feeding of the multitude (6:1-15); the raising of Lazarus (11:1-44); the surprising catch of fishes (21:1-8).

Q. What do these signs have in common?

A. Each of them in some way contributes to the abundance of life that Jesus announced as the purpose of his ministry: "I came that they may have life, and have it abundantly" (10:10).

Q. How does the gospel according to John differ from the Synoptics?

A. It mentions three Passovers, the others but one, and thus suggests a longer ministry than they describe; in the Synoptics, Jesus, after his boyhood visit to the temple, is in Jerusalem only once; in John he goes there frequently; of its seven signs, the only one it has in common with the Synoptics is the feeding of the multitude.

Q. Why does the gospel according to John place the cleansing of the temple at the beginning of Jesus' career rather than, as in the Synoptics, at the end?

A. Perhaps to show that the circumstances of Jesus' passion and crucifixion were not confined to a single week but characterized the whole of his public life and work.

Q. Why does the gospel according to John have no account of the temptation of Jesus?

A. Although it has no dramatic story, such as Matthew (4:1-11) and Luke (4:1-13), it does show how temptation beset Jesus at every stage of his career. In the gospel according to John, Jesus is not tempted to turn the stones into bread, but he is tempted by his mother to make a display of his power (John 2:3f). In the gospel according to John, Jesus is not tempted to win people by leaping from the pinnacle of the temple, but is tempted by his own brothers to go to the capital city prematurely (7:1-8). In the gospel according to John, Jesus is not tempted to gain the kingdoms of the world by falling down to worship Satan; he is urged by the multitudes to accept their offer of kingship (6:15).

Q. Did the author of the gospel according to John know and use the Synoptic gospels?

A. It is clear that he knew such traditions about Jesus as are included in the Synoptics; it is not clear that he used any of the Synoptics themselves.

Q. What use does the gospel according to John make of the kind of materials found in the Synoptics?

A. The Synoptics contain the parable of the lost sheep (Luke 15:3-7), the gospel according to John has the portrait of the good shepherd (10:1-18). The Synoptics remember the saying, "You are the light of the world" (Matthew 5:14); the gospel according to John reports a sermon of Jesus on the text, "I am the light of the world" (8:12-20). The Synoptics record Jesus' word to the disciples, "unless you turn and become like children, you will never enter the kingdom of heaven" (Matthew 18:3); the gospel according to John reports a discourse of Jesus revolving about the words, "You must be born anew" (3:1-21). The Synoptics speak of judgment to come (Matthew 25:31-46); the gospel according to John, of judgment that has already come (3:19). The Synoptics report a visit of Jesus to a Samaritan village, where he was inhospitably received (Luke 9:51-56); the gospel according to John describes Jesus' visit to a Samaritan community where he was acknowledged to be "the Savior of the world" (4:4-42). The Synoptics report that, upon the death of Jesus, some who had died appeared in the streets (Matthew 27:52f); the gospel according to John has Jesus say (5:25): ". . . the hour is coming, and now is, when the dead will hear the voice of the Son of God, and those who hear will live." The Synoptics report the case of Lazarus, a poor man who "died and was carried by the angels to Abraham's bosom"; the rich man who had earlier despised him pleaded to have Lazarus return to earth to warn his brothers (Luke 16:19-31); the gospel according to John reports (11:1-44) how Lazarus was summoned from the tomb. Jesus says in the Synoptics (Matthew 26:18): "My time is at hand"; the gospel according to John reports that the authorities were unable to arrest him "because his hour had not yet come" (8:20; compare 13:1), and that he said to his friends, "My time has not yet come, but your time is always here" (7:6).

Q. What is the Prologue to the gospel according to John?

A. Verses 1-18 of Chapter 1, a passage that sets the great themes of the gospel: light and life and truth.

Q. The Synoptics report that Jesus, in a "great loving act of communion with our misery," submitted to baptism at John's hand (Mark 1:9-11; Matthew 3:13-17; Luke 3:21f); the fourth evangelist does not mention this; instead, he has John the Baptizer from the beginning deprecating his own importance (1:19-28); why this difference?

A. Although John the Baptizer wished all his followers to become disciples of Jesus, we learn from Acts 18:24-26 that they did not all do this. At a time when there was a continuing "John-the-Baptist" sect, a rival to Christianity, it was important to play down the significance of the Forerunner.

Q. Concerning the crucifixion of Jesus, the Synoptics say: "they compelled a passerby, Simon of Cyrene . . . to carry his cross" (Mark 15:21); why then does John say (19:17): "he went out, bearing his own cross"?

A. The scandal of the cross as a form of punishment was so great that some in the early church denied that Jesus was ever crucified, saying that he traded places with Simon and it was Simon who was crucified, while the Lord stood to one side and laughed at the executioners. This was part of the effort to deny the humanity of Jesus. In stressing the reality of the crucifixion, John insists that Jesus really had a cross placed on his back and went out to the place of execution.

Q. What method of discourse does Jesus use in the gospel according to John?

A. Although the Synoptics relate of Jesus, ". . . he did not speak to them without a parable" (Mark 4:34), John contains no parables, but rather allegories, such as 10:1-18 and 15:1-11.

Q. How does allegory differ from parable?

A. A parable is the placing of one thing alongside another so that clarification may come by comparison; usually it is only one point of the analogy that is emphasized. Allegory is longer and more contrived, with symbolic meaning to be found in many details.

Q. What else is distinctive in Jesus' manner of speaking in the gospel according to John?

A. A number of discourses are reported beginning with the formula "I am" (e.g., 8:12; 10:7; 11:25). Also, Jesus in this gospel sometimes introduces his discourses with "Truly, truly," a solemn repetition of the "Amen" that usually occurs at the end of a prayer or sober statement.

Q. Why is John represented in Christian art by the eagle?

A. From earliest times the answer has been that he has "taken a higher flight" than the other evangelists.

Q. What are some tributes that have been paid to the gospel according to John?

A. Luther called it "the chiefest of the Gospels"; William Temple, "the profoundest of all writings"; Magregor, "the Holy of Holies of Christian literature."

Q. What incidents in John have no parallel in the Synoptics?

A. The marriage at Cana (2:1-11); the Samaritan woman at Jacob's well (4:1-42); the infirm man at the pool of Bethzatha (5:2-9); the raising of Lazarus (11:1-44).

Q. How does Jesus' attitude toward himself, as pictured by John, differ from that in the Synoptics?

A. In the Synoptics, Jesus is reticent about making known his Messiahship (Mark 1:44; 3:12; 5:43; 7:36; 8:30; 9:9; Matthew 8:4; 9:30; 12:16; 16:20; 17:9; Luke 5:14; 9:21). In John, openly and from the very beginning, Jesus sets forth his messianic claims (4:26; 5:46; 9:37).

Q. How do John and the Synoptics differ with respect to the element of humility in the ministry of Jesus?

A. In the Synoptics, Jesus often enjoins meekness and humility (Matthew 5:5; 18:4; 20:25-27; Mark 10:42-44; Luke 14:11). In John the single injunction to humility is by example (13:3-16) rather than by precept; throughout John, Jesus boldly asserts his own pre-eminence (8:23; 6:35,48,51; 7:37; 14:6; 15:1; 10:11,7; 8:12; 11:25).

Q. Why has John been called "the gospel of the rejection"?

A. Because of the numerous references to circumstances in which Jesus was not received as he ought to have been (1:11; 3:11,32; 12:37; 5:43).

Q. What has John done with the apocalyptic elements in the message of Jesus?

A. He gives them immediate, rather than long-range, application. For him, the day of judgment is not something far off and remote; every day is a day of judgment: "this is the judgment, that the light has come into the world, and men loved darkness rather than light, because their deeds were evil" (3:19). Conversely, the life of the ages is not simply a future hope but a present possession: "whoever believes . . . may have eternal life" (3:15); "I am the resurrection and the life; he who believes in me, though he die, yet shall he live, and whoever lives and believes in me shall never die" (11:25).

Q. Why is John spoken of as the gospel of the Holy Spirit?

A. Because more than any other it reports Jesus' promises regarding the coming of the Spirit (14:16-25; 16:7-15).

Q. What section of John is known as Jesus' high priestly prayer?

A. Chapter 17.

Q. What verses from John are frequently quoted in support of the ecumenical movement?

A. "And I have other sheep, that are not of this fold; I must bring them also, and they will heed my voice. So there shall be one flock, one shepherd" (10:16). "I do not pray for those only, but also for those who . . . believe in me through their word, that they may all be one; even as thou, Father, art in me, and I in thee, that they also may be in us, so that the world may believe that thou hast sent me" (17:20,21).

Q. What is distinctive about the treatment accorded Peter in the gospel according to John?

A. He who had three times denied (18:15-27) has the opportunity three times to reaffirm his love and devotion (21:15-19).

Q. In what way does the author make it clear that he has made selection from much that had to be left untold?

A. "But there are also many other things which Jesus did; were every one of them to be written, I suppose that the world itself could not contain the books that would be written" (21:25).

Q. When is John remembered in the Christian year?

A. December 27 commemorates St. John, Apostle and Evangelist.

THE ACTS OF THE APOSTLES

Q. What is the meaning of the word *Acts* in the title?

A. *Acts* translates the single word that serves as the title in Greek; it means "Doings" or "Deeds." The volume recounts the travels, sermons, and persecutions of those in the early church whose designation *apostles* means "Sent Ones" or "Those who have been sent."

Q. Which apostles principally figure in the story?

A. Peter is the main character in the earlier chapters, and Paul in the latter. John is mentioned three times as the companion of Peter, and the death of James is reported; more space is given to Stephen, Philip, Timothy, and Silas, none of whom was originally designated as an apostle, than to those upon whom the title had been earlier bestowed. "Some Acts of Some Apostles" would be a more precise designation; since the emphasis is upon what God was doing in and through and for his church, it could appropriately be called "The Acts of the Holy Spirit" or "The Acts of the Risen Lord"; the work is the first missionary handbook, the first book in church history.

Q. Who is the author of Acts?

A. The opening phrases, "In the first book, O Theophilus" (1:1), indicate that it is the second part of a two-volume work by Luke (see Luke 1:3).

Q. When was Acts written?

A. The church had become established in many communities, but the heresies apparent in later New Testament books had not become a problem; a date between 80 and 90 A.D. would seem to accord with the facts.

Q. Where was Acts written?

A. Much of the work was set down contemporaneously with the events it describes: the "we" passages (16:10-18; 20:5-16; 21:1-16; 27:1-28:15) evidently incorporate Luke's travel diary; he seems also to have made use of traditions gathered from the churches in Philippi, Ephesus, Corinth, Caesarea; the whole could have been compiled in Antioch, Rome, or Ephesus.

Q. To whom is Acts addressed?

A. Theophilus (1:1) is addressed in Luke 1:3 as "most excellent" [perhaps equivalent to our "right honorable"] Theophilus." *Theophilus* means "lover of God," and has sometimes been thought to be a symbolic name for any believer. More general is the belief that Theophilus was a Roman official; the fact that the title "most excellent" is dropped in the second volume has suggested that, by the time the sequel was written, Theophilus had himself become a member of the believing community.

Q. What evidences are there within the book itself of the author's special concern with the Roman empire?

A. Alone among New Testament writers, Luke mentions a Roman emperor by name (11:28; 18:2; cf. Luke 2:1; 3:1); lesser Roman officials appear with some frequency: "the proconsul Sergius Paulus" (13:7); Claudius Lysias, "the tribune of the cohort" (21:31; 23:26); Felix the governor (23:24); Porcius Festus, successor to Felix (24:27). Luke identifies Philippi as "a Roman colony" (16:12), and refers in certain legal matters to "the custom of the Romans" (25:16; cf. 16:21; 22:25-29); historical study has generally confirmed the accuracy of these allusions to the geography and administration of the empire.

Q. Why would a gospel writer and church historian address his work to a Roman magistrate?

A. Perhaps to demonstrate to an official of the Roman government that Christianity, like other religions, should be tolerated and not outlawed.

Q. What other purpose did the author have?

A. To narrate, in the Old Testament manner, the early history of the Christian church; 1:8 outlines the sequence: "you shall be my witnesses in Jerusalem and in all Judea and Samaria and to the end of the earth."

Q. What are the themes of the sermons in Acts?

A. A reference to some prophetic word in the history of Israel pointing forward to the present scene; the affirmation that in Christ this has been fulfilled; "this Jesus God raised up, and of that we all are witnesses" (2:32); a challenge to the bystander: "Repent and be baptized" (2:38; cf. 3:11-26; 7:1-53; 13:16-41).

Q. What items of church organization appear in Acts?

A. To bring the number of the apostles up to twelve, Matthias is chosen to replace Judas (1:23-26); when the church grew in numbers and "the Hellenists murmured against the Hebrews because their widows were" inadequately cared for (6:1), the twelve arranged to appoint seven men to superintend "the daily distribution"; the twelve "prayed and laid their hands upon them" (6:6); when Barnabas and Saul were to be set apart for missionary work, the "prophets and teachers" at Antioch "laid their hands on them and sent them off" (13:3); Paul and Barnabas visited Lystra, Iconium, and Antioch: "and when they had appointed elders for them in every church, with prayer and fasting, they committed them to the Lord" (14:23).

Q. What name is commonly given to Christianity in Acts?

A. It is repeatedly referred to as "the Way" (9:2; 18:25; 19:9,23; 22:4; 24:22); members of the believing community also are "witnesses" (1:8,22; 2:32; 3:15; 5:32; 10:39).

Q. Where did the Christian missionaries generally begin their approach to the communities they visited?

A. Because they regarded Christianity as the logical and necessary sequel to Judaism, they went first to the synagogue for a hearing (9:20; 13:5,14; 14:1; 17:1f,10; 18:4; 19:8), although they were often physically thrown out and had then to seek other quarters (17:5-9; 18:7; 19:9).

Q. How does the narrative in Acts begin?

A. With Jesus presenting "himself alive after his passion" (1:3) and the disciples, still misunderstanding the nature of his mission, asking, "Lord, will you at this time restore the kingdom to Israel?" (1:6); while the believing company was together at Jerusalem, "there appeared to them tongues as of fire, distributed and resting on each one of them"

(2:3); thus came the power to break the language barrier in imparting the truth: "each heard them speaking in his own language" (2:6).

Q. What is the theme of Peter's address on the day of Pentecost?

A. That the words of the prophet Joel (Joel 2:28-32) have received glorious fulfilment (2:14-21).

Q. What is the reaction to Peter's sermon?

A. "They were cut to the heart, and said . . . 'what shall we do?' " (2:37); "and there were added that day about three thousand souls" (2:41).

Q. What was the effect of this upon the members?

A. "They sold their possessions and goods and distributed them to all, as any had need" (2:45; 4:32-37).

Q. Did all the members adhere to this arrangement?

A. Ananias and Sapphira, having not only "kept back some of the proceeds" (5:2), but lied about it, "fell down and died" (5:5,10).

Q. What treatment was given the lame man at the gate of the temple?

A. Peter said, " 'I have no silver and gold, but I give you what I have . . .' and immediately his feet and ankles were made strong. And leaping up he stood and walked and entered the temple" (3:1-10).

Q. How did Peter explain "by what means this man has been healed"? (4:9).

A. "By the name of Jesus Christ of Nazareth, whom you crucified, whom God raised from the dead, by him this man is standing before you well" (4:10).

Q. What first led to the arrest of Christian missionaries?

A. The Jerusalem authorities were "annoyed because they were teaching the people and proclaiming in Jesus the resurrection from the dead" (4:2).

Q. What impressed the authorities about the missionaries?

A. "Now when they saw the boldness of Peter and John, and perceived that they were uneducated, common men, they wondered; and they recognized that they had been with Jesus" (4:13; cf. 4:31).

Q. What was the attitude of the missionaries toward the authorities?

A. "Whether it is right in the sight of God to listen to you . . . you must judge; for we cannot but speak of what we have seen and heard" (4:19f); "we must obey God rather than men" (5:29).

Q. What advice did Gamaliel give regarding the strange new doctrine?

A. Gamaliel, "a teacher of the law, held in honor by all the people" (5:34), said: ". . . if this plan or this undertaking is of men, it will fail; but if it is of God, you will not be able to overthrow them." (5:39).

Q. What assistance did the missionaries have in their conflict with the authorities?

A. "At night an angel of the Lord opened the prison doors and brought them out" (5:19); "Peter was sleeping between two soldiers, bound with two chains, and sentries . . . were guarding the prison; and behold, an angel of the Lord . . . struck Peter on the side and woke him. . . . And the chains fell off his hands" (12:6f). "But about midnight Paul and Silas were praying and singing hymns to God, and the prisoners were listening to them, and suddenly there was a great earthquake, so that the foundations of the prison were shaken; and immediately all the doors were opened and everyone's fetters were unfastened" (16:25f).

Q. What devices did the people use to put themselves in touch with the life-giving power that streamed from the apostles?

A. "They even carried out the sick into the streets, and laid them on beds and pallets, that as Peter came by at least his shadow might fall on some of them" (5:15). "God did extraordinary miracles by the hands of Paul, so that handkerchiefs or aprons were carried away from his body to the sick" (19:11f).

Q. What charge did the authorities bring against Stephen?

A. "We have heard him speak blasphemous words . . . Jesus of Nazareth will destroy this place, and will change the customs which Moses delivered to us" (6:11,14).

Q. What defense did Stephen make?

A. After recounting the history of the Hebrew people from the call of Abraham to the days of Solomon (7:2-50), he said: "You stiff-necked people, uncircumcised in heart and ears, you always resist the Holy Spirit. As your fathers did, so do you" (7:51).

Q. What effect did this discourse have upon the people?

A. "Then they cast him out of the city and stoned him" (7:58), thus making Stephen the first Christian martyr.

Q. What was the sequel to Stephen's death?

A. Among those who witnessed the stoning was "a young man named Saul," at whose feet the executioners laid their garments; he heard the dying Stephen pray: "Lord, do not hold this sin against them" (7:60). Saul then began to persecute the church, dragging men and women off to prison (8:3); "still breathing threats and murder," he started for Damascus, to wipe out the church already established there (9:1f); en route to Damascus, no doubt pondering the fact that Stephen died as Christ died, breathing forgiveness upon his tormentors, Saul was struck by a blinding light and heard a voice, "I am Jesus, whom you are persecuting" (9:5). Going on to Damascus, Saul regained his sight (9:10-18), was baptized, and "in the synagogues immediately he proclaimed Jesus" (9:20; other accounts of Saul's conversion are found in 22:6-21 and 26:12-18).

Q. What commission is given the converted Saul (also called Paul)?

A. Through Ananias the word of the Lord is spoken: ". . . he is a chosen instrument of mine to carry my name before the Gentiles and kings and the sons of Israel" (9:15).

Q. What kind of reception did Paul receive in Damascus?

A. The Christians were uneasy about him: "I have heard from many about this man, how much evil he has done" (9:13), and "the Jews plotted to kill him" (9:23); this plot he escaped when "his disciples took him by night and let him down over the wall, lowering him in a basket" (9:25); when Paul reached Jerusalem the followers of Jesus "were all afraid of him, for they did not believe that he was a disciple" (9:26).

Q. What part did Philip play in the spreading of Christianity?

A. He "went down to a city of Samaria, and proclaimed to them the Christ" (8:5); Simon the magician was converted by his preaching (8:9-24); Philip explained to an Ethiopian official how to read the Old Testament in the light of "the good news of Jesus" (8:26-39).

Q. What is told of Peter's ministry at Lydda and Joppa (modern Jaffa)?

A. At Lydda he healed the bedridden Aeneas (9:32-35); at Joppa he prayed over the body of Dorcas and "presented her alive" (9:36-42); in the house of Simon the tanner, he learned through a vision "that God shows no partiality, but in every nation any one who fears him and does what is right is acceptable to him" (10:1-11:18).

Q. What is told us regarding the ministry of Barnabas?

A. He took Paul to the Jerusalem apostles, vouching for the genuineness of his conversion (9:27); he brought Paul to Antioch, where "the disciples were for the first time called Christians" (11:26); he and Paul took to Jerusalem the famine relief contribution made in Antioch (11:27-30); Barnabas was, in short, "a good man, full of the Holy Spirit and of faith" (11:24).

Q. What befell Herod who "laid violent hands upon some who belonged to the church" (12:1), "killed James the brother of John" (12:2), and "proceeded to arrest Peter also" (12:3); then "put on his royal robes, took his seat upon the throne, and made an oration" (12:21)?

A. "An angel of the Lord smote him, because he did not give God the glory; and he was eaten by worms and died" (12:23).

Q. What happened to Elymas the magician who sought "to turn away the proconsul [Sergius Paulus] from the faith"?

A. "Mist and darkness fell upon him and he went about seeking people to lead him by the hand" (13:11).

Q. How was the gospel received in Lystra?

A. When Paul enabled a man, crippled from birth, to stand up and walk (14:8-10), the people wanted to worship Paul and Barnabas, saying, "The gods have come down to us in the likeness of men!" (14:11). Paul's response was: "We also are men, of like nature with you, and bring you good news" (14:15).

Q. What issue was debated at Jerusalem?

A. When some said, "Unless you are circumcised according to the custom of Moses, you cannot be saved" (15:1), "The apostles and elders were gathered together to consider this matter" (15:6); this first church council ever held resolved to lay upon the Gentiles "no greater burden than . . . that you abstain from what has been sacrificed to idols and from blood and from what is strangled and from unchastity" (15:28f).

Q. What led Paul to cross from Asia into Europe?

A. A "vision" of the night in which "a man of Macedonia was . . . saying, 'Come over to Macedonia and help us' " (16:9).

Q. Why did Paul at Philippi not follow the usual practice of the apostles and go first to a synagogue?

A. At Philippi there evidently was no synagogue, ten heads of families, or elders, being necessary before one could be established; in the absence of a synagogue, there was "a place of prayer" outside the gate down by the river, and thither Paul went (16:11-13).

Q. Who was the first convert in Philippi?

A. Lydia, "a seller of purple goods," an immigrant from Thyatira, gave "heed to what was said by Paul" and "was baptized, with her household" (16:14f). Since this was the first visit to Europe by a Christian missionary, Lydia became the first convert in the Western world.

Q. To what business venture in Philippi did Paul and Silas bring bankruptcy?

A. The owners of a demented slave girl were exploiting her as a soothsayer. Paul exorcised the demon; "when her owners saw that their hope of gain was gone . . . they brought them to the magistrates," who imprisoned them (16:16-24).

Q. What communities did Paul visit following his release from jail in Philippi?

A. Thessalonica, where "the people and the city authorities were disturbed" (17:8); Beroea, where "they received the word with all eagerness" (17:11); Athens, where, seeing an altar inscribed "To an unknown God," Paul said: "What therefore you worship as unknown, this I proclaim to you" (17:23); Corinth, where, making his headquarters in the home of fellow tentmakers, Aquila and Priscilla (18:1-3), he "stayed a year and six months, teaching the word of God" (18:11); Ephesus, where he found some disciples who knew only the baptism of John (19:1-7), and "those who practiced magic arts brought their books together and burned them" (19:19), and the idol-makers' guild instigated a riot (19:23-41); to Troas where, during one of Paul's addresses, "a young man named Eutychus . . . sank into a deep sleep . . . and . . . fell down from the third story" (20:7-12).

Q. What was the burden of Paul's farewell to the elders of Ephesus?

A. "I did not shrink from declaring to you the whole counsel of God" (20:27).

Q. Where did Paul go following his departure from Ephesus?

A. To Tyre (21:1-6); Ptolemais (21:7); Caesarea (where he stayed in the home of Philip the evangelist—21:8-14); Jerusalem (where "they were trying to kill him"—this gave Paul an opportunity to explain to the tribune, the council, and the people why he had become a Christian—

21:17-23:10); to avoid a plot to kill Paul, the tribune remanded him to the authorities in Caesarea (23:12-34).

Q. What happened in Caesarea?

A. Felix, the governor, had hoped that money would be given him by Paul, but at the time of Felix's retirement and succession by Festus, Paul still remained in prison. Standing on his rights as a Roman citizen, Paul appealed to Caesar. Festus invited King Agrippa to review the case on the ground that it seemed "unreasonable, in sending a prisoner, not to indicate the charges against him" (25:27). Agrippa's verdict is: "This man could have been set free if he had not appealed to Caesar" (26:32).

Q. How does the Acts conclude?

A. With an account of the voyage to Rome, with what has become a classical account of a shipwreck (27:4-44); the escape of the shipwrecked persons to the island of Malta, where Paul was taken for a god (28:2-6); the resumption of the voyage when winter had passed (28:11-13); the landing at Rhegium and Puteoli (modern Pozzuoli); the overland journey to Rome, with the meeting of friends at Three Taverns (28:15f); Paul is placed under house detention in Rome (28:16), where he explains to visitors: ". . . it is because of the hope of Israel that I am bound with this chain" (29:20); there he lived on "two whole years at his own expense, and welcomed all who came to him, preaching the kingdom of God and teaching about the Lord Jesus Christ quite openly and unhindered" (28:30f).

An Introduction to Paul

Q. Who was Paul?

A. An early and indefatigable missionary; the first interpreter of the gospel to the Gentile world; the author of more New Testament books than any other writer.

Q. What is the significance of his name?

A. When we first meet him (Acts 7:58-8:1) he is Saul; Acts 13:9 describes him as "Saul, who is also called Paul." This tells us a significant thing about him. As a Hebrew, he bore the name of Israel's earliest king; as a free citizen of the Roman world, he bore a Roman name.

Q. What was Paul's native place?

A. He proudly identifies himself as "a Jew, from Tarsus, in Cilicia, a citizen of no mean city" (Acts 21:39). This accounts for his dual citizenship. Citizens of Tarsus, whatever their race, had the right to be called Romans, and Paul stands on his rights as "a Roman citizen" (Acts 22:25-29). Tarsus was a center of learning, and perhaps Paul there acquired a knowledge of philosophy from local and itinerant Greek scholars.

Q. What additional training did Paul have?

A. He studied at the rabbinical school conducted in Jerusalem by Gamaliel (Acts 22:3); Paul could thus boast of having been "educated according to the strict manner of the law of our fathers" (Acts 22:3).

Gamaliel taught his students to drink from Greek vases as well as from Jewish water jars.

Q. To what group in Hebrew society did Paul belong?

A. He was "a Pharisee, a son of Pharisees" (Acts 23:6); "as to the law a Pharisee" (Philippians 3:5).

Q. To what course of conduct did his informed Pharisaism lead?

A. He sought desperately to exterminate Christianity, which he regarded as a rival of the true faith: "I persecuted this Way to the death, binding and delivering to prison both men and women" (Acts 22:4; cf. 26:11).

Q. What happened to Paul en route to Damascus to wipe out Christianity there?

A. "Now as he journeyed he approached Damascus, and suddenly a light from heaven flashed about him"; a voice said, "I am Jesus, whom you are persecuting" (Acts 9:3f).

Q. What effect did this have upon his life?

A. He reports how the Christians of one community could say: " 'He who once persecuted us is now preaching the faith he once tried to destroy.' And they glorified God because of me" (Galatians 1:23,24).

Q. What does he say of the journeys he thereafter took for the gospel?

A. "On frequent journeys, in danger from rivers, danger from robbers, danger from my own people, danger from Gentiles, danger in the city, danger in the wilderness, danger at sea, danger from false brethren; in toil and hardship, through many a sleepless night, in hunger and thirst, often without food, in cold and exposure" (II Corinthians 11:26,27).

Q. What was the purpose of these travels?

A. To make converts and establish churches.

Q. Why did Paul write letters?

A. To keep in touch with the churches he had founded, seeking to make application of the timeless gospel to the timely needs of the congregations newly called out of heathendom.

Q. How are the Hebrew elements in Paul's background brought out in his correspondence?

A. He knows the Law thoroughly, and in its exegesis often employs the methods of the rabbis (Acts 23:6-9; 24:14f: 26:3; Galatians 4.21-31; I Corinthians 10:4).

Q. How are the Greek elements in Paul's background revealed in his correspondence?

A. He is the master of a powerful Greek style; most of his metaphors are drawn from the life of the Hellenized cities (I Corinthians 4:9; 9:24; Philippians 3:14; Romans 1:32; II Corinthians 2:14; 1:22; 5:5; Colossians 2:15); he uses some of the terminology of popular Stoic teaching (Romans 1:26; 2:14,27; 11:24; I Corinthians 11:14; Galatians 2:15; 4:8).

Q. What do we know of Paul's physical appearance?

A. Nothing can be certainly known about this. An early apocryphal work, *The Acts of Paul and Thekla,* describes him thus: "A man of middling size, and his hair was scanty, and his legs were a little crooked, and his knees were far apart; he had large eyes, and his eyebrows met and his nose was somewhat long; and he was full of grace and mercy; at one time he seemed like a man, and at another he seemed like an angel."

Q. When is Paul remembered in the Christian year?

A. January 25 commemorates the Conversion of St. Paul.

Q. What was Paul's distinctive contribution to Christianity?

A. Besides having created some of its loveliest literature (such as I Corinthians 13 and Romans 12), he made explicit for all time what he had learned through his own experience, namely, the impossibility of a man's ever attaining through the Law right standing before God, and the utter necessity that one should trust in God's grace made known in Christ: "For by grace you have been saved through faith; and this is not your own doing, it is the gift of God—not because of works, lest any man should boast" (Ephesians 2:8,9).

THE LETTER OF PAUL TO THE
ROMANS

Q. Who is the author of the Letter of Paul to the Romans?

A. The writer identifies himself as "Paul . . . an apostle" (1:1).

Q. To whom is this letter addressed?

A. "To all God's beloved in Rome" (1:7).

Q. When was this letter written?

A. Probably between 56 and 58 A.D.

Q. Where was this letter written?

A. Corinth has often been identified as the place of writing (Acts 20:2f); the claims of Philippi have also been put forward.

Q. The letter was evidently written while Paul was en route; where was he going?

A. He was on his way to Jerusalem, taking with him the contributions made in Greece and Macedonia for the poor in the mother church (15:25-27).

Q. Had Paul visited the church in Rome?

A. No; but he here writes of his wish to visit the Christians in the capital city of the empire: "I long to see you" (1:11); "I am eager to preach the gospel to you also who are in Rome" (1:15); "since I have longed for many years to come to you, I hope to see you in passing as I go to Spain" (15:23f).

Q. Did Paul carry out the proposed visit to Spain?

A. There is no record of it.

Q. Did Paul get to Rome?

A. Yes, but not as he had hoped. He intended to come as an evangelist; when he finally got there, he was a prisoner (Acts 28:16).

Q. There is a saying in many languages, "When in Rome, do as the Romans do." Did Paul agree with this?

A. No. Paul says: "Do not be conformed to this world"—that is, do not do as your fellow Romans do. (12:2)

Q. What is the purpose for which this letter was written?

A. To exhibit the gospel as "the power of God for salvation to every one who has faith, to the Jew first and also to the Greek" (1:16).

Q. How is this purpose carried out?

A. In the most systematic treatise we have from the pen of Paul, he treats of God's sovereign power, of the efficacy of faith, of God's loving purpose embracing both Jew and non-Jew.

Q. Is this letter a unity?

A. Many ancient copies end with verse 33 of Chapter 15, which forms a natural conclusion: "The God of peace be with you all. Amen." It is likely therefore that what we know as Chapter 16 was a separate document, fastened on to the Roman letter to round out the papyrus roll. In some manuscripts the closing doxology of 16:25-27 appears after

14:23; this shortened form of the letter appears to have been extant in the second century.

Q. What is the nature of Chapter 16?

A. It seems to be a letter of introduction for Phoebe, a deaconess of the church at Cenchreae, as she set out to visit other churches.

Q. What is the gospel that Paul proclaims in Romans?

A. ". . . concerning his Son, who was descended from David according to the flesh and designated Son of God in power according to the Spirit of holiness by his resurrection from the dead, Jesus Christ our Lord, through whom we have received grace and apostleship to bring about the obedience to the faith for the sake of his name among all the nations" (1:3-5).

Q. What picture does Paul give of the world without the gospel?

A. He describes it as ungrateful, immoral, untruthful, worshiping "the creature rather than the Creator . . . full of envy, murder, strife, deceit," and many other forms of wickedness (1:18-32).

Q. What is the purpose of God's kindness?

A. "To lead you to repentance" (2:4).

Q. What is the wrath of God (1:18; 3:5; 4:15)?

A. The other side of holy love, God's wrath is his opposition to evil.

Q. What is the position of the Gentiles who did not know the Law of Moses?

A. They have God's law written on the conscience (2:13-16).

Q. What is Paul's attitude toward the Jewish Law?

A. Thoroughly acquainted with it from his youth, he learned that efforts to keep it left him with a sense of futility: "Wretched man that I am! Who will deliver me from this body of death?" (7:24).

Q. What has Christ done to the Law?

A. "Christ is the end of the law, that every one who has faith may be justified" (10:4); "love is the fulfilling of the law" (13:10).

Q. What is Paul's attitude toward the Jewish people?

A. "Brethren, my heart's desire and prayer to God for them is that they may be saved. I bear witness that they have a zeal for God, but it is not enlightened" (10:1f).

Q. Who is now the true Jew?

A. "He is a Jew who is one inwardly, and real circumcision is a matter of the heart" (2:29).

Q. What advantages did Jews have in earlier times?

A. They had been "entrusted with the oracles of God" (3:2); "to them belong the sonship, the glory, the covenants, the giving of the law, the worship, and the promises; to them belong the patriarchs, and of their race, according to the flesh, is the Christ" (9:4f).

Q. Had this brought redemption?

A. "No human being will be justified . . . by works of the law" (3:20); God "justifies him who has faith in Jesus" (3:26).

Q. What position is assigned to Abraham?

A. His faith "was reckoned to him as righteousness" (4:3,22); he is the father of all "who share the faith of Abraham" (4:16).

Q. Did not Abraham obey the spirit of the Law?

A. Paul makes it clear that Abraham's saving faith was demonstrated before he was circumcised; Abraham, at the time he set out on the life of faith, was, in effect, a Gentile (4:9-15).

Q. How is justification now obtained?

A. Through faith (5:1).

Q. What position is assigned to Christ?

A. "Through him we have obtained access to this grace in which we stand" (5:2); "death no longer has dominion over him" (6:9); "There is therefore now no condemnation for those who are in Christ Jesus" (8:1).

Q. What is the proof of God's love?

A. God shows his love for us in that while we were yet sinners Christ died for us" (5:8).

Q. What part is played by Adam?

A. "Because of one man's trespass, death reigned" (5:17); but Christ is, so to speak, a second "first man" or "Adam," and men receive "the free gift of righteousness . . . through the one man Jesus Christ" (5:17).

Q. What autobiographical touches appear in this letter?

A. In 7:15-20 the author gives a frank picture of a tortured inner self: "I do not understand my own actions"; in 11:1 he recounts his ancestry: "an Israelite, a descendant of Abraham, a member of the tribe of Benjamin"; in 15:21 he tells us that it was his policy to seek out places where Christ had not yet been preached, "lest I build on another man's foundation."

Q. What philosophy of suffering is set forth?

A. "I consider that the sufferings of this present time are not worth comparing with the glory that is to be revealed to us" (8:18). "We know that in everything God works for good with those who love him" (8:28).

Q. What striking figures of speech appear in this letter?

A. The potter and the clay (9:19-21) suggest God's providential ordering of human life; the grafting of a wild olive shoot (11:17-24) suggests how God can be kind to all; "the armor of light" must replace "the works of darkness" (13:11-14).

Q. What is Paul's attitude toward civil government?

A. "Let every person be subject to the governing authorities. For there is no authority except from God . . . rulers are not a terror to good conduct, but to bad" (13:1,3).

Q. What is the duty of the believing citizen?

A. "Pay . . . taxes to whom taxes are due, revenue to whom revenue is due, respect to whom respect is due, honor to whom honor is due" (13:7).

Q. On matters of conscience, what is to be the believer's attitude toward others?

A. "Then let us no more pass judgment on one another, but rather decide never to put a stumbling block or hindrance in the way of a brother" (14:13).

Q. What are some notable passages in Romans?

A. "God shows no partiality" (2:11); "For the wages of sin is death, but the free gift of God is eternal life" (6:23); "For all who are led by the Spirit of God are sons of God" (8:14); the passage describing man's inseparability from God (8:31-39); "For there is no distinction between Jew and Greek; the same Lord is Lord of all and bestows his riches upon all who call upon him" (10:12); "O the depth of the riches and wisdom and knowledge of God! How unsearchable are his judgments and how inscrutable his ways!" (11:33); Chapter 12; "None of us lives to himself, and none of us dies to himself" (14:7); "Let us then pursue what makes for peace and for mutual upbuilding" (14:19); "whatever does not proceed from faith is sin" (14:23b); "We who are strong ought to bear the failings of the weak, and not to please ourselves" (15:1).

THE FIRST LETTER OF PAUL TO THE
CORINTHIANS

Q. Who is the author of I Corinthians?

A. The writer identifies himself in 1:1 as "Paul . . . an apostle," and associates with him in the writing "our brother Sosthenes."

Q. Who was Sosthenes?

A. Acts 18:17 reports that the authorities "seized Sosthenes, the ruler of the synagogue, and beat him in front of the tribunal."

Q. To whom is this letter addressed?

A. "To the church of God which is at Corinth" (1:2); Corinth has been called the "Vanity Fair" of the ancient world.

Q. Who had founded the church in Corinth?

A. Paul, on one of his missionary journeys, spent eighteen months there (cf. Acts 18:2).

Q. What was the condition of the church in Corinth at the time Paul wrote?

A. It was divided into factions, some claiming Paul as their model, others claiming Peter, others Apollos.

Q. What is Paul's answer to factionalism?

A. That the church ought to rejoice in all its leaders, since the leaders belong to the church, not the church to the leaders: "all things are yours, whether Paul or Apollos or Cephas . . . all are yours; and you are Christ's; and Christ is God's (3:21-23).

Q. How did Paul hear of these dissensions?

A. Through "Chloe's people" (1:11).

Q. Who was Chloe?

A. Perhaps a woman of means whose servants had brought messages to Paul.

Q. When was this letter written?

A. Probably in 54 or 55 A.D.

Q. Where was this letter written?

A. From Ephesus (16:8).

Q. What was the author's purpose in writing this letter?

A. To eliminate dissensions in the church; to give directions regarding ethical problems arising from life in a pagan city; to emphasize those aspects of the gospel especially relevant to a congregation newly called out of heathendom.

Q. How does the author carry out this threefold purpose?

A. The first by passionate entreaty (1:10); the second by giving the soundest advice his wisdom could summon (as in 7:8,10,12,25); the third by contrasting worldly wisdom with Christianity's crucial fact (1:22-24).

Q. What is the significance of 11:23-26?

A. It is the earliest description of the observance by the church of the Lord's supper.

Q. What class of people made up the church in Corinth?

A. "Not many of you were wise according to worldly standards, not many were powerful, not many were of noble birth" (1:26).

Q. What divine principle does Paul see illustrated by this fact?

A. "God chose what is foolish in the world to shame the wise, God chose what is weak in the world to shame the strong, God chose what is low and despised in the world, even things that are not, to bring to nothing things that are" (1:27f).

Q. How had Paul conducted himself when in Corinth?

A. "I was with you in weakness and in much fear and trembling; and my speech and my message were not in plausible words of wisdom, but in demonstration of the Spirit and power" (2:3f).

Q. Who was Apollos (4:6)?

A. An eloquent teacher from Alexandria, well instructed in the Jewish Scriptures.

Q. Why should men refrain from boasting of their gifts and achievements?

A. "What have you that you did not receive? If then you received it, why do you boast as if it were not a gift?" (4:7).

Q. Did Paul boast of his achievements?

A. On the contrary, he says: ". . . we have become, and are now, as the refuse of the world, the offscouring of all things" (4:13).

Q. What were some of the moral problems in Corinth?

A. Incest, adultery, homosexuality, gluttony, greed, and drunkenness.

Q. What help does Paul give in overcoming these?

A. "Do you not know that your body is a temple of the Holy Spirit within you, which you have from God? You are not your own; you were bought with a price. So glorify God in your body" (6:19f).

Q. Chapter 7 begins with a reference to "the matters about which you wrote"; what were these?

A. Since their letter has not survived, we can only make surmises from the nature of the reply—but the matter is not wholly clear; we could understand the reply better if we knew what the questions were.

Q. What is "the impending distress" of 7:26?

A. This is not certain; among the possibilities are the expected end of the age; the famine that beset parts of the Mediterranean world at that time (Acts 11:28); persecution at the hands of the Roman government. Again, our understanding of Chapter 7 would be clarified if we knew its background.

Q. What were some of the problems faced by Christian citizens in Corinth?

A. The question as to whether matters in dispute should be taken into the civil courts ("To have lawsuits at all with one another is defeat for you"—6:7); the question as to whether meat, part of which had been consecrated to idols, should be purchased and eaten ("if food is a cause of my brother's falling, I will never eat meat, lest I cause my brother to fall"—8:13).

Q. Why was this meat a problem?

A. Worshipers at pagan shrines in Corinth would offer animals in sacrifice; the pagan priests would take their portion, and the rest could be sold in the market. To eat meat from an animal, some of which had been "offered to an idol," was for many a problem of conscience. Paul is sure it would do no harm to eat this meat—but Paul is never one to stand on his rights in matters of this kind.

Q. In what other way did Paul forego his rights?

A. As a preacher of the gospel, he was entitled to get his "living by the gospel," but he refused to accept support from needy congregations, "that in my preaching I may make the gospel free of charge" (9:14,18).

Q. What phases of life in Corinth are reflected in the letter?

A. 9:24-27 is an allusion to the Corinthian games, held in honor of Poseidon; the licentiousness of the Corinthians is suggested by the fact that some wanted to "drink the cup of the Lord and the cup of demons" (10:21); even at the Lord's Supper "each one goes ahead with his own meal, and one is hungry and another is drunk" (11:21); the injunction, "the women should keep silence in the churches" (14:34), has reference to the fact that ritual prostitution flourished at the temple of Aphrodite in Corinth: it seemed the part of wisdom for Christian women not to be too conspicuous, lest their position be misunderstood.

Q. What figures of speech does Paul use in this letter regarding the church?

A. "We are fellow workmen for God; you are God's field, God's building" (3:9); "Now you are the body of Christ and individually members of it" (12:27).

Q. What is Paul's opinion of speaking in tongues?

A. "In church I would rather speak five words with my mind, in order to instruct others, than ten thousand words in a tongue" (14:19).

Q. What family words does Paul use in describing his relationship with the Corinthians?

A. Paul refers to the Corinthians as "babes in Christ. I fed you with milk, not solid food" (3:1f); "do not be children in your thinking" (14:20); "I became your father in Christ Jesus through the gospel. I urge you, then, be imitators of me" (4:15f).

Q. What does this letter disclose about worship in the early church?

A. When the congregation assembles, "each one has a hymn, a lesson, a revelation, a tongue, or an interpretation" (14:26). "On the first day of every week, each of you is to put something aside . . . as he may prosper" (16:2).

Q. What are some notable passages in this letter?

A. Two of the most famous sections in all the writings of Paul are found here: the description of what love is and does (Chapter 13), and the section dealing with the resurrection, enumerating appearances of the risen Christ and marshaling arguments from history, nature, philosophy, and personal experience to establish the significance of the resurrection (Chapter 15, the only such argument in the New Testament). Other significant passages are the section dealing with various gifts of the Spirit by which the church is enriched (Chapter 12); an account of the power of speaking with tongues, and how these are to be interpreted (14:2-33); the picture of the church as a growing thing: "I planted, Apollos watered, but God gave the growth" (3:6); "Let all that you do be done in love" (16:14).

THE SECOND LETTER OF PAUL TO THE
CORINTHIANS

Q. Who is the author of II Corinthians?

A. The writer speaks of himself as "Paul an apostle" and associates with him "Timothy our brother" (1:1).

Q. Who was Timothy?

A. Paul's associate, traveling companion, and perhaps amanuensis; Acts 16:1 describes Timothy's mother as a convert from Judaism to Christianity, and his father as a Greek; in II Timothy 1:5 mention is made of Timothy's "sincere faith, a faith that dwelt first in your grandmother Lois and your mother Eunice"; Timothy often served as Paul's messenger to the churches.

Q. To whom is this letter addressed?

A. "To the church of God which is at Corinth, with all the saints who are in the whole of Achaia" (1:1).

Q. Where was Achaia?

A. The southernmost of the two Roman provinces now constituting Greece, the other being Macedonia.

Q. When was this letter written?

A. Probably in 55 or 56 A.D.

Q. Where was this letter written?

A. Probably from Ephesus.

Q. Is this letter regarded as a unity?

A. There was evidently an extended interchange of letters between Paul and the Corinthian church. Even I Corinthians contains (5:9) a reference to a letter sent earlier. II Corinthians 2:3f refers to a previous letter, written "out of much affliction and anguish of heart and with many tears"; this same letter is evidently alluded to in II Corinthians 3:1 and 7:8. Many suppose either that part of I Corinthians or II Corinthians 10:1-13:10 is the "severe letter" thus referred to. The dislocations in arrangement would result from a copyist's need to fill out the available papyrus roll. 10:7-12 throws an interesting light on Paul as letter writer.

Q. What was Paul's purpose in writing this letter?

A. 13:11 summarizes this: "Mend your ways, heed my appeal, agree with one another, live in peace, and the God of love and peace will be with you."

Q. What autobiographical notes are included here?

A. A necessary shift in travel arrangements leads Paul to ask: "Do I make my plans like a worldly man?" (1:17); faithfulness to the gospel sometimes requires him to say stern things, but "if I cause you pain, who is there to make me glad but the one whom I have pained?" (2:2); he denies that he is like the itinerant dispensers of philosophy of the time: "we are not, like so many, peddlers of God's word" (2:17); "our sufficiency is from God, who has qualified us to be ministers of a new covenant" (3:5f); "what we preach is not ourselves, but Jesus Christ as Lord, with ourselves as your servants for Jesus' sake" (4:5); "I, Paul, myself entreat you, by the meekness and gentleness of Christ—I who am humble when face to face with you, but bold to you when I am away!" (10:1); 10:16 reveals Paul's pioneering spirit; 12:1-10 describes a mystic vision and its results.

Q. What evidences are there of Paul's trade as tentmaker?

A. Chapter 5:1 speaks of "the earthly tent we live in" as contrasted with the "house not made with hands."

Q. What was Paul's "thorn in the flesh"? (12:7).

A. Some unspecified physical affliction is described thus; the Greek word suggests a stake or tent peg driven into his body; a lesser man would have given us all the gory details.

Q. What is Paul's attitude toward the Old Testament?

A. Paul felt that these earlier Scriptures speak of Christ in references not understood by Jews, "but when a man turns to the Lord the veil is removed" (3:16).

Q. What philosophy of suffering is set forth in this letter?

A. "As we share abundantly in Christ's sufferings, so through Christ we share abundantly in comfort, too" (1:5); "as you share in our sufferings, you will also share in our comfort" (1:7).

Q. What account does Paul give of his own sufferings?

A. Referring to the "afflictions we experienced in Asia," he says: ". . . we were so utterly, unbearably crushed that we despaired of life itself" (1:8); the catalogue of these and other of his afflictions is given in 11:24-33, one of the most moving passages in literature (compare 6:4-10; 7:5).

Q. What advice does Paul give regarding marriage?

A. "Do not be mismated with unbelievers" (6:14).

Q. What does the letter disclose regarding economic conditions in the early church?

A. "In a severe test of affliction, their abundance of joy and their extreme poverty have overflowed in a wealth of liberality" (8:2).

Q. What theological point does this suggest to Paul?

A. "For you know the grace of the Lord Jesus Christ, that though he was rich, yet for your sake he became poor, so that by his poverty you might become rich" (8:9).

Q. What are some memorable passages in this letter?

A. "For it is God who said, 'Let light shine out of darkness,' who has shone in our hearts to give the light of the knowledge of the glory of God in the face of Christ" (4:6). "But we have this treasure in earthen vessels, to show that the transcendent power belongs to God and not to us" (4:7). "We are afflicted in every way, but not crushed; perplexed, but not driven to despair; persecuted, but not forsaken; struck down, but not destroyed" (4:8f); "the things that are seen are transient, but the things that are unseen are eternal" (4:18); "we walk by faith, not by sight" (5:7); "the love of Christ controls us" (5:14); "if any one is in Christ, he is a new creation" (5:17); "God was in Christ, reconciling the world to himself . . . and entrusting to us the message of reconciliation" (5:19); "he who sows sparingly will also reap sparingly, and he who sows bountifully will also reap bountifully" (9:6); "God loves a cheerful giver" (9:7); "even Satan disguises himself as an angel of light" (11:14); "we cannot do anything against the truth, but only for the truth" (13:8).

THE LETTER OF PAUL TO THE
GALATIANS

Q. Who is the author of the letter to the Galatians?

A. The writer identifies himself in 1:1 as "Paul an apostle," and associates with himself an unnamed company summed up as "all the brethren who are with me."

Q. When was the letter written?

A. Probably between 49 and 51 A.D.

Q. Where was the letter written?

A. Probably from Syrian Antioch; Corinth and Ephesus are other possibilities.

Q. To whom was the letter written?

A. "To the churches of Galatia" (1:2).

Q. How does this destination differ from that of Paul's other letters?

A. Other letters are addressed to particular congregations; this alone is a circular letter (forerunner of the modern encyclical letter).

Q. Where were the churches of Galatia?

A. Galatia was the name of a Roman province in Asia Minor; it is not clear whether the letter is directed to the churches in the northern or southern part of that region.

Q. Who had founded the churches of Galatia?

A. Paul, who visited the region first in the company of Barnabas (Acts 13:14-14:23) and on two other occasions (Acts 16:1-6; 18:23).

Q. Why was Galatians written?

A. To protest against the Judaizing process that was under way in the Galatian churches; false teachers were insisting that, in order to become Christians, believers must first submit to circumcision and other ceremonial requirements of Judaism: "there are some who trouble you and want to pervert the gospel of Christ" (1:7b).

Q. Were the false teachers gaining a following?

A. Paul expresses surprise at how easily they had led his friends astray: "I am astonished that you are so quickly deserting him who called you" (1:6); "O foolish Galatians! who has bewitched you?" (3:1).

Q. Who were the false teachers?

A. Unnamed individuals who could claim the support of other leaders in the apostolic church.

Q. Who were these other leaders?

A. Paul points out how at Antioch he had been compelled to oppose Peter "to his face, because he stood condemned" (2:11), and "even Barnabas was carried away by their insincerity" (2:13).

Q. What was the crucial issue between Paul and the Judaizers?

A. The question of table fellowship: Peter had formerly been willing to eat with the Gentiles, but when "certain men came from James . . . he drew back and separated himself" (2:12).

Q. What was Peter's motive in refusing to eat with Gentiles?

A. Paul says that Peter was "fearing the circumcision party" (2:12) and so was "not straightforward about the truth of the gospel" (2:14).

Q. Why does Paul regard this as so great an evil?

A. Because it means the attempt to win God's favor by carrying out the ceremonial law; the gospel is that "a man is not justified by works of the law but through faith in Jesus Christ" (2:16).

Q. Was Paul's low view of the law a result of ignorance?

A. No; he makes it clear that he had been familiar with it from childhood, and, he says (1:14), "I advanced in Judaism beyond many of my own age among my people, so extremely zealous was I for the traditions of my fathers."

Q. What accounts for Paul's vigorous resistance to the imposition of the ceremonial law?

A. The vision on the Damascus Road (Acts 9:1-9) meant that life for him had a new starting point, a new center, and a new goal.

Q. In his interpretation of the revelation granted to him on the Damascus Road, did Paul consult those who had been in Christ before him?

A. He makes it clear that in the formulation of his gospel he "did not confer with flesh and blood" (1:16); "I did not receive it from man, nor was I taught it" (1:12).

Q. Does Paul recognize the authority of anyone else in the church?

A. He states that, after his vision and a period of lonely contemplation in the desert of Arabia, he "went up to Jerusalem to visit Cephas" (1:18—the Greek verb suggests the words "look him over"); he saw also "James the Lord's brother" (1:19); he insists, however, that he learned nothing "from those who were reputed to be something" (2:6).

Q. Why does Paul in this letter omit the phrases of gratitude and felicitation with which he usually begins his correspondence?

A. Because of the seriousness of the situation to which he addresses himself; it was not simply that his own authority had been questioned, but that the gospel itself was being subverted.

Q. Was Paul uniformly scornful of the Law?

A. So far as in good conscience he could do so, he deferred to it, perhaps for the sake of weaker brethren. Possibly he even allowed Titus, a Greek, to be circumcised (2:3)—though he would not have allowed it if it had been made a necessary condition of accepting Titus into the believing community.

Q. Does Paul hope, by deferring on such occasions as this, to "win friends and influence people"?

A. On the contrary, he asks, "Am I trying to please men? If I were still pleasing men, I should not be a servant of Christ" (1:10).

Q. What position does Paul now assign to the Law?

A. The Law "was our custodian until Christ came" (3:24); those who still "rely on works of the law are under a curse" (3:10).

Q. How is the Law summarized?

A. "For the whole Law is fulfilled in one word, 'You shall love your neighbor as yourself.' " (5:14).

Q. What does Paul mean when he says, "I went up by revelation" (2:2)?

A. Acts 15:2 states that this visit was by appointment of the church. Paul sees in the judgment of his brethren a revelation and affirmation of the purposes of God as he understands them.

Q. What division of labor was recognized in the early church?

A. Paul was "entrusted with the gospel to the uncircumcised, just as Peter had been entrusted with the gospel to the circumcised" (2:7).

Q. What is the significance of the use of the two words, "Abba! Father!" (4:6)?

A. *Abba* is the Aramaic word for "Father." "Father" translates the Greek word. The early church was made up of people from Greek background as well as from Jewish; the name that each used in address to the Deity was caught up in the prayers of the community, where all racial distinctions were obliterated.

Q. What is the believer's responsibility to his teacher?

A. "Let him who is taught the word share all good things with him who teaches" (6:6).

Q. What does Paul say in this letter about faith?

A. He sets in a new context the words of the prophet Habakkuk: "He who through faith is righteous shall live" (3:11 quotes Habakkuk 2:4).

Q. Who was the originator of faith?

A. Although Abraham is the father of the faithful ("It is men of faith who are the sons of Abraham"—3:7), Paul is sure that in Christ everything had a new beginning and he can speak of the era prior to Christ as the time "before faith came" (3:23).

Q. What part does Abraham play in Paul's thought?

A. Recalling Abraham's two wives, Paul employs rabbinical methods of interpretation to exhibit the human situation. Hagar represents "Mount Sinai, bearing children for slavery" (4:24); her children are in bondage to the Law. Sarah's offspring is the child of promise. Those whom Christ has set free "are not children of the slave but of the free woman" (4:31).

Q. What other figure of speech does Paul use in referring to Abraham?

A. That of a will or testament or covenant which, once ratified, continues to have binding force (3:15-18).

Q. What place does Paul assign to circumcision?

A. He regards it as useless, actually no better than the mutilation practices of pagan cults (5:12; cf. 5:6; 6:15).

Q. How does Paul represent the difference between life lived under Law and life lived under Grace?

A. Life lived under Law produces a harvest of riotous confusion (5:19-21); life lived under Grace produces a bountiful crop of good fruit (5:22f).

Q. How are we to understand the seeming contradiction between 6:2 ("Bear one another's burdens") and 6:5 ("Each man will have to bear his own load")?

A. The latter refers to the soldier's pack, something that no one else may carry—each individual must bear his full share of the common load. The former refers to the burdens of grief, anguish, perplexity, etc., of which—through understanding sympathy—we may in some measure relieve those who are struggling under them.

Q. In sealing the letter, Paul says: "I bear on my body the marks of Jesus" (6:17); what were these?

A. The Greek word *stigmata* refers to the identification marks placed by a master on the body of his slave. Paul is proud to bear the marks of Christ's slave; these are probably the scars resulting from the tortures he has endured for the sake of the gospel; he enumerates these in II Corinthians 11:24f.

Q. What does Paul tell us in this letter about his own physical condition?

A. He says: "It was because of a bodily ailment that I preached the gospel to you at first" (4:13); some infer from this that the thorn in the flesh referred to in II Corinthians 12:7 was malarial fever, requiring him to go into the highlands for cure. In Galatians he says also (4:15): ". . . if possible, you would have plucked out your eyes and given them to me"; this suggests that Paul's affliction was eye trouble. Those who hold the latter interpretation refer also to 6:11: "See with what large letters I am writing to you with my own hand," the implication being that only by doing so could one with eye trouble see what he was doing.

Q. What else does Paul tell us about himself in this letter?

A. The ideas here come tumbling so fast that grammar is ignored; the letter has been called "a veritable torrent . . . like a mountain stream in full flow, such as may often have been seen by his Galatians"; the continuous outpouring of his emotions reaches a climax in the ejaculation of 1:20: "before God, I do not lie" (compare Matthew 5:33-37); he recalls his former life as a persecutor of Christians (1:13,23); he is sure that, like Jeremiah, he has come to his present position by God's appointment (1:15; cf. Jeremiah 1:5); though he is adamant on the validity and originality of his gospel, he nevertheless lays his position before the Jerusalem authorities, "lest somehow I should be running or had run in vain" (2:2); the sympathy he continues to feel for the troubled brethren is revealed in 4:16: "Have I then become your enemy by telling you the truth?" and 4:19f: "My little children, with whom I am again in travail until Christ be formed in you! I could wish to be present with you now and to change my tone, for I am perplexed about you" (compare 4:12).

Q. What are some memorable passages in Galatians?

A. "I have been crucified with Christ; it is no longer I who live, but Christ who lives in me" (2:20). "There is neither Jew nor Greek, there is neither slave nor free, there is neither male nor female; for you are all one in Christ Jesus" (3:28). "For freedom Christ has set us free; stand fast, therefore, and do not submit again to a yoke of slavery" (5:1). "Do not be deceived; God is not mocked, for whatever a man sows, that he will also reap" (6:7). "And let us not grow weary in well-doing, for in due season we shall reap, if we do not lose heart" (6:9). "So then, as we have opportunity, let us do good to all men, and especially to those who are of the household of faith" (6:10). "But far be it from me to glory except in the cross of our Lord Jesus Christ, by which the world has been crucified to me, and I to the world" (6:14).

THE LETTER OF PAUL TO THE

EPHESIANS

Q. Who wrote the letter to the Ephesians?

A. The author refers to himself as "Paul, an apostle" (1:1); many contemporary students believe that it was written in Paul's name by a disciple of Paul, and that it actually represents a covering letter for the first collection of Paul's correspondence ever made; there is nothing in the letter that Paul could not have written.

Q. What internal evidence is there for thinking that this was written by a Paulinist rather than by Paul himself?

A. It was Paul's custom to address himself to particular situations in the young congregations, especially situations where trouble has arisen; this letter deals only with matters of a sublime and general character. Further, Paul habitually names in his letters many individuals to whom he sends greetings; no individual is mentioned in this letter except Tychicus, a "faithful minister" (6:21); since Paul had spent between two and three years in Ephesus (Acts 19 and 20), it is difficult to believe he could have addressed a letter to the Christians there without mentioning any by name.

Q. To whom is the letter addressed?

A. "To the saints who are also faithful in Christ Jesus" (1:1).

Q. Where did those "saints" live?

A. If this is a covering letter for the first edition of Paul's correspondence, they would be residents of every community to which the collection might come. Some early manuscripts, by the quotation "To the saints who are at Ephesus and faithful," indicate that one particular city was the destination. Some suppose that as a circular letter the address would be left blank and each congregation could insert its own name. Colossians 4:16 records the injunction: ". . . when this letter has been read among you, have it read also in the church of the Laodiceans; and see that you read also the letter from Laodiceans." Marcion, about 140 A.D., regarded "Ephesians" as "the letter from Laodiceans."

Q. When was this letter written?

A. Probably in 61 or 62 A.D.; if by a Paulinist, perhaps in 65 A.D.

Q. Where was this letter written?

A. It has been traditionally listed among the prison epistles, which are thought to have been sent from Rome (cf. Acts 28:16,30f). However, arguments have been put forward to suggest that Paul's imprisonment letters were composed while he was under detention in Ephesus (I Corinthians 15:32) or Caesarea (Acts 25:4).

Q. What evidence is there that the letter was sent from prison?

A. In 3:1 he refers to himself as "a prisoner for Christ Jesus" and in 4:1 as "a prisoner for the Lord"; he also wants his friends "not to lose heart over what I am suffering for you" (3:13).

Q. What is the purpose of this letter?

A. To exhibit the glorious things God has accomplished for the church through Christ; to praise him for "the immeasurable greatness of his power in us who believe" (1:19); to summon believers to gratitude appropriate for recipients of such bounty (3:20f); to call believers to a life of praise, "that through the church the manifold wisdom of God might now be made known to the principalities and powers in the heavenly places" (3:10).

Q. What is to be the attitude of believers in a church for which God has done such great things?

A. They must "lead a life worthy of the calling to which you have been called, with all lowliness and meekness, with patience, forbearing one another in love, eager to maintain the unity of the Spirit in the bond of peace" (4:1-3).

Q. What position is assigned to God's love in this letter?

A. God "destined us in love to be his sons" (1:5; cf. 3:11); believers are to be "rooted and grounded in love" (3:17); the love of Christ "surpasses knowledge" (3:19); believers are to speak "the truth in love" (4:15); the church "upbuilds itself in love" (4:16).

Q. What position is assigned to grace in this letter?

A. Grace, "freely bestowed on us in the Beloved" (1:6), has been "lavished upon us" (1:8); "by grace have you been saved" (2:8); by grace was Paul "made a minister" (3:7); by grace is he permitted "to preach to the Gentiles the unsearchable riches of Christ" (3:8); "grace was given to each of us according to the measure of Christ's gift" (4:7).

Q. What position is assigned to the Holy Spirit in this letter?

A. The Spirit is "the guarantee of our inheritance until we acquire possession of it" (1:14); the word translated "guarantee" is a term used in real estate transactions to denote down payment.

Q. What position is assigned to faith?

A. Faith is itself a manifestation of God's grace; it, too, "is the gift of God" (2:8).

Q. If God's grace is everything, what place is there for good works?

A. God has created us in Christ Jesus for good works, "which God prepared beforehand, that we should walk in them" (2:10).

Q. What position is assigned to Christ?

A. God has "raised him from the dead and made him sit at his right hand in the heavenly places, far above all rule and authority and power and dominion" (1:20f); it is through Christ's resurrection that believers, once dead in sin, have been made alive (2:1,5); Christ has put an end to all racial distinctions (2:14); Christ is the cornerstone of the new and living temple (2:21); "the measure of the stature of the fulness of Christ" is the pattern of mature manhood (4:13); we are to "walk in love, as Christ loved us and gave himself up for us" (5:2); husbands are to love their wives "as Christ loved the church" (5:25).

Q. How does this letter deal with ideas treated in Paul's other letters?

A. Galatians 1:15 refers to God who "set me apart before I was born"; Ephesians 1:4 speaks of him who chose us "before the foundation of the world." Colossians 1:17 refers to Christ as the one in whom "all things hold together," Ephesians 1:10 to God's plan "to unite all things in him, things in heaven and things on earth." In 1 Corinthians 3:2 Paul speaks of having "fed you with milk"; he here speaks of their attaining "mature manhood" (4:13). II Corinthians 5:17 says: ". . . if any one is in Christ, he is a new creation"; Ephesians 4:24 says: ". . . put on the new nature." Philippians 2:15 says that, "in the midst of a crooked and perverse generation," believers "shine as lights in the world"; Ephesians 5:8 says: ". . . now you are light in the Lord."

Q. What position is assigned to the Gentiles?

A. Once "alienated from the commonwealth of Israel" (2:12), they are "no longer strangers and sojourners" but "fellow citizens with the saints and members of the household of God" (2:12,19).

Q. What gifts or offices are there in the church?

A. Apostles, prophets, evangelists, pastors and teachers (4:11).

Q. What function is assigned to the church leaders?

A. They are to equip "the saints, for the work of ministry" (4:12).

Q. What injunctions are there for the life of the believer?

A. "Be angry, but do not sin" (4:26); "be kind to one another, tenderhearted, forgiving one another, as God in Christ forgave you" (4:32); "look carefully then how you walk" (5:15); "do not get drunk with wine" (5:18).

Q. What suggestions are given here for worship?

A. "Addressing one another in psalms and hymns and spiritual songs, singing and making melody to the Lord with all your heart, always and for everything giving thanks in the name of our Lord Jesus Christ to God the Father" (5:19f).

Q. What is the believer's true strength?

A. "Be subject to one another out of reverence for Christ" (5:21).

Q. Who are bidden to be in subjection?

A. Believers to each other, wives to husbands (5:22), slaves to masters (6:5).

Q. In what way does this letter go beyond the Ten Commandments?

A. Exodus 20:15 says, "You shall not steal"; Ephesians 4:28 says: "Let the thief no longer steal, but rather let him labor, doing honest work . . . so that he may be able to give to those in need." Exodus 20:12 says, "Honor your father and your mother"; Ephesians 6:4 adds: "Fathers, do not provoke your children to anger, but bring them up in the discipline and instruction of the Lord."

Q. What military metaphor is employed?

A. In 6:10-17 Paul pictures in detail the panoply of the Christian warrior; the several items of accoutrement—both defensive and offensive —were perhaps suggested by the gear of the Roman soldier set to guard him (Acts 28:16).

THE LETTER OF PAUL TO THE
PHILIPPIANS

Q. Who is the author of this letter?

A. The senders are identified as "Paul and Timothy, servants of Christ" (1:1).

Q. What was Timothy's part in the writing?

A. He was evidently Paul's companion and supporter; Paul says in 2:22: "Timothy's worth you know, how as a son with a father he has served with me in the gospel."

Q. To whom is this letter addressed?

A. "To all the saints in Christ Jesus who are at Philippi" (1:1).

Q. Where was Philippi?

A. It was a community along the Aegean Sea, founded by Philip of Macedon; it is identified in Acts 16:12 as "the leading city of the district of Macedonia, and a Roman colony."

Q. Where was Macedonia?

A. The northern section of the Greek peninsula, lying between the Adriatic and the Aegean.

Q. What were Paul's earlier associations with Philippi?

A. Philippi has the distinction of being the first city in the Western world in which the gospel was preached. Impelled by a vision of the night (Acts 16:9), Paul crossed from Troas to Philippi and proclaimed Christ for the first time in Europe. Paul's feelings for the believing community there are expressed in 1:8: "God is my witness, how I yearn for you all with the affection of Christ Jesus."

Q. Why does Paul yearn "with the affection of Christ" rather than with the "affection of Paul"?

A. Because for Paul, "to me to live is Christ" (1:21).

Q. Who was the first convert in Europe?

A. "Lydia, from the city of Thyatira, a seller of purple goods" (Acts 16:14); Paul found her and others worshiping outside the gate by the river (Acts 16:13) and "the Lord opened her heart to give heed to what was said by Paul" (Acts 16:14).

Q. Is the fact that Christianity in Europe began with a woman revealed in the letter to Philippians?

A. Women in Philippi appear to have had a position of freedom and dignity different from that of women in Corinth. In the letter to Philippians, two women, Eudoia and Syntyche, are mentioned by name (4:2), and Paul adds: ". . . help these women, for they have labored side by side with me in the gospel" (4:3).

Q. What other evidences are there of women's influence in Philippi?

A. The letter reveals that a messenger had made his way from Philippi to Paul's place of imprisonment, bringing gifts and messages. This ministry to a faraway prisoner can be thought of as history's first "Red Cross" activity; it is not unlikely that the errand of mercy was inspired by the imaginative sympathy characteristic of women. In 4:18 Paul describes "the gifts you sent, a fragrant offering, a sacrifice acceptable and pleasing to God."

Q. When was the letter to Philippians written?

A. Probably in 61 or 62 A.D.

Q. Where was the letter to Philippians written?

A. It is one of Paul's prison letters.

Q. What references are there in the letter to Paul's imprisonment?

A. Chapter 1:13 discloses that "it has become known throughout the whole pretorian guard . . . that my imprisonment is for Christ." Chapter 4:22 says: "All the saints greet you, especially those of Caesar's household." It is apparent that members of a crack regiment, the pretorian guard, took turns supervising Paul's imprisonment; having completed their tour of duty, they returned to the emperor's palace, and thus the gospel reached the highest station in the Empire.

Q. Why was the letter to Philippians written?

A. To express Paul's gratitude for their remembrance of him in prison. The letter contains no rebuke, deals with no controversy, and has therefore been described as "Paul's love letter." The tone is set in 1:5: ". . . thankful for your partnership in the gospel from the first day until now."

Q. Who was the messenger of mercy delegated by the Philippian church to visit Paul?

A. Epaphroditus (4:17), whose name, based on the name of Aphrodite, Greek goddess of love and beauty, suggests that a man of pagan background had been won to the gospel.

Q. What was Paul's relationship to Epaphroditus?

A. He describes him (2:25) as "my brother and fellow worker and fellow soldier"; the devotion that Epaphroditus had for Paul is indicated in 2:30: "for he nearly died for the work of Christ, risking his life to complete your service to me."

Q. What was the relationship of Epaphroditus to the Philippian church?

A. Paul describes him as "your messenger and minister to my need" (2:25); the affection Epaphroditus had for the sending church is suggested in 2:26: "for he has been longing for you all, and has been distressed because you heard that he was ill."

Q. What are some of the distinctive theological ideas in the letter to Philippians?

A. Chapter 1:6 contains what is probably the best argument for immortality: "he who began a good work in you will bring it to completion"; 2:5-11 contains Paul's doctrine of the Incarnation, interpreting it in terms of Christ's self-emptying; 1:12 contains a remarkable statement of how God's Providence can take evil circumstances and turn them to good account: "what has happened to me has really served to advance the gospel"; the letter is replete, too, with the deep and abiding joy that the believer has even in the midst of adversity (1:4; 1:19; 2:2,29; 3:1; 4:1,4,10).

Q. Why is 2:5-11 known as the *kenosis* passage?

A. From the Greek word meaning "empty," used in verse 7.

Q. What are some of the best-known passages in Philippians?

A. "For me to live is Christ, and to die is gain" (1:21). "Finally, brethren, whatever is true, whatever is honorable, whatever is just, whatever is pure, whatever is lovely, whatever is gracious, if there is any excellence, if there is anything worthy of praise, think about these things" (4:8); "The grace of the Lord Jesus Christ be with your spirit (4:23).

Q. Philippians 3:1 begins, "Finally, my brethren." Philippians 4:8 says, "Finally, brethren." Why does Paul have such a hard time bringing the letter to a conclusion?

A. Perhaps his overflowing affection made it hard for him to break off; more prosaically, some have held this to be evidence that two or more brief notes, written at different times, are here combined.

THE LETTER OF PAUL TO THE
COLOSSIANS

Q. Who is the author of the letter to the Colossians?

A. The writer identifies himself in 1:1 as "Paul, an apostle . . . and Timothy our brother."

Q. To whom is the letter addressed?

A. "To the saints and faithful brethren in Christ at Colossae" (1:2).

Q. Where was Colossae?

A. In the province of Asia Minor, northeast of the island of Rhodes; it was an inland city, in New Testament times, a city that had known better days economically.

Q. When was the letter to Colossians written?

A. Probably in 62 or 63 A.D.

Q. Where was Colossians written?

A. From Paul's imprisonment; 4:3 declares that he is in prison for Christ's sake, and the concluding words of the letter are a plea to "remember my fetters."

Q. What is the purpose of the letter to the Colossians?

A. To combat false doctrines that had already overtaken the church.

Q. What were these false doctrines?

A. That Christ had not yet come (Paul counters this by describing how God has already "delivered us from the dominion of darkness and transferred us to the kingdom of his beloved Son"—1:13); that Creation had come by a series of emanations from some primal spirit (Paul counters this by insisting that Christ is "the image of the invisible God, the first-born of all creation; for in him all things were created"—1:15f); that man's life might be under the influence of the stars, "insisting on self-abasement and worship of angels" (2:18—Paul counters this by affirming that in Christ "all the fulness of God was pleased to dwell—1:19); that ascetic regulations—"Do not handle, Do not taste, Do not touch" (2:21)—might be a way of winning God's favor (Paul counters this by pointing out that such rules "are of no value in checking the indulgence of the flesh"—2:23).

Q. What are significant theological ideas in Colossians?

A. That Christ "is before all things, and in him all things hold together" (1:17); that in Christ "are hid all the treasures of wisdom and knowledge" (2:3); that "Christ in you" is "the hope of glory" (1:27); that in Christ "there cannot be Greek and Jew, circumcised and uncircumcised, barbarian, Scythian, slave, free man, but Christ is all, and in all" (3:11).

Q. What are some of the figures of speech Paul uses in this letter?

A. "Buried with him [i.e., Christ] in baptism" (2:12); "canceled the bond which stood against us" (2:14); "disarmed the principalities and powers" (2:15).

Q. What are some memorable phrases in this letter?

A. "Set your mind on things that are above, not on things that are on earth" (3:2); "you have died, and your life is hid with Christ in God" (3:3); "as the Lord has forgiven you, so you also must forgive" (3:13); "above all these put on love, which binds everything together in perfect harmony" (3:14); "whatever you do, in word or deed, do everything in the name of the Lord Jesus" (3:17).

Q. What groups are given special advice?

A. Parents, children, masters, slaves.

Q. What injunction sums up advice to these groups?

A. "Whatever your task, work heartily, as serving the Lord and not men" (3:23).

Q. Who was Epaphras (1:7)?

A. Paul describes him as "our beloved fellow servant . . . a faithful minister of Christ on our behalf" (1:8). He appears to have been an associate of Paul who founded the church in Colossae. In 4:12 Paul says, "Epaphras . . . greets you, always remembering you earnestly in his prayers."

Q. What is revealed in this letter about the organization of the early church?

A. Reference to "Nympha and the church in her house" (4:15) discloses that the early church, before it was able to afford buildings of its own, met in the homes of believers. The house congregations were an effective means of propagating the gospel.

Q. What does this letter tell about worship in the early church?

A. Chapter 3:16 no doubt reflects the teaching and praise in which

Christians engaged each time they came together: "Let the word of Christ dwell in you richly, as you teach and admonish one another in all wisdom, and as you sing psalms and hymns and spiritual songs with thankfulness in your hearts to God."

Q. What does this letter tell about the mechanics of Paul's correspondence?

A. The conclusion begins: "I, Paul, write this greeting with my own hand" (4:18), implying that the body of the letter had been set down by an amanuensis. Like a modern executive, Paul takes pen in hand to sign a document prepared by someone else.

Q. What does this letter disclose about the formation of the New Testament?

A. Chapter 4:16 says: ". . . when this letter has been read among you, have it read also in the church of the Laodiceans; and see that you read also the letter from Laodicea." So far as we know, this represents the earliest beginning of the New Testament as such. Paul's letters were passed from congregation to congregation, perhaps each keeping a copy. Paul's collected letters were the nucleus of the New Testament. By the time II Peter 3:15f was written, they had attained a status in the churches that ranked them with "the other scriptures"—by which was meant what we call the Old Testament.

Q. What is "the letter from Laodicea"?

A. Marcion, about the middle of the second century, thought it was our letter to Ephesians; we have no other information.

Q. Who is Onesimus (4:9)?

A. He may be the runaway slave whom Paul returned to his master (see the letter to Philemon); there is a theory that Onesimus was the first to assemble a collection of Paul's letters. This he did out of gratitude for what Paul had done for him in changing his relationship with Philemon from that of slave and master to that of brother and brother.

Q. What does Colossians disclose about the relationship between Paul and Mark?

A. It is evident that Paul and Mark, who had earlier had a falling out (Acts 15:37-39), have been wholly reconciled. Paul commends Mark to the church at Colossae and lists him among those "who have been a comfort to me" (4:10f).

THE FIRST LETTER OF PAUL TO THE
THESSALONIANS

Q. Who is the author of this letter?

A. The salutation is from "Paul, Silvanus, and Timothy" (1:1); Timothy had been dispatched by Paul from Athens to strengthen the faith of the Thessalonians (3:2).

Q. Who was Silvanus?

A. Some consider him to be identical with Silas (listed in Acts 16:19-40 as a sharer in one of Paul's more exciting adventures); Acts 18:5 reports that Silas and Timothy joined Paul in Corinth. I Peter 5:12 discloses that Silvanus had a significant part in the composition of that document; perhaps Silvanus played an important role in the reconciliation between Paul and Peter (cf. Galatians 2:11).

Q. To whom is the letter addressed?

A. "To the church of the Thessalonians" (1:1).

Q. Where was Thessalonica?

A. In Macedonia, at the head of the western arm of the Aegean Sea.

Q. What is the modern name of Thessalonica?

A. Salonika.

Q. Who had founded the church in Thessalonica?

A. Paul, on a journey described in Acts 17:1-9.

Q. When was the letter written?

A. About 50 A.D.

Q. Where was the letter written?

A. Probably in Corinth.

Q. What was the occasion of the writing of the letter?

A. The perplexity of the Thessalonian Christians regarding what would happen to those of their number who had died between Christ's resurrection and expected return (4:13).

Q. What is Paul's solution of this problem?

A. The assurance that God is always to be trusted and "will bring with him those who have fallen asleep" (4:14).

Q. What does Paul suggest as the best way to make ready for the Lord's expected return?

A. "So then let us not sleep as others do, but let us keep awake and be sober" (5:6).

Q. For what purpose was the letter written?

A. To recall the believers in that community to the truths Paul had proclaimed while he had earlier been among them.

Q. What response did the gospel meet when first proclaimed in Thessalonica?

A. Its inhabitants "turned to God from idols, to serve a living and true God" (1:9).

Q. What example of the Christian life did Paul cite?

A. "You learned from us how you ought to live and to please God" (4:1); "you became imitators of us and of the Lord" (1:6).

Q. How did Paul conduct himself in Thessalonica?

A. "We worked night and day, that we might not burden any of you, while we preached to you the gospel" (2:9).

Q. What terms of affection does Paul use in recalling his ministry among the Thessalonians?

A. "We were gentle among you, like a nurse taking care of her children" (2:7); "like a father with his children, we exhorted each one of you" (2:11); "since we were bereft [Greek, "orphaned"] of you, brethren, for a short time . . . we endeavored the more eagerly . . .to see you" (2:17).

Q. What words of praise has Paul for the Thessalonians?

A. "You became an example to all the believers in Macedonia and in Achaia. For not only has the word of the Lord sounded forth from you in Macedonia and Achaia, but your faith in God has gone forth everywhere" (1:7f).

Q. At what points did the Thessalonians need to be reminded of the pristine wonder of their enlistment in Christ's cause?

A. Paul had warned that afflictions would be the lot of the believer (3:3f); apparently some had been tempted to turn back when the going became hard (3:5). Although Paul is grateful for their "work of faith and labor of love and steadfastness of hope" (1:3), there are elements in their faith that are undeveloped or lacking (3:10): their sympathies needed to be enlarged (3:12) and their lives made more blameless (3:13); the relationship between the sexes needed to be freed from immorality (4:3-8); some members of the community were not busy but busybodies (4:11f); jealousy and quarrelsomeness needed to be eliminated (5:12f).

Q. What are the obligations of believers to weaker members of the community?

A. "Admonish the idle, encourage the fainthearted, help the weak, be patient with them all" (5:14).

Q. How are we to understand the injunction, "pray constantly" (5:17)?

A. In the light of 2:9: ". . . you remember our labor and toil, brethren; we worked night and day"; he who enjoins constant prayer is he who works the hardest.

Q. What are some memorable phrases from this letter?

A. "We speak, not to please men, but to please God who tests our hearts" (2:4). "See that none of you repays evil for evil, but always seek to do good to one another and to all" (5:15); "give thanks in all circumstances" (5:18); "test everything; hold fast what is good, abstain from every form of evil" (5:20f); "May the God of peace himself sanctify you wholly; and may your spirit and soul and body be kept sound and blameless at the coming of our Lord Jesus Christ" (5:23).

Q. What does Paul disclose in this letter about the relationship of his own inner life to that of his friends?

A. "You are our glory and joy" (2:20); "we live, if you stand fast in the Lord" (3:8).

THE SECOND LETTER OF PAUL TO THE
THESSALONIANS

Q. Who is the author of this letter?

A. The salutation is from "Paul, Silvanus, and Timothy" (1:1— see I Thessalonians).

Q. To whom is it addressed?

A. "To the church of the Thessalonians" (1:1).

Q. When was it written?

A. Probably in 50 A.D.

Q. Where was it written?

A. Probably in Corinth.

Q. What is the purpose of the letter?

A. To correct misunderstandings of the gospel and to rebuke those who, under false notions of Christ's return, had given up their jobs and were parasites on the community.

Q. How does Paul preface the rebuke he must administer?

A. By finding as many things as possible in their lives concerning which to give thanks: "your faith is growing abundantly, and the love of every one of you for one another is increasing" and they had been steadfast under persecution (1:3f).

Q. What were the misunderstandings that needed to be corrected?

A. The idea that "the day of the Lord has come" (2:2), with the result that some were "living in idleness" (3:6), "mere busybodies, not doing any work" (3:11).

Q. How had these misunderstandings arisen?

A. Evidently they had been deliberately cultivated by some who forged letters in Paul's name. He warns against being misled "by letter purporting to be from us" (2:2), and is particularly careful at the conclusion to identify this as a genuine letter: "I, Paul, write this greeting with my own hand. This is the mark in every letter of mine; it is the way I write" (3:17).

Q. What is Paul's remedy for these abuses?

A. He recalls "the traditions which you were taught" by him when he had been among them and subsequently by letter (2:15; 3:6); he reminds them of his own example, "how you ought to imitate us; we were not idle when we were with you" (3:7); he summons them "in the Lord Jesus Christ to do their work in quietness and to earn their own living" (3:12).

Q. What form of discipline is enjoined for the recalcitrant?

A. Discipline by isolation: "keep away from any brother who is living in idleness" (3:6).

Q. Was this withdrawal of fellowship to be permanent?

A. No, it was rather designed to lead him to penitence: "have nothing to do with him, that he may be ashamed. Do not look on him as an enemy, but warn him as a brother" (3:14f).

Q. Who is "the man of lawlessness" (2:3)?

A. Some otherwise unidentified incarnation of evil—perhaps a magistrate or other high official, perhaps a false teacher of personal magnetism, "who . . . exalts himself" (2:4).

Q. What is the restraining force that prevents the lawless one from doing even greater iniquity?

A. Paul says (2:6), ". . . you know what is restraining him." We do not know: perhaps the reference is to the Pax Romana, perhaps to the Spirit of God, perhaps to the concerted resistance of believers.

Q. What is conceived to be the ultimate destiny of the lawless one?

A. The "Lord Jesus will slay him with the breath of his mouth" (2:8).

Q. What are some memorable passages in this letter?

A. "We always pray for you, that our God may make you worthy of his call, and may fulfil every good resolve and work of faith by his power" (1:11). "If any one will not work, let him not eat" (3:10). "Brethren, do not be weary in well-doing" (3:13).

The Pastoral Letters

Q. Why are I Timothy, II Timothy, and Titus called the Pastoral Letters?

A. Unlike other correspondence attributed to Paul, they are not addressed to congregations but to missionary assistants. They are more concerned with sound church order and effective ecclesiastical procedures than with the leadership of the Spirit or ventures into abstract thought. As dealing with the realities of parish life, they represent interests best summarized as "pastoral."

Q. Who is the author of the Pastoral Letters?

A. "Paul, an apostle of Jesus Christ by command of God our Savior and of Christ Jesus our hope" (I.1:1); "Paul, an apostle of Christ Jesus by the will of God according to the promise of the life which is in Christ Jesus" (II.1:1); "Paul, a servant of God and an apostle of Jesus Christ" (Titus 1:1)—these opening phrases, so different from those of Galatians, Romans, Philippians, etc., suggest someone—sometimes called the Pastor—writing in Paul's name. Undoubtedly the books contain reminiscences of the Apostle, but in keeping with ancient literary practices, it is likely that a younger associate of Paul has expanded these into their present form.

Q. When were the Pastoral Letters written?

A. They appear to reflect organized church life about 100 A.D.

Q. Where were the Pastoral Letters written?

A. There is no clear evidence, but tradition has it that Timothy carried out his ministry in Ephesus, where he served as bishop of the Christian community until martyred by the populace whom he tried to dissuade from taking part in the pagan orgies of Dionysus.

Q. What experiences in Paul's life are alluded to in the Pastorals?

A. "Christ Jesus . . . judged me faithful by appointing me to his service, though I formerly blasphemed and persecuted and insulted him" (I.1:12f). "I was appointed a preacher and apostle (I am telling the truth, I am not lying), a teacher of the Gentiles in faith and truth" (I.2:7); "the gospel for which I am suffering and wearing fetters, like a criminal" (II.2:9). "Now you have observed . . . my persecutions, my sufferings, what befell me at Antioch, at Iconium, and at Lystra, what persecutions I endured" (II.3:10f). "I was rescued from the lion's mouth" II.4:17).

Q. What events in the Pastorals are difficult to reconcile with the chronology of Paul's life as outlined in Acts?

A. The visits to Ephesus (I.1:3), to Malta (II.4:20), to Troas (II.4:13), to Crete (Titus 1:5) are not recorded in Acts. Indeed, Acts 27:7 says that his nearest approach to Crete was when "we sailed under the lee of Crete."

Q. What other ideas in the Pastorals are treated differently in Paul's correspondence with the churches?

A. "Let a woman learn in silence with all submissiveness" (I.2:11) sounds not unlike I Corinthians 14:34; yet the reason for this ("Adam was formed first, then Eve; and Adam was not deceived, but the woman was deceived and became a transgressor"—I.2:13f) is quite unlike I Corinthians 15:22: "For as in Adam all die . . ." The author of I Timothy 1:15 says: "I am the foremost of sinners"; this goes beyond I Corinthians 15:9: "I am the least of the apostles" and Ephesians 3:8: "I am the very least of all the saints."

Q. What type of organization is reflected in the Pastoral Letters?

A. There appear to be two orders of clergy, bishops (I.3:1) or elders (I.5:17), and deacons (I.3:8); and an order of widows (I.5:9).

Q. What are the requirements for one who would hold the office of bishop?

A. He must be married and able to "manage his own household well" (I.3:4), "temperate, sensible, dignified, hospitable, an apt teacher, no drunkard, not violent but gentle, not quarrelsome, and no lover of money" (I.3:2f); a convert tried and true and of good reputation in the community (I.3:6f).

Q. What is said regarding the duties of the elders?

A. They are to be appointed in every town (Titus 1:5); they are to be "blameless," and good family men (Titus 1:6); they are to "labor in preaching and teaching," and those "who rule well" are to "be considered worthy of double honor" (I Timothy 5:17); they are to "attend to the public reading of scripture, to preaching, to teaching" (I.4:13).

Q. What are the requirements for admission to the office of deacon?

A. "Deacons must be serious, not double-tongued, not addicted to much wine, not greedy for gain" (I.3:8); married and able to "manage their children and their households well" (I.3:12).

Q. What are the requirements for one to be a member of the order of widows?

A. She must have been married only once and have attained the age of sixty (I.5:9); "she must be well attested for her good deeds, as one who has brought up children, shown hospitality, washed the feet of the saints, relieved the afflicted, and devoted herself to doing good in every way" (I.5:10).

Q. Why were younger widows not to be enrolled?

A. Their hearts may be set on capturing another husband (I.5:11f). "Besides that, they learn to be idlers, gadding about from house to house, and not only idlers but gossips and busybodies, saying what they should not" (I.5:13).

Q. What Old Testament passage does the author invoke as suggesting the church's duty to provide for its clergy?

A. "You shall not muzzle an ox when it is treading out the grain" (I.5:18) is a quotation from Deuteronomy 25:4.

Q. What is the idea of God in the Pastoral Letters?

A. "To the King of ages, immortal, invisible, the only God, be honor and glory for ever and ever" (I.1:17). "God our Savior . . . de-

sires all men to be saved and to come to the knowledge of the truth"
(I.2:3f); "there is one God" (I.2:5); "we have our hope set on the living
God, who is the Savior of all men, especially of those who believe"
(I.4:10); "the blessed and only Sovereign, the King of kings and Lord
of lords, who alone has immortality and dwells in unapproachable light,
whom no man has ever seen or can see" (I.6:15f); "who saved us and
called us with a holy calling, not in virtue of our works but in virtue of
his own purpose and the grace which he gave us in Christ Jesus" (II.1:
9); "God who never lies" (Titus 1:2); "the grace of God has appeared
for the salvation of all men" (Titus 2:11); "when the goodness and loving kindness of God our Savior appeared, he saved us, not because of
deeds done by us in righteousness, but in virtue of his own mercy"
(Titus 3:4f).

Q. What position is assigned to Christ in these letters?

A. "Christ Jesus came into the world to save sinners" (I.1:15);
"there is one mediator between God and man, the man Christ Jesus,
who gave himself as a ransom for all" (I.2:5f); "who abolished death
and brought life and immortality to light through the gospel" (II.1:10);
"I know whom I have believed" (II.1:12). "Remember Jesus Christ,
risen from the dead, descended from David, as preached in my gospel"
(II.2:8); "Jesus Christ who is to judge the living and the dead" (II.4:1);
"our blessed hope, the appearing of the glory of our great God and
Savior Jesus Christ, who gave himself for us to redeem us from all iniquity" (Titus 2:13f).

Q. What is the author's doctrine of the church?

A. "The household of God, which is the church of the living God,
the pillar and bulwark of the truth" (I.3:15); Jesus Christ "gave himself . . . to purify for himself a people of his own who are zealous for
good deeds" (Titus 2:14).

Q. What is the author's teaching about ordination?

A. "Do not be hasty in the laying on of hands" (I.5:22). "Do not
neglect the gift you have, which was given you by prophetic utterance
when the elders laid their hands upon you" (I.4:14). "I remind you to
rekindle the gift of God that is within you through the laying on of my
hands" (II.1:6).

Q. What ideas about family religion are inculcated in the Pastoral
Letters?

A. "I am reminded of your sincere faith, a faith that dwelt first in your grandmother Lois and your mother Eunice and now, I am sure, dwells in you" (II.1:5). "If a widow has children or grandchildren, let them first learn their religious duty to their own family and make some return to their parents" (I.5:4). "If any one does not provide for his own relatives, and especially for his own family, he has disowned the faith and is worse than an unbeliever" (I.5:8).

Q. What is the author's attitude toward the young?

A. "Let no one despise your youth, but set the believers an example in speech and conduct, in love, in faith, in purity" (I.4:12). "Show yourself in all respects a model of good deeds, and in your teaching show integrity, gravity, and sound speech" (Titus 2:7f).

THE FIRST LETTER OF PAUL TO
TIMOTHY

Q. To whom was the letter sent?

A. "To Timothy, my true child in the faith" (1:2); Timothy, son of a Greek father and a Jewish mother (Acts 16:1; II Timothy 1:5), trained in the Hebrew Scriptures (II.3:15), was a Christian convert of Lystra (Acts 14; 16:1f); desiring to have Timothy accompany him, Paul "circumcised him because of the Jews who were in those places" (Acts 16:3). In Philippians 2:22 Paul speaks of Timothy: ". . . how as a son with a father he has served with me in the gospel." Some suppose that Timothy, delegated by Paul to oversee certain churches and prizing the notes he had received from his mentor, expanded these into the Pastoral Letters.

Q. What is the purpose of I Timothy?

A. To combat false notions summed up as "godless and silly myths" (4:7).

Q. What were some of these false notions?

A. Misinterpretation of the Old Testament Law: some desired to be "teachers of the law, without understanding what they are saying or the thing about which they make assertions" (1:7); others, boasting of their freedom from Law and engaged in antinomian practices, are reminded that the Law is necessary for the control of immoral conduct and is "in accordance with the glorious gospel" (1:8-11). Still others stressed "myths and endless genealogies" (1:4)—that is, imaginative theories of Gnosticism or speculation regarding descent from the patriarchs; others laid claim to special forms of knowledge that the author calls "the godless chatter and contradictions of what is falsely called knowledge" (6:20); others engaged in ascetic practices (4:3f; 5:23), perhaps denying the possibility of salvation for women (2:8-15).

Q. What ideas in I Timothy differ from those generally associated with Paul?

A. In view of Romans 7:7-25, it would be strange if Paul could write "the law is good" (1:8); in view of Galatians 2:20 it would be strange if Paul could talk of "the sound words of our Lord Jesus Christ" (6:3) or bid Titus "teach what befits sound doctrine" (Titus 2:1); in view of Galatians 1:8 it would be strange if Paul should speak of "the elect angels" (5:21); in view of Philippians 1:21-23 it would be strange if Paul should speak of remaining "unstained and free from reproach until the appearing of our Lord Jesus Christ" (6:14); in view of Philippians 3:12 it would be strange if he should advise people to "guard what has been entrusted to you" (6:20); there is here, too, a distinctive vocabulary: the terms "godliness" (in the Pastoral Letters nine times) and "gravity" (three times) do not occur elsewhere in letters attributed to Paul.

Q. How does the author sum up the religion he urges?

A. "The aim of our charge is love that issues from a pure heart and a good conscience and sincere faith" (1:5).

Q. What does the author envision as the duty the believer owes the state?

A. "I urge that supplications, prayers, intercessions, and thanksgivings be made for all men, for kings and all who are in high positions, that we may lead a quiet and peaceable life, godly and respectful in every way" (2:1f).

Q. What style in women's attire is recommended?

A. "Women should adorn themselves modestly and sensibly in seemly apparel, not with braided hair or gold or pearls or costly attire but by good deeds" (2:9f).

Q. What is the author's opinion of athletic activity?

A. "While bodily training is of some value, godliness is of value in every way" (4:8).

Q. What duty is enjoined upon slaves?

A. "Let all who are under the yoke of slavery regard their masters as worthy of all honor" (6:1).

Q. What judgment does the author pronounce upon anyone who teaches a doctrine different from his own?

A. "He is puffed up with conceit, he knows nothing; he has a morbid craving for controversy and for disputes about words" (6:4).

Q. What is the author's teaching about worldly competence?

A. "We brought nothing into this world, and we cannot take anything out of the world; but if we have food and clothing, with these we shall be content" (6:7f).

Q. What about the craving for possessions?

A. "Those who desire to be rich fall into temptation. . . . For the love of money is the root of all evils" (6:9f). "As for the rich in this world, charge them not to be haughty, nor to set their hopes on uncertain riches. . . . They are to do good, to be rich in good deeds" (6:17f).

THE SECOND LETTER OF PAUL TO

TIMOTHY

Q. To whom was this letter addressed?

A. "To Timothy, my beloved child" (1:2).

Q. Why was this letter sent?

A. To encourage the recipient ("I remember you constantly in my prayers"—1:3; "Do not be ashamed then of testifying to our Lord"—1:8; "guard the truth that has been entrusted to you"—1:14); to instruct him in effective procedures for church life ("what you have heard from me before many witnesses entrust to faithful men who will be able to teach others also"—2:2); and to warn against perversions of the gospel ("the time is coming when people will not endure sound teaching"—4:3).

Q. What is to be the attitude of believers?

A. "God did not give us a spirit of timidity but a spirit of power and love and self-control. Do not be ashamed then of testifying to our Lord . . . but take your share of suffering for the gospel" (1:7f; cf. 2:3); "avoid disputing about words. . . . Do your best to present yourself to God as one approved, a workman who has no need to be ashamed, rightly handling the word of truth" (2:15). "Let every one who names the name of the Lord depart from iniquity" (2:19). "So shun youthful passions and aim at righteousness, faith, love, and peace" (2:22).

Q. What metaphors does the author use regarding the faithfulness of believers?

A. "No soldier on service gets entangled in civilian pursuits. . . . An athlete is not crowned unless he competes according to the rules. It is the hard-working farmer who ought to have the first share of the crops" (2:4-6).

Q. What characteristics mark the "Lord's servant"?

A. He "must not be quarrelsome but kindly to every one, an apt teacher, forbearing, correcting his opponents with gentleness" (2:24f); he must "preach the word, be urgent in season and out of season, convince, rebuke, and exhort, be unfailing in patience and in teaching" (4:2); "always be steady, endure suffering, do the work of an evangelist, fulfil your ministry" (4:5).

Q. What does the author envision as marking the end-time?

A. "In the last days there will come times of stress. For men will be lovers of self, lovers of money, proud, arrogant, abusive, disobedient to their parents, ungrateful, unholy, inhuman, implacable, slanderers, profligates, fierce, haters of good, treacherous, reckless, swollen with conceit, lovers of pleasure rather than lovers of God, holding the form of religion but denying the power of it" (3:1-5).

Q. What is the author's doctrine of Scripture?

A. "All scripture is inspired by God and profitable for teaching, for reproof, for correction, and for training in righteousness" (3:16).

Q. What kind of life does the author expect for believers?

A. "Indeed all who desire to live a godly life in Christ Jesus will be persecuted" (3:12).

Q. Who are some of the persons mentioned in II Timothy?

A. Onesiphorus ("he often refreshed me"—1:16); Hymenaeus and Philetus ("who have swerved from the truth"—2:18); Demas ("in love with this present world, has deserted me"—4:10); Mark ("he is very useful in serving me"—4:11); Alexander the coppersmith ("did me great harm"—4:14).

Q. Who are the Jannes and Jambres referred to in 3:8?

A. Jewish tradition gave these as the names of Pharaoh's magicians mentioned in Exodus 7:11.

THE LETTER OF PAUL TO
TITUS

Q. Who is the Titus to whom this letter is addressed?

A. A Greek of whom Paul made a test case concerning circumcision (Galatians 2:3); he served as Paul's representative to the church at Corinth: "he is my partner and fellow worker in your service" (II Corinthians 8:23; cf. II Corinthians 7:6,13; 8:6,16). Tradition affirms that Candia, Crete, was his birthplace and that he became bishop of the church in Crete ("That is why I left you in Crete"—1:5).

Q. What other link does the letter have with Crete?

A. Chapter 1:12 quotes "One of themselves, a prophet of their own," who said: "Cretans are always liars, evil beasts, lazy gluttons" (the line is attributed to Epimenides, a Cretan of the sixth century B.C., reputedly the author of many poems and oracles).

Q. What other proverbial saying is quoted?

A. "To the pure all things are pure" (1:15).

Q. What is the purpose of the letter to Titus?

A. "To further the faith of God's elect and their knowledge of the truth which accords with godliness" (1:1).

Q. What advice is given to the aged?

A. "Bid the older men be temperate, serious, sensible, sound in faith, in love, and in steadfastness. Bid the older women likewise to be reverent in behavior, not to be slanderers or slaves to drink" (2:2f).

Q. What conduct is expected of the young marrieds?

A. The young women are to "love their husbands and children, to be sensible, chaste, domestic, kind, and submissive to their husbands. . . . Likewise urge the younger men to control themselves" (2:5f).

Q. What conduct is expected of slaves?

A. "They are not to be refractory, nor to pilfer, but to show entire and true fidelity" (2:9f).

Q. In what spirit are believers to undertake the tasks of the common life?

A. They are "to be ready for any honest work . . . careful to apply themselves to good deeds" (3:1,8).

Q. What is to be the motive of such work?

A. "Let our people learn to apply themselves to good deeds, so as to help cases of urgent need, and not to be unfruitful" (3:14).

Q. What treatment is prescribed for obstreperous members of the community?

A. "As for a man who is fractious, after admonishing him once or twice, have nothing more to do with him" (3:10).

THE LETTER OF PAUL TO
PHILEMON

Q. Who is the author of this letter?

A. The author identifies himself as "Paul, a prisoner for Christ," and associates with him "Timothy our brother" (verse 1).

Q. To whom is this letter addressed?

A. "To Philemon . . . and Apphia . . . and Archippus . . . and the church in your house" (verse 1f).

Q. What is distinctive about this address?

A. Paul's other letters are addressed to the believers in a particular city (Corinth, Philippi, Thessalonica) or a particular region (Galatia); this alone is addressed to a house congregation, the one that met in the home of Philemon.

Q. Who were Philemon, Apphia, and Archippus?

A. Relatives or close friends of one another, perhaps husband, wife, and son.

Q. Where did they live?

A. Probably in Colossae, since Onesimus (verse 10) and Epaphras (verse 23) are mentioned here as well as in the letter to Colossae. Perhaps Philemon was a businessman in that city.

Q. Were there many house congregations in the early church?

A. New Testament references to them (Acts 12:12; Romans 16:5; Colossians 4:15) suggest that this was the only organization and the only meeting-place the early church possessed.

Q. When was this letter written?

A. Probably in 62 A.D.

Q. Where was this letter written?

A. From prison.

Q. What are the evidences of its having been sent from prison?

A. The author indicates from the outset that he is "a prisoner for Christ" (verse 1); he states of Onesimus: "whose father I have become in my imprisonment" (verse 10); he lists Epaphras as "my fellow prisoner" (verse 23); he hopes that the prayers of his friends will avail for his release (verse 22).

Q. Who was Epaphras?

A. Perhaps the founder of the church in Colossae (Colossians 1:7; 4:12).

Q. What is the purpose of the letter?

A. To return Onesimus, a runaway slave, to his master, Philemon, and to get the slaveowner, on his part, to establish a new relationship with Onesimus: "no longer a slave, as a beloved brother" (verse 16).

Q. What compensation does Paul offer the slaveowner?

A. "If he has wronged you at all, or owes you anything, charge that to my account" (verse 18). How Paul, in prison, would pay such a debt he does not explain; he has complete trust that no such payment will be exacted, since the slaveowner is "owing me even your own self" (verse 19).

Q. How does Paul prepare the way for this request?

A. By giving thanks for all the good he and others have received at the hands of the addressees: "For I have derived much joy and comfort from your love, my brother, because the hearts of the saints have been refreshed through you" (verse 7).

Q. What is the meaning of the name Onesimus?

A. It is from the Greek term for "useful," and Paul does not fail to make a play on the word. Verse 11 means: ". . . he who once was Useless to you has become Useful to you and to me" (this is echoed in the "benefit" of verse 20).

Q. What passages sum up the spirit in which Paul makes the unusual request?

A. "I preferred to do nothing without your consent in order that your goodness might not be by compulsion but of your own free will" (verse 14). "Confident of your obedience, I write to you, knowing that you will do even more than I say" (verse 21).

THE LETTER TO THE

HEBREWS

Q. Who is the author of the Letter to the Hebrews?

A. A completely anonymous work, from the seventh century onward it was attributed by some to Paul. Its style, vocabulary, and argument, however, are quite unlike those of Paul (Origen noted that it "has not the Apostle's roughness of utterance"). Other guesses as to its authorship have included Luke, Barnabas, Apollos, Priscilla, Silas, Philip, Aristion, Clement of Rome; perhaps Origen, about 225 A.D., spoke the final word on the subject: "God only knows."

Q. In what other ways does Hebrews differ from Paul?

A. Although continually concerned with the pre-existence of Christ, it contains more references to the earthly life of Jesus than all the ten letters of Paul. The writer insists that the gospel, "declared at first by the Lord . . . was attested to us by those who heard him" (2:3.) Paul never tired of stressing the firsthand character of his experience of the risen Christ (cf. I Corinthians 15:8; Galatians 1:11f).

Q. Who are the Hebrews to whom the letter is addressed?

A. Persecuted Christians of Jewish background who lived in Rome, Jerusalem, Ephesus, Alexandria, or some other community, or perhaps were scattered in many communities. The reference to "Those who come from Italy" have led many to favor Rome.

Q. When was the letter to Hebrews written?

A. During a time of persecution, either around 68 A.D. or around 96 A.D. References to the Jerusalem temple have been held to imply that that structure had not been destroyed, as it was in 70 A.D., but this is inconclusive because it is always the ideal temple ("the pattern which was shown you on the mountain"—8:5) that is in view.

Q. Where was the letter to Hebrews written?

A. No indication is given, though some think its use of Alexandrian philosophy suggests that the Egyptian city of Alexandria is its source.

Q. What is the wider significance of the appearance in Hebrews of ideas related to Alexandrian philosophy?

A. Christianity for the first time begins to reckon with ancient philosophy and education.

Q. What evidences are there that the readers were familiar with persecution?

A. "You endured a hard struggle with sufferings" (10:32); "let us be grateful for receiving a kingdom that cannot be shaken" (12:28).

Q. Why was the letter to Hebrews written?

A. To establish the superiority of Christ to every legal or ceremonial regulation, every order of priesthood or angelic being.

Q. What is the literary form of the document?

A. Its epistolary style is purely conventional; much of its consists of short Bible readings taken from the Greek version of the Psalter and the five books of Moses; it has been called also the first example of Christian literary art, harbinger of the literary skill later to be associated with those who wrote and spoke for the faith. Some think it originally a series of sermons put into letter form, and that Chapters 3 and 4 may be our best examples of early Christian homilies.

Q. It has been said that the letter to Hebrews "comes nearer to being a systematic treatise" than any other book in the Bible; what is its thesis?

A. "In many and various ways God spoke of old to our fathers by the prophets; but in these last days he has spoken to us by a Son, whom he appointed the heir of all things" (1:1f).

Q. What ascetic practices are rejected?

A. "Let marriage be held in honor among all" (13:4). "Do not be led away by diverse and strange teachings, for it is well that the heart be strengthened by grace, not by foods, which have not benefited their adherents" (13:9).

Q. What Aristotelian idea is adopted to illustrate the development of Christianity from Judaism, the perfecting through suffering of Christ himself, and the growth of the Christian through discipline?

A. The idea of the *telos,* or final end (2:10; 5:8f).

Q. What notion from Platonic philosophy is in the background?

A. "For since the law has but a shadow of the good things to come instead of the true form of these realities, it can never, by the same sacrifices which are continually offered year after year, make perfect those who draw near" (10:1).

Q. How does the author work out in detail the superiority of Christ?

A. Christ is superior to the prophets, through whom revelation was fragmentary (1:1); to angels (1:4-2:9), who occupied a prominent part in Jewish thought of the time ("Are they not all ministering spirits sent forth to serve, for the sake of those who are to obtain salvation?"— 1:14); to Moses (3:1-4:10), the Hebrew law giver; to Aaron, the representative high priest (5:1-10:25)—again using the analogy of Greek philosophy, the author argues that Jesus was the ideal high priest who offered the ideal sacrifice in the ideal sanctuary; to Melchizedek (6:20-7:22)—Christ "has become a priest, not according to a legal requirement concerning bodily descent but by the power of an indestructible life. . . . This makes Jesus the surety of a better covenant" (7:16,22).

Q. What inferences does the author draw from the superiority of Christ?

A. A stronger commitment is required ("we must pay the closer attention to what we have heard"—2:1; "For we share in Christ, if only we hold our confidence firm to the end"—3:14. "Since then we have a great high priest who has passed through the heavens, Jesus, the Son of God, let us hold fast our confession"—4:14); the life of faith becomes more exciting ("faith is the assurance of things hoped for, the conviction of things not seen"—11:1); a more solemn responsibility devolves upon the living ("let us run with perseverance the race that is set before us"— 12:1); practical duties become imperative ("let us consider how to stir one another up to love and good works"—10:24; "Let brotherly love continue. Do not neglect to show hospitality to strangers. . . . Remember those who are in prison. . . . Keep your life free from love of money"—13:1-5).

Q. What is the author's doctrine of the person and work of Christ?

A. "He reflects the glory of God and bears the very stamp of his nature" (1:3); "crowned with glory and honor because of the suffering of death, so that by the grace of God he might taste death for every one" (2:9). "For because he himself has suffered and been tempted, he is able to help those who are tempted" (2:18). "Although he was a Son, he learned obedience through what he suffered" (5:8); "we have been sanctified through the offering of the body of Jesus Christ once for all" (10:10); "the pioneer and perfecter of our Faith, who for the joy that was set before him endured the cross, despising the shame, and is seated at the right hand of the throne of God" (12:2). "Jesus Christ is the same yesterday and today and forever" (13:8).

Q. What does the author teach about God?

A. "By faith we understand that the world was created by the word of God" (11:3); "before him no creature is hidden, but all are open and laid bare to the eyes of him with whom we have to do" (4:13). "God is not so unjust as to overlook your work and the love which you showed for his sake in serving the saints" (6:10); "it is impossible that God should prove false" (6:18). "It is a fearful thing to fall into the hands of the living God" (10:31). "It is for discipline that you have to endure. God is treating you as sons; for what son is there whom his father does not discipline?" (12:7); "let us offer to God acceptable worship, with reverence and awe; for our God is a consuming fire" (12:28f).

Q. What description does the author give of the word of God?

A. It is "living and active, sharper than any two-edged sword, piercing to the division of soul and spirit, of joints and marrow, and discerning the thoughts and intentions of the heart" (4:12).

Q. What reference is made to the idea of the covenant?

A. Christ is "the mediator of a new covenant" (9:15).

Q. Whom does the author cite as examples of the faith without which "it is impossible to please" God?

A. Abel, Enoch, and Noah; Abraham, Isaac, and Jacob; Joseph, Moses, Gideon, Barak, Samson, Jephthah, "David and Samuel and the prophets" (11:4-32).

Q. How does the author summarize the accomplishments of those who lived by faith?

A. They "conquered kingdoms, enforced justice, received promises, stopped the mouths of lions, quenched raging fire, escaped the edge of the sword, won strength out of weakness, became mighty in war, put foreign armies to flight" (11:33f).

Q. Were God's best gifts bestowed upon old-time heroes?

A. "God had foreseen something better for us" (11:40).

THE LETTER OF
JAMES

Q. Who is the author of the Letter of James?

A. He identifies himself as "James, a servant of God and of the Lord Jesus Christ" (1:1); Mark 6:3; 15:40; Luke 6:16 reveal that more than one man bore the name of James; since one was the brother of Jesus, it is often assumed that this letter is by that James. In that case, three questions arise: Why did one who had known Jesus so intimately content himself with writing a letter instead of a gospel? Why does it manifest no interest in such theological ideas as Messiahship, Incarnation, and Resurrection? Why would the brother of Jesus not claim that distinction rather than simply referring to himself as "a servant of the Lord Jesus Christ"? To the latter, perhaps, a due sense of modesty could be the answer.

Q. What passage might have special point if written by the Lord's brother?

A. The discussion of what the tongue can do (3:6-12) would have particular poignancy if written by the James who evidently misunderstood Jesus (see Mark 3:31-35).

Q. When was the letter written?

A. Tradition has it that James, the Lord's brother, who prayed so continuously that he had knees like a camel's, was martyred in 62 A.D. Some would date the book before that, even as early as 45 A.D. Others, believing it to reflect conditions in the early church, would place it in the second century.

Q. What situations referred to in the letter suggest a late date?

A. Whereas the church in Paul's time had not many who were well-to-do (I Corinthians 1:26f), now the presence of the wealthy has become a problem: ". . . if a man with gold rings and in fine clothing comes into your assembly . . ." (2:2); "show no partiality as you hold the faith of our Lord Jesus Christ" (2:1).

Q. Where was the letter written?

A. No indication is given.

Q. To whom was the letter written?

A. "To the twelve tribes in the dispersion" (1:1), meaning that it is a general letter, addressed to widely scattered groups of believers.

Q. What is the purpose for which the letter was written?

A. To warn the church against becoming "conformed to this world," and to recall it to the elemental purity and simplicity of the original gospel. Its message is summed up in 1:22: "But be doers of the word, and not hearers only, deceiving yourselves."

Q. What is the literary form of the document?

A. Although superficially a letter, it has been variously described as a collection of sermon notes, "an ethical scrapbook," and a Christian adaptation of the Cynic-Stoic diatribe.

Q. What passages seem to echo the Sermon on the Mount?

A. Chapter 5:12 is similar to Matthew 5:34-37; 1:10f is similar to Matthew 6:30-34; 1:12 is similar to Matthew 5:11f.

Q. What does the author regard as the test of one's religion?

A. Its effectiveness in the work-a-day world: ". . . faith apart from works is dead" (2:26).

Q. What is the author's definition of religion?

A. "Religion that is pure and undefiled before God and the Father is this: to visit orphans and widows in their affliction, and to keep oneself unstained from the world" (1:27).

Q. How does the author's interpretation of faith differ from that of Paul?

A. Paul's emphasis had been on the origin of religion; James' is on its outreach; Paul condemns a religion of work-righteousness; James is sure that faith must show itself in works. However, Paul is sure that life in the Spirit must produce fruits (Galatians 5:22f), and it is precisely these fruits that James refers to as works. That the conflict between Paul and James is more apparent than real is indicated by the fact that both of them cite Abraham as the exemplar of the truths they are proclaiming (Galatians 3:6-9; James 2:21-24).

Q. What is the author's idea regarding law?

A. In 2:8-11 he summarizes the Ten Commandments as "the royal law," but concludes: "So speak and so act as those who are to be judged under the law of liberty" (2:12; cf. 1:25).

Q. What is the author's point of view with respect to persecution?

A. "Count it all joy, my brethren, when you meet various trials, for you know that the testing of your faith produces steadfastness" (1:2f). "Blessed is the man who endures trial, for when he has stood the test he will receive the crown of life" (1:12). "As an example of suffering and patience, brethren, take the prophets who spoke in the name of the Lord" (5:10).

Q. What ethical injunctions are found in the book?

A. "Let every man be quick to hear, slow to speak, slow to anger" (1:19). "For where jealousy and selfish ambition exist, there will be disorder and every vile practice" (3:16). "Resist the devil and he will flee from you" (4:7). "Do not speak evil against one another . . . who are you that you judge your neighbor?" (4:11f). "Whoever knows what is right to do and fails to do it, for him it is sin" (4:17).

Q. What does the author regard as the source of temptation?

A. "Each person is tempted when he is lured and enticed by his own desire" (1:14).

Q. What does the author regard as the cause of wars?

A. "You desire and do not have; so you kill. And you covet and cannot obtain; so you fight and wage war" (4:2).

Q. What attitude does the author enjoin regarding the future?

A. "What is your life? For you are a mist that appears for a little time and then vanishes. Instead you ought to say, 'If the Lord wills' " (4:14f).

Q. What judgment is pronounced upon the rich?

A. "Weep and howl for the miseries that are coming upon you . . . the wages of the laborers . . . which you kept back by fraud, cry out . . . you have fattened your hearts in a day of slaughter" (5:1-6).

Q. What agrarian example suggests the need for patience?

A. "Behold, the farmer waits for the precious fruit of the earth, being patient over it until he receives the early and the late rain" (5:7).

Q. Which of the seven sacraments owes its origin to this book?

A. Extreme unction finds its Biblical basis in 5:13-16.

Q. What type of confessional is envisioned?

A. "Confess your sins to one another, and pray for one another, that you may be healed" (5:16).

Q. What claim has James to be the most modern book in the New Testament?

A. The issues with which it deals—democracy, philanthropy, and social justice—are precisely those that are to the fore in our time.

THE FIRST LETTER OF

PETER

Q. Who is the author of I Peter?

A. The writer refers to himself as "Peter, an apostle of Jesus Christ" (1:1), but in 5:12 says: "By Silvanus, a faithful brother as I regard him, I have written briefly to you."

Q. Who was Silvanus?

A. He is thought to have been the same person as the man referred to elsewhere in the New Testament (Acts 15:40; 16:19; 17:4, etc.) as Silas.

Q. What part did Silvanus play in the writing of I Peter?

A. In accordance with literary practices of the time, he could have performed any one of several roles: that of Peter's amanuensis, setting down what Peter dictated; that of Peter's interpreter, writing out ideas imparted by Peter; that of Peter's representative, setting forth what he believed Peter would say to the existing situation.

Q. Why is it unlikely that Silvanus was merely an amanuensis?

A. In Acts 4:13 Peter and John are described as "uneducated, common men"; Peter's provincial speech gave him away the night of Jesus' arrest ("your accent betrays you"—Matthew 26:73)—in view of which it is assumed that the excellent literary style of the letter must be due to someone other than the Galilean fisherman.

Q. What personal reminiscences of Peter appear in the book?

A. "By his great mercy we have been born anew to a living hope through the resurrection of Jesus Christ from the dead" (1:3; cf. 1:23) may well recall Jesus' post-resurrection message to Peter in Mark 16:7. "Always be prepared to make a defense to any one who calls you to account for the hope that is in you" (3:15) may well be from one who was not always ready (see Matthew 26:58,69-75). "I beseech you as aliens and exiles" (2:11) may well be from a Galilean peasant who, though called to preach in Rome, was never able to feel at home in the capital of empire.

Q. What ecclesiastical term, in use today, is derived from this thought of the Christians as unprotected residents of a hostile world?

A. The English word *parish* is derived from the Greek term translated "exile" (1:1); a parish is a group of dislocated people.

Q. To whom was the letter written?

A. "To the exiles of the dispersion in Pontus, Galatia, Cappadocia, Asia, and Bithynia"—that is, to Christians scattered in these Near Eastern communities; it is a circular letter, perhaps with the several regions listed in the order in which they were to be visited by its bearer.

Q. Where was the letter written?

A. Chapter 5:13 states that "She who is at Babylon . . . sends you greetings." Babylon, the Mesopotamian region where the Hebrews suffered the torture of exile, came to stand for a community of suffering and could have been used, in an era of persecution, to conceal the fact that the letter was written from Rome; others suppose that Babylon is a cipher for a Roman garrison city on the Nile, near the site of present-day Cairo.

Q. When was the letter written?

A. Obviously during a time of persecution ("do not be surprised at the fiery ordeal which comes upon you"—4:12); the Christians suffered under Nero in 64 A.D., but the persecution under Domitian, about 95 A.D., was more widespread and organized; there is no certain way to tell which persecution is meant.

Q. Why was the letter written?

A. To strengthen and encourage those undergoing persecution by putting their afflictions in the context of Christ's sufferings: "Since therefore Christ suffered in the flesh, arm yourselves with the same thought" (4:1); "rejoice in so far as you share Christ's sufferings" (4:13); "to this you have been called, because Christ also suffered for you" (2:21).

Q. What disciplinary effect may suffering have?

A. "So that the genuineness of your faith, more precious than gold which though perishable is tested by fire, may redound to praise and glory and honor at the revelation of Jesus Christ" (1:7).

Q. What perspective is given by reference to the Hebrew prophets?

A. Assurance and strength could be found because "they were serving not themselves but you" (1:12).

Q. What is the literary form of the document?

A. Although it has the conventional form of a letter, it has been variously interpreted as a commentary on the Lord's Prayer; a "microcosm of Christian faith and duty, the model of a pastoral charge, composed of divers materials and many themes"; a collection of sermons; a discourse delivered by a bishop to candidates for baptism (1:3-4:11), with epistolary additions.

Q. What use does the author make of the Old Testament?

A. To support his doctrine of the imperishable character of the divine message, he quotes (2:24f) Isaiah 40:6-9. To support his idea of the church as a structure that will endure, he cites (2:4) Psalm 118:22; Isaiah 28:16; 8:14f. For his doctrine of the Christian community ("you are a chosen race, a royal priesthood, a holy nation, God's own people" —2:9), he cites Exodus 23:22 and Hosea 2:23; for his description (3:10-12) of God's care of those who love him, he cites Psalm 34:12-16.

Q. What is the believer's duty to the state?

A. "Be subject for the Lord's sake to every human institution" (2:13; cf. 2:17).

Q. What is the author's idea of freedom?

A. "Live as free men, yet without using your freedom as a pretext for evil" (2:16).

Q. Upon what groups is submission enjoined?

A. Servants to their masters (2:18-25); wives to their husbands (3:1-6); the younger to the older (5:5).

Q. What conduct is expected of husbands?

A. "Live considerately with your wives, bestowing honor on the woman as the weaker sex, since you are joint heirs to the grace of life" (3:7).

Q. What Old Testament circumstance does the author regard as the prototype of baptism?

A. "The building of the ark, in which a few, that is, eight persons, were saved through water" (3:20).

Q. What passage is used by the church in support of the doctrine of Christ's descent into hell?

A. "He went and preached to the spirits in prison" (3:19).

Q. How are believers to live in a pagan society?

A. "Maintain good conduct among the Gentiles" (2:12); "hold unfailing your love for one another . . . Practice hospitality ungrudgingly" (4:8f).

Q. What is to be the believer's attitude toward the expected end of the age?

A. "Keep sane and sober for your prayers" (4:7).

Q. What instruction is given to church officers?

A. "Tend the flock of God . . . not by constraint, but willingly, not for shameful gain but eagerly, not as domineering over those in your charge but being examples to the flock" (5:2f).

Q. What creature from the animal world is pictured as representing evil?

A. "Your adversary the devil prowls around like a lion, seeking someone to devour" (5:8).

Q. What advice is given to believers in an age of danger and bewilderment?

A. "Humble yourselves . . . under the mighty hand of God. . . . Cast all your anxieties on him, for he cares about you" (5:6f).

THE SECOND LETTER OF

PETER

Q. Who is the author of II Peter?

A. The author speaks of himself as "Simon Peter, a servant and apostle of Jesus Christ" (1:1).

Q. Why is this regarded by some as a pen name?

A. Ancient authors, in order to pay tribute to a well-loved mentor, sometimes chose to write in his name; John Calvin thought a follower of Peter might here have written at Peter's command.

Q. To what event in Peter's life is reference made?

A. "We are eyewitnesses of his majesty . . . for we were with him on the holy mountain" (1:16,18) alludes to the Transfiguration, an experience Peter was privileged to share with Jesus (Mark 9:2-7).

Q. When was the letter written?

A. Chapter 3:15f speaks of how "our beloved brother Paul wrote to you . . . speaking of this as he does in all his letters. There are some things in them hard to understand, which the ignorant and unstable twist to their own destruction, as they do the other scriptures." That Paul's letters had not only been written and collected but had also attained a status comparable to that of the Old Testament, indicates a time not earlier than the first decades of the second century.

Q. Where was the letter written?

A. No clue is given; some in the early church thought it originated in Egypt.

Q. To whom is the letter written?

A. No particular destination or recipients are mentioned; it is addressed generally "to those who have obtained a faith of equal standing with ours in the righteousness of our God and Savior Jesus Christ" (1:1); the recipients also have been instructed in the Christian life, and the author wishes "to arouse you by way of reminder" (1:13).

Q. Why was the letter written?

A. To oppose and expose "false teachers . . . who . . . secretly bring in destructive heresies" (2:1), "follow cleverly devised myths" (1:16), and put forth false notions regarding the end of the age.

Q. In what terms does the author speak of the heretical teachers?

A. "These are waterless springs and mists driven by a storm . . . uttering loud boasts of folly, they entice with licentious passions of the flesh men who have barely escaped from those who live in error" (2:17f).

Q. What other New Testament book does this resemble?

A. The letter of Jude.

Q. What is the purpose of God's "precious and very great promises" (1:4)?

A. "That through these you may escape from the corruption that is in the world because of passion, and become partakers of the divine nature" (1:4).

Q. What psychological description does the author give of development in the life of the believer?

A. "Make every effort to supplement your faith with virtue, and virtue with knowledge, and knowledge with self-control, and self-control with steadfastness, and steadfastness with godliness, and godliness with brotherly affection, and brotherly affection with love" (1:5).

Q. What is the author's teaching regarding Biblical inspiration and interpretation?

A. "No prophecy of scripture is a matter of one's own interpretation . . . men moved by the Holy Spirit spoke from God" (1:20f).

Q. What events in Hebrew history does the author cite as suggesting the inexorable doom that falls upon wickedness?

A. The flood in the time of Noah, and the obliteration of Sodom and Gomorrah (2:5-10).

Q. What of those in the author's own time who were living as did Noah's contemporaries?

A. "These, like irrational animals . . . will be destroyed in the same destruction" (2:12).

Q. What Old Testament proverb does the author quote as applicable to those who, having once confessed the Gospel, have lapsed into old ways of living?

A. "The dog turns back to his own vomit, and the sow is washed only to wallow in the mire" (2:22; cf. Proverbs 26:11).

Q. How does the author explain the delay in Christ's expected return?

A. "With the Lord one day is as a thousand years, and a thousand years as one day" (3:8).

Q. What reason is given for the delay?

A. "The Lord . . . is forbearing toward you, not wishing that any should perish, but that all should reach repentance" (3:9).

Q. How was the dropping of the first atomic bomb reflected in a quotation from II Peter before the British Association for the Advancement of Science?

A. In the reading of 3:10: "But the day of the Lord will come like a thief, and there the heavens will pass away with a loud noise, and the elements will be dissolved with fire, and the earth and the works that are upon it will be burned up."

Q. What follows from the possible imminence of destruction?

A. "Since all these things are thus to be dissolved, what sort of persons ought you to be in lives of holiness and godliness . . . ?" (3:11).

Q. What concluding wish has the author for his readers?

A. That they may "grow in the grace and knowledge of our Lord and Savior Jesus Christ" (3:18).

THE FIRST LETTER OF
JOHN

Q. Who wrote I John?

A. The author nowhere identifies himself; similarity to the fourth gospel leads many to believe I John to have been written by the same man.

Q. How does I John resemble the gospel according to John?

A. Some regard the former as a condensed version of the latter, and others as its complement, showing how the truths about God, which in this gospel are illustrated in the person of Christ, must be realized in the lives of Christ's followers; others hold that his gospel intends to demonstrate that Jesus is the Christ, the letter that Christ is Jesus—that is to say, the Messiah, long hoped for, is identical with Jesus of Nazareth.

Q. To whom was I John written?

A. To Christians in general, with special reference perhaps to those who lived in the Roman province of Asia.

Q. When was I John written?

A. No identifiable date is mentioned, although some hold that 2:18 and 4:3 point to a time just before the destruction of Jerusalem in 70 A.D. Others believe the letter to have been written closer to the end of the first century A.D.

Q. What is the purpose of the letter?

A. To combat false notions of the Gospel and to emphasize that "God is love"; Paulus and Michaelis, in the nineteenth century, held that the allusions to light and darkness were designed to correct the Zoroastrian philosophy of religion.

Q. How does the letter seek to accomplish its purpose?

A. By recalling believers to the initial wonder of the faith, "that which was from the beginning" (1:1; 2:7,24; 3:11), and by emphasizing how God in Christ has supremely made himself known.

Q. What words does this author use to describe the essential nature of Deity?

A. "God is light" (1:5); "God is love" (4:8,16).

Q. What Gnostic notions are combatted?

A. The denial that Jesus came in the flesh (2:22; 4:2; 5:5); the minimizing of the significance of Christ's death (1:7; 5:6,8).

Q. With what senses, according to this author, can the historical Christ be understood?

A. Sound ("which we have heard"), sight ("which we have seen with our eyes"), touch ("which we have . . . touched with our hands") 1:1.

Q. What compels the author to write as he does?

A. "That our joy may be complete" (1:4).

Q. What practical truths does the author deduce from the doctrine that "God is light"?

A. "If we say we have fellowship with him while we walk in darkness, we lie" (1:6). "He who loves his brother abides in the light" (2:10); "he who hates his brother is in the darkness and walks in the darkness, and does not know where he is going, because the darkness has blinded his eyes" (2:11).

Q. What cosmic significance does the author see in Christ's death?

A. "He is the expiation for our sins, and not for ours only but also for the sins of the whole world" (2:2).

Q. For what groups in the believing community does the author have special messages?

A. "Little children" (2:12,18,28; 3:7; 4:4; 5:21); "fathers" (2:13f); "young men" (2:14).

Q. Who are the "little children" to whom so much of the letter is addressed?

A. Probably immature believers, of whatever age.

Q. What contrast is there between love of the world and love for the Father?

A. "The world passes away, and the lust of it; but he who does the will of God abides for ever" (2:17).

Q. How did the professors of certain false beliefs identify themselves?

A. "They went out from us . . . if they had been of us, they would have continued with us" (2:19).

Q. How does God's love manifest itself?

A. "That we should be called children of God" (3:1).

Q. What effect does the realization of his divine sonship have upon the individual?

A. "Every one who thus hopes in him purifies himself as he is pure" (3:3).

Q. What is this author's definition of sin?

A. "Sin is lawlessness" (3:4). "All wrongdoing is sin" (5:17).

Q. How does the author explain the first murder?

A. Cain "murdered his brother . . . because his own deeds were evil and his brother's righteous" (3:12).

Q. How can the believer be sure of his salvation?

A. "We know that we have passed out of death into life, because we love the brethren" (3:14); "and by this we know that he abides in us, by the Spirit which he has given us" (3:24).

Q. What is "the spirit of antichrist"?

A. Failure to acknowledge that "Jesus Christ has come in the flesh" (4:2).

Q. How is God's love supremely made known?

A. "Not that we loved God but that he loved us and sent his Son to be the expiation for our sins" (4:10).

Q. What effect should this have upon human life?

A. "If God so loved us, we also ought to love one another" (4:11); "he who loves God should love his brother also" (4:21).

Q. What is the relationship between love and fear?

A. "There is no fear in love, but perfect love casts out fear" (4:18).

Q. What is "the victory that overcomes the world"?

A. Life lived in this faith (5:4,5).

Q. How else does this life of faith and love manifest itself?

A. "This is the confidence which we have in him, that if we ask anything according to his will he hears us" (5:14).

Q. What was John Wesley's judgment upon I John?

A. He referred to it as "that compendium of all the holy Scriptures."

THE SECOND LETTER OF
JOHN

Q. Who is the author of II John?

A. One who identifies himself simply as "the elder" (1:1).

Q. To whom does he write?

A. The letter is addressed "to the elect lady and her children whom I love in the truth" (verse 1); the identity of the individual is unknown; some suppose her to be the personification of a particular congregation; "the children of your elect sister greet you" (verse 13) would seem to imply that one congregation sends its greetings to another.

Q. When was the letter written?

A. There is no hint as to date, and no mention of any identifiable historical situation.

Q. Why was the letter written?

A. To warn against a situation in which purveyors of false doctrine were deliberately setting out to distort the truth.

Q. What protection does the author set against this perversion?

A. To obey the commandment "we had from the beginning, that we love one another" (verse 5).

Q. How are the believers to defend themselves from the dispensers of falsehood?

A. "If any one comes to you and does not bring this doctrine, do not receive him into the house or give him any greeting" (verse 10).

Q. What relationship has II John to other Johannine literature?

A. It has been called "a miniature edition of I John," and may be the communication referred to in III John 9: "I have written something to the church."

THE THIRD LETTER OF
JOHN

Q. Who is the author of III John?

A. He identifies himself simply as "the elder" (verse 1).

Q. To whom is the letter addressed?

A. "To the beloved Gaius, whom I love in the truth" (verse 1); Gaius was a fairly common name in New Testament times (cf. Acts 19:29; 20:4; I Corinthians 1:14; Romans 16:23), and the identity of this Gaius is not further disclosed.

Q. When was the letter written?

A. As in the case of II John, no datable event is reported; it was a time, however, when formal ecclesiastical authority was developing.

Q. Where was the letter written?

A. The author says in his conclusion, "The friends greet you" (verse 15), but who or where these friends were is not specified.

Q. What was the purpose of the letter?

A. To rebuke a defiant and self-seeking member of the early Christian community: "Diotrephes, who likes to put himself first, does not acknowledge my authority" (verse 9).

Q. How did the insubordination of Diotrephes manifest itself?

A. The writer speaks of him as "prating against me with evil words. And not content with that, he refuses himself to welcome the brethren, and also stops those who want to welcome them and puts them out of the church" (verse 10f).

Q. What does the author say regarding itinerant missionaries in the early church?

A. "We ought to support such men" (verse 8).

Q. Who was Demetrius (verse 12)?

A. Perhaps the bearer of this letter, he was doubtless one of the itinerant missionaries earlier referred to.

Q. What psychosomatic insight is contained in the letter?

A. "I pray that . . . you may be in health; I know that it is well with your soul" (verse 2).

THE LETTER OF
JUDE

Q. Who is the author of Jude?

A. One who refers to himself as "Jude, a servant of Jesus Christ and brother of James" (verse 1); tradition identifies this Jude with the brother of Jesus mentioned in Mark 6:3. If this is true, it is impressive evidence of Jesus' influence upon him that he does not claim the status of "brother of Jesus," but only of "servant of Jesus Christ." Jude, however, was a not uncommon name (cf. Luke 6:16; Acts 1:13; 15:22,23), and we cannot be certain of which Jude this is.

Q. To whom was the letter written?

A. Addressed simply to "those who are called" (verse 1), this must be described as a general letter to unknown Christians.

Q. When was the letter written?

A. Since the author urges his readers to "remember . . . the predictions of the apostles" (verse 17) regarding the end-time, refers to "love feasts" (verse 12—a developed accompaniment of the eucharist), and summons all to "contend for the faith which was once for all delivered to the saints" (verse 3), a period toward the end of New Testament times is indicated, 90 to 125 A.D.

Q. Where was Jude written?

A. No indication is given; probably from somewhere in Palestine.

Q. Why was the letter written?

A. To awaken the church to the dangers it was facing through troublemakers who wished to replace the historic faith with false teaching. The troublemakers are picturesquely described as clouds that bring no rain, trees that bear no fruit, waves that end in foam (verse 12f).

Q. To what other book in the New Testament is Jude related?

A. It has close affinities with II Peter; some consider that it is a condensation of that letter; others, that II Peter is an expansion of Jude.

Q. What are the sources of the author's imagery?

A. As suggesting God's judgment upon disobedience, the author alludes to the wilderness wanderings of the Hebrews (verse 5), the belief in angels that rebelled (verse 6), and the wickedness of Sodom and Gomorrah (verse 7). He mentions Cain, Balaam, and Korah (verse 11), all of whom are Old Testament figures. He also quotes the intertestamental book of Enoch (verse 14). The mention of the archangel Michael, "contending with the devil" for the body of Moses (verse 9), may be an allusion to a book now unknown.

Q. What significance does the author see in the evil circumstances of his time?

A. "In the last time there will be scoffers, following their own ungodly passions" (verse 18).

Q. What is the duty of believers in such a situation?

A. "Build yourselves up on your most holy faith. . . . Convince some, who doubt; save some, by snatching them out of the fire; on some have mercy with fear, hating even the garment spotted by the flesh" (verses 20, 22, 23).

Q. What does it mean to "contend for the faith once for all delivered to the saints?"

A. Traditionally this has been interpreted as the preservation of a body of dogma, handed on from age to age and to be kept intact by each generation. Contemporary existentialists have given the words a different meaning: are we in our time willing to struggle and sacrifice for our faith as the apostles did for theirs?

Q. What is the distinctive contribution of this letter to worship?

A. The doxology with which it concludes, verses 24 and 25, is often used as a benediction: "Now to him who is able to keep you from falling and to present you without blemish before the presence of his glory with rejoicing, to the only God, our Savior through Jesus Christ our Lord, be glory, majesty, dominion, and authority, before all time and now and forever. Amen."

THE REVELATION TO JOHN

Q. Who was the author of Revelation?

A. The author, frequently called "Seer," refers to himself (1:4,9) as John, but John was as common a name in the ancient world as in the modern, and which John this is cannot with certainty be determined; radical difference in literary style indicates that the author is not the author of the gospel according to John.

Q. When was Revelation written?

A. At a time of organized persecution, probably about 96 A.D.

Q. Where was Revelation written?

A. The author says: "I John . . . was on the island called Patmos on account of the word of God and the testimony of Jesus" (1:9). Patmos, an island in the Mediterranean, was a concentration camp for political prisoners of the Roman empire.

Q. For whom was Revelation written?

A. The author says (1:9), "I John, your brother, who share with you in Jesus the tribulation and the kingdom and the patient endurance"; he is evidently addressing fellow Christians who, like himself, were undergoing persecution. Seven communities were named; probably there were many more in his mind.

Q. What was the author's purpose in writing?

A. To assure those suffering at the hands of the Roman state that, however evil the times, evil cannot be permanently victorious, God having already won the decisive victory: "The kingdom of the world has become the kingdom of our Lord and of his Christ, and he shall reign for ever and ever" (11:15). "Here is a call for the endurance and faith of the saints" (13:10; cf. 14:12).

Q. To what art forms has Revelation been compared?

A. To an opera in three acts, a symphony in three movements, a surrealistic painting.

Q. To what type of literature does the book belong?

A. The title, "Revelation," translates a Greek word that is transliterated as *Apocalypse;* it means "unveiling" or "disclosure"; as shown by Zephaniah, Joel, Daniel, and Ezekiel, apocalyptic was a common type of literature among the Hebrews. Within the apocalyptic framework of Revelation, the epistolary form is also employed, and there are (2:1-3:22) letters to seven churches.

Q. What is characteristic of apocalyptic literature?

A. It employs highly symbolic language to disclose what the author believes to be the signs of the times.

Q. What are the sources of the imagery used in Revelation?

A. The Greek alphabet ("I am the Alpha and the Omega"—1:8; 21:6); the temple and sacrificial system of the Hebrew community ("seven golden lampstands"—1:12; "a Lamb standing as though it had been slain—5:6; cf. 5:12f); the works of earlier apocalyptists ("the four living creatures" of 4:6-8; 5:8 are from Ezekiel 1:5-10; the locusts of 9:3-11 are from Joel 1:4; 2:3-5; eating the bitter-sweet scroll, in 10:10, is similar to Ezekiel 3:1-3); the realm of imaginary beings ("a great red dragon, with seven heads and ten horns"—12:3; a "horse, bright red" —6:4; "a pale horse, and its rider's name was Death"—6:8; a beast with "ten horns and seven heads," a beast "like a leopard, its feet were like a bear's, and its mouth was like a lion's"—13:1f; "a scarlet beast which was full of blasphemous names"—17:3); Hebrew angelology ("the seven angels who stand before God"—8:2; "Michael and his angels" —12:7); the plagues that were heaped upon Pharaoh and the Egyptians ("hail and fire"—8:7; "a third of the sea became blood"—8:9); the heavenly bodies: sun, moon, and stars (12:1; 2:28; 22:16), plus the rainbow (4:3), "flashes of lightning" and "peals of thunder" (4:5); the realm of husbandry: "Put in your sickle . . . for its grapes are ripe' (14:18).

Q. What use of numerical symbolism is made in Revelation?

A. Since three stands for heaven and four for the earth, then seven, the number of perfection, represents God's presence in the universe with men; the number of the redeemed, 144,000 (7:4) is made up of 12,000 from each of the twelve tribes of Israel, and symbolizes the completeness of the household of God; 666, "the number of the beast" (13:18), is the Hebrew numerical value of *Neron Caesar,* the Greek name of the Roman emperor hero.

Q. What evidence is there within Revelation that its primary application is to the immediate situation of the first readers?

A. The opening words are: "The revelation of Jesus Christ, which God gave him to show . . . what must soon take place" (1:1); 1:3 insists that "the time is near"; the last chapter says: ". . . the Lord, the God of the spirits of the prophets, has sent his angel to show his servants what must soon take place" (22:6).

Q. What communities are specifically addressed?

A. The churches in Ephesus, Smyrna, Pergamum, Thyatira, Sardis, Philadelphia, Laodicea, cities in Asia Minor.

Q. What is the message to the church in Ephesus?

A. At the conclusion of Paul's three-year ministry in Ephesus, the elders "all wept and embraced Paul and kissed him" (Acts 20:37); Paul warned them: ". . . after my departure, fierce wolves will come in among you, not sparing the flock; and from among your own selves will arise men speaking perverse things, to draw away the disciples" (Acts 20:29f). This, tragically, had come true, and the Seer's word to this church is: ". . . you have abandoned the love you had at first. Remember then from what you have fallen, repent and do the works you did at first" (2:4f).

Q. What is the message to the church in Smyrna?

A. To a church facing persecution (Polycarp suffered martyrdom there about 150 A.D.), the Seer says: "Do not fear what you are about to suffer. . . . Be faithful unto death, and I will give you the crown of life" (2:10).

Q. What is the message to the church in Pergamum?

A. To a congregation harboring a group that ate food offered to idols and engaged in immoral practices, the Seer says: "Repent" (2:16).

Q. What is the message to the church in Thyatira?

A. To a community famed as the center of the dyeing trade (Acts 16:14f), where Christians were taking part in licentious dinners, the Seer writes: "I am he who searches mind and heart, and I will give to each of you as your works deserve" (2:23).

Q. What is the message to the church in Sardis?

A. To a community whose life of luxury and indulgence had affected the church, the Seer says: "I know your works; you have the name of being alive, and you are dead. Awake, and strengthen what remains" (3:1f).

Q. What is meant by "the book of life" (3:5)?

A. In Exodus 32:32f God says to Moses, "Whoever has sinned against me, him will I blot out of my book"; the reference appears to be to a listing of living Israelites; to be blotted out of this scroll was to die (cf. Psalm 69:28; Daniel 12:1).

Q. What is the message to the church in Philadelphia?

A. To a city rich in missionary opportunities, the Seer says: "I have set before you an open door, which no one is able to shut" (3:8).

Q. What is the message to the church in Laodicea?

A. To a community whose devotion was halfhearted, the Seer says: ". . . you are neither cold nor hot. Would you were cold or hot! So, because you are lukewarm . . . I will spew you out of my mouth" (3:15f).

Q. What does the Seer envision in heaven's throne room?

A. ". . . one seated on the throne!" (4:2) surrounded by twenty-four other thrones, on which elders sit praising God (4:4-6,9-11), and "four living creatures" continually singing, "Holy, holy, holy, is the Lord God Almighty" (4:8).

Q. What was "in the right hand of him who was seated on the throne" (5:1)?

A. A scroll "sealed with seven seals" (5:1). It is assumed that "the Lion of the tribe of Judah . . . can open the scroll and its seven seals" (5:5); it is not the Lion, however, but the Lamb that is worthy to open the seals (5:6-7:3) and disclose the number of those whose names were sealed within the book: twelve thousand from each of Israel's twelve tribes. "And after this I looked, and behold, a great multitude which no man could number, from every nation, from all tribes and peoples and tongues, standing before the throne" (7:9) and offering praise to God (7:10-12).

Q. What follows the opening of the seals?

A. The seven angels blow their trumpets, one after the other (8:6-21; 11:15-18), each trumpet blast ushering in a plague upon those who did not "repent of their murders or their sorceries or their immorality or their thefts" (9:21).

Q. Who are "the seven angels who stand before God" (8:2)?

A. The seven archangels of Hebrew tradition (the number is probably the result of Babylonian influence) where Michael (who appears in Daniel 10:13 and Jude 9 as the champion of Israel—cf. Revelation 12:7); Gabriel (the messenger of God—cf. Luke 1:26; Daniel 8:16); Raphael (the minister of healing); Uriel; Raguel; Sariel; Remiel—each of these names ends with the syllable denoting the name of God—these are the heavenly beings who "stand in the presence of God" (Luke 1:19).

Q. What is the vision of the little scroll?

A. It is brought by an angel, "his right foot on the sea, and his left foot on the land" (10:2); the Seer eats the scroll, which, he says, proves "sweet as honey in my mouth, but when I had eaten it my stomach was made bitter" (10:10); this suggests the bitter-sweet role of him who is called upon to speak for God: "You must again prophesy about many peoples and nations and tongues and kings" (10:11).

Q. What conflict is seen to rage in heaven?

A. A "woman clothed with the sun, with the moon under her feet, and on her head a crown of twelve stars" (12:1), gives birth to "a male child, one who is to rule all the nations" (12:5); "a great red dragon, with seven heads and ten horns" lies in wait to devour the child. "Now war arose in heaven, Michael and his angels fighting against the dragon. . . . And the great dragon was thrown down" (12:7-9).

Q. What future is predicted for those who worship the beast "with ten horns and seven heads . . . and a blasphemous name upon its heads" (13:1)?

A. "He also shall drink the wine of God's wrath" (14:10).

Q. What vision follows this warning?

A. "Seven angels with seven plagues" (15:1); the angels are commanded to "Go and pour out on earth the seven bowls of the wrath of God" (16:1-21).

Q. What is symbolized by "the woman, drunk with the blood of the saints and the blood of the martyrs" (17:6)?

A. "The great city which has dominion over the kings of the earth" (17:18)—Rome appears to be meant, though the name Babylon, scene of an earlier persecution of the Hebrew people, is cited.

Q. What is the fate of this city?

A. "Fallen, fallen is Babylon the great!" (18:2). Her business is destroyed: no one any longer buys what her merchants offer (18:11-17); sailors and all whose trade is on the sea . . . saw the smoke of her burning" (18:18); music and crafts and family life all are ended (18:22f).

Q. What is the sequel to the city's destruction?

A. Hymns of praise ("Hallelujah! For the Lord our God the Almighty reigns"—19:6); the emergence of One who "is called Faithful and True . . . King of kings and Lord of lords" (19:11,16); "the great supper of God" (19:17); the chaining of the dragon (20:1-3); the triumph of those who had been martyred (20:4-6); the destruction of the last enemy: "Then Death and Hades were thrown into the lake of fire" (20:14).

Q. What links has the last book in the Bible with the first?

A. Genesis 1:1 tells the story of what happened "in the beginning"; since God in Christ enabled man to make a fresh start, Jesus is, at Revelation 3:14, spoken of as "the beginning of God's creation." Genesis 2:9 pictures God as placing, amid the other green and growing things, "the tree of life also in the midst of the garden"; Revelation 2:7 contains the promise: "To him who conquers I will grant to eat of the tree of life, which is in the paradise of God."

Q. With what vision does Revelation conclude?

A. "A new heaven and a new earth" (21:1), with God dwelling among his people (21:3f), his people living in a new city that has no temple, "for its temple is the Lord God the Almighty and the Lamb" (21:22). "And night shall be no more" (22:5). Into this city "the kings of the earth shall bring their glory" (21:24). Through the city flows a river, on either side of which stands the tree of life, whose leaves are "for the healing of the nations" (22:2). To this well-watered community all are welcomed: "And let him who is thirsty come, let him who desires take the water of life without price" (22:17).

INDEX